Information Technology and Law Series

Volume 33

More information about this series at http://www.springer.com/series/8857

Elif Kiesow Cortez
Editor

Data Protection Around the World

Privacy Laws in Action

ASSER PRESS

Springer

Editor
Elif Kiesow Cortez
International and European Law
The Hague University of Applied Sciences
The Hague, The Netherlands

ISSN 1570-2782 ISSN 2215-1966 (electronic)
Information Technology and Law Series
ISBN 978-94-6265-406-8 ISBN 978-94-6265-407-5 (eBook)
https://doi.org/10.1007/978-94-6265-407-5

Published by T.M.C. ASSER PRESS, The Hague, The Netherlands www.asserpress.nl
Produced and distributed for T.M.C. ASSER PRESS by Springer-Verlag Berlin Heidelberg

This T.M.C. ASSER PRESS imprint is published by the registered company Springer-Verlag GmbH, DE part of Springer Nature
The registered company address is: Heidelberger Platz 3, 14197 Berlin, Germany

Series Information

The *Information Technology & Law Series* was an initiative of IT*e*R, the national programme for Information Technology and Law, which was a research programme set up by the Dutch government and The Netherlands Organisation for Scientific Research (NWO) in The Hague. Since 1995 IT*e*R has published all of its research results in its own book series. In 2002 IT*e*R launched the present internationally orientated and English language *Information Technology & Law Series*. This well-established series deals with the implications of information technology for legal systems and institutions. Manuscripts and related correspondence can be sent to the Series' Editorial Office, which will also gladly provide more information concerning editorial standards and procedures.

Editorial Office

T.M.C. Asser Press
P.O. Box 30461
2500 GL The Hague
The Netherlands
Tel.: +31-70-3420310
e-mail: press@asser.nl

In loving memory of Nalan Celik

Preface

The EU General Data Protection Regulation (GDPR) was adopted in April 2016 and came into force in May 2018 to supersede the outdated Data Protection Directive 95/46/EC of 1995. The drafters of the GDPR announced that it would adhere to the EU Digital Single Market Strategy, which aims to create incentives for digital networks and services to flourish by providing trustworthy infrastructure and effective regulations. The European Data Protection Supervisor described it as the "gold standard" for the protection of personal data. However, as national legislation around the world has increasingly defined the right to the protection of personal data, the stringency of the EU-based gold standard led to many objections from certain interest groups. Academics and practitioners struggle to pinpoint applicable laws, especially for transnational cases that might infringe the right to the protection of personal data.

This book provides a snapshot of privacy laws and practices from a varied set of jurisdictions in order to offer guidance on national and international contemporary issues regarding the processing of personal data. It also serves as an up-to-date resource on the applications and practice relevant examples of data protection laws in different countries. Our objective was to show the applications of the GDPR within European countries and a selection of national data protection laws from different continents with a focus on how the GDPR has influenced these laws. The jurisdictions covered in this book include European countries—Belgium, Estonia, France, Greece and the Netherlands—as well as Indonesia, Tanzania, Turkey, and USA.

The authors of this book offer an in-depth analysis of the national data protection legislation of various countries across different continents, not only including country-specific details but also comparing the idiosyncratic characteristics of these national privacy laws to the GDPR. Valuable comparative information on data protection regulations around the world is provided in one concise volume.

It was a challenging task to fully capture and track new developments in national legislation given the fast-changing regulatory landscape regarding data protection and privacy. At the same time, this surely makes this an exciting legal field which is likely to continue evolving with continuing efforts being made to safeguard legal protections in the face of myriad changes related to the modern data economy. I would like to thank all the contributors for the submission of their chapters which are excellent reference sources both for practitioners and researchers. I would like to also thank family, friends and colleagues for their guidance, THUAS Cybersecurity Center of Expertise for the research appointment and Ms. Anne Hillmer for providing research assistance.

The Hague, The Netherlands
June 2020

Elif Kiesow Cortez

Contents

Editor and Contributors

About the Editor

Dr. Elif Kiesow Cortez is a senior lecturer and researcher in data protection and privacy regulation in the International and European Law Program at The Hague University of Applied Sciences (THUAS), the Netherlands. Dr. Kiesow Cortez is the coordinator of the Legal Technology Minor and the Cybersecurity Minor at THUAS. Before joining THUAS, she was a John M. Olin Fellow in Law and Economics at Harvard Law School. Her doctoral research at the Institute of Law and Economics, University of Hamburg, Germany, was funded by the German Research Association (DFG). During her doctoral studies, Dr. Kiesow Cortez was a visiting fellow at Harvard Business School and a visiting scholar at Berkeley School of Law.

Her research is focused on utilizing the economic analysis of law to provide recommendations for solving cooperation problems between public and private actors in the domains of data protection and privacy. Since 2018, Dr. Kiesow Cortez is an advisory board member for the CIPP/E Exam Development Board of the IAPP and she is currently a Transatlantic Technology Law Forum Fellow at Stanford Law School.

Contributors

Godelieve Alkemade The Hague University of Applied Sciences, The Hague, The Netherlands

Ambrogino G. Awesta Windesheim University of Applied Sciences, Almere, The Netherlands

Georgios Bouchagiar Tilburg Institute for Law, Technology, and Society (TILT), Tilburg University, Tilburg, The Netherlands

Els De Busser Institute of Security and Global Affairs, Leiden University, The Hague, The Netherlands

Başak Erdoğan MEF University, Maslak, Sarıyer, Istanbul, Turkey; Galatasaray University, Istanbul, Turkey

Muge Fazlioglu International Association of Privacy Professionals, Portsmouth, NH, USA

Tanel Kerikmäe Tallinn University of Technology, Tallinn, Estonia

Nikos Koutras School of Business and Law, Edith Cowan University, Joondalup, WA, Australia

Aurelien Lorange The Hague University of Applied Sciences, The Hague, The Netherlands

Edmon Makarim Faculty of Law, University of Indonesia, Depok, Indonesia

Alex B. Makulilo Open University of Tanzania, Dar es Salaam, Tanzania

Nele Nisu Estonian Ministry of Social Affairs, Tallinn, Estonia

Kärt Salumaa-Lepik Tallinn University of Technology, Tallinn, Estonia

Joeri Toet Vrije Universiteit Amsterdam, Amsterdam, The Netherlands

Chapter 1
Data Protection Around the World: An Introduction

Elif Kiesow Cortez

Contents

Abstract This book serves as an up-to-date resource on the applications and practice-relevant examples of data protection laws in different countries. The snapshot of privacy laws and practices from a varied set of jurisdictions it provides reflects national and international contemporary issues regarding the processing of personal data. The ever-increasing emergence of privacy violations, due to evolving technology and new lifestyles linked to an intensified online presence of ever more individuals, has required the design of a novel data protection and privacy regulation. The contributors to this book offer an in-depth analysis of the national data protection legislation of various countries across different continents, not only including country-specific details but also comparing the idiosyncratic characteristics of these national privacy laws to the EU General Data Protection Regulation (GDPR). Valuable comparative information on data protection regulations around the world is provided in one concise volume.

Keywords Data protection around the world · GDPR · Privacy · European data protection · Privacy law · Right to privacy

1.1 Introduction

Evolving technology and new lifestyles linked to an intensified online presence of ever more individuals have put privacy increasingly at risk. An individual's personal

---

E. Kiesow Cortez (✉)
The Hague University of Applied Sciences, Johanna Westerdijkplein 75, 2521 EN The Hague, The Netherlands
e-mail: e.kiesowcortez@hhs.nl

E. Kiesow Cortez (ed.), *Data Protection Around the World*, Information Technology and Law Series 33, https://doi.org/10.1007/978-94-6265-407-5_1

data is an extremely profitable resource for companies and a tool to increase government surveillance. It is very difficult to balance these interests against an individual's fundamental right to privacy and protection of personal data. People have little control over their personal data and sometimes even lack knowledge of which personal data is collected and when and what conclusions governments and companies can draw from collected personal data. The resulting information asymmetry between individuals and the companies that collect their data makes it easy for companies to infringe individual fundamental rights without individuals even knowing the infringement has occurred. To address this problem, the EU General Data Protection Regulation (GDPR) was adopted in April 2016 and came into force in May 2018 to supersede the outdated Data Protection Directive 95/46/EC of 1995. The drafters of the GDPR announced that it would cohere to the EU Digital Single Market Strategy,[1] which aims to create incentives for digital networks and services to flourish by providing trustworthy infrastructure and effective regulations. The efforts aimed at supporting the privacy respecting practices through the GDPR enforcement also meant that administrative fines were issued in the first year of the GDPR and several organizations updated their privacy policy to become compliant with the GDPR.[2] A significant part of this was to create the conditions that would lead EU citizens to trust digital services enough to use them. GDPR has been seen as having created new control mechanisms that allow individuals to decide how much data they are willing to share and with whom.

Following the GDPR's first application year, the UK Information Commissioner's Office reported that individuals were taking more control of their data. For example, between 25 May 2018 and 1 May 2019, the commissioner received 14,000 personal data breach reports, more than quadruple the 3000 the office received in the prior year.[3] Likewise, supervisory authorities of 11 European economic area countries already imposed fines under the GDPR amounting to a total of approximately €56 million fines.[4] GDPR has extraterritorial application as well, which has led the European Data Protection Supervisor to describe it as the "gold standard" for the protection of personal data.[5] However as national legislation around the world has increasingly defined the right to protection of personal data, the stringency of the EU-based gold standard led to many objections from lobbying groups.[6] Academics and practitioners struggle to pinpoint applicable laws, especially for transnational cases that might violate the right to the protection of personal data.

Regulating the right to protection of personal data requires attention to the normative dimensions of privacy as a concept. There are benefits as well as risks in the

[1] European Commission 2015.

[2] European Union Agency for Fundamental Rights 2019.

[3] Information Commissioner's Office 2019.

[4] European Data Protection Board 2019.

[5] Buttarelli G (April 2016) The EU GDPR as a clarion call for a new global digital gold standard. https://edps.europa.eu/press-publications/press-news/blog/eu-gdpr-clarion-call-new-global-digital-gold-standard_fr. Accessed 25 February 2020.

[6] Schwartz 2013.

large-scale collection and processing of personal data.[7] The benefits include a more connected society, fast access to products and services and receiving customized, tailored suggestions for products and services. Risks of commercial uses of personal data include being profiled and having limited access to products and services due to the relevant profiling. Law enforcement uses may have greater risks, which have led to right to privacy discussions where significant attention was devoted to the potential *privacy vs. security trade-off*. As of early 2020, an important debate takes place with respect to governments' objective to collect individual's personal data regarding coronavirus infections. Especially relevant in this context is individual's right to protection of their health data which under the GDPR is categorized as sensitive personal data. This recent development showed that right to protection of personal data is also at the center of the discussion on potential *privacy vs. public health trade-offs*.

This book provides a snapshot of privacy laws and practices from a varied set of jurisdictions in order to offer guidance on national and international contemporary issues regarding the processing of personal data. It also serves as an up-to-date resource on the applications and practice-relevant examples of data protection laws in different countries. Our objective was to show the applications of the GDPR within European countries and a selection of national data protection laws from different continents with a focus on how the GDPR has influenced these laws. The jurisdictions covered in this book include European countries—Belgium, Estonia, France, Greece and the Netherlands—as well as Indonesia, Tanzania, Turkey, and United States.

The authors of this book offer an in-depth analysis of the national data protection legislation of various countries across different continents, not only including country-specific details but also comparing the idiosyncratic characteristics of these national privacy laws to the GDPR. Valuable comparative information on data protection regulations around the world is provided in one concise volume.

1.2 Overview

In Chap. 2, Els De Busser provides an overview of the application of data protection regulation in Belgium. As she explains, the Belgian Privacy Commission has taken a proactive approach to GDPR implementation. Indeed, Belgium created a special function within the government, the Secretary of State for Privacy (later Federal Minister), that oversees implementation. To explain the impact of this, Dr. De Busser describes how the country's Privacy Commission became the Belgian Data Protection Authority and the high-profile case it subsequently brought against Facebook in 2015.

In Chap. 3, Kärt Saluuma-Lepik, Tanel Kerikmae and Nele Nisu cover GDPR implementation issues and related topics from an Estonian perspective, as Estonia is one of the recognized pioneers and leaders concerning modern digital society. The

[7]For a discussion of the economic value of right to privacy see Posner 1981, 1983. For counterarguments, see Solove 2007.

authors explain the roots of Estonian data protection and provide an overview of the latest developments related to GDPR and case law in that matter. After clarifying how GDPR interacts with Estonian jurisdiction and the most notable differences and similarities, the authors conclude by highlighting the most prominent issues in Estonian jurisdiction regarding data protection regulations with a focus on e-governance.

In Chap. 4, Aurelien Lorange focuses on the data protection law and practices in France by providing a detailed overview on the policy origins and evaluation. The author highlights the importance of the role of the French Data Protection Authority, which received more competences and a territorial application than it had before the GDPR, leading to better definition of and maintenance of its role of controlling the regime of the most sensitive data (justice and police) and informing individuals of their rights with respect to their data. As Chap. 4 explains, the French Data Protection authority created many informative sources in the first application year of the GDPR and has since moved on to enforcement and increased cooperation with the other national authorities in charge of protection of personal data in the European Union.

In Chap. 5, Georgios Bouchagiar and Nikos Koutras deliver a detailed analysis of the data protection law in Greece. They provide an overview of case law of the Supreme Administrative Court and the Supreme Civil and Criminal Court, as well as indicating the relevant national laws and passages of the Constitution of Greece. They then explain the core concepts that have driven this body of law, such as "control" and "consent." The analysis highlights the similarities and differences between the GDPR and Greek law. The conclusion examines the risks emerging from new technologies. It underlines ignorance and confusion that may affect people with respect to these issues, referencing data portability as a trust-enhancing tool that could strengthen controllership and promote transparency in the interests of data subjects.

In Chap. 6 Edmon Makarim explores Indonesia's data protection regulations. He provides an overview of the data protection laws implemented by the Communication and Informatics Ministry Regulation No.20 in 2016 about personal data protection in e-systems. Chapter 6 also provides an in-depth analysis of the Bill for Personal Data Protection introduced in the Indonesian legislature in 2008, explaining how it responds to GDPR and existing information and communication laws in Indonesia.

The first section of Chap. 7 discusses the existing generic personal data protection regime in the Netherlands and recent and expected legislative changes in and related to this regime. Godelieve Alkemade and Joeri Toet then provide an informative overview of sector specific personal data protection legislation and explain key distinguishing elements of the Dutch personal data protection environment, focusing specifically on the latitude the GDPR provides member states for implementation or deviation. The chapter concludes with the authors' expectations as to how GDPR will affect these prominent issues in the Netherlands.

In Chap. 8, Alex Makulilo offers an overview of the influence the GDPR on the Tanzanian data privacy law and practice. The author states that the Constitution of the United Republic of Tanzania provides for constitutional protection of individual privacy even if the country has no general data protection legislation. The country's constitution states that all people are entitled to respect and protection of their persons; the privacy of their own person, family, and matrimonial lives; and respect and protection of their residence and private communications. The author lays out the limitations of these rights and provides an in-depth analysis of whether these limitations align with the GDPR.

In Chap. 9, Başak Erdoğan dissects Turkey's approach to personal data protection and compares it to the GDPR by analysing the current state of affairs after the adoption of Law no. 6698 on the Protection of Personal Data in 2016 and the establishment of the Turkish Data Protection Authority. The chapter analyses Turkey's main laws and regulations and case-law with regard to the protection of personal data, then compares of Turkish data protection law with the GDPR. Following a review of prominent issues with regard to data protection in Turkey, the chapter concludes with discussing the possible application of the GDPR in Turkey and its impact on Turkish data protection law.

In Chap. 10, Muge Fazlioglu focuses on U.S. information privacy and data protection laws and compares them to the GDPR as well as discussing how the GDPR is likely to affect privacy and data protection in the United States in the years ahead. The author explains that U.S. privacy laws are "sectoral" in nature, meaning that businesses in different economic sectors are subject to different privacy rules and regulations, which differs from the EU's omnibus approach to data protection. The author provides a thorough analysis regarding the interaction between the GDPR and U.S. law, the interplay between the right to be forgotten and the protection of speech and of the press provided by the First Amendment. The chapter concludes with insights on understanding the interaction of state-level consumer privacy laws, such as the California Consumer Privacy Act of 2018 and legislative efforts at the federal level.

In Chap. 11, Ambrogino Awesta first elaborates on the meaning and scope of the concept of privacy in the EU. Subsequently the applicability of privacy in relation to technologies that are employed for tracking and targeting in cyberspace is scrutinized. The author concludes by focusing on the impact of obligations that are imposed on digital enterprises by the new legal instruments and the actual effectiveness of these instruments in protecting and securing the privacy of users against the technologies deployed by digital enterprises.

In the final chapter, Elif Kiesow Cortez shares an overview of selected future challenges for the protection of personal data in the domains of automated decision making and artificial intelligence, blockchain technology, and also with respect to the newly emerged discussions on public health with regards to the coronavirus pandemic and contact tracing apps. The chapter focuses on providing an analysis of these three new and emerging areas based on the relevant guidelines of the European Data Protection Board.

The present volume aims to shed light on the fast-moving legal field of data protection regulation. It aims to provide practitioners and scholars alike with information on the distinct ways with which different jurisdictions across the globe approach this thorny subject whose relevance is expected to continue to grow, given the ongoing transformation towards more digital economies and the cultivation of social ties occurring increasingly via electronic means.

Parallel to the interaction of national privacy laws and the GDPR we are witnessing GDPR itself consolidating and evolving in response to unforeseen challenges linked to dynamic behavioral responses, external factors like the COVID-19 pandemic and interplay involving citizens and firms. The worldwide impact of the GDPR will likely not be fully uniform but rather adapted to and filtered through the national legal landscape of privacy laws in occasionally unexpected ways, yielding country-specific reactions and results. The present collection of chapters aims to illustrate how this process can take place in a variety of jurisdictions and what specific commonalities and potential frictions exist between GDPR and national legal privacy regimes.

References

European Commission (2015) Communication from the Commission to the European Parliament, the Council, the European Economic and Social Committee and the Committee of the Regions: a digital single market strategy for Europe. https://ec.europa.eu/digital-single-market/en/news/digital-single-market-strategy-europe-com2015-192-final. Accessed 25 February 2020

European Data Protection Board (2019) 2019 Annual report: working together for stronger rights. https://edpb.europa.eu/sites/edpb/files/files/file1/edpb_annual_report_2019_en.pdf.pdf. Accessed 25 February 2020

European Union Agency for Fundamental Rights (2019) The General Data Protection Regulation – One year on. Civil society: awareness, opportunities and challenges. https://fra.europa.eu/sites/default/files/fra_uploads/fra-2019-gdpr-one-year-on_en.pdf. Accessed 25 February 2020

Information Commissioner's Office (2019) GDPR: One year on, May 2019, Version 1.0. https://ico.org.uk/media/about-the-ico/documents/2614992/gdpr-one-year-on-20190530.pdf. Accessed 25 February 2020

Posner R (1981) The economics of privacy. Am Econ Rev 71(2):405–409

Posner R (1983) The economics of justice. Harvard University Press, Cambridge

Schwartz P (2013) The EU-US privacy collision: a turn to institutions and procedures. Harvard Law Rev 126:1

Solove D (2007) "I've got nothing to hide" and other misunderstandings of privacy. San Diego Law Rev 44:745

Dr. Elif Kiesow Cortez is a senior lecturer and researcher in data protection and privacy regulation in the International and European Law Program at The Hague University of Applied Sciences (THUAS), the Netherlands.

Chapter 2
Data Protection Around the World: Belgium

Els De Busser

Contents

Abstract The GDPR is not fully new. Data controllers and processors, who are compliant with the current law, will be able to use this approach as a valid starting point for the implementation of the GDPR. This was the message of the Belgian Privacy Commission in the introductory text to their 13-step-plan to GDPR implementation. An accurate consideration, since Belgium has had a detailed data protection act in place since 1992. This act was amended in order to bring it in line with Directive 95/46/EC. The GDPR implementation law was finally enacted in the shape of a framework act encompassing more than just the GDPR in the summer of 2018 so after the period for transposition expired. Thanks to the proactive attitude of the Belgian Privacy Commission however, publishing recommendations to comply with specific parts of the GDPR, Belgian data controllers and processors received clear guidance even before the implementation law was published. In 2015,

E. De Busser (✉)
Institute of Security and Global Affairs, Leiden University, Turfmarkt 99, 2511 DP The Hague, The Netherlands
e-mail: e.de.busser@fgga.leidenuniv.nl

E. Kiesow Cortez (ed.), *Data Protection Around the World*, Information Technology and Law Series 33,
https://doi.org/10.1007/978-94-6265-407-5_2

Belgium also was the first country in the world to create the function of Secretary of State for Privacy. This unique government post, together with the pending GDPR implementation law and two main developments are highlighted: the reform of the Privacy Commission into a Data Protection Authority that was adopted in 2017 and a high-profile case initiated by the Privacy Commission against Facebook. The latter concerned Facebook's tracking of Internet users by means of cookies and pixels in breach of the Belgian data protection act of 1992 and contained a significant question regarding which national law applies to the company. Facebook has announced to appeal its conviction by a Brussels court but the applicability of the GDPR may make the question moot.

Keywords Data protection · Belgium · Personal data · Privacy · Facebook · Data breaches

2.1 Background[1]

At first sight, the Kingdom of Belgium can hardly be called a forerunner in the development of data protection laws. Introducing a genuine right to privacy in the Belgian Constitution took as long as 1994. Obviously, that does not mean that personal data and privacy were unprotected before. Specific national laws together with international human rights provisions were relied upon. It was the international pressure that would lead Belgium to make haste and catch up with its national legal framework on privacy and data protection. The direct cause was the establishment of the Schengen area abolishing internal border controls, which increased cross-border crime necessitating more cross-border data transfers for the purpose of criminal investigations. The result was a comprehensive 1992 Law on the Protection of Personal Data (further: the 1992 law)[2] followed by a list of royal decrees amending and executing the law.

Yet, this late awakening of the Belgian institutions to the right to privacy and data protection stands in stark contrast with the renowned role they have taken on in recent years. The country quickly developed from the last-minute follower to a recognized leader thanks to its dedicated Privacy Commission—turned Data Protection Authority (further: DPA)—and the creation of a special government post for privacy. One would think that this transformation would make the country also be a forerunner in implementing the new EU data protection legal framework. Nonetheless, the Belgian government took its time in presenting the actual implementation laws for the GDPR and the Directive on data protection for law enforcement purposes. On 5 September 2018—months after the implementation period had passed—an extensive framework act was published covering the GDPR, the related Directive on data

[1]Preparation of this chapter was finalized in Spring 2019.

[2]Act on the Protection of the Private Life concerning the Processing of Personal Data, B.S. 18.03.1993.

protection for law enforcement purposes and more specific provisions on the protection of data by intelligence and security authorities (further: the Framework Act).[3] Earlier, a substantial part of the GDPR—covering the setting up of a DPA—was implemented in a separate act adopted on 3 December 2017[4] in order to enter into force on the day the GDPR came into effect. The purpose of this act is reforming the Belgian Privacy Commission into a DPA.

Besides these two implementation laws, this chapter will zoom in on a number of particular characteristics of the Belgian data protection legal framework, including the function of Secretary of State for Privacy and two cases that significantly shaped the Belgian data protection landscape. With Belgium endorsing to the monist doctrine, the GDPR technically did not need to be transposed into national law. However, as the GDPR is not a regulation in the traditional sense of the word several provisions do need a national implementation as they grant the national legislator a rather wide margin of interpretation. Several examples of how the Belgian national legislator filled in this margin are discussed in Sect. 2.3.2. It should be pointed out though—as also announced by the Belgian Privacy Commission in the introductory text to their proactively released 13-step-plan to implement the GDPR—the data processors and controllers who were already compliant with the 1992 law could use that approach as a starting point for GDPR compliance.

2.2 The Belgian Data Protection Landscape Pre-GDPR

The fact that the Belgian implementation laws for the GDPR and the Directive on data protection for law enforcement purposes were implemented after the transposition deadline was passed is contradictory to the pronounced stance that the Belgian government and the Privacy Commission—turned DPA—have taken in the past years. Being the first country to dedicate a special government post to privacy and being the leading country in sanctioning Facebook for privacy violations, it is remarkable to note that transposing the new EU legal framework on data protection in Belgium was a fairly slow process. It is a reminder of the slow enactment of the first comprehensive data protection law—the 1992 law—in the country.

[3] Act on the Protection of Natural Persons concerning the Processing of Personal Data, B.S. 05.09.2018.

[4] Act establishing the Data Protection Authority, B.S. 10.01.2018.

2.2.1 *The Belgian Constitution*

The Belgian Constitution of 1831 did not include a right to privacy as such. It did however provide in a right to protect the home[5] in relation to search and seizure for law enforcement purposes. The original Article 22[6] only protected the confidentiality of letters. Both can be said to safeguard aspects of what we call privacy today but a general right to a private life did not receive constitutional protection until 1994.[7] Before that time, safeguarding privacy was done by relying on the general protection of Article 8 ECHR in conjunction with specific branches of law—criminal law, civil law and labor law—that would include privacy protection provisions in their respective codes. With the exception of specific legal acts such as the law concerning the national population register or the royal decree on a database for government staff,[8] the term data protection was unfound in Belgian laws before 1992.

2.3 Data Protection Act of 1992

In spite of attempts to create the first national law on the protection of personal data in the 70s, the proposals hit a wall of political opposition and were never realized.[9] The introduction of the general 1992 law on the protection of personal data[10] was thus rather late; although it should be pointed out that a list of more specific laws and royal decrees covering data protection in certain sectors[11] acted as predecessors to the comprehensive 1992 law. Yet, the late adoption of the first general Belgian data protection law together with the late ratification of the Council of Europe's convention on data protection in 1993 demonstrated an—at first—unfavorable climate for personal data safeguards in the country whereas the international pressure on Belgium to make the necessary legal steps was high.[12] After all, the Belgian ratification of the Council of Europe's mother convention on data protection ran parallel to the entry into force of the 1990 Schengen Implementation Convention. The founding states of the Schengen zone had agreed to each adopt a data protection law before ratifying the Schengen Implementation Convention. This put additional pressure on the then

[5]Article 10 in the original version, Article 15 in the current version of the Constitution: Consolidated Constitution of 17.02.1994, B.S. 17.02.1994.

[6]Current Article 29 of the Constitution.

[7]De Hert and Gutwirth 2013, pp. 28 and 44.

[8]De Hert 2003, pp. 42–43.

[9]De Hert 2003, pp. 42–43.

[10]Act on the Protection of the Private Life concerning the Processing of Personal Data, B.S. 18.03.1993.

[11]For a full list, see De Hert 2003, pp. 43–43.

[12]De Hert and Gutwirth 2013, p. 35.

government to draw up a legislative proposal that would eventually lead to the 1992 law.[13]

When EU Directive 95/46 was adopted just two years after the enactment of the Belgian law, the government adjusted its policy where needed by means of royal decrees.[14] Finally in 1998 the 1992 law was the subject of a significant amount of amendments due to a full implementation of Directive 95/46.[15]

Based on these efforts to bring Belgian national law in line with Directive 95/46, the overhaul of the EU's data protection legal framework by the GDPR should not cause too much concern on a legislative level.

2.3.1 Secretary of State for Privacy

In 2014, the Belgian government was the first in Europe to introduce a special function within the federal government: a Secretary of State for privacy, the fight against social fraud and the North Sea attached to the Minister of Social Affairs and Public Health. This means that one of his responsibilities is legislation on the protection of personal privacy. Since 2016, a former member of the European Parliament, Philippe De Backer, takes up this function. His task is simply and widely defined as "competent for legislation on the protection of privacy", which was included in this portfolio when he became Federal Minister of Digital Agenda, Telecommunication and Postal Services in 2018.[16]

Compared to other countries, it is exceptional to have a separate government portfolio dedicated to privacy policy. Its main advantage is ensuring that the inevitably policy-overarching theme receives the appropriate attention in the decision-making process of other legislative acts or policies rather than being a side-note. In addition, the function of Secretary of State also gave visibility to a debate that was—especially in the months leading up to the entering into effect of the GDPR—assisting awareness among citizens and reassuring companies that the government recognized the investments they were making to be compliant.

2.3.2 Prominent Data Protection Authority

Commonly known as the Privacy Commission, the Commission for the Protection of Privacy is reformed since 25 May 2018 into the DPA.[17] The change in name may

[13]De Hert and Gutwirth 2013, p. 36.

[14]De Hert 2003, p. 43.

[15]Act transposing Directive 95/46/EG of 24 October 1995 on the protection of natural persons concerning the processing of personal data and the free movement of these data, B.S. 03.02.1999.

[16]Royal Decree establishing certain ministerial competences, B.S. 10.02.2015.

[17]Act establishing the Data Protection Authority, B.S. 10.01.2018.

sound trivial but corresponds better with the role of supervisory and sanctioning authority rather than a mere advisory organ. Nevertheless, it must be pointed out that even before the reform, the Belgian Privacy Commission has had a prominent role in data protection issues that drew international attention: the financial message data transfers between SWIFT and the US authorities in 2007 and the more recent court case against Facebook. The latter will be the focal point of Sect. 2.5.2. Under this heading, the key characteristics of the reformed DPA will be discussed.

In accordance with the 1992 law the Belgian Privacy Commission had wider competences compared to the scope of the GDPR, for example the GDPR excludes activities that fall outside the scope of Community law and data processing for the purpose of prevention, investigation, prosecution of criminal offences and the execution of sentences. The Council of State (*Conseil d'État*) therefore underlined in its opinion on the recent Act establishing the Data Protection Authority that it should be made clear what the (territorial) competences of the DPA would be.[18] The aforementioned Secretary of State clarified that the powers of the DPA will be further extended to cover the additional areas. With regard to data processing covered by other laws than the implementation law, Article 4, §1 of the act establishing the DPA refers to all acts containing provisions on protecting data processing activities.

In the original legislative proposal, the DPA organ that decides on cases and determines the consequences was referred to as an "administrative judicial body". Such formulation caused confusion and made the Council of State doubt the judicial nature of the body.[19] On the one hand the legislative proposal uses terminology such as judges, penalty and registry, which are commonly used in a judicial context. On the other hand, the proposal states that the body can impose administrative fines, which leads to the assumption that it is an administrative body. Following the reasoning of the GDPR though, the Council of State concluded that the DPA organ in question was meant to be an administrative authority. Following the Council of State's advice to clarify the matter, the adopted act now refers in its Article 32 to the administrative dispute organ. All other confusing terminology was removed. Categorizing the dispute organ as an administrative authority had another remarkable consequence. The Council of State referred to the 2015 Schrems case before the Court of Justice of the EU to point out that if the dispute organ is not a judicial body, it will not be able to refer requests for a preliminary ruling to the Court of Justice based on Article 267 of the TFEU. In this case §65 of the Schrems ruling[20] could give inspiration for a different type of procedure should the DPA doubt the validity of the European Commission's adequacy decision. The adopted act establishing the DPA does not seem to have remedied this situation.

---

[18]See Chambre, 2648/001, Travaux Préparatoires, Proposed Act establishing the Data Protection Authority, 23.08.2017, pp. 103–133.

[19]Council of State, Opinion 61.267/2/AG, 27.06.2017, on the Proposed Act establishing the Data Protection Authority, pp. 43–47.

[20]CJEU 6.10.2015, C-362/14, Schrems.

2.4 New GDPR-Related Issues

The Belgian Framework Act implementing the GDPR was published in September 2018 including also the implementation of the Directive on data protection for law enforcement purposes.[21] The approval by the federal Council of Ministers in May 2018 already announced what the key points are of the implementation law as well as the government's choice for a Framework Act rather than a set of amendments in specific laws. In accordance with the GDPR, the Framework Act's key points are accountability, transparency and enhanced supervision by the DPA. In view of that last point, a new law was enacted on 3 December 2017 reforming the Belgian Privacy Commission into the DPA (see supra, Sect. 2.3.2). In the Council of State's opinion to the draft text of the act, two substantial points were raised. The first point regarding the nature of the DPA's supervision—judicial or administrative—was dealt with in the previous subsection. The second point raised by the Council of State is related to Belgium's federal structure and presents the issue of more supervisory authorities within different competence spheres. This subsection therefore zooms in on the latter argument before raising two further questions related to the Belgian GDPR implementation: legal basis of data processing activities and exercising data protection rights online. Lastly, this subsection covers the Belgian implementation of specific GDPR provisions that left the national legislator enough margins to widen their scope.

2.4.1 *Belgium's Federal Structure*

As one of the smaller member states of the EU, the Kingdom of Belgium often draws attention due to its complex federal structure joining a federal legislator with legislators on the level of the communities and regions. Even though the protection of personal data is a matter that falls within the scope of the federal government's legislative powers, the introduction of the new data protection legal framework by the EU has consequences on the level of the Flemish and Walloon governments. The Flemish and Walloon decrees enacted on the basis of the 1992 law and referring to provisions of the law, all need to be amended in view of the GDPR's implementation as well. The Flemish government already took the first steps in bringing its decrees in line with the GDPR; even before the Belgian Framework Act was ready.[22]

However, this was not the only point of contention with regard to the GDPR. When the federal government submitted its proposed law on the establishment of the DPA—effectively reforming the existing Privacy Commission in accordance with

[21] Act on the Protection of Natural Persons concerning the Processing of Personal Data, B.S. 05.09.2018.

[22] Council of State, Opinion 62.834/3 on the proposed decree by the Flemish Community and the Flemish Region concerning the amendments to the decrees based on Regulation (EU) 2016/679, 19.02.2018.

the GDPR—to the Council of State for advice, a question on the autonomy of the communities and regions took center stage, namely whether or not the establishment of the authority by the federal government infringes upon the competences of the communities and regions.[23] Since 2010 a Flemish supervisory authority is operational for electronic administrative data traffic.[24] The proposed act establishes a data protection authority that has competence over all operators regardless of the matter that is dealt with or the public authority that is involved, even if the operators fall under the scope of the communities and regions. Referring to the jurisprudence of the Constitutional Court on Article 22 of the Belgian Constitution, the Council of State stressed that the federal government is competent for the general provisions on the right to a private life. The communities and regions can regulate the right to a private life with regard to areas that fall within their competence taking the federal rules into consideration. In view of these specific rules, the communities and regions can establish specific supervisory authorities, but it is the federal government that remains competent for setting up an authority supervising the general rules. Concluding the argument, the Council of State mentions that in case of supervisory authorities on these different levels, a cooperation agreement should be made as soon as possible.[25]

2.4.2 Legal Basis of Data Processing Activities

The launch of the GDPR made the Belgian DPA present an early step-by-step plan[26] informing mostly companies—data processors and data controllers—of their new obligations and how they should start preparations to be compliant. Even before the Belgian implementation law, the GDPR had direct effect, meaning data processors and controllers risk repercussions in case of non-conformity with the GDPR's provisions.

The Belgian DPA recognized the fact that under the 1992 law many companies and organizations had not defined a legal basis for their data processing activities. Whereas this did not have far-reaching consequences under the 1992 law, it does make a difference under the GDPR since the rights of the citizen in question can vary depending on the legal basis of the specific data processing activity.[27] The types of legal bases remain the same—consent or an exception based on the necessity of the processing—but the consequences for the data processor or controller's accountability are different. When consent is the legal basis of a data processing activity,

---

[23] Council of State, Opinion 61.267/2/AG, 27.06.2017, on the Proposed Act establishing the Data Protection Authority, pp. 30–37.

[24] Flemish Decree on electronic administrative data traffic, B.S. 29.10.2008.

[25] Council of State, Opinion 61.267/2/AG, 27.06.2017, on the Proposed Act establishing the Data Protection Authority, p. 37.

[26] Belgian Privacy Commission 2016 GDPR, Prepare yourself in 13 steps. https://www.gegevensbeschermingsautoriteit.be/bereid-je-voor-13-stappen. Accessed 6 May 2019.

[27] Ibid.

the Belgian DPA acknowledges that the GDPR's mentioning of consent and explicit consent is unclear. Still, it makes a strong recommendation to data controllers to create an audit trail in order to demonstrate consent being given by the data subject.

2.4.3 Exercising Data Protection Rights Online

The Belgian DPA rightfully points out that in general, citizens have the same rights under the GDPR in comparison to the 1992 law with the exception of a few improvements. At the same time the DPA welcomes the new right to data portability but points out that many companies and organizations have already introduced such right on their own initiative. These companies and organizations are however invited to revise their current systems and—at least—make the right to data portability a fully digital procedure. A similar recommendation is made by the DPA for the procedures to request access to data. Apart from the new deadlines, the GDPR imposes additional information duties in this context and this can require significant investments such as a possibility for the citizen to access their data online. The companies and organizations in question are therefore encouraged to conduct a cost-benefit analysis of an online procedure.[28] Considering the language laws of the country,[29] Belgian companies and organizations face additional investments making their online information and procedures available in at least two languages.

The Belgian Framework Act provides in legal remedies for possible infringements on data processing. A case can be brought to court not only by the data subject but also by the DPA or by a body or organization that acts on behalf of the data subject. Such body or organization should be active in the field of data protection for at least three years.[30]

2.4.4 Interpretations in the Belgian Implementation Law

As the GDPR left considerable room for the EU member states to widen the scope of specific provisions, this subsection will touch upon a number of instances where the Belgian legislator made the choice to increase protection on particular points and to specify provisions on other points.

The minimum age for giving consent to data processing is 16 years in accordance with the GDPR. Every child younger than that needs the permission of a parent or the person who has parental responsibility. However, the member states are allowed to lower the threshold as long as it is not lower than the age of 13. The Belgian Secretary

---

[28] Ibid.

[29] With Article 4 of the Constitution as the legal basis.

[30] See Article 220 of the Act on the Protection of Natural Persons concerning the Processing of Personal Data.

of State clarified in the *travaux préparatoires* that the choice for the minimum age of 13 was made in accordance with opinions expressed by the Commissioner for Children's Rights, the Councils for Youth and the competent Community Ministers.[31]

The text of the GDPR left the member states with significant leeway to allow for the processing of sensitive data. Accordingly, the Belgian Framework Act contains several exceptions to the general rule that sensitive data should not be processed.

Specific public authorities are allowed to process sensitive data for the purpose of their mandate. This includes the processing of data concerning race and ethnicity, political and religious views, union membership, genetic data, health data, sexual preferences and data concerning criminal convictions by the intelligence authorities for the purpose of security clearances.[32] In the *travaux préparatoires* this provision is clarified by highlighting risks of radicalization that could be revealed by allowing the use of data on political or religious views and risks of mental illness that could be retrieved by processing health data.[33] Three types of organizations can legitimately process sensitive data: institutions for the purpose of defending human rights, the organization Child Focus and institutions set up for the purpose of assistance to sexual offenders.[34] Thus, the exception allowing processing of sensitive personal data for reasons of substantial public interest of Article 9 §2, g) of the GDPR was interpreted by the Belgian legislator in an exhaustive manner without doing detriment to the requirement of a substantial public interest. The travaux préparatoires clarify however that the list of organizations is in and of itself not sufficient. Additional requirements include the proportionality of the data to the purpose of their processing, the essence of the right to data protection should be respected and specific measures should be taken to protect the rights and fundamental interests of the persons involved.[35]

Sensitive data can also be processed by the Belgian Coordination Organ for Threat Analysis OCAD (*Orgaan voor de Coördinatie en de Analyse van de Dreiging*). The mandate of OCAD consists of analysis and assessment of potential threats to the security of the country and its citizens based on the information that it receives from a number of national supporting services. Taking into account that the legal framework on the intelligence and security authorities as well as OCAD provide in strong supervisory mechanisms, the exceptions to the general prohibition of processing of sensitive data is clearly overruled by the authorities' mandate.

---

[31] Chambre, 3126/003, Travaux Préparatoires, Proposed Act on the Protection of Natural Persons concerning the Processing of Personal Data, 06.07.2018, p. 5.

[32] See Article 110 of the Act on the Protection of Natural Persons concerning the Processing of Personal Data.

[33] Chambre, 3126/003, Travaux Préparatoires, Proposed Act on the Protection of Natural Persons concerning the Processing of Personal Data, 06.07.2018, pp. 53–54.

[34] Chambre, 3126/003, Travaux Préparatoires, Proposed Act on the Protection of Natural Persons concerning the Processing of Personal Data, 06.07.2018, p. 5 and Article 8 §1 of the Act on the Protection of Natural Persons concerning the Processing of Personal Data.

[35] Chambre, 3126/001, Travaux Préparatoires, Proposed Act on the Protection of Natural Persons concerning the Processing of Personal Data, 11.06.2018, pp. 20–21.

Designating a data protection officer is mandatory for all federal government services. This obligation was laid down in Article 21 of the Framework Act. Nevertheless, the corresponding provision in the GDPR—Article 37—permits member states to define other controllers or processors who should designate a data protection officer. The Belgian legislator made a deliberate choice to impose such requirement also on all private companies that process personal data on behalf of government services and all private companies that receive personal data from government services. The Belgian DPA's opinion on the proposed Framework Act inspired the legislator to limit the designation duty to high-risk data processing only.[36]

2.5 Data Protection Disputes in Belgium

The Belgian DPA has drawn much attention to its work due to two high profile international cases. In 2006, a group of US journalists revealed that Belgium based company SWIFT was transferring mass amounts of financial messaging data to the US authorities in the framework of the Terrorist Finance Tracking Program.[37] The Belgian DPA stepped forward with an in-depth analysis of the case, which eventually led to an EU-US agreement on sharing such data. From 2015 onwards, the same DPA was involved in a complicated legal battle with US company Facebook. As the case could be resolved for the moment with a hefty incremental fine on the social network and a requirement to destroy the illegitimately collected data, the entry into effect of the GDPR sheds new light on the matter.

2.5.1 SWIFT and the Terrorist Finance Tracking Program

SWIFT is a company based in the Brussels region that does not handle money transfers as such, rather it manages more than 90% of the world's money transfers by sending so-called financial messaging data between financial institutions. The data that are not encrypted—and are thus visible to SWIFT—include data on the holder of the account from which money is transferred, the holder of the receiving account, the receiving bank and the date and time of the transfer. By means of Executive Order 13224[38] issued by the US Department of the Treasury (further: UST), a secret program was started shortly after the 11 September 2001 attacks on US territory. In the context of this program, the financing of terrorism was investigated by following

[36]Chambre, 3126/001, Travaux Préparatoires, Proposed Act on the Protection of Natural Persons concerning the Processing of Personal Data, 11.06.2018, pp. 46–47.

[37]Lichtblau and Risen 2006 Bank data is sifted by U.S. in secret to block terror. https://www.nytimes.com/2006/06/23/washington/23intel.html. Accessed 5 May 2019.

[38]Executive Order 13224, Blocking Property and Prohibiting Transactions with Persons Who Commit, Threaten to Commit, or Support Terrorism, 23 September 2001.

money trails. For that purpose, administrative subpoenas were sent to SWIFT to hand over financial messaging data related to suspects.[39]

The fact that the UST subpoenas were addressed to the American SWIFT operation center does not annul the applicability of the Belgian law. The main seat is based in Belgium and the company is officially registered in Belgium. Furthermore, the Article 29 Data Protection Working Party pointed out that the critical decisions on the processing of personal data and transfer of data to the UST were decided by the head office in Belgium.[40] One of the key points of contention was SWIFT's role in the data transfers. While SWIFT maintained that it was the data processor,[41] the Belgian DPA concluded that SWIFT is a data controller based on the authority SWIFT has to take decisions on the purposes and the means of processing personal data.[42]

In its qualification as the authority transferring personal data to a third state from the EU, SWIFT should have complied with the requirement of checking the adequate level of data protection of the receiving authority's data protection regime in accordance with Directive 95/46 and the applicable Belgian law. After a detailed analysis of the workings of SWIFT and the transfers in question, the DPA stressed that the amount of data transferred to the UST was exceptionally large and disproportionate considering the general scope of the subpoenas and the average number of messages that pass through SWIFT's system on a daily basis every day.

Ultimately, the DPA recognized that SWIFT had been caught in a conflict of laws between the EU data protection legal framework on the one hand and the US subpoena on the other. Acknowledging this difficult position, the DPA concluded that SWIFT made grave errors in transferring substantial amounts of data for several years to the UST in secret without legitimate purpose and an independent supervision in accordance with EU and Belgian law.[43]

The SWIFT case functioned as an eye-opener for the position internationally active companies can find themselves in when they are processing personal data in accordance with one country's laws and receive an order to hand over such data under another country's laws. In 2007, the solution developed for the transfer of financial messaging data from SWIFT to the UST was—after several failed attempts—an ad

---

[39] For an in-depth analysis, see De Busser 2009, pp. 384–399.

[40] Article 29 Data Protection Working Party (2006) WP 128, 01935/06, Opinion 10/2006 on the processing of personal data by the Society for Worldwide Interbank Financial Telecommunication (SWIFT).

[41] González Fuster et al. 2008, pp. 194–195.

[42] Belgian Privacy Commission (2006) Opinion RG 37/2006.

[43] Belgian Privacy Commission (2006) Opinion RG 37/2006.

hoc agreement.[44] In 2018, the US as well as the EU introduced more permanent solutions[45] but instead of choosing international agreements, both rely on laws applicable on their own territory with international repercussions.

2.5.2 Belgian DPA Versus Facebook

The Belgian DPA drew worldwide attention initiating a brave court case against Facebook in 2015. After failed attempts to reach an agreement with the company concerning their practice of tracking users as well as non-users, the DPA entered a three-year legal battle that is not necessarily over yet. Points of contention were the use of social plug-ins and the so-called "datr" cookie. The latter allows Facebook to track surfing behavior of non-users by means of social plug-ins installed on websites outside the domain of the company's social network.[46]

The DPA initiated summary proceedings as well as proceedings on the merits before the Court of First Instance in Brussels. Even though Facebook claimed a lack of jurisdiction on the part of the Belgian courts—instead stating the Irish courts as competent due to the EU headquarters of Facebook having their seat in Dublin, Ireland—the Court in the summary proceedings recognized their jurisdiction. The DPA had elaborated on this topic in its recommendation basing its argument for jurisdiction on Facebook Inc. being the only data controller—not Facebook Ireland—and on Article 4, §1, a) of Directive 95/46 stating that a controller should ensure that its establishments on the territory of several member states comply with the obligations laid down by the applicable national law. In first instance, the Court sentenced Facebook to an incremental penalty based on a breach of the Belgian law of 1992 as well as the Belgian implementation act of Directive 2002/58, the so-called e-privacy Directive.[47]

When Facebook appealed the summary proceedings, the Brussels Court of Appeal agreed with them that the Belgian courts did not have jurisdiction; moreover, that the required urgency for initiating summary proceedings could not be invoked as the DPA had waited three years before taking their complaint to court.[48]

[44]Agreement between the European Union and the United States of America on the processing and transfer of Financial Messaging Data from the European Union to the United States for the purposes of the Terrorist Finance Tracking Program, O.J. L 195, 27.07.2010.

[45]The US Clarifying Lawful Overseas Use of Data Act or CLOUD Act (H.R. 4943) and the Proposal for a Regulation on European Production and Preservation Orders for Electronic Evidence in Criminal Matters, COM (2018) 225 final.

[46]Belgian Privacy Commission (2015) Recommendation no. 04/2015.

[47]Law on Electronic Communication, B.S. 20.06.2005. Court of First Instance Brussels, 9.11.2015, 15/57/C https://www.gegevensbeschermingsautoriteit.be/sites/privacycommission/files/documents/Vonnis%20Privacycommissie%20v.%20Facebook%20-%2009-11-2015.pdf.

[48]Court of Appeal Brussels, 29.06.2016, 2016/KR/2, https://www.gegevensbeschermingsautoriteit.be/sites/privacycommission/files/documents/arrest%20Facebook.pdf.

On 16 February 2018, the Court of First Instance dealt with the procedure on the merits agreeing with the DPA on the question of jurisdiction as well as on the claimed violations of the 1992 law and the Belgian implementation of the e-privacy Directive. The Court emphasized the lack of consent and the unfair and disproportionate processing of data by Facebook.[49]

The decision received backing by the Advocate-General of the Court of Justice of the EU when he presented his opinion in a German case that raised a similar question regarding jurisdiction: as long as a company conducts commercial activities on the territory of a member state, that member state can apply its own privacy provisions on that company's practices. The Court followed its Advocate-General on this point.[50] The Court will soon have to take a stand on how the entry into effect of the GDPR affects the Belgian case against Facebook because on 27 and 28 March 2019 this case was plead before the Court of Appeals in Brussels. With both parties sticking to their arguments, the Court of Appeals recognized the difficult questions that the application of the GDPR now adds to the case. Not only is the consent requirement sharper under the GDPR, also the one-stop-shop-mechanism is now in effect. The latter means that companies such as Facebook that have a presence in several member states, can rely on the DPA of their main EU establishment to act as their lead DPA. The lead DPA is required to cooperate and coordinate with the DPAs of the other member states where this particular company may have other establishments. In the case of Facebook this will mean that the Irish DPA is the lead DPA but will have to liaise with—inter alia—the Belgian and the German DPAs in the context of the aforementioned issues. Therefore, on 8 May 2019, the Court of Appeals did not rule on the merits of the case. Rather, the Court of Appeals requested the Court of Justice of the EU for a preliminary ruling on whether the Belgian DPA can proceed with its claims against Facebook.[51]

2.6 GDPR Forecast

Due to the Belgian government's hesitant position on data protection before the 1992 Law was adopted, it is remarkable to see the prominent role that the Belgian DPA has

[49] Court of First Instance Brussels, 16.02.2018, 2016/153/A, https://www.gegevensbeschermingsautoriteit.be/sites/privacycommission/files/documents/Facebook_vonnis_16022018_0.pdf.

[50] CJEU 24.10.2017, C-210/16, Opinion, §128 and Judgment 05.06.2018.

[51] See Data Protection Authority (2019) Het Hof van Beroep van Brussel beslist om de zaak Facebook door te verwijzen naar het Hof van Justitie van de Europese Unie [The Court of Appeals of Brussels decides to refer the Facebook case to the Court of Justice of European Union]. https://www.gegevensbeschermingsautoriteit.be/nieuws/het-hof-van-beroep-van-brussel-verwijst-de-zaak-facebook-door-naar-het-hof-van-justitie. Accessed 11 May 2019.

taken in more recent years. In particular the DPA's continuing fight against unlawful data processing by Facebook, culminating in a favorable judgment in spring of 2018, was a strong endorsement of the DPA's position in actively pursuing better data protection. Followed by a reference to the Court of Justice of the EU, the DPA seems to feel strengthened in its pursuit of lawful data protection by large private companies such as Facebook. In addition, the Belgian DPA has also taken up a proactive stance with regard to the entry into effect of the GDPR. Publishing a 13-step-plan to be GDPR compliant and elaborate analyses for laymen as well as for legal experts on its website, the DPA anticipated the later adopted Belgian implementation law. What is more, aiming to provide data controllers with the necessary guidance on how to make a data protection impact assessment in accordance with the GDPR, the DPA published a detailed report in February 2018. The DPA did this on its own initiative and draws heavily on the guidance offered by the Article 29 Data Protection Working Party.

It can be expected that the Belgian DPA will continue to provide Belgian data controllers and processors guidance in complying with the GDPR but it can also be expected that the DPA will be uncompromising when it comes to those controllers and processors that do not comply.

References

Belgian Privacy Commission (2016) GDPR, Prepare yourself in 13 steps. https://www.gegevensbeschermingsautoriteit.be/bereid-je-voor-13-stappen. Accessed 6 May 2019

De Busser E (2009) EU-US data protection in criminal matters. Maklu, Antwerp

De Hert P (2003) Handboek Privacy: Persoonsgegevens in België [Privacy Handbook, Personal Data in Belgium]. Politeia, Brussels

De Hert P, Gutwirth S (2013) Anthologie Privacy [Privacy Anthology] ASP, Brussels

González Fuster G, De Hert P, Gutwirth S (2008) SWIFT and the vulnerability of transatlantic data transfers. IRLCT 2008 22:191–202

Lichtblau E, Risen J (2006) Bank Data Is Sifted by U.S. in Secret to Block Terror. https://www.nytimes.com/2006/06/23/washington/23intel.html. Accessed 5 May 2019

Dr. Els De Busser, Assistant Professor, Institute of Security and Global Affairs, Leiden University, The Netherlands.

Chapter 3
Data Protection in Estonia

Kärt Salumaa-Lepik, Tanel Kerikmäe and Nele Nisu

Contents

This text was compiled at the end of 2018 and therefore does not reflect the developments and changes introduced by the new Estonian Personal Data Protection Act, which entered into force in 2019.

K. Salumaa-Lepik (✉) · T. Kerikmäe
Tallinn University of Technology, Akadeemia tee 3, 12618 Tallinn, Estonia
e-mail: kart.salumaa-lepik@taltech.ee

T. Kerikmäe
e-mail: tanel.kerikmae@taltech.ee

N. Nisu
Estonian Ministry of Social Affairs, Tallinn, Estonia

E. Kiesow Cortez (ed.), *Data Protection Around the World*,
Information Technology and Law Series 33,
https://doi.org/10.1007/978-94-6265-407-5_3

Abstract The GDPR, which took effect on 25 May 2018, is an ambitious legal act aimed at harmonizing personal data protection and the free flow of data in the European Union. This chapter covers GDPR implementation issues and related topics from an Estonian perspective. The first section (Sect. 3.1) explains the roots of Estonian data protection and gives an overview of the latest developments related to the GDPR and the relevant case law. Section 3.2 offers readers an indication as to how the GDPR interacts with Estonian jurisdiction and identifies the most notable differences and similarities. Section 3.3 focuses on the most prominent issues within Estonian jurisdiction regarding data protection regulations. The main topic in this section is e-governance and the fact that Estonia is one of the recognized pioneers and leaders among modern digital societies. Taken from the perspective of the GDPR, some practices need to be re-evaluated (the cross-use functioning of national databases, the implementation of the "once-only" principle, the openness of state databases, etc.). Section 3.4 gives an overview of the envisaged application of the GDPR within Estonian jurisdiction and the possible problems that may occur when implementing GDPR provisions.

Keywords GDPR · Estonia · Personal data protection · Legislation · Privacy · Personal Data Protection Act

3.1 Data Protection Regulations and Case Law in Estonian Jurisdiction: Origin and Development of Estonian Data Protection Related Legislation and the Personal Data Protection Act

3.1.1 Introduction

Data protection law[1] is a relatively young area compared to more traditional branches of law. Samuel Warren and Louis Brandeis, in 1890, were the first to significantly address "the right to privacy," considering that right primarily as a "right to be let alone."[2] Since then, for more than a hundred years, this area has seen many new developments which have also reached Estonia and shaped its domestic privacy and data protection law.

Estonia became a member of the Council of Europe on 14 May 1993, shortly after regaining its independence from the Soviet Union in August 1991. This entailed

[1]This work was supported by Estonian Research Council grant PUT 1628.

[2]Warren and Brandeis 1890.

building up a wholly new and modern national legal order.[3] Estonia became a member state of the European Union (EU) on 1 May 2004; subsequently, the country has also been involved in the process of developing and negotiating the EU's legal framework, including the new EU data protection framework, of which the GDPR is a component.

The center of personal data protection in the Estonian domestic legal system lies within the Estonian Constitution which addresses some specific issues in the following articles:

- Article 26 stipulates the inviolability of family and private life.
- Article 33 stipulates the inviolability of the home.
- Article 42 forbids government authorities, local governments and officials from gathering or storing information about the beliefs of Estonian citizens against their free will.
- Article 43 stipulates the secrecy of communication channels. Everyone has the right to confidentiality of messages sent or received by him or her by post, telegraph, telephone or other commonly used means. Derogations from this right may be made in cases and pursuant to a procedure provided by law if they are authorized by a court and if they are necessary to prevent a criminal offence, or to ascertain the truth in a criminal case.
- Article 44 foresees the right to free access to information disseminated for public use.

These articles and rights as a whole form the constitutional integrity of Estonian data protection law and give the general mandate to further identify these matters within more specific laws and provisions. Before the GDPR, its predecessor (Directive 95/46/EC[4] on the protection of personal data) was transposed into Estonian domestic jurisdiction by the Estonian Personal Data Protection Act ("EDPA"). The first version of the EDPA[5] entered into force in 1996. Pertinent legislation of Germany and Finland was used as an example when drafting the EDPA.[6]

In addition to the aforementioned domestic legislation, the Estonian Public Information Act ("EPIA")[7] has been adopted. The EPIA, which entered into force in 2001, fulfils the idea of Article 44 of the Estonian Constitution that foresees the right to free access to information disseminated for public use. According to the EPIA § 3(1), public information is information which is recorded and documented in any manner and on any medium and which is obtained or created upon performance of public duties provided by law or legislation issued on the basis thereof. According to

[3] See Kerikmäe et al. 2017.

[4] Directive 95/46/EC of the European Parliament and of the Council of 24 October 1995 on the protection of individuals with regard to the processing of personal data and on the free movement of such data.

[5] First text of EDPA (in Estonian only)—Estonian Personal Data Protection Act/Isikuandmete kaitse seadus RT I 1996, 48, 944 (1996). https://www.riigiteataja.ee/akt/862756. Accessed 1 December 2018.

[6] Nõmper 2017.

[7] Estonian Public Information Act/Avaliku teabe seadus RT I 2000, 92, 597 (2000). https://www.riigiteataja.ee/en/eli/516102017007/consolide. Accessed 1 December 2018.

the EPIA § 3(2), access to information may be restricted pursuant to the procedure provided by law.

The EPIA also addresses the important issue of re-using of public information since 2016 when the relevant additions and amendments to the Act entered into force. According to the EPIA § 3^1(1), the re-use of information is defined as the use of such public information, the public use of which is not restricted by law or pursuant to the procedure established by law (open data), by natural persons or legal persons for commercial or non-commercial purposes other than the initial purpose within the public duties for which the information was obtained or produced. The exchange of information between holders of information for the performance of their public duties does not constitute re-use of information. This part of the EPIA is linked to the directive on the re-use of public sector information, also known as the PSI Directive (Directive 2003/98/EC) which entered into force in 2003. It was revised by the Directive 2013/37/EU, which entered into force in 2013.

In addition to the main laws on the protection of personal data, many more specific data processing provisions are regulated in Estonian special laws. For instance, Estonian Insurance Activities Act's[8] § 218 regulates situations where the processing of personal data may take place without the consent of the data subject.

Processing of sensitive personal data (special categories as per the GDPR) is permitted without the consent of the data subject in the following cases:

(1) processing of sensitive personal data specified in clause 4 (2) 3) of the EDPA for determining the obligation to perform an insurance contract by an insurance undertaking and the scope thereof and for exercising the right of recourse if the insured event is the death of the data subject or if determining the obligation to perform the insurance contract and the scope thereof and exercising the right of recourse requires processing of data on the state of health or disability of the data subject;

(2) processing of sensitive personal data specified in clause 4 (2) 8) of the EDPA for determining the obligation to perform an insurance contract by an insurance undertaking and the scope thereof and for exercising the right of recourse.

3.1.2 The History of the Estonian Data Protection Inspectorate

Article 51(1) of the GDPR stipulates that each EU member state shall provide for one or more independent public authorities to be responsible for monitoring the application of the GDPR, in order to protect the fundamental rights and freedoms of natural persons in relation to processing and to facilitate the free flow of personal data within the EU ("supervisory authority"). The predecessor of the GDPR (Directive 95/46/EC and its Article 28) contained a similar requirement: each EU member state

[8]Estonian Insurance Activities Act/Kindlustustegevuse seadus RT I, 07.07.2015, 1 (2015). https://www.riigiteataja.ee/en/eli/529012018003/consolide. Accessed 1 December 2018.

had to make one or more public authorities responsible for monitoring the application within its territory of the provisions adopted by the member states pursuant to Directive 95/46/EC.

Although Estonia was not yet a member state of the EU in 1995 when Directive 95/46/EC was approved by the EU member states, Estonia was actively preparing to become one. For example, before joining the EU, Estonia adjusted its domestic laws—including personal data protection provisions—according to EU requirements. From January 1995 to December 1997, the country made preparations for accession to the EU and adapted domestic laws to the internal market, i.e., the start of the harmonization process.[9] Directive 95/46/EC was also at the center of attention during this period. Hence, establishing national data protection supervisory authority was also on Estonia's agenda during the 1990s.

Estonia's independent data protection authority, *Andmekaitse Inspektsioon* (the Data Protection Inspectorate), was finally founded in 1999. From January 1997 to February 1999, data protection in Estonia was supervised by the Data Protection Department of the Ministry of Internal Affairs. The department's activities were controlled by the Legislative Committee of Estonia's parliament, in accordance with the requirements of the country's Act on Databases. However, the legal status of the department was not appropriate for the authority which implemented national supervisory functions. In addition, the solution did not comply with Estonia's Personal Data Protection Act, or the legislation of the European Union in this area. It was acknowledged that an independent authority within the framework of the Interior Ministry was needed; to fill this need, the Data Protection Inspectorate was established on 18 February 1999.[10]

For 2018, the Inspectorate set the following goals:

(1) comply with the obligations of the data protection authority in the implementation of the new data protection law (GDPR);
(2) comply with these obligations in a balanced manner, taking into account the openness of society in Estonia and the small size of its business institutions;
(3) help increase the level of information management and information security in enterprises and institutions, synchronizing with the adoption of the European Union Network and Information Security Directive 2016/1148.[11]

The Inspectorate carries out an active role in supervising the public sector. However, the short-term sectoral guidelines will not be in the Inspectorate's plan for the near future. At the same time, the Inspectorate is ready to advise business and professional associations if they want to create self-help manuals. The general regulation provides rules for both voluntary codes of conduct (guidelines for good practice) and data protection certificates (labels, etc., as per GDPR Articles 40–43).

[9]Estonian Ministry of Foreign Affairs 2009 Estonia's way into the European Union. http://vm.ee/sites/default/files/content-editors/web-static/052/Estonias_way_into_the_EU.pdf. Accessed 1 December 2018.

[10]The Estonian Data Protection Inspection (2000) The history of the organization. http://www.ebaltics.com› doc_upl › The_Estonian_Inspection. Accessed 1 December 2018.

[11]Peep 2018.

The Inspectorate has recommended that data protection, consumer protection and information security issues be reconciled.[12] It has stated that the new GDPR and national implementation standards form a very voluminous and complex area, with the choices leading to greater administrative burdens and increased legal risks. At the same time, the new *acquis* provides opportunities for a balanced and flexible implementation. The flexibility of the judicial area should be taken into account in digital development in Estonia and it should provide support for the small size of institutions.[13]

From the legal perspective, issues relating to establishment, functioning and supervision—in addition to supervisory authorities' powers since 25 May 2018 (the GDPR's application date)—can be found in the GDPR. As well, the GDPR creates the corresponding legal basis for covering the aforementioned topics. Until then, the EDPA in light of Directive 95/46/EC has stipulated relevant legal basis. More specifically, Chap. 6 and §§ 32–41 of the EDPA covered areas such as supervision and its measures, tasks of the Inspectorate, reporting and powers.

3.1.3 The Latest Estonian Data Protection Legislation Related to the GDPR

The GDPR became applicable from 25 May 2018 and it applies to the processing of personal data in the context of the activities of a controller or a processor in the EU, regardless of whether the processing takes place in the EU. Until the adoption of the entire package of new domestic GDPR-related legislation, the old laws remain applicable insofar as they do not contradict with GDPR requirements.

Paragraph 1 of Estonian Rules for Good Legislative Practice and Legislative Drafting[14] stipulates that a legislative intent must be compiled for the approval of the need to prepare a draft act. The legislative intent[15] for implementing the GDPR (and transposing Directive 680/2016) more specifically in Estonian domestic legislation was compiled by the Estonian Ministry of Justice and sent to coordination round in the first half of 2017. This legislative intent focused on specific GDPR articles and their application in Estonian domestic legislation. For example, the legislative intent addressed conditions applicable to a child's consent in relation to information society services originating from Article 8 of the GDPR. Article 8(1) stipulates that where point (a) of Article 6(1) applies, in relation to the offer of information society

[12] Ibid.

[13] Ibid.

[14] Estonian Rules for Good Legislative Practice and Legislative Drafting/Hea õigusloome ja normitehnika eeskiri RT I, 29.12.2011, 228 (2011). https://www.riigiteataja.ee/en/eli/508012015003/consolide. Accessed 1 December 2018.

[15] Estonian Ministry of Justice (2017) Legislative intent for implementing GDPR and directive 680/2016 into Estonian law/Isikuandmete kaitse uue õigusliku raamistiku kontseptsioon. https://eelnoud.valitsus.ee/main/mount/docList/db80bf57-35ca-41e3-be15-827a2f056fdd. Accessed 1 December 2018.

services directly to a child, the processing of a child's personal data will be lawful where the child is at least 16 years old. Where the child is below the age of 16 years, such processing shall be lawful only if and to the extent that consent is given or authorized by the holder of parental responsibility over the child. The last sentence of the GDPR, Article 8, states that EU member states may provide by law for a lower age for those purposes provided that such lower age is not below 13 years. Estonian legislative intent regarding the implementation of the GDPR addressed that issue and proposed 13 years as the age limit—a position that was also supported by the national supervisory authority.

The legislative intent addressed other issues, including:

- possible changes and amendments to be considered by the stakeholders such as a Data Protection Officer institution in the Estonian context;
- changes to special laws other than the new EDPA;
- processing of personal data of deceased persons;
- personal data protection certification procedures;
- administrative fines and the starting point for their more specific regulation in the Estonian context;
- amendments to special laws that make reference to the old EDPA;
- representation of data subjects originating from Article 80 of the GDPR;
- restrictions to the application of the GDPR originating from Article 23;
- processing criminal records data; and
- possible mandatory consultation obligation and authorization requirement with the Inspectorate.

The legislative intent was followed by the draft act of a new EDPA in the second half of 2017. The draft act for the new EDPA addressed topics brought under discussion by the legislative intent in a draft act form.

The draft changes are also planned in relation to data on the deceased, as this part is outside the scope of the GDPR. Recitals 27 and 158 state that the GDPR does not apply to the personal data of deceased persons. Member states may provide for rules regarding the processing of personal data of deceased persons. Although the conditions and the procedure for the establishment of death and the cause of death are regulated in the Establishment of Cause of Death Act,[16] the entire package of new domestic GDPR-related legislation should also be arranged, taking into account, *inter alia*, the necessity to protect the data of deceased persons. Currently a broader picture and an interdisciplinary coherent approach across sectors and between different legal acts is missing. For example, the protection of personal data relating to deceased persons, especially in the case of hereditary diseases, should also be protected. Disclosure of such data, especially health records, may affect the protection of the privacy of related persons (close relatives). Therefore, the use of data from national databases is limited even after the death of a person. Although the protection of data

---

[16]Establishment of Cause of Death Act/Surma põhjuse tuvastamise seadus RT I 2005, 24, 179 (2005). https://www.riigiteataja.ee/en/eli/ee/525062018018/consolide/current. Accessed 1 December 2018.

on deceased persons remains broadly similar (with some new aspects) to the law in force (the EDPA), certain exceptions are also laid down in specific laws. The privacy of individuals can be violated even if their data is not processed. It is important to assess the impact of several legal acts, including in the context of the EPIA. Because the EPIA also addresses the re-using of such of information, the legal area has to support balanced solutions and foresee the necessary restrictions in specific laws.

Pursuant to the general principle of the EPIA, public information is freely available, unless access is restricted and limited in accordance with the specific law. EPIA § 2(2) point 4) precludes the application of this law where restrictions and access rules are provided under specific legislation. On the one hand, the right to receive information prevails (§ 44 of the Constitution); on the other hand, the individual has the right to privacy (§ 26 and § 19 of the Constitution). The solution must be found through a reasonable balance between the various rights. When issuing data or disclosing data, access restrictions (private, family, etc.) must be evaluated every time, if specific rules do not exist. The implementation of Ethics Committees set-up, which Estonia has done in the past, may also provide additional protection in personal data processing. Recital 33 of the GDPR states that data subjects should be allowed to give their consent to certain areas of scientific research when in keeping with recognized ethical standards for scientific research. In this regard, Estonia has kept its current principles unchanged, specifying and harmonizing the principles whereby and how research ethics should be assessed.

The new draft legislation (for the implementation of the new EDPA, (the first new EDPA draft 650 SE[17] dropped from the proceedings, followed by draft 778 SE)[18] has *inter alia* addressed issues concerning the review of the personal data processing purposes stipulated in already existing legislative acts, the review of deadlines for data retention and the re-examination and designation of controllers (if not already brought out clearly in previous legislation). The main purpose of this exercise was to better perform the administrative tasks foreseen for a public sector data controller. Some of the relevant issues (*inter alia*) are listed below:

- EPIA § 43^5 stipulates that the regulation of the databases must include the composition of data collected in the database, the deadline for data retention and other organizational issues related to the maintenance of the database, while—in some cases in Estonian legislation—it was still not clear what data and how long exactly it may be processed (for instance, in a number of tax and customs applications).
- The Estonian Archives Act[19] regulates the access and use of archival records (§ 10). The new draft legislation states more specifically that after the death of

---

[17]Estonian Parliament (2018) History of readings in Parliament of the draft 650 SE. https://www.riigikogu.ee/tegevus/eelnoud/eelnou/96c37d10-383c-40ad-87be-a8583008b994/Isikuandmete%20kaitse%20seaduse%20rakendamise%20seadus. Accessed 1 December 2018.

[18]Estonian Parliament (2018) History of readings in Parliament of the draft 778 SE. https://www.riigikogu.ee/tegevus/eelnoud/eelnou/9d1420bb-b516-4ab1-b337-17b2c83eedb1/Isikuandmete%20kaitse%20seaduse%20rakendamise%20seadus Accessed 20 December 2018.

[19]Archives Act/Arhiiviseadus RT I, 21.03.2011, 1 (2011). https://www.riigiteataja.ee/en/eli/ee/504032016002/consolide/current. Accessed 1 December 2018.

the data subject, access to the records containing the data subject's personal data shall be available to a third party such as successor, spouse, descendant, ascendant, relative, brother or sister.

New amendments occurred after the second reading of the draft legislation (650 SE). As a result, information on the activities of a public authority and persons related to it during the period of occupation will not be subject to access restrictions arising from the EPIA. The amendment seeks to state more clearly that the information related to the authority's activities—even when carried out by a natural person, for instance the person working or otherwise. However, the new draft as a final draft did not include this distinction of data processing in the period of occupation (778 SE).

- Issues have also arisen in relation to the salaries of individuals who work in the public sector under an employment contract (whether this data should be public or not).

In addition, there have been significant disputes regarding the implementation of the new EDPA (draft legislation 778 SE) and the new EDPA itself (draft legislation 679 SE[20]) which regulates personal data protection issues directly linked to the GDPR. One example is discussions related to deceased persons' data in general. Who should be given the right to decide upon the processing of the deceased person's data? Should it should be a successor or, as before, a family member? And how long should the data be protected after the data subject's death? Disputes regarding the new legislation and future personal data processing have also been linked to the processing of personal data for journalistic purposes. The wording of one sentence has received a lot of attention. Should data processing for journalistic purposes be justified if there is predominant public interest or just a public interest? The solutions and answers to these topics will be given with the new Estonian data protection legislation.

3.1.4 Data Protection Case Law Within Estonian Jurisdiction

Over the years, Estonian court practice regarding personal data protection and privacy law has become more diverse and comprehensive. The following section of this chapter is a selection of Estonian Supreme Court (*Riigikohus*) rulings concerning personal data and personal data protection.

Pursuant to judgment **3-3-1-98-06**[21] of the Supreme Court, information about alcohol consumption (intoxication by alcohol) can be considered as sensitive personal data. This position is also supported by EDPA § 4 paragraph 2 point 3 which indicates to data on the state of health or disability as sensitive personal data. The judgment

[20]Estonian Parliament (2018) History of readings in Parliament of the draft 679 SE. https://www.riigikogu.ee/tegevus/eelnoud/eelnou/5c9f8086-b465-4067-841e-41e7df3b95af/Isikuandmete%20kaitse%20seadus. Accessed 1 December 2018.

[21]Supreme Court (*Riigikohus*) (2007) Case 3-3-1-98-06. https://rikos.rik.ee/?asjaNr=3-3-1-98-06. Accessed 1 December 2018.

focused on health data as sensitive personal data from the perspective of data disclosure. In addition, it addresses the issue of legal ground for personal data disclosure because personal data disclosure can be seen as personal data processing. The Court stated that disclosure of personal data by a public body may be legitimate only in cases clearly stipulated by law; because such processing under attention was not clearly stipulated by the law, it was not approved by the Supreme Court.

In another judgment (3-15-2079/28),[22] the Supreme Court *inter alia* gave an assessment to two issues related to personal data protection: the right of data subjects to obtain information and personal data concerning them (EDPA § 19); and the right of the data subject to demand the correction (rectification) of inaccurate or misleading data (EDPA § 6 p. 7). In this case, the Estonian Financial Supervision Authority (*Finantsinspektsioon*) rejected the data subject's access request to personal data by using the argument of confidentiality and refused to give out information. Therefore it also became impossible for the data subject to implement the right to rectification. *Finantsinspektsioon* explained its decision not to hand over the personal data requested with the reservation foreseen by the Estonian Financial Supervision Authority Act[23] § 54. The § 54 of the aforementioned act stipulates that proceedings conducted by the Supervision Authority for the conduct of financial supervision shall not be public and that information obtained in the course of financial supervision from the subjects of financial supervision or other persons or agencies—including data, documents and other information, certificates, reports and precepts prepared in the course of financial supervision, and other documents on any type of data media containing information on the results of financial supervision—shall be confidential. Additional provisions in the aforementioned act further specify the concept and therefore give *Finantsinspektsioon* the right to operate under confidentiality. The judgment also mentioned that the confidentiality obligation for supervision does not prevent data subjects from obtaining—and supervisory authority from providing—personal data in situations where it is linked to authority's supporting activities, e.g., business administration, personnel (p 22 of the judgment). Because the data subject in the context of this specific judgment asked for information concerning financial supervision, his request was denied. The Court also found that given the specifics of the financial supervision system regarding the obligation to maintain professional secrecy and the confidentiality of the communication, the applicant (data subject) had no right to request rectification in the current case. Hence, the Court declared that the right to request rectification of personal data is not unlimited and therefore not an absolute right.

In the case 3-3-1-85-15[24] about media coverage (by *Äripäev*—one of Estonia's most influential newspapers), the personal data issue was related to investors and

---

[22] Supreme Court (*Riigikohus*) (2018) Case 3-15-2079/28. https://rikos.rik.ee/LahendiOtsingEriVaade?asjaNr=3-15-2079/28. Accessed 1 December 2018.

[23] Financial Supervision Authority Act/Finantsinspektsiooni seadus RT I 2001, 48, 267 (2001). https://www.riigiteataja.ee/en/eli/529012018006/consolide. Accessed 1 December 2018.

[24] Supreme Court (*Riigikohus*) (2016) Case 3-3-1-85-15. https://rikos.rik.ee/?asjaNr=3-3-1-85-15. Accessed 1 December 2018.

investments (ranking "TOP 50 of Estonian stock market investors"). Because the data was published in a newspaper, the supervisory authority checked first whether the conditions for disclosure were met according to EDPA § 11(2) and whether the disclosure of such data was not disproportionate and did not disproportionally affect the data subject's right to a private life. EDPA § 11(2) stipulates that personal data may be processed and disclosed in the media for journalistic purposes without the consent of the data subject, if there is predominant public interest and this is in accordance with the principles of journalism ethics.

The applicant's defense was built on the following argumentation (p 4 of the judgment). The applicant noted that before the publication of the article, the journalist had contacted him, after which the applicant stated that he did not wish to publish his personal data in such a way. The publication of the data did not have a journalistic purpose, as the applicant works as a patent attorney, and his day-to-day activities are not generally related to public tasks. Also, investing is a private activity and the applicant cannot be considered as a major investor. The applicant is not a public figure considered to be a person who exercises public authority or is capable of influencing politics or economics.

The Court, instead, found (p 6 of the judgment) that the articles of *Äripäev* had a journalistic purpose to provide a comprehensive overview of the changes in investment activity that took place during the previous year. Given the value of the applicant's investment, it cannot be assumed that he had no economic power at all. Only the name and the value of his investments in comparison between the years 2013 and 2014, as well as the reference to the improvement of the ranking compared to previous comparisons, were published and the data was presented in a neutral form. The Court also found that this sort of interference with the applicant's private sphere was not intense. It was found in the present case that the disclosure of the personal data originated from the volume of the applicant's investments. Hence, the Court indicated that it is not in itself important whether there is a reason to consider the applicant as a public figure in a broader context (for example, because of the occupation of the applicant as a patent attorney).

The Court additionally indicated that the data *Äripäev* used for media coverage originated from public sources. More specifically, it came from the database where data is being published according to the Estonian Securities Register Maintenance Act. Hence, the newspaper received its data from public sources. Therefore, the Court reached a conclusion that there was no infringement in the case and the disclosure of data was lawful in the current context of the case.

Case **3-3-1-3-12**[25] is also about publishing personal data in an article, although the background and context are somewhat different than described in the previous case concerning the disclosure of investment data. In this case, the dispute was over the disclosure of data concerning a prisoner held in prison; the data was printed in *Vangla Ekspress* (a publication distributed free of charge within the prison administration mostly between public servants, under the coordination of the Estonian Ministry of

[25] Supreme Court (*Riigikohus*) (2012) Case 3-3-1-3-12. https://rikos.rik.ee/?asjaNr=3-3-1-3-12. Accessed 1 December 2018.

Justice). The published information relating to the prisoner (data subject) concerned the applicant's relations with the prison authorities and with the detainees; it also cited the applicant's recorded telephone conversations and a diary. Although the article was published under the administration of the Ministry of Justice, in particular within the framework of the prison system's internal communication system, a large number of public servants received access to the data. It was also not ruled out that the article might have been spread outside the system. Thus, the number of people who had accessed that article remained unknown in that case.

The Court stated that such administrative measures affecting fundamental rights can only be legitimate if they are: based on the legal basis provided by law; in accordance with procedural and substantive law; and necessary (proportional) in a democratic society. The Court also found that the article's data about the applicant, including telephone extracts and diary entries, was published in the public criminal hearing.

The Court considered it important to state that the mere fact that the information had previously been disclosed in some form on the basis of consent of the data subject or by law should not result in a conclusion that additional disclosure (further processing) may not have significant consequences for the data subject. Initial and repeated disclosure of the data may take place in a very different format and with varying intensity, depending on the identity of the transmitter, the information channel, the context, the auditorium, etc. For example, the new publication of the data published at the hearing by the press will, as a general rule, broaden the circle of informed persons. Point 24 of the judgment also makes a reference to several European Court of Human Rights (ECtHR) rulings stating that the ECtHR has repeatedly emphasized that the disclosure of data in court proceedings does not give blanket power to publish information in the media (judgments of 17 January 2012 in case 33497/07 *Krone Verlag and Others v. Austria*, p. 49, and case 3401/07: *Kurier/Austria*, p. 44; Decision of 10 February 2009 in case No 3514/02: *Eerikäinen* et al./*Finland*, p. 63).

A proportionate interference in the private life of an individual is not the case where the necessary and moderate limited disclosure would always be accompanied by an unlimited opportunity to process the data repeatedly. Such a possibility would be manifestly contrary to the purpose limitation principle, the data minimalization principle and the principle of restricted use. Hence, the Court found accordingly that the data subject has the right, under certain conditions, to demand the termination of further processing of previously disclosed personal data, including refraining from disclosure in the future. The Court also found that in the current context, the disclosure of a data subject's personal data was not inevitably necessary. Thus, the Court declared such disclosure of personal data unlawful.

3.2 Interaction Between Estonian Data Protection Legislation and the GDPR—Similarities and Differences

3.2.1 Similarities of the GDPR and the Estonian Jurisdiction

Because both the GDPR and the Estonian pre-GDPR personal data protection legal framework are based on Directive 95/46/EC, many similarities can be found between the GDPR and the Estonian domestic jurisdiction regarding personal data protection.

First, similar understandings of the definitions laying down the common understanding of personal data protection existed in the past and are currently in place.

Second, the principles for processing personal data are applicable now with the GDPR in both the Estonian and the EU legal frameworks. The newest addition to this list is the principle of *data protection "by design" and "by default"* which became a similarity with the application of the GDPR (because the GDPR is directly applicable).

It is also possible to raise the question whether it is even proper to mention Estonian and GDPR jurisdiction in separate contexts because after 25 May 2018, the GDPR is part of the Estonian legal framework.

At the time of writing this section (at the beginning of December 2018), the authors were not able to finalize the list of similarities and differences because the Estonian domestic legal act implementing more specific provisions of the GDPR had still not yet been approved by the Parliament (*Riigikogu*).[26] Recital 8 of the GDPR declares that where this Regulation (GDPR) provides for specifications or restrictions of its rules by member state law, member states may—as far as necessary for coherence and for making the national provisions comprehensible to the persons to whom they apply—incorporate elements of this Regulation into their national law. Because the domestic law is only halfway approved by the time of writing this section, it is too early to draw final conclusions regarding the exhaustive list of all similarities and differences.

[26]Only the so-called "new general framework data protection legal act" has been approved (by 12 December 2018), but without more specific implementing provisions concerning domestic special laws. Therefore, the full extent of the impact is still not known at the time of the writing of this chapter.

3.2.2 Differences Between the GDPR and the Estonian Jurisdiction

3.2.2.1 Administrative Fines Versus Misdemeanor Procedure

The most overwhelming challenge relates to GDPR recital 151 considering the fact that Estonia's legal system does not allow for administrative fines as set out in the GDPR.

As of today, GDPR fines have not yet been imposed in Estonia. The maximum amount of an imposed fine as per GDPR's Article 83 is up to 20,000,000 EUR or, in the case of an undertaking, up to 4% of the total worldwide annual turnover of the preceding financial year, whichever is higher. It is remarkable that fines for personal data protection infringements by the supervisory authority in Estonia were imposed on only three[27] occasions in 2017, according to the latest statistics published by the Inspectorate. The future will show whether this number will see an increase.

3.2.2.2 Obligation to Designate a Data Protection Officer (*DPO*)

The obligation to designate a DPO, according to Article 37 of the GDPR, can be seen as a difference between the GDPR and the Estonian pre-GDPR domestic legal system where the institution of a DPO as such was unknown. The pre-GDPR legislation and the § 27 of the EDPA stipulated the obligation to register the processing of sensitive personal data. When a processor of personal data had not appointed a person responsible for the protection of personal data, the processor of personal data was required to register the processing of sensitive personal data with the Inspectorate. DPOs constituted a new functionality in the Estonian personal data protection legal framework.

3.2.2.3 Legal Grounds for Personal Data Processing

The basics of processing have not changed substantially compared to the predecessor directive. As Article 9(4) of the GDPR stipulates, member states may maintain or introduce further conditions, including limitations, with regard to the processing of genetic data, biometric data or health data. However, this should not prevent the free flow of personal data in cross-border processing.[28] Because the genetic data of individuals is of a sensitive nature, its processing should be protected with different guarantees.

---

[27] Estonian Data Protection Inspectorate 2018c Statistics. https://www.aki.ee/et/inspektsioon/statistika. Accessed 1 December 2018.

[28] GDPR rec 53—However, this should not hamper the free flow of personal data within the Union when those conditions apply to cross-border processing of such data.

The Estonian Human Genes Research Act (HGRA)[29] lays down the conditions for the processing of tissue samples, descriptions of DNA, descriptions of state of health and genealogies in the Gene Bank, as well as rights and obligations of gene donors and restrictions on the use of tissue samples, descriptions of DNA, descriptions of state of health and genealogies collected in the Gene Bank (HGRA § 1(2)). The objectives of this Act are to regulate the establishment and maintenance of a Gene Bank, to organize the genetic research, etc., but also to protect persons from misuse of genetic data and from discrimination based on interpretation of the structure of their DNA and the genetic risks arising therefrom. The Gene Bank may be used only for scientific research, research into and treatment of illnesses of gene donors, public health research and statistical purposes. Use of the Gene Bank for other purposes, especially to collect evidence in civil or criminal proceedings or for surveillance, is prohibited (HGRA § 16(1)). The latter may be interpreted as a nationally preserved distinction in the sense of Article 9(4) of the GDPR. In addition, if the GDPR includes the "right to know" and the "right to be forgotten," HGRA refers also to the "right not to know." Therefore, a person is able to become a gene donor, but after donating blood, he or she has the right not to know his own gene data (HGRA § 11(1) and § 12(4)(4)).

Regarding the Ethics Committees, Estonia didn´t achieve what was initially planned—a comprehensive coverage of Ethics Committees and requirements applicable to them. It eventually did not become part of the new EDPA, and the EDPA draft only upgraded the existing principles in specific law. There are distinct ethics committees foreseen for the health information system (Health Services Organisation Act § 59^4)[30] and the Gene Bank (HGRA § 29). The law states that the aim of the respective Committee is to ensure the preventive protection of the fundamental rights of persons, the harmonization of the evaluation principles applied to surveys in order to safeguard the rights of the defense and the obligation of researchers to observe these safeguards. The main goal of the Ethics Committees is to assess the ethical risks of the research and the background of the researcher, striking a balance between data protection and public interest as one of the important purposes for processing.

However, in the light of the new EDPA, the role of the Ethics Committees has decreased considerably. Even if certain principles are harmonized in the field of health data, there is no longer double control in the area of health research. On the basis of § 16 of the current EPIA, if the research is conducted without the person's consent, it is necessary to obtain permission from the Inspectorate and the Ethics Committee, if the latter is created in this area. In the draft of the new EPIA, the law provides for the intervention of the Inspectorate only if there is not a specific committee. This will reduce the bureaucracy in this area and give the Data Protection Inspectorate more time to deal with more serious violations, but on the other hand,

[29] Human Genes Research Act/Inimgeeniuuringute seadus RT I 2000, 104, 685 (2000). https://www.riigiteataja.ee/en/eli/ee/518062014005/consolide/current. Accessed 1 December 2018.

[30] Health Services Organisation Act/Tervishoiuteenuste korraldamise seadus RT I 2001, 50, 284 (2001). https://www.riigiteataja.ee/en/eli/508042019003/consolide. Accessed 1 December 2018.

the double checks are eliminated and the importance of committees will increase. There is a clear distinction between situations that are subject to either the research rules or the analysis of the institution task in the public sector in the new EDPA. Doubts have been expressed as to whether the analysis of an administrative body can be considered as "research" and can therefore be subject to § 16. So far, the provision in the new EDPA is included according to which analyses and research are carried out by the executive authorities for the purpose of policy-making which are also considered as "research" (new EDPA, § 6(5)). The Inspectorate shall verify the fulfillment of the conditions provided in the EDPA, unless the regulation of the processing of personal data is regulated in the specific legal act.

It may be the case that, although the person whose privacy should be protected has died, the processing of sensitive data related to the deceased person can harm the privacy or become harmful to his or her family or other relatives. Although, on the one hand, the protected period is significantly shortened with the new EDPA draft, the draft also provides for an additional option. The new EDPA draft makes it possible for the person to extend the referred terms, by making such a declaration in, for example, health data in the health information system or in the data subject's will. As health-related data is very sensitive, the greatest fears are associated with this type of data. Therefore, if the new EDPA comes into effect, the person will be able to determine in advance some of his or her data processing.

3.3 The Most Prominent Issues in the Estonian Jurisdiction Regarding Data Protection Regulations: eGovernance and National Databases in Conjunction with the GDPR

3.3.1 Introduction

Data protection is an interdisciplinary field, which is based not only on law and jurisprudence, but also on information technology and ethics. The relationship with information technology can especially be addressed in the light of an important 2016 decision of the Court of Justice of the European Union (CJEU) where the Court ruled that IP addresses can also qualify as personal data.[31] Data, information and knowledge are the raw material in this age of knowledge and networks, and are commonly referred to as the "oil of the 21st century."[32] The GDPR, according to the European Commission, has rules designed to encourage innovation: the GDPR

[31] CJEU Judgment Case C-582/14 19 October 2016 (*Breyer*).

[32] Schweighofer et al. 2017.

is technology neutral.[33] This is very important when the functioning of eGovernance and the reputation of e-Estonia are at stake.

Effective eGovernment can provide a wide variety of benefits, including: more efficiency and savings for governments and businesses; increased transparency; and greater participation of citizens in political life.[34] However, it can also increase potential privacy risks. As the General Director of the Estonian Data Protection Inspectorate stated: "Part of the data protection is security of information—without it, the rules are worthless."[35]

The Digital Economy and Society Index (DESI) is a composite index that summarises relevant indicators on Europe's digital performance and tracks the evolution of EU member states in digital competitiveness. Denmark, Sweden, Finland and the Netherlands have the most advanced digital economies in the EU followed by Luxembourg, Ireland, the UK, Belgium and Estonia. Romania, Greece and Italy have the lowest scores on the DESI.[36] Therefore, Estonia can be considered as one of the leading EU member states when it comes to digital performance and digital competitiveness.

In achieving good results in digital competitiveness, the Estonian X-Road system has played a significant role. Estonia's current e-solution environment includes a full range of services for the general public and, because each service has its own database, they all use X-Road. To ensure secure transfers, all outgoing data from X-Road is digitally signed and encrypted, and all incoming data is authenticated and logged. Originally, X-Road was simply used to send queries to different databases. Now it has developed into a tool that can also write to multiple databases, transmit large data sets and perform searches across several databases simultaneously. X-Road was designed with growth in mind, so it can be scaled up as new e-services and new platforms come online. Today, X-Road is also implemented in Finland, Azerbaijan, Namibia and the Faroe Islands. X-Road is also the first data exchange platform in the world that allows data to be automatically exchanged between countries. Since June 2017, automatic data exchange capability has been established between Estonia and Finland.[37] X-Road also enables citizens and officials to operate via different portals and applications (document management systems, institutional information systems) in a more efficient and flexible manner. Even though X-Road was originally created by the "I ask you, you answer me" principle, it now has become a main component of the state information system, offering integrated e-services in addition to data exchange

---

[33]European Commission 2018g The GDPR: new opportunities, new obligations. https://ec.europa.eu/commission/sites/beta-political/files/data-protection-factsheet-sme-obligations_en.pdf. Accessed 1 December 2018.

[34]European Commission 2018d eGovernment & Digital Public Services. https://ec.europa.eu/digital-single-market/en/policies/egovernment. Accessed 1 December 2018.

[35]Peep 2018.

[36]European Commission 2018c The digital economy and society index (DESI). https://ec.europa.eu/digital-single-market/en/desi. Accessed 1 December 2018.

[37]E-Estonia 2018 X-Road. https://e-estonia.com/solutions/interoperability-services/x-road/. Accessed 1 December 2018.

and file exchange.[38] Hence, X-Road is an essential key-player when processing personal data and also a facilitator for following GDPR personal data processing norms.

As Digital Agenda 2020 says: "Both individuals and companies find that public e-services help them to save time and money and are largely satisfied with the provision of public services." According to the Agenda, the major strength to date of the national ICT policy is the systematic development of the state information system and ensuring its security, as well as appropriate data security and data exchange and the use of strong authentication tools.[39] These elements—the digital solutions of both the public and private sectors—have captured international attention and created a growing reputation for Estonia as a leading e-country.[40]

As stated in the European Commission blog "E-Governance and E-Guidance. The Example of Estonia",[41] some of the best e-solutions that have led to Estonia becoming one of the world's most developed digital societies are the following.

1. **X-Road**. More than 900 organizations and enterprises in Estonia use X-Road daily.
2. **Digital ID**. As a digital access card for every secure e-service in Estonia.
3. **e-Tax**. Electronic tax filing system where 95% of tax declarations are filled in only 3 min.
4. **e-Residency**. Secure access to Estonian e-services for foreign citizens. The owner of the e-resident's digital ID card can digitally sign documents and log into all the portals and information systems that recognize the Estonian ID-card.
5. **e-Health**. The patient owns his or her personal health data. Another unique aspect is the fact that, since 2008, hospitals and doctors in Estonia have been required to digitize data and make it available in the e-Health record.
6. **e-Prescription**. This centralized paperless system for issuing and handling medical prescriptions is used in 99% of cases. E-Prescription does not require digital skills; the patient only needs to call the doctor and collect their medication from the closest pharmacy.
7. The **i-Voting** system. This system allows citizens to vote anywhere, no matter how far they are from a polling station, because the ballot can be cast from any internet-connected computer anywhere in the world.
8. Entrepreneurs can: **register businesses** in as little as 20 min; check vital company, property and legal records online; and integrate their own secure services with the ones offered by the state.

[38]Estonian Information System Authority 2018 Riigi Infosüsteemi teejuht. https://www.ria.ee/teejuht/eesti-it-edulood/2013-aastal-tehti-x-teel-ule-280-miljoni-infoparingu. Accessed 1 December 2018 (link no longer active).

[39]Ministry of Economic Affairs and Communications 2018 Digital agenda 2020. https://www.mkm.ee/sites/default/files/digital_agenda_2020_estonia_engf.pdf. Accessed 1 December 2018.

[40]Ibid.

[41]European Commission 2018f The example of Estonia. https://ec.europa.eu/epale/en/blog/e-governance-and-e-guidance-example-estonia. Accessed 1 December 2018.

Citizens' main data source for communicating with the state is the Estonian population register which allows the organization of state e-services and ensures the use of personal data on a uniform basis throughout the country. The population register, which is the property of the state, is maintained as an electronic database. The maintenance of the registry has to follow GDPR and personal data protection principles, for example, protection of private life, access on the basis of law. The main user of this register is the public sector while carrying out its duties. Exchanging the registry data with other state databases through X-Road allows this solution to always link the correct person's data with his or her data in the other database. This data plays a very important role, for example, in Estonia's e-voting. The data in the population register is the base used for calculating the number of voters, to create polling lists and updated voter cards. The data in the population register is provided by county governments and local government units, notaries, clergy, medical institutions, foreign representations, the Ministry of the Interior, the Ministry of Foreign Affairs, the Police and Border Guard Board, the courts and the Road Administration, as well as the persons themselves. The population register contains the birth and death data of a person, as well as their personal identification code and revised versions of the code. The rest of the databases can therefore rely on the basis of the population register's central data—marital property register, land register, social services and benefits registry, state databases related to public health, motor register, the criminal records database, etc. Of course, each separate database plays its more specific role in the daily work of the respective administrative body and each personal data processing activity must also follow the GDPR and other personal data protection and security norms.

Cross-usage of personal data reduces the data subject's obligation to provide state authorities and the public sector with different pieces of personal data more than once. However, it still may not be easy to do so on the international level and also in the EU. Due to the lack of a common transnational exchange of data, Estonia must negotiate with each country separately in order to achieve those goals both internationally and domestically. Although Estonia has become a leader in electronic identity management internationally, its effective maintenance and development still require a lot of work and effort in order to stay in the top tier of global digital successful players.

Managing well-developed databases and information systems will also benefit society in the wider context. The Estonian data collections with open data can be found on a special portal: "*Eesti avaandmete portal*" (as Estonian open information portal).[42] The EPIA gives an explanation of open data. EPIA § 3^1(1) stipulates that this data be in a machine-readable format and available to everyone for free and public use. Open data can bring diverse benefits to governments, businesses and individuals. It has the power to help improve services and grow economies.[43] The reduction of administrative burden (for example, reduced number of information requests) as well

---

[42]Estonian Open Government Data Portal (2018) https://opendata.riik.ee/ Accessed 1 December 2018.

[43]Read further from the European Data Portal: https://www.europeandataportal.eu/en/homepage. Accessed 1 December 2018.

as the transition to future technologies is also considered to be an advantage in using open data. At the same time, the principle of open data is specified in the draft package (778 SE). The second reading of the new draft legislation brought an amendment regarding that topic. The explanatory part specifies that if such data contains personal information, the general use of such information must be restricted if it significantly impairs the individual's privacy. In personal data re-usage for purposes other than for which it was collected initially, the potential consequences for the data subject must be taken into account. These principles are also supported by the current law in EPIA (§ 3^1(7) and (8)).

As also mentioned earlier, Estonia has successfully implemented many e-services. The following is an illustration of how the exchange of driving licenses can take place without visiting several institutions in person and how it is possible to receive a new license via post.

- First, the health service provider forwards the medical certificate data to the Road Administration electronically on the conditions of and in accordance with the procedure established on the basis of the HSOA. Patients/data subjects are allowed to forward their health declarations to health care providers through the Health Information System (HSOA § 59^2(1^2)).
- After completing the declaration, the data subject must make an appointment and visit a family doctor.
- To renew the license in e-service on the self-service web page of the Estonian Road Administration, a data subject needs to provide a valid medical certificate, digital photo, signature and proof of residence in Estonia. The provided data is verified by data from the population register and (for the health certificate) from the health information system.
- The data subject can choose a picture from the Police and Border Guards database (which is used when preparing identity documents) or from the motor register[44] and can then pay the state fee in order to renew the license.
- The driving license will be mailed to the data subject's address indicated in the e-service system.

This driving license example illustrates how the data subject's personal data may be processed easily, comfortably and transparently with only a little effort on the part of the data subject.

[44] See further: https://eteenindus.mnt.ee/juht.jsf.

3.3.2 The Application and Possibilities of the "Once-Only" Principle in Light of the GDPR

Building smarter cities and improving access to eGovernment, eHealth services and digital skills will result in one digital European society.[45] Individuals who want to benefit from the opportunities provided by the European Single Market for travelling, working, doing business and living abroad are generating significant demands for public services in cross-border situations. Recognizing that data (including personal data) can be obtained in many different ways leads to the Once Only principle (OOP). In the context of the public sector, the OOP means that citizens and businesses should supply information only once to a public administration in the EU. The importance of the OOP is also reflected by the fact that it is described in the eGovernment Action Plan 2016–2020[46] and seen as a key indicator. It means that citizens and businesses provide diverse data only once in contact with public administrations, while public administration bodies take actions to internally share and re-use these data, while respecting data protection regulations.

In Estonia, the need for the implementation of the OOP has also emerged as a result of a nationally initiated project, the so-called "zero-bureaucracy." It became part of the action program of the Government of the Republic of Estonia for 2016–2019.[47] The Minister of Economic Affairs and Infrastructure—together with the Minister of Entrepreneurship, the Minister of Finance and the Minister of Public Administration—initiated an ambitious project to reduce the bureaucratic burden on businesses.[48] A summary of the proposal's analysis included a proposal for the implementation of the OOP, recognizing that people themselves want to apply this principle in practice to reduce the time spent on communication. In essence, different initiatives have led to the same result—Estonians want to gain and derive as much as possible from a growing digital society. Therefore, the implementation of the OOP will not only facilitate the communication of citizens with the state but also the interactions of the administrations with society, including across Europe when interoperability principles will be implemented on a larger scale in order to benefit EU citizens.

An Estonian proverb says that a good child has several names. In Estonia, the OOP is also known as the "one door method." Submitting data to one administrative body, for example, to receive a grant, it is possible to use the same data as a second

[45]European Commission 2018a Creating a digital society. https://ec.europa.eu/digital-single-market/en/policies/creating-digital-society. Accessed 1 December 2018.

[46]European Commission 2018e EU-wide digital once-only principle for citizens and businesses. Policy options and their impacts. Executive Summary, 2015/0062. https://ec.europa.eu/digital-single-market/en/news/eu-wide-digital-once-only-principle-citizens-and-businesses-policy-options-and-their-impacts. Accessed 1 December 2018.

[47]Action program of the Government of the Republic of Estonia for 2016–2019/Vabariigi Valitsuse tegevusprogramm 2016–2019 (2016). https://www.riigiteataja.ee/aktilisa/3280/4201/8008/111k_lisa.pdf. Accessed 1 December 2018.

[48]Ministry of Economic Affairs and Communications 2017 Zero-bureaucracy. https://www.mkm.ee/en/zero-bureaucracy-0. Accessed 1 December 2018.

grant application. The Work Ability Allowance Act[49] § 6(2) and Social Benefits for Disabled Persons Act[50] § 2^2(2) regulate situations in which a person may submit an application only once by choosing either the Unemployment Insurance Fund or the Social Insurance Board.

The Work Ability Allowance Act stipulates that a person may submit an application for assessment of work ability to the unemployment insurance fund through the Social Insurance Board if the application is submitted together with an application for determination of the degree of severity of disability submitted to the Board on the basis of the Social Benefits for Disabled Persons Act. Under the Social Benefits for Disabled Persons Act, a person may also submit an application for determination of the degree of severity of disability through the Estonian Unemployment Insurance Fund if the application is submitted together with an application for assessment of work ability submitted to the unemployment insurance fund on the basis of the Work Ability Allowance Act. Hence, the assessment of work capacity and the identification of disability may be submitted together to the Unemployment Insurance Fund or to the Social Insurance Board—one application and one evaluation.

Data is successfully re-usable if it can be shared in machine-readable format, i.e., can be automatically processed by information systems. Data re-using is made possible by the creation of national information systems and registries. The collected data must be of high quality, relying on agreed-upon data standards, classifications, lists and other requirements. For example, health data in Estonia is entered into the eHealth system and the existing source data is used. In the Estonian eHealth Strategic Development Plan 2020,[51] the same principle is mentioned. Health data is essential for the processing of the service, and the data already collected should always be used in the context of health care. Data is collected by default for all health services according to the legal basis. Based on the legislation, it is assumed that a person agrees to the processing of their health information when using the service (opt-out). Outside the eHealth system, the opt-in principle is applied.[52]

HSOA § 4^1(2) stipulates that the use of the classifications, directories, address details of the State Information Systems and standards of the Health Information System is mandatory in maintaining health care service records. Health care providers are required to submit medical documents information and images to the Health Information System (HSOA § 59^2(1)). In addition, they must maintain confidentiality arising from law and have the right to process personal data required for the provision of a health service (HSOA 4^1(1)). Similarly, patients as data subjects have the right to prohibit the access of a health care provider to their personal data in the Health

[49] Work Ability Allowance Act/Töövõimetoetuse seadus RT I, 13.12.2014, 1 (2014). https://www.riigiteataja.ee/en/eli/ee/518122017009/consolide/current. Accessed 1 December 2018.

[50] Social Benefits for Disabled Persons Act/Puuetega inimeste sotsiaaltoetuste seadus RT I 1999, 16, 273 (1999) https://www.riigiteataja.ee/en/eli/ee/518122017011/consolide/current. Accessed 1 December 2018.

[51] Ministry of Social Affairs (2018) Estonian eHealth Strategic Development Plan 2020. https://www.sm.ee/sites/default/files/content-editors/sisekomm/e-tervise_strateegia_2020_15_en1.pdf. Accessed 1 December 2018.

[52] Ibid.

Information System (HSOA § 59^3(3)). Other persons have access to personal data in the Health Information System if such right arises from law (§ 59^3(6)). This solution has worked quite effectively for the past ten years: the system has operated in a secure manner and has always given data subjects access to their personal health data. Of course, the modernization in personal data protection and privacy law and the development of technologies should not be disregarded in order to maintain the achieved level of the existing system.

Controlling whether or not a person is suitable for a mandatory military service in Estonia is one example of this. The Estonian Military Service Act[53] 14(6) gives doctor the right to receive information with the consent of a person, from the Health Information System, about the person's state of health. If a person does not grant consent for the use of his or her health information entered into the Health Information System (or there is no information in the Health Information System concerning him or her), the information will be provided on paper or in a format which can be reproduced in writing (§ 14(10)). Therefore, the data already collected is preferably used for several different purposes (where, of course, there is a legal basis and an existing purpose for the processing of personal data). However, it cannot be denied that the implementation of the OOP principle creates more pressure on the use of sensitive personal data. As the amounts of data get larger and with the spread of innovation, the use of already collected data for other purposes may also increase. It is up to the legislator to decide which derogations could be created by law in order to implement the OOP principle.

While Estonia is facing the question of whether data cross-usage between different databases using X-Road is always ethical and reasonable, the development of existing e-services remains as one of Estonia's top priorities as a digital nation. All the European Union member states and EFTA countries signed the 'eGovernment Declaration' in Tallinn on 6 October 2017, which marks a new political commitment on the EU level. The member states reaffirmed their commitment to progress in linking up their public eServices and implementing the eIDAS regulation and the OOP in order to provide efficient and secure digital public services.[54]

The EU is moving forward with several innovative projects and initiatives, including a proposal for a Single Digital Gateway, the European e-Justice Portal and the Single Electronic Mechanism for registration and payment of VAT.[55] EU member states have also agreed to start with the exchange of health data between

[53]Military Service Act/Kaitseväeteenistuse seadus RT I, 10.07.2012, 1 (2012). https://www.riigiteataja.ee/en/eli/ee/511072018002/consolide/current. Accessed 1 December 2018.

[54]European Commission 2017 Ministerial Declaration on eGovernment—the Tallinn Declaration. https://ec.europa.eu/digital-single-market/en/news/ministerial-declaration-egovernment-tallinn-declaration. Accessed 1 December 2018.

[55]European Commission 2016 Communication from the Commission, EU eGovernment Action Plan 2016–2020, Brussels. https://ec.europa.eu/digital-single-market/en/news/communication-eu-egovernment-action-plan-2016-2020-accelerating-digital-transformation. Accessed 1 December 2018.

the member states which have joined the project.[56] The aforementioned agreement, adopted by the eHealth Network, aims at establishing an European Interoperability Framework for Cross-border eHealth Information Services (CBeHIS) with a view to achieving a high level of trust and security, enhancing continuity of care, and ensuring access to safe and high-quality health care in the Union as provided for by Directive 2011/24/EU on the application of patients' rights in cross-border health care. The EU depends on the exchange of personal data concerning patients' health, in conjunction with the existing electronic health care information systems residing with the member states.[57] This is why it is so difficult to implement the OOP across Europe; however, we must recognize that the Commission's past steps cannot be underestimated. Estonia continues to pursue a similar principle in cross-border exchange of health data. As the patient/data subject has the right to prohibit the access of a health care provider in Estonia, the person is able to stop the exchange of his/her personal data to other country. Hence, the data subject can exercise control over his or her personal data.

What is more, many actions in the Estonian legal system can be done in an e-environment (*E-toimik*[58]) which saves time and money for law enforcement institutions as well as for citizens. Sectoral solutions—including, for example, in the police area—enable fast access to important information about the citizen's place of residence, vehicle information or insurance and other necessities, thereby saving the police time and making the process less time-consuming and less bureaucratic for the data subject. Such a sectoral database system approach has been chosen consciously—to reduce risks that may be realized if the data is accessed by non-authorized external parties.

3.3.3 Legal Bases for Personal Data Processing: GDPR Art 6 Interaction with Pre-GDPR Conditions in Estonia

Although Directive 95/46/EC had to be transposed by the member states before the GDPR came into force, the final word on how to do this is in practice was left to the member states. What was interesting about Estonian pre-GDPR EDPA that transposed Directive 95/46/EC was that it did not include all the legal bases for

[56] Agreement between National Authorities or National Organisations responsible for National Contact Points for eHealth on the Criteria required for the participation in Cross-Border eHealth Information Services.

[57] Article 29 Data Protection Working Party (2018) Subject: Agreement between National Authorities or National Organisations responsible for National Contact Points for eHealth on the Criteria required for the participation in

Cross-Border eHealth Information Services. https://ec.europa.eu › newsroom › article29 › document. Accessed 1 December 2018.

[58] *E-toimik* allows participants in the proceeding and their representatives to participate in civil, administrative, criminal and misdemeanor proceedings electronically. The parties to the proceedings are able to follow the procedure, receive and submit documents, and access the digital files.

personal data processing as was foreseen by the directive—at least not explicitly. Article 7 of Directive 95/46/EC settles the following grounds for processing:

(a) the data subject has unambiguously given his or her consent;
(b) processing is necessary for the performance of a contract to which the data subject is party or in order to take steps at the request of the data subject prior to entering into a contract; or
(c) processing is necessary for compliance with a legal obligation to which the controller is subject; or
(d) processing is necessary in order to protect the vital interests of the data subject; or
(e) processing is necessary for the performance of a task carried out in the public interest or in the exercise of official authority vested in the controller or in a third party to whom the data are disclosed; or
(f) processing is necessary for the purposes of the legitimate interests pursued by the controller or by the third party or parties to whom the data are disclosed, except where such interests are overridden by the interests of the data subject's fundamental rights and freedoms which require protection under Article 1.

If Article 7(1) of Directive 95/46/EC stipulates six legal grounds for personal data processing, then the pre-GDPR EDPA did so for only two legal grounds. Paragraph 10 of the EDPA settles:

(1) Processing of personal data is permitted only with the data subject's consent unless otherwise provided by law.
(2) An administrative authority shall process personal data only in the course of performance of public duties in order to perform obligations prescribed by law, an international agreement or directly applicable legislation of the Council of the European Union or the European Commission.
(3) The conditions of and procedure for the processing of personal data as provided for in subsection 2 (3) of this Act shall be established by a regulation of the Government of the Republic.

The Government has not used its mandate for a more detailed regulation. Certain grounds can be derived from the other provisions of the EDPA itself. For example, under the § 14(1)(4) of the EDPA which corresponds to directive article 7(b), § 14(2)(1) of the EDPA which corresponds to article 7(c) of the directive or § 14(1)(3) and § 14(2)(2) which corresponds at least partly to article 7(d) of the directive, as the EDPA settles that "if the data subject has not been able to give his or her consent". Therefore, a large part of the legal grounds for personal data processing has been regulated more specifically in specific laws, based on EDPA § 10(1)—unless otherwise provided by law. The legitimate interest has clearly been brought out for example in the Population Register Act (§ 4(3), § 44(3)(4), § 46, 51), Marital Property Register Act (§ 6), Vital Statistics Registration Act (§ 15), Land Register Act (§ 74), and Traffic Act (§ 184(4)). These legal grounds in Estonian domestic legislation correspond to the directive 95/46/EC article 7(f). If processing is necessary for the performance of a task carried out in the public interest under directive article 7(e), the corresponding ground to this was § 10(2) of the EDPA. Whether such wording is understandable and fully complies with the objectives of the directive 95/46/EC has remained a controversial matter of opinion.

3.3.4 The Estonian Electronic Communications Act and Data Retention

Personal data protection is not only provided by the GDPR. In addition, other legal acts regulate different special areas of personal data protection. One of these areas is the field of electronic communications. The legal act of the EU that regulated the area before 2014 was Directive 2006/24/EC (Data Retention Directive).

Article 1 of the Data Retention Directive declared that the aim of that directive was to harmonize member states' provisions concerning the obligations of the providers of publicly available electronic communications services or of public communications networks with respect to the retention of certain data which are generated or processed by them. The goal was to ensure that the data is available for the purpose of investigating, detecting and prosecuting serious crime, as defined by each member state in its national law. In Estonia, the directive was transposed with the Electronic Communications Act.[59]

In joined Cases C-293/12 and C-594/12 *Digital Rights Ireland and Seitlinger and Others*, the Court of Justice of the European Union (CJEU) declared Directive 2006/24/EC on retention of data retroactively invalid because of several shortcomings. *Inter alia*, the Data Retention Directive did not provide a definition of a serious criminal offense, and there was no established procedure for handing over data to surveillance institutions. In addition, the Data Retention Directive made no difference between data subjects; in other words, the regime applied equally to those who had connections with crime and to those who had not. The CJEU declared in the judgment that the EU legislature had exceeded the limits imposed by compliance with the principle of proportionality in the light of Articles 7, 8 and 52(1) of the Charter. Following the judgment *Digital Rights Ireland and Seitlinger and Others*, the Commission started to monitor developments at the national level, in particular as regards the assessment by EU member states of their data retention legislation.[60]

---

[59] Electronic Communications Act/Elektroonilise side seadus RT I 2004, 87, 593 (2004). https://www.riigiteataja.ee/en/eli/530052018001/consolide. Accessed 1 December 2018.

[60] European Commission 2018b Data retention. https://ec.europa.eu/home-affairs/what-we-do/policies/police-cooperation/information-exchange/data-retention_en. Accessed 1 December 2018.

3.3.5 The Data Retention Directive

The Data Retention Directive was transposed into Estonian legislation via paragraph 111^1 of the Electronic Communications Act. The provisions transposing the Data Retention Directive in this Act are still in force while writing this chapter and since the invalidation of the Data Retention Directive. The authors of this chapter consider this to be a legal shortcoming because the CJEU has expressed the views that the provisions laid down in the Data Retention Directive do not meet the proportionality criterion. The CJEU has also concluded, in the *Tele2 Sverige* judgment, that all domestic legislation that does not comply with the Charter is in conflict with EU law.[61] Proportionality criteria brought out by the CJEU also need to be evaluated in Estonia and in the Electronic Communications Act. At the time of the writing of this chapter, the Electronic Communications Act 111^1 still stipulated the obligation to preserve data that is not in accordance with the relevant CJEU court practice. Hence, Estonian legislators need to take the necessary steps to overcome the current negative situation and amend the current law in force by taking into account the recommendations given by relevant court practice. The Estonian Human Rights Centre[62] and other prominent Estonian lawyers[63] have constantly turned government's attention to this topic which needs to be resolved in the very near future.

3.4 Application of the GDPR in the Jurisdiction of Estonia

3.4.1 GDPR Application in Estonia: Will the Enormous Fines for Data Breaches Make Data Controllers and Processors in Estonia Take Personal Data Protection and Privacy Issues and Requirements More Seriously?

Before the application of the GDPR, personal data protection could be thought of by some as a *niche* area without proper and uniform sanction mechanisms. However, consistent enforcement of the data protection rules is central to a harmonized data

[61] P 134(1) of the ruling says that "Charter of Fundamental Rights of the European Union, must be interpreted as precluding national legislation which, for the purpose of fighting crime, provides for general and indiscriminate retention of all traffic and location data of all subscribers and registered users relating to all means of electronic communication".

[62] Estonian Human Rights Centre 2017 On data retention and Estonia. https://humanrights.ee/en/2017/12/data-retention-estonia/. Accessed 1 December 2018.

[63] E.g., Lõhmus 2016.

protection regime.[64] Therefore, the rationale for having administrative fines harmonized on the EU level is to have a uniform and standardized approach to personal data protection infringements and penalties.

Directive 95/46/EC did not stipulate uniform administrative fine rates, unlike the current GDPR. This represents progress for the EU member states and for the uniform application of fine rates in the EU. The guidelines on the application and setting of administrative fines for the purposes of the GDPR also state that the EDPB and individual supervisory authorities agree on using this agreed-upon guideline as a common approach.[65] These commonly agreed guidelines assist supervisory authorities and create more legal clarity due to the fact that the same assessment criteria are used throughout the EU when considering the application of administrative fines.

Although the Estonian legal system does not include administrative fines as such, GDPR recital 151 stipulates *expressis verbis* that in Estonia the fine is imposed by the supervisory authority in the framework of a misdemeanour procedure, provided that such an application of the rules has an equivalent effect to administrative fines imposed by supervisory authorities. The lack of administrative fines in the Estonian legal system can be seen as one deviation from the comprehensive GDPR system. However, it should not be seen as an obstacle to the application of fines because the legal mechanism—framework of misdemeanor procedure—is in place.

The second substantial topic regarding administrative fines determined in the GDPR is definitely the number of administrative fines and the great difference between the maximum amounts of fines which may be imposed under the GDPR and the pre-GDPR amounts of fines possible under Estonian law. The difference between them is, indeed, enormous. According to the pre-GDPR EDPA which replaces Directive 95/46/EC, a person who commits any of the following three violations—failing to register the mandatory processing of sensitive personal data, failing to meet the requirements regarding security measures for the protection of personal data, or failing to meet other requirements for the processing of personal data—was punishable by a fine of up to 300 fine units (1200 EUR). However, the same act, if committed by a legal person, is now punishable by a fine of up to 32,000 EUR. Hence, the GDPR entails a large-scale leap in maximum amounts of fines for these types of offenses committed in Estonia.

Mr. Viljar Peep, Director General of the Estonian Data Protection Inspectorate 2008–2018, had stated that the option of imposing huge fines would be a last-resort measure.[66] However, in future, the Estonian Data Protection Inspectorate will be required to impose fines similarly and on the same bases as other data protection authorities in the EU because of the harmonized approach to personal data protection on the EU level. The same position is also enshrined in the GDPR recital 10 according

[64] Article 29 Working Party (2017) Guidelines on the application and setting of administrative fines for the purposes of the Regulation 2016/679. https://ec.europa.eu/newsroom/article29/item-detail.cfm?item_id=611237. Accessed 1 December 2018.

[65] Ibid.

[66] Estonian Data Protection Inspectorate 2018a Don't panic! How to be compliant with the new GDPR in 5 steps. http://www.aki.ee/et/node/1471. Accessed 1 December 2018.

to which the level of protection of the rights and freedoms of natural persons with regard to the processing of such data should be equivalent in all member states in order to ensure a consistent and high level of protection of natural persons and to remove the obstacles to flows of personal data within the EU.

This understandable ambition is also confirmed by the data gathered by the Estonian Data Protection Inspectorate concerning the number of designated Data Protection Officers (DPOs) in Estonia that need to be registered in the Estonian Business Register (*Äriregister*). By 25 July 2018, Estonia had 1598[67] registered DPOs. Although this might not seem to be a huge number, considering that the population of Estonia is 1.3 million, it is a significant number of officers.

In the first year under the GDPR, more than 100 personal data breach notifications have been brought to the Estonian Data Protection Authority[68] and this number is constantly increasing. Although the Authority has started several investigation procedures over GDPR compliance, no fines have yet to be imposed in Estonia. The Estonian Data Protection Authority has also noted in its Yearbook 2018[69] that it will not turn into a "fine factory" and will use the option to impose a fine as a last resort. Hence, Estonia is still in a standby mode for its first big GDPR fine.

Although there are no examples of big GDPR fines in Estonia to date, the awareness of the GDPR is at a reasonable level. According to the Special Eurobarometer 487a report on the General Data Protection Regulation (March 2019),[70] 58% of respondents in Estonia have at least heard of the GDPR. Estonia is in a relatively good position compared to other EU countries when it comes to data subjects exercising their rights. For example, in 20 EU countries at least one in five have exercised the right to access their data, with those in Estonia (39%), Latvia (29%), Finland and Lithuania (both 27%) the most likely to have done so.[71] In addition, in 11 countries at least one in five have exercised the right to correct their data, with respondents in Estonia (36%), Latvia (28%) and the Netherlands (25%) the most likely to have done so.[72] What is more, in Estonia, 13% of respondents to the Eurobarometer survey have also exercised the right to have a say when decisions are automated.[73] Of course,

---

[67] Estonian Data Protection Inspectorate 2018b Ettevõtjaportaalis on registreeritud ligi 1600 andmekaitsespetsialisti [Almost 1,600 data protection specialists are registered in the company portal]. https://www.aki.ee/et/uudised/pressiteated/ettevotjaportaalis-registreeritud-ligi-1600-andmekaitsespetsialisti. Accessed 1 December 2018.

[68] Estonian Data Protection Inspectorate 2019a Rikkumisteadete arv ületas 100 piiri [The number of infringement notifications exceeded 100]. https://www.aki.ee/et/uudised/uudiste-arhiiv/rikkumisteadete-arv-uletas-100-piiri. Accessed 25 August 2019.

[69] Estonian Data Protection Inspectorate 2019b Soovitused aastaks 2019 [Recommendations for 2019]. https://www.aki.ee/sites/www.aki.ee/files/elfinder/article_files/Aastaraamat.%202018%20kohta.%20Soovitused%20aastaks%202019.pdf. Accessed 25 August 2019.

[70] European Commission (2019) Special Eurobarometer 487a report on the General Data Protection Regulation. https://ec.europa.eu/commfrontoffice/publicopinion/index.cfm/survey/getsurveydetail/instruments/special/surveyky/2222. Accessed 25 May 2018.

[71] Ibid.

[72] Ibid.

[73] Ibid.

even better results are expected with the next surveys when more time has passed from the adoption of the GDPR and best practices have had even more time to evolve.

3.4.2 The GDPR—Data Protection Awareness-Raising Masterpiece?

The Director General of the Estonian Data Protection Inspectorate has expressed the opinion that the main challenges faced by personal data controllers and processors in the Estonian context in light of the GDPR are actually very similar to those in the other European countries: data portability, carrying out impact assessments, making sure that all the processes and the documents meet the requirements of the new legal order.[74]

As a background to the above, the authors of this chapter would not claim that the GDPR is solely responsible for the increased awareness of personal data protection in Europe and thus in Estonia. Of course, enormous fines are one reason why the GDPR and personal data protection have brought these topics into the limelight. Because nobody wants to get fined and in order to raise awareness, many personal data protection and GDPR trainings, conferences, courses, etc., have been carried out in Estonia and also by the authors of this chapter. Tallinn University of Technology's Law School has also arranged several longer-term DPO trainings in order to fill the new knowledge gap in the Estonian data protection community.

It should be noted that this new and popular trend of GDPR training in Estonia originates from Article 39(1)b of the GDPR which stipulates that one task of a DPO is *inter alia* awareness-raising and training of staff involved in personal data processing operations. No such requirement existed previously in Estonian legislation. This new requirement is having the following effect: the trained and designated DPOs in Estonian data processors and controllers (whether in-house or outsourced) start spreading the knowledge of personal data protection and the GDPR within the organizations they work for, which enhances the level of awareness universally. This is another notable development in the area of Estonian data protection.

3.4.3 Let's Clean up the Room: GDPR Implementing Regulation in Estonia. Will It Solve All the Questions?

The GDPR has given Estonian personal data protection a new presence and has definitely shaken the area out of its previous comfort zone. For example, in the submission process of breaches in data processing (GDPR, Article 33), the minimum age for the consent of the child in e-services (GDPR, Article 8), etc., has been regulated

[74]Estonian Data Protection Inspectorate 2018a Don't panic! How to be compliant with the new GDPR in 5 steps. http://www.aki.ee/et/node/1471. Accessed 1 December 2018.

due to GDPR requirements. The Estonian draft law (778 SE) on implementing the new EDPA covered amendments of approximately 130 sectoral laws and made two additional amendments to ministerial and Government regulations.

The GDPR has also raised somewhat unexpected questions in Estonia. For example: Who owns the data that is collected into the database? Is it the data holder (controller, processor) or is it the data subject? According to GDPR recital 7, natural persons should have control of their own personal data. Should medical data belong to a hospital or a natural person? All the Estonian legal acts that have been in force so far have stipulated what is personal data and personal data categories regarding the specific area, as well as what constitutes processing; however, in many cases, not much more has been stipulated. The authors of this chapter do of course support the starting point where personal data (it is also important to distinguish between whether we are talking about a person's data or personal data)—as it is in the real sense of the words—should be understood as the person's data. The data subject should have the chance to decide upon the usage of personal data and, where appropriate, the use of corresponding remedies. Processing of personal data is not an "ownership" of personal data. This is also supported by the view that regardless of the legal basis for the processing of personal data (as right to use), all the data subject's rights can still be exercised by a natural person whose personal data are processed (GDPR article 16–18, 20, 21, 77–80, 82 and national legislation).

The "right to be forgotten" may raise a new dilemma. The state or local government agency or a legal person in public law who receives a document (letter), must register it in the documents register pursuant to EPIA § 11(1). There are theoretical examples where, for example, data is collected on the basis of law, but the person would like to stop the collection of data on the basis of "right to be forgotten." Is it possible to say no to the state if your tax data is collected for calculating the coefficient for future pensions or to offer family allowances?[75] Such processing is definitely in the public interest. Secondly, it is not solely related to the person's own rights, but also to those of his or her family, including children. Most likely, the person would be unable to successfully exercise the right to be forgotten in this area of data processing.

The provisions of GDPR Article 25 (data protection by design and by default) are amongst the most innovative and ambitious norms of the European Union's newly reformed data protection regime. They are directed essentially at information systems development.[76] The European Court of Human Rights has been relatively early in embracing ideals similar to those in GDPR Article 25 already under the convention.

In the 2008 *I v Finland* case,[77] the Court unanimously found Finland to have violated its positive obligations to secure respect for private life pursuant to article 8 of

[75]The state adds 4% to the mandatory funded pension (II step) out of the current social tax that is paid by the employee in Estonia. The parental benefit amount is calculated based on the person's last year's income for which an employer has paid social tax (salary, bonuses, etc.) according to the Family Benefits Act, § 7(2).

[76]Bygrave 2017.

[77]European Court of Human Rights, Case of *I v. Finland*, 17 July 2008, no. 20511/03.

the European Convention for the Protection of Human Rights and Fundamental Freedoms, due to its failure to secure, through technological-organizational measures, the confidentiality of patient data in a public hospital. The applicant was a woman who was infected with HIV and who suspected that unauthorized third persons had accessed her medical records generated while she was hospitalized. The Court held that Finland had to provide more than data protection *de jure* and an opportunity to claim compensation for damages caused by an alleged unlawful disclosure of personal data.

As Lee Bygrave indicates, on the basis of this judgment, the protection is a *vital* principle in the legal systems, crucial not just for the privacy of the data subject but also for preserving data subjects' confidence, for example, in the medical profession and in the health services in general.[78] The measures referred to in GDPR Article 25(1) are not just technical but also organizational. In other words, they embrace more than just the design and operation of software or hardware, but also business strategies and other organizational-managerial practices.[79] The GDPR Article 25 duty plays a role in the application of numerous other GDPR provisions, although this is (unhelpfully) not made clear in article 25 itself (GDPR Article 6(4)(e); 34(3)(a) and see recitals 87 and 88; 83(2)(d)).[80] Regardless of the importance of this article, its implementation requires the availability of resources more so than changes in the legal area. This approach is likely to apply in Estonia as well as elsewhere.

But there is one indicator that is very specific to Estonia. Currently, 119,887 active companies in Estonia have less than 10 employees, and only about 200 companies have more than 250 employees.[81] The costs associated with the GDPR implementation and changes can have a particularly strong impact on these small Estonian enterprises.

As with most of the issues, the scope for reimbursement of damages will also be set by practice. Article 5 of the GDPR, in accordance with section 2, settles that the controller must, where appropriate, prove that he or she has complied with the rules and principles of the regulation. Therefore, the defendant must prove that he or she complied with all the GDPR rules.[82]

In the context of non-patrimonial damage, the most intriguing question will arise in light of GDPR recital 146. Should we consider that the rules on the processing of personal data are always addressed observing the non-patrimonial interest of the data subject? Is it reasonable to assume that the rights of the data subject are violated and, consequently, non-patrimonial damage is caused? An example would be a situation where the data controller does not give the data subject information within the sufficient time frame on what information the controller has collected, or does not inform the data subject about the data processing and its conditions

[78] Ibid.

[79] Bygrave 2017.

[80] Ibid.

[81] Statistics Estonia 2017 Majanduslikult aktiivsed ettevõtted töötajate arvu järgi [Economically active enterprises by number of employees]. Accessed 1 December 2018. https://www.stat.ee/68771.

[82] Sein et al. 2018.

before the personal data processing begins. Also, information should be provided as to what extent national law provides additional restrictions.[83] Due to different legal justifications of the member states, it can be assumed that a coherent interpretation of the rules on data protection cannot be easy and fast in this matter as well.[84] Public institutions, on the one hand, enjoy very wide-ranging flexibility clauses which take into account differences between countries, but it does not allow achieving a certain level of coherence. According to Austrian data protection expert W. Kotschy, the uniformity of data protection achieved by the GDPR is very superficial.[85] In addition, Professor A. Roßnagel from Kassel University gives a rather negative evaluation of the GDPR. According to his opinion, the regulation is disappointing, primarily because it does not include new data protection rules; it is just for further development of the directive. The decision-making space (flexibility clauses) is very wide and does not guarantee the goal of harmonization.[86]

The GDPR leaves many data protection nuances to be regulated by the EU member states. As well, the new reality in data protection will not be the originally advertised single harmonized set of rules; rather, it will remain a scattered overall picture. This raises a question about the applicable law,[87] especially regarding a pan-European exchange of data and an open e-market. In fact, the GDPR does not resolve the dilemmas of the applicable law between member states.[88] There are topics which are left to be clarified and solved by the European Data Protection Board, the European Data Protection Supervisor and the Court of Justice. So, there is no fully harmonized "one continent, one law",[89] because 28 (or without the Brexiteers, 27) different regulations exist due to the fact that every EU member state can present their exemptions (see Article 23). "Same rules for all companies"[90] will not happen in its entirety because domestic regulations can differ around the EU and it is not possible to unequivocally state that the new GDPR solution is cheaper for companies to do their business in the EU. Confusion is also caused by the fact that some of the GDPR provisions concerning applicable law are written in the context of a processor (e.g., GDPR Article 28(3)(a)), whereas others are written in the context of a controller (e.g., Article 14(5)(c)).[91] During the writing of this chapter, without the corresponding practice and the additional guidance, there is no clear and final understanding of the processing in a cross-border context, although the increase of data exchange is expected from member states which is a bit of a worrying factor. Therefore, the service provider must take into account the specifics of each country, which the GDPR also allows

[83]Ibid.

[84]Ibid.

[85]Tupay 2016.

[86]Ibid.

[87]See further: Pormeister and Nisu 2018; Brkan 2016.

[88]Pormeister and Nisu 2018.

[89]European Commission 2018h Questions and Answers—Data protection reform package. https://europa.eu › rapid › press-release_MEMO-17-1441_en. Accessed 1 December 2018.

[90]Ibid.

[91]Pormeister and Nisu 2018.

to do. Hopefully, it will be possible in the near future to have the opportunity to draw more comprehensive conclusions about GDPR implementation. Then it will be possible to make more precise mid-term reviews of whether the desired and set goals were achieved or whether there were shortcomings.

References

Brkan M (2016) Data Protection and Conflict-of-laws: A Challenging Relationship. European Data Protection Law Review 2016/3, p. 324–341

Bygrave L A (2017) Data protection by design and by default: Deciphering the EU's legislative requirements. Oslo L Rev 4:105–120

E-Estonia (2018) X-Road. https://e-estonia.com/solutions/interoperability-services/x-road/. Accessed 1 December 2018

Estonian Data Protection Inspectorate (2018a) Don't panic! How to be compliant with the new GDPR in 5 steps. http://www.aki.ee/et/node/1471. Accessed 1 December 2018

Estonian Data Protection Inspectorate (2018b) Ettevõtjaportaalis on registreeritud ligi 1600 andmekaitsespetsialisti [Almost 1,600 data protection specialists are registered in the company portal]. https://www.aki.ee/et/uudised/pressiteated/ettevotjaportaalis-registreeritud-ligi-1600-andmekaitsespetsialisti. Accessed 1 December 2018

Estonian Data Protection Inspectorate (2018c) Statistics. https://www.aki.ee/et/inspektsioon/statistika Accessed 1 December 2018

Estonian Data Protection Inspectorate (2019a) Rikkumisteadete arv ületas 100 piiri [The number of infringement notifications exceeded 100]. https://www.aki.ee/et/uudised/uudiste-arhiiv/rikkumisteadete-arv-uletas-100-piiri. Accessed 25 August 2019

Estonian Data Protection Inspectorate (2019b) Soovitused aastaks 2019 [Recommendations for 2019]. https://www.aki.ee/sites/www.aki.ee/files/elfinder/article_files/Aastaraamat%202018%20kohta.%20Soovitused%20aastaks%202019.pdf. Accessed 25 August 2019

Estonian Human Rights Centre (2017) On data retention and Estonia. https://humanrights.ee/en/2017/12/data-retention-estonia/. Accessed 1 December 2018

Estonian Information System Authority (2018) Riigi Infosüsteemi teejuht [State Information System Guide]. https://www.ria.ee/teejuht/eesti-it-edulood/2013-aastal-tehti-x-teel-ule-280-miljoni-infoparingu. Accessed 1 December 2018 (link no longer active)

Estonian Ministry of Foreign Affairs (2009) Estonia's way into the European Union. http://vm.ee/sites/default/files/content-editors/web-static/052/Estonias_way_into_the_EU.pdf. Accessed 1 December 2018

European Commission (2016) Communication from the Commission, EU eGovernment action plan 2016–2020, Brussels. https://ec.europa.eu/digital-single-market/en/news/communication-eu-egovernment-action-plan-2016-2020-accelerating-digital-transformation. Accessed 1 December 2018

European Commission (2017) Ministerial declaration on eGovernment - the Tallinn Declaration. https://ec.europa.eu/digital-single-market/en/news/ministerial-declaration-egovernment-tallinn-declaration. Accessed 1 December 2018

European Commission (2018a) Creating a digital society. https://ec.europa.eu/digital-single-market/en/policies/creating-digital-society. Accessed 1 December 2018

European Commission (2018b) Data retention. https://ec.europa.eu/home-affairs/what-we-do/policies/police-cooperation/information-exchange/data-retention_en. Accessed 1 December 2018

European Commission (2018c) The digital economy and society index (DESI). https://ec.europa.eu/digital-single-market/en/desi. Accessed 1 December 2018

European Commission (2018d) eGovernment & digital public services. https://ec.europa.eu/digital-single-market/en/policies/egovernment. Accessed 1 December 2018

European Commission (2018e) EU-wide digital once-only principle for citizens and businesses. Policy options and their impacts. Executive summary, 2015/0062. https://ec.europa.eu/digital-single-market/en/news/eu-wide-digital-once-only-principle-citizens-and-businesses-policy-options-and-their-impacts. Accessed 1 December 2018

European Commission (2018f) The example of Estonia. https://ec.europa.eu/epale/en/blog/e-governance-and-e-guidance-example-estonia. Accessed 1 December 2018

European Commission (2018g) The GDPR: New opportunities, new obligations. https://ec.europa.eu/commission/sites/beta-political/files/data-protection-factsheet-sme-obligations_en.pdf. Accessed 1 December 2018

European Commission (2018h) Questions and answers – Data protection reform package. https://europa.eu › rapid › press-release_MEMO-17-1441_en. Accessed 1 December 2018

Kerikmäe T, Joamets K, Rodina A, Pleps J, Berkmanas T, Gruodytė E (2017) The law of the Baltic states. Springer-Verlag, Heidelberg

Lõhmus U (2016) The saga of retaining electronic data has been resolved, yet not in Estonia. Juridica 10:698–708

Ministry of Economic Affairs and Communications (2017) Zero-bureaucracy. https://www.mkm.ee/en/zero-bureaucracy-0. Accessed 1 December 2018

Ministry of Economic Affairs and Communications (2018) Digital agenda 2020. https://www.mkm.ee/sites/default/files/digital_agenda_2020_estonia_engf.pdf. Accessed 1 December 2018

Nõmper A (2017) Personal data protection regulation in Estonia and Directive 95/46/EC. Taylor & Francis Group, London

Peep V (2018) Data protection law seen through the eyes of a data protection authority. Juridica 2018/2:116–124

Pormeister K, Nisu N (2018) Dilemma of the law applicable within the EU in the General Data Protection Regulation. Juridica 2:125–135

Schweighofer E et al. (2017) Privacy by design data exchange between CSIRTs, GDPR & ePrivacy. Springer International Publishing https://doi.org/10.1007/978-3-319-67280-9_6

Sein K et al. (2018) Pilguheit andmesubjekti õiguskaitsevahenditele uues isikuandmete kaitse üldmääruses [A look at the data subject's remedies in the new General Data Protection Regulation]. Juridica 2:94–115

Statistics Estonia (2017) Majanduslikult aktiivsed ettevõtted töötajate arvu järgi [Economically active enterprises by number of employees]. https://www.stat.ee/68771. Accessed 1 December 2018

Tupay P K (2016) On the right to privacy up to the General Data Protection Regulation, i.e. the right of an unidentified person to the protection of personal data. Juridica 2016/4:227–240

Warren S D, Brandeis L D (1890) The right to privacy. Harv L Rev 4: 193–220

Kärt Salumaa-Lepik, PhD candidate at TalTech Law School, Tallinn University of Technology, Estonia.

Prof. Dr. Tanel Kerikmäe, Director of TalTech Law School, Tallinn University of Technology, Estonia.

Nele Nisu, Legal Advisor at the Estonian Ministry of Social Affairs, Tallinn, Estonia.

Chapter 4
GDPR in France: A Lot of Communication for a Jurisdiction Well Experienced in the Protection of Personal Data

Aurelien Lorange

Contents

A. Lorange (✉)
The Hague University of Applied Sciences, Johanna Westerdijkplein 75, 2521 EN The Hague, The Netherlands
e-mail: a.lorange@hhs.nl

E. Kiesow Cortez (ed.), *Data Protection Around the World*,
Information Technology and Law Series 33,
https://doi.org/10.1007/978-94-6265-407-5_4

Abstract France has been a pioneer country in terms of the protection of personal data, as demonstrated by the Informatique et Libertés law of 1978 and the creation of the national authority known as the CNIL. However, the first harmonization with the European framework of the Directive 95/46/CE occurred late, in 2004. By transposing (incorporating) the EU's GDPR into French law, via an emergency procedure a few days before its coming into force in the European Union as a whole, France managed to modernize the protection of data with the rise of awareness among companies and public authorities. The CNIL, which received more competences and a better defined territorial application, maintains its role of controlling the regime of the most sensitive data (justice and police) while reminding individuals of the possible use of their rights on their data. Updating the Informatique et Libertés law of 1978 into the GDPR framework without changing its structure creates the problem of readability and confusion which increases the work of communication and requires the CNIL to repeatedly remind simply the new framework in cases. Considering that the grace period for companies to respect the GDPR is over, the CNIL will start its second year of applying the GDPR by moving from primarily informing and warning to sanctions (often for conserving the personal data of users without their consent) and increasing its cooperation with the other national authorities responsible for protecting personal data in the European Union.

Keywords CNIL · French data protection authority · GDPR · EU data protection · Privacy law · EU privacy

4.1 An Update of the Existing Protection of Personal Data Needed with the Application of the GDPR in France

4.1.1 An Accelerated Procedure of Adoption of the GDPR in France and a Few Changes in the Law of 1978

On 13 December 2017, the French Minister of Justice (commonly called Garde des Sceaux in the French government) presented a draft law on the protection of personal data.[1] This was an adaptation of the law dated 6 January 1978,[2] called the "Informatique et Libertés" law, to the European Union (EU) Law. This draft law transposed the General Data Protection Regulation (GDPR), which entered into force on 25 May 2018, and the Directive 2016/680 on the protection of physical persons to

[1]Ministère de la Justice (2017) Projet de loi relatif à la protection des données personnelles [Draft law on the protection of personal data]. http://www.justice.gouv.fr/la-garde-des-sceaux-10016/projet-de-loi-relatif-a-la-protection-des-donnees-personnelles-31094.html. Accessed 11 August 2019.

[2]Legifrance (2019) Loi n° 78-17 du 6 janvier 1978 relative à l'informatique, aux fichiers et aux libertés [Law n ° 78-17 of 6 January 1978 relating to data processing and freedoms]. https://www.legifrance.gouv.fr/affichTexte.do?cidTexte=JORFTEXT000000886460. Accessed 11 August 2019.

the treatment of personal data relating to the penal system into French law. The text was examined in an accelerated procedure (one reading only) between December 2017 and May 2018.

On 14 May 2018, the French Parliament adopted the new legislation concerning the protection of personal data.[3] The GDPR was mentioned 56 times in national laws. For this reason, the new French law has been amended to become fully applicable.

Although Germany had already transposed the new European text into its national legislation in 2017,[4] the French Commission "Informatique et Libertés" (CNIL) had some doubts concerning the delay of the process of transposing the law in France.[5] Merely 11 days before the GDPR entered into force, the Parliament adopted the new text in an emergency procedure.[6]

Proposed by the government at the French National Assembly, the draft law had as its goal to adapt the Law of 6 January 1978 ("Informatique et Libertés") by transposing the new European framework of the GDPR into it. The directive on the protection of personal data entered into force on 25 May 2018.

The French government chose not to abrogate the 1978 law. Instead, the GDPR was inserted into the existing French framework of Data Protection, highlighting the practical and technical elements of its implementation.

The main modification of this new legal framework is the change from a system of a preliminary authorization administered by the CNIL[7] to a system wherein actors are responsible for the processing of data.[8] The preliminary formalities will therefore be replaced by an obligation on the part of entities to treat personal data so as to ensure that a certain minimal level of protection is maintained at all times. They will have to prove their compliance with the new system of responsibilities.

4.1.2 More Competencies for the CNIL and a Better Defined Territorial Application

The government gives more missions to the CNIL and redefines the framework whereby CNIL agents and members can intervene in cases involving control on the

[3]Legifrance (2018) Loi n° 2018-493 du 20 juin 2018 relative à la protection des données personnelles [Law n° 2018-493 of 20 June 2018 on the protection of personal data]. https://www.legifrance.gouv.fr/affichLoiPubliee.do?idDocument=JORFDOLE000036195293&type=general&legislature=15. Accessed 11 August 2019.

[4]Ritzer et al. (2017) Germany's parliament approves local data protection law to operate alongside GDPR. https://www.dataprotectionreport.com/2017/05/germanys-parliament-approves-local-data-protection-law-to-operate-alongside-gdpr/. Accessed 11 August 2019.

[5]Commission Nationale Informatique et Libertés 2017a.

[6]Assemblée Nationale (2017) Projet de loi relatif a la protection des données personnelles (procédure accélérée) [Draft law on the protection of personal data (accelerated procedure)]. http://www.assemblee-nationale.fr/15/projets/pl0490.asp. Accessed 11 August 2019.

[7]Commission Nationale Informatique et Libertés 2018f.

[8]Banck et al. 2018.

treatment of data in the following three situations: on field; on documents; or online in case of the use of assumed identity.[9]

Some modifications have been made to the CNIL's power of investigation and the type of cooperation the CNIL has with the other controlling authorities of the European Union.[10] The CNIL is able to add a preliminary question to the EU Court of Justice in its conclusions to have a study on the compliance of the legislation of the states outside of the EU with the EU Law.[11] The CNIL is also able to ask the Conseil d'État (France's highest administrative court) to order the suspension or the cessation of a transfer of data out of the EU.[12]

Title II of the draft law contains the margins given to the Member State by the regulation to make the best adaptation to the new legal framework. In this text, the national law applies to a person in France, even when the person in charge of the treatment of data is not on the territory of the French Republic in cases involving differences between legislations of EU Member States.[13]

4.2 Precisions Given to the Processing of Sensitive Information and Derogations

The new legislation specifies the types of processing of certain types of sensitive data, such as that relating to the penal system and to infractions.[14] Such processing of data can be used by private entities collaborating with the public service of justice such as associations helping victims or associations of reinsertion.[15] For data having a public interest, the CNIL—after consulting with the National Institute for Health Data—can adopt rules and methodology of reference which will be the general rule. Even in questions of health care, CNIL authorizations will be the exception.[16]

Again, within the margin given to the EU Member States, the legislation makes it possible to set derogatory measures to apply to the execution of certain personal

---

[9] Rees M (2018) Le RGPD expliqué ligne par ligne (articles 1 à 23) [The GDPR explained line by line (Articles 1 to 23)]. https://www.nextinpact.com/news/106135-le-rgpd-explique-ligne-par-ligne-articles-1-a-23.htm. Accessed 11 August 2019.

[10] Chapter VII, Regulation (EU) 2016/679 of the European Parliament and of the Council of 27 April 2016 on the Protection of Natural Persons with Regard to the Processing of Personal Data and on the Free Movement of Such Data, and Repealing Directive 95/46/EC.

[11] Sénat 2019b Projet de loi relatif à la protection des données personnelles.

[12] Chapter V, Regulation (EU) 2016/679 of the European Parliament and of the Council of 27 April 2016 on the Protection of Natural Persons with Regard to the Processing of Personal Data and on the Free Movement of Such Data, and Repealing Directive 95/46/EC.

[13] Commission Nationale Informatique et Libertés 2019a.

[14] Bohic C (2018) RGPD: les données pénales épinglées par le Conseil constitutionnel [GDPR: criminal data pinned down by the Constitutional Council]. https://www.itespresso.fr/loi-rgpd-donnees-penales-conseil-constitutionnel-192294.html. Accessed 11 August 2019.

[15] Vie Public, Direction de l'information légale et administrative 2018.

[16] Guillemain 2019.

rights (right to be informed, right of access, right of rectification, right to erase, right of portability, right of opposition, etc.) in order to guarantee some objectives of public interest such as security and national defence, and the independence of the justice system and judiciary procedures.[17] These derogations will be defined by a Conseil d'État's decree.[18]

Use and defence of rights by the persons and entities.

The legislation also mentioned that anybody can give mandate to an association or an organization for the exercise of his or her rights for a reclamation claim to the CNIL.[19]

4.2.1 Legislation and Practice Before 2018 on the Protection of Personal Data

4.2.1.1 A Strong System in Place Since 1978 with Difficulties Regarding Readability

Proposed by the government at the French National Assembly, the draft law had the purpose of adapting the Law of 6 January 1978 ("Informatique et Libertés") to transpose the new European framework of the GDPR and the directive on the protection of personal data that entered into force on 25 May 2018.[20]

The French government chose not to abrogate the 1978 law. Instead, the GDPR was inserted into the existing French framework of Data Protection, highlighting the practical and technical elements of its implementation. As the Minister said, the intelligibility and readability of the "Informatique et Libertés" law is a reason to maintain the architecture of the legislation.[21] There is a codification, through ordinance, in the law of 6 January 1978, that offers a clear and readable legal framework because of structure.

[17]Chapter III, Regulation (EU) 2016/679 of the European Parliament and of the Council of 27 April 2016 on the Protection of Natural Persons with Regard to the Processing of Personal Data and on the Free Movement of Such Data, and Repealing Directive 95/46/EC.

[18]Drey F, Le village de la justice (2018) RGPD, point d'étape a la suite de l'harmonisation de la loi informatique et liberté [GDPR, point of step following the harmonization of the data protection law]. https://www.village-justice.com/articles/rgpd-point-etape-suite-harmonisation-loi-informatique-Libertés,29185.html. Accessed 11 August 2019.

[19]Chapter IV, Regulation (EU) 2016/679 of the European Parliament and of the Council of 27 April 2016 on the Protection of Natural Persons with Regard to the Processing of Personal Data and on the Free Movement of Such Data, and Repealing Directive 95/46/EC.

[20]Commission Nationale Informatique et Libertés 2018e.

[21]Conseil des Ministres du Gouvernement 2017.

4.3 The Initiative of Protecting Personal Data and Facing the Administrative Necessity of Simplification

Coming back to the law of 1978, it is important to mention that this legislation, adopted by the French Presidency of Valery Giscard D'Estaing, was one of the primary pieces of legislation relating to the modernization of French society, together with the law legalizing the volunteered abortion.

The 1978 law was about information, files, and rights. This major legislation dealt with the processing of personal data by both administrative entities and private organizations, which would be responsible for administering databases of personal information. The French government believed that it would be impossible to dissociate the information society from the possible consequences on personal data.

The elaboration of the "Informatique et Libertés" law in 1978 began during a sitting of the National Assembly in 1970 when the French Member of Parliament, Michel Poniatowski, proposed to create a "comité de surveillance" and a court for information technology.[22] However, this suggestion was rejected. In 1971, the INSEE (French national institute for statistics), enjoying the change from printed cards to magnetic tapes, decided to centralize in Nantes, where the country's identification database was located. Until the 1990s in France, most of the questions dealing with ID cards and passports for all French citizens were dealt with in Nantes at the regional level. Centralization was done by the SAFARI Project (an electronic system for administrative files about individual persons), in order to get a better interconnection between files, based on the Social Security Number (released by INSEE for every French citizen).[23] The administrative services tried to aggregate three data areas: ID; the administration of pensions; and Social Security data, managed by the Ministry of Home Affairs.

The general public perceived this project as an obstacle to freedom and it became a public scandal when *Le Monde* wrote about the "SAFARI or the hunt after French citizens" on 21 March 1974.[24] This newspaper article provoked a huge political reaction. Jacques Chirac, the new minister for Home Affairs, had just arrived from the Ministry of Agriculture; he was responsible for dealing with the problem. On 2 April 1974, President Georges Pompidou died and Valery Giscard d'Estaing became President, thanks to the support of Chirac who became Prime Minister. Chirac asked Mr. Poniatowski to become Minister of Home Affairs. Mr. Poniatowski resumed Chirac's idea by creating the CNIL and initiating the law "Informatique et Libertés" before he resigned in 1977.[25]

---

[22]Le Monde, Archives (1970) M. Poniatowski propose la création d'un "Comité de Surveillance" de l'Informatique [M. Poniatowski proposes the creation of an IT Supervisory Committee]. https://www.lemonde.fr/archives/article/1970/11/09/m-poniatowski-propose-la-creation-d-un-comite-de-surveillance-de-l-informatique_2658184_1819218.html. Accessed 12 August 2019.

[23]Tribalat 2016.

[24]Boucher 1974.

[25]Gouvernement.fr, Archives 1978.

4.4 Early Initiative and Late Involvement for a European Harmonization of France

The French government launched one of the first three European initiatives concerning the question of protection of personal data, after the land of Hessen in Germany (1971)[26] and Sweden (1973).[27] This made France a leader in promoting this initiative at the Economic European Union in 1981, inspiring the Convention of the Council of Europe on the Protection of Personal Data in 1981[28] and the Guidelines for the Regulation of Computerized Personal Data Files, as adopted by General Assembly resolution 45/95 of 14 December 1990.[29] However, France would be the last Member State to transpose the European directive of 1995 in 2004,[30] which significantly modified the law of 1978, replacing the words "nominative information" with "data with personal characteristic"; as a result, Article 2 contained a definition of these terms in order to avoid the strange interpretations of this notion and to cover most of the possible situations/scenarios. Moreover, the "Informatique et Libertés" law focused on new Information Technology and specified that the law was not applicable to temporary copies of files and instead defined the exact conditions of legality regarding the treatment of personal data. A distinction was also made between treatment by the public sector and treatment by the private sector; currently, the same procedure applies to both sectors.

It is important to mention that the lawmakers, whose initial goal was limited to recognizing new rights for citizens on the centralized systems of information owned by the administration, did not imagine the creation of the Internet; however, they still succeeded in creating legislation that is a pillar of regulations pertaining to electronics.

[26]Kosta 2013.

[27]Gonzalez Fuster 2014.

[28]Convention for the Protection of Individuals with regard to Automatic Processing of Personal Data [1981], CETS No. 108.

[29]Guidelines for the Regulation of Computerized Personal Data Files [1990], General Assembly resolution 45/95.

[30]Legifrance (1995) Directive 95/46/CE du Parlement européen et du Conseil du 24 octobre 1995 relative à la protection des personnes physiques à l'égard du traitement des données à caractère personnel et à la libre circulation de ces données [Directive 95/46/EC of the European Parliament and of the Council of 24 October 1995 on the protection of individuals with regard to the processing of personal data and on the free movement of such data]. https://www.legifrance.gouv.fr/affichTexte.do?cidTexte=JORFTEXT000000697074. Accessed 12 August 2019.

4.5 Attention on the Most Sensitive Data to Be Under Special Regimes (Police, Justice, Secret Services)

A first modification dealing with sensitive data was implemented by a governmental decree on 14 October 1991.[31] This text reorganized the files of the Renseignements Généraux (Secret Services) allowing the "collection, conservation and the treatment of the RG files about adult persons having particular objective inalterable physical signs" and "political, philosophical, religious or trade union activities" (Article 2). These data could be collected if they deal with "physical or moral persons who asked, used, executed a political, trade union, economic mandate or who play a significant political, economic, social or religious role, under the condition that these data are necessary for the Government, its services the means to appreciate the political social or economic situation and foresee its evolution" (Article 3). But in this case, they cannot be communicated to the police (attached to the Ministry of Home Affairs) or to the gendarmerie (military police, at that time attached to the Ministry of Defence) (Article 5). This decree also provides an examination, every five years, of the legitimacy of the data detained, under the control of the CNIL (Article 6).

Another modification was made to the law of 6 August 2004, which was a late transposition of the Directive 95/46/EC on the protection of personal data. This transposition modified the 1978 law, substantially expanding the domain of data deemed to qualify as "personal data" (Article 2). The legal regime was simplified and the sanctions were made more severe in the Penal Code (Article 226-16 and Article 226-24). At that time, the CNIL acquired even more powers of investigation and sanctions.

4.6 A Structure of the "Informatique et Libertés" Law in 1978 in Compliance with the French Constitutional and Administrative Law

The 1978 law has 13 parts, of which only the first three (principles, definitions, conditions of legality of treatment of personal data, CNIL) are about citizens. The law's first Article mentions the compliance with Human Rights ("Droits de l'Homme", to differentiate it from the treatment of personal data under the Vichy regime).

[31] Legifrance (2009) "Décret n°91-1051 du 14 octobre 1991 portant application aux fichiers informatisés, manuels ou mécanographiques gérés par les services des renseignements généraux des dispositions de l'article 31, alinéa 3, de la loi n° 78-17 du 6 janvier 1978 relative à l'informatique, aux fichiers et aux libertés [Decree n ° 91-1051 of 14 October 1991 applying to computerized, manual or mechanographic files managed by the general information services of the provisions of article 31, paragraph 3, of law n ° 78-17 of 6 January 1978 relating to computers, files and freedoms]. https://www.legifrance.gouv.fr/affichTexte.do?cidTexte=JORFTEXT000000173238&categorieLien=cid. Accessed 12 August 2019.

The second Article provides the framework of application to the larger extent. Then specifications about the obligations of a person responsible for the treatment of personal data and the persons designated by that treatment (Article 3) are introduced. It also specifies which data can be collected. The following types of information are forbidden to be collected, because they are considered sensitive (except if justified as per Articles 8 and 26): "racial", ethnic origins, political, philosophical or religious opinions, membership in a trade union, health- or sexual-related data. In addition, it specifies. how the data must be collected (Articles 6 and 7). Article 6 defines the principle of "finalité" (goal), the principle of proportionality, and the principle of accuracy. Article 7 details the need to obtain the consent of the person concerned for use of their data or to satisfy certain listed conditions.

The law to allow treatment of data by the CNIL lists several declaration procedures:

- request for authorization (Article 25) when the treatment of data can be dangerous for a person's private life. Data can be used only after being formally authorized by the CNIL;
- request for opinion (Article 26 and Article 27) only for treatment by the public sector;
- simplified norms, with a simple act of commitment from the CNIL;
- unique authorizations; and
- commitment of conformity with a decree of Conseil d'État (since 2012).

In France, special attention is given to data relating to police or judiciary needs. In Articles 9 and 10, the law mentions that only courts, public authorities, persons managing a public service or assisting lawmakers can treat data about infractions, convictions, and imprisonment. Furthermore, justice decisions cannot be based on personal data, thereby protecting such irregular practices.

Moreover, Article 26 mentions that the treatment of personal data concerning the "security of State, Defence or public security" or having as its object the "prevention, investigation, statement or pursuit of penal infractions or the execution of penal sanctions" must be authorized by arrest (public at) taken after justified opinion given by the CNIL is published in the *Journal Officiel* (official administrative journal). The data transferred to the CNIL can be less than other kind of files (since the law of 23 January 2006 on terrorism (Article 13)).

When sensitive data is involved (in the case of the Renseignements Généraux, for example, or EDVIGE database, DNA database), the treatment must be authorized by a decree from the Conseil d'État, taken after justified and published opinion from the CNIL.

Currently, authorization for these data treatments can be provided simply through publication in the *Journal Officiel* with a decree from the Conseil d'État. Until now, this procedure was used only for files concerning the Renseignements Généraux, not for police-justice files.

In terms of sanctions, the CNIL has different levels:

- warning (Article 45);

- injunction to stop the treatment or withdraw the authorization (Article 45);
- the locking of some data (Article 45);
- request to the Prime Minister or to justice to take the necessary measures to stop the treatment (Article 45); and
- financial administrative sanction to a maximum of 150,000 euros and 300,000 euros in case of recidivation.

The CNIL's administrative sanctions can be argued only in front of the Conseil d'État.

4.7 The Main Rights of Citizens Are Recognized by the French Legislation

This legislation recognizes several citizens' rights, including:

- the right to information;
- the right of opposition;
- the right of access; and
- the right of rectification.

Entities which receive requests are required to execute these rights (the administrators of personal data) within two months and to verify the identity of the person requesting the right (to avoid communication of data about a third party).

Concerning the right to information, mentioned in Article 3, every person has the right to know if he/she is listed in a database and, if it is the case, in which file. This is the fundamental basis of the other rights.

The right of opposition allows anybody to oppose, with a legitimate reason, being listed in a file. Moreover, the person can refuse, without needing to provide justification, any use of data about themselves for prospection, particularly for commercial purposes. Some companies, which are members of the French federation of distance-selling companies, created the "Robinson" database; this database allows everybody to be removed from the database of all the companies that are federation members.[32] France Telecom (now Orange), the telecommunications company, has set up a similar system for its clients who do not want to have their telephonic data commercialized, but still want to be in the phone books.[33]

Files from the public sector (databases of the tax administration, police, justice, and passengers' databases) are not, for the most part, concerned by this right of opposition. This is true despite a decision by the Conseil d'État on 20 July 2010 in

[32] Commission Nationale Informatique et Libertés 2019b.

[33] Ibid.

the file from the Ministry of Education which noticed a contradiction between some acts of the Ministry and Article 38 of the Informatique et Libertés law.[34]

The right of access is complementary to the right of information because in justifying the identify, it is possible to have access to personal data. This right can also enable the right of accuracy, and it is possible to obtain a copy of the data. This right is limited because if the person responsible for the treatment considers that the right of access is used in an abusive way or if the data are conserved in a regular manner, this right can be refused. If the data deals with the security of the State, defence, or public security (police, gendarmerie), a member of the CNIL is designated to verify the data and in some cases modify the data if this modification does not jeopardize national security. Treatments carried out by public administrations, as well as by persons in charge of public service and tax services, are also concerned by this measure.

Finally, the right of rectification complements the right of access, allowing anybody to rectify, complete, update, lock, or ask that incorrect personal data concerning him/her be erased. Essentially, this is accomplished by sending a written letter to the organization owner of the data. The person responsible for the treatment must show evidence of the rectification requested and send a copy of the modified records (Article 40).

4.8 Incomplete Harmonization of the Rules and Procedures Between Databases of the Private and Public Sectors

Before the transposition of the GDPR in 2018, the most important modification to the 1978 law was the transposition of directive 95/46/EC, which took place on 6 August 2004.

This 2004 change resulted in a better harmonization between public sector databases and private sector databases. The rules of declaration in the public sector became similar to those in the private sector: a simple declaration, and the person requesting data only needs to wait for the CNIL's written authorization before gaining effective use of the file. This distinction between public person and private person has not totally disappeared has a request for opinion concerning sensitive data is imposed to the public sector.

4.9 Personal Data Officer to Data Protection Officer

When talking about the Directive's new obligation in 2018 to have a Data Protection Officer in place in every entity administering databases of personal data, the law of 6

[34]Rome S, Mediapart (2010) Le ministère de l'Education recale par le Conseil d'État [The Ministry of Education received by the Council of State]. https://blogs.mediapart.fr/sebastien-rome/blog/060710/le-ministere-de-leducation-recale-par-le-conseil-detat. Accessed 12 August 2019.

August 2004 in France introduced the possibility for private or public organizations to designate a "correspondant à la protection des données à caractère personnel" (personal data officer) usually named "correspondant informatique et libertés" or "CIL."[35] This officer is in charge of ensuring the correct application of the law in the organization. The procedures of declaration to the CNIL are simplified except for the most sensitive data (such as biometric data or data dealing with the security of the State). In general, the officer advises the company on all personal data questions. Designated by the company, this officer (who can be an employee or someone hired externally) must act independently of the company and can alert the CNIL. (Such positions already exist in various forms, for example, Datenschutzbeauftragter in Germany,[36] functionaris gegevensbescherming in the Netherlands,[37] and the person-uppgiftsombud in Sweden.[38]) Since 2007, the Institut supérieur d'électronique de Paris [Higher Institute of Electronics of Paris] (Grande École) has offered a Master's degree specializing in the CIL.[39] On 23 March 2010, a proposition of law in its Article 3 raised the possibility of making the existence of such an officer compulsory in every organization (the President of the CNIL was in favour of such a requirement).[40] The Data Protection Officer position created by the GDPR is an evolution of the CIL existing in France.

Finally, that modification of the 1978 law formally established the requirement that visits of the CNIL to offices of private and public organizations occur only between 6 am and 9 pm.[41]

4.10 Changes Brought by the GDPR to the French Legal Framework

4.10.1 Limited Modifications to the Law of 1978 Towards More Administrative Simplifications

The different changes brought by the GDPR in France in 2018 are limited, due to the long development since the 1970s of a legal framework of protection of personal data. It is important to highlight that an additional right (data portability) has been

[35]Sfez B, Village de la Justice (2011) Le correspondant Informatique et Libertés, garant de la conformité des traitements de données personnelles a la loi [The IT and Liberties correspondent, guarantor of the compliance of personal data processing with the law]. https://www.village-justice.com/articles/Correspondant-Informatique-Libertes,11311.html. Accessed 12 August 2019.

[36]Custers et al 2019.

[37]Ibid.

[38]Ibid.

[39]Institut supérieur d'électronique de Paris 2019.

[40]Sénat 2010.

[41]Commission Nationale Informatique et Libertés 2018a.

given to citizens and that the goal of administrative simplification desired by several successive governments has been partially achieved in this reform.

The framework, which is unified with the one of the other Member States concerning personal data, applies to all the companies wherever they are based, as soon as goods and services are offered to persons having a residence on the territory of the European Union. This adds a new right for the French citizen, not existing before 2018, which is the portability of personal data.[42] The concrete application of this portability in France was the possibility of having access (via the Internet) to French TV channels outside of the French territory by (without limitation by IP address, as was the case previously).[43] This possibility applies only to paid services. This legal framework provides a clearer idea and potential trust of citizens in the use of their personal data.

Moreover, the law provides a simplification of the rules applied to the economic actors while maintaining a high level of protection for citizens. The a priori system of control, based on the system of declarations and authorization, is replaced by the a posteriori system of control, which is based on the Data Protection Officer's evaluation of the risks regarding treatment of the data. As a counterpart, the CNIL's powers are strengthened and the sanctions are increased to a maximum of 20 million euros or 4% of (global) sales revenue.[44]

Nevertheless, some a priori procedures are maintained for the processing of the most sensitive data, for example, the biometric data necessary for identification or for control of the identity of persons, or those using the INSEE number (Social Security number).[45]

Persons under 16 years old are also better protected. The consent of both parents is necessary for a young person's personal data to be treated by the IT companies, such as the social networks.[46]

Concerning the police-justice data, a right of information is created with a direct exercise of the right of access, the right of rectification, and the right of removing the data. New rules are included also for the transfer of data to third states.

4.11 Powers of the CNIL Clarified and Strengthened

The French law added the following new dispositions:

- New missions for the CNIL in order to improve the legal environment with more flexible instruments in a gradual manner (Article 1);

[42] Commission Nationale Informatique et Libertés 2017b.

[43] Centre Européen des Consommateurs France 2018.

[44] Commission Nationale Informatique et Libertés 2019c.

[45] INSEE 2019.

[46] Commission Nationale Informatique et Libertés 2018b.

- The possibility for CNIL members to make decisions without the presence of agents of the commission (the presence of governmental representatives is optional, and no longer compulsory) (Article 3);
- More details about the framework of intervention by on-site CNIL agents and members, communication of all documents, possible use of fake identity during controls online, etc.) (Article 4);
- The French Law is applicable as soon as a person has a residence in France, including when the person responsible for the treatment is not based in France in case of divergences between the legislations of the EU Member States due to the margins of manoeuvre left to them (Article 8).

4.11.1 Controversies and Pending Issues of the Protection of Data in France

4.11.1.1 A Few Last Controversies Solved by the New Legislation

While discussing the text in Parliament, two elements have been raised by Members of Parliament:

- the right to transparency about the criteria used by the system of allocation of students to universities after high school (much criticized on its efficiency since it was first put in place);[47] and
- the use of contracts by companies to include the pre-installation of applications on mobile devices to collect the personal data of its employees using these devices.

"Parcourssup", the name of the system using algorithms to allocate future students to the universities accepting them, has been highly criticized. Although many Members of Parliament have asked about the possibility of making the reasons and criteria behind allocating or not allocating students to a university or school transparent and available to the future students, this has been rejected.

The question regarding the pre-installed application on devices used by employees also has been brought forward by MP Cedric Villani (the most recent French winner of the Fields Medal for Mathematics). It has been decided that it will be an illegal act to make the possibility of such pre-installation part of a job contract.[48]

---

[47] Villani 2018.

[48] Sénat 2019a.

4.11.1.2 Pending Issues in France on the Administration of Personal Data: Database Owned by International Organizations Having Headquarters in France

Interpol is the international organization of cooperation of criminal police based in Lyon, France, since 1989. This organization—proposed by Albert 1st of Monaco in 1923, organized by Austria, having a dark period during the Second World War, and operating under a Chart in 1955—has been in conflict with the French government ever since the passage of the Informatique et Libertés law in 1978.

In the 1970s, Interpol decided to computerize its large database (at that time based in Saint-Cloud, near Paris). The French government said that the Informatique et Libertés law applied to the organization and that the CNIL should have access to the venue for controls.[49] Interpol replied that the Informatique et Libertés law was not applicable because the data are owned by Interpol Member States and not by Interpol which is only in possession of them. As a result, the data are foreign data; making this data available to French authorities would prevent good international police cooperation, because some of the 182 Member States would refuse to communicate information to which France would have direct access.[50]

In 1983 and 1984, a proper text was signed between France and Interpol for the organization's legal framework which prevents France from having access to Interpol documents and creates an internal authority of database control in Interpol.[51]

The former conflict between France and Interpol is a possible source of worry for future international organizations that are thinking about moving their headquarters to France; this is because they may have concerns relating to the application of the Informatique et Libertés law. The 1983 and 1984 text thereby offers these organizations a high level of protection of personal data.

[49]Commission Nationale Informatique et Libertés 2015.

[50]Lebrun 1997.

[51]Commission Nationale Informatique et Libertés 1988.

4.11.1.3 Choice of Retaining the Architecture of the Law of 1978, Problem for Readability in the Long Term

The National Assembly has highlighted a problem of readability of the law of 1978 with its multiple insertions of modifications; the most recent reform occurred in 2018.[52] This complexity is due to the French government's choice of a fast adoption procedure, as was the case of the Directive of 1995 that was transposed only in 2004 in French legislation. This combination of a European regulation and national texts is aggravated by choices of legal terms, which shows the difference of approach (for example, between the Data Protection Officer and the "correspondant CIL"). The French government chose to include only the indispensable modifications for the execution of the Regulation and the Directive in France, postponing the rewriting of the law of 1978 to a latter ordinance, according to the empowerment foreseen in Article 23 of the law.

Meanwhile, the difficulty in reading the law of 1978 may induce mistakes in the meaning of the rights and obligations. Some dispositions of the law of 1978 still not modified are actually not applicable because they have been replaced in their field of application by dispositions from European regulation (for example, in the areas of consent, the legal basis of treatments, or the meaning of recognized personal rights), while some new rights are not explained yet in the text.

For these reasons, the National Assembly requested a fast adoption of the ordinance in order to have a rewriting of the law of 1978 and, if possible, a full new examination of the protection of personal data in France for treatment both within and outside the field of the EU.

4.11.1.4 Application of the GDPR in France and Possible Evolution

Pioneer in Data Protection in Europe and New Rights for Citizens

France has been one of the European pioneers in setting a legal framework for the protection of personal data, due to both political moves and the administrative needs of restructuring the functioning of the state. However, due to some complications and diminished interest in the evolution of the law of 1978, France was one of the last countries to transpose and implement the new modifications intervened with the Directive of 1995 (transposition made in 2004) and the GDPR (transposition made a few days before the entry into force).

As mentioned by the Senate in its report on the project of the law transposing the GDPR in French law, French authorities want to keep the possibility of adopting national measures and foreseeing the faculty of citizens to use their rights under the

[52] Assemblée Nationale (2017) Projet de loi relatif a la protection des données personnelles [Draft law on the protection of personal data]. http://www.assemblee-nationale.fr/15/projets/pl0490-ei.asp. Accessed 12 August 2019.

country's national authority of control (the CNIL).[53] France welcomes the harmonization of the applicable rules on the territory of the European Union and the introduction of new rights (right to be forgotten, obligation of portability of personal data, express consent, limitation of profiling, creation of the data protection officer). However, French authorities want to maintain additional national measures for guaranteeing these rights in their application (for example, more obligations of transparency on the Internet browser companies concerning the right to be forgotten and a better balance with the freedom of expression and more investigative powers for the CNIL).

Ongoing Need for Clarification of the Police Justice Data and Need of Guarantee of the Rights for Citizens

As mentioned in the previous section, in light of its conflict with Interpol in the past, France keeps asking for a clarification on the applicable regime on some administrative police files and the consequences of exclusion of the European databases in dealing with security questions (Europol, Eurojust or Frontex), from the field of application of the directive.

Due to the late entry of the legislative measures of applications of the GDPR in France and due to the administrative, technical, and financial burden generated by the changes, difficulties arise for the actors in France who did not anticipate the new obligations coming into effect. This is especially true for the small territorial collectives such as small and medium-size cities as well as departments, which rarely have the necessary financial and technical means for dealing with these obligations.

With the margin of manoeuvre provided by the regulation in order to maintain special regimes for the most sensitive data, France considers that the reform of 2018 is beneficial for maintaining more protective measures on a national basis. France is very careful to maintain a high level of national protection without placing more burden on small and medium-size companies.[54]

It is important to highlight that the main discussions in the French National Assembly on the GDPR were focused on issues that did not result in any modification to the legal framework. These issues included the age of consent,[55] algorithms used,[56] the obligations on the Internet browser companies,[57] and the data's heritage.[58] On the age of consent, the possibility that the European Regulation would bring the age to lower than 16 is still being discussed in French society. It is recognized as an open topic because of young peoples' lack of consideration on the actual exchanges between/among them on the Internet at an earlier age as well as a lack of awareness of the risks due to uncontrolled communication of personal data.

---

[53] Sénat 2016.

[54] Assemblée Nationale (2017) Projet de loi relatif a la protection des données personnelles [Draft law on the protection of personal data]. http://www.assemblee-nationale.fr/15/projets/pl0490-ei.asp. Accessed 12 August 2019.

[55] Ibid.

[56] Ibid.

[57] Ibid.

[58] Ibid.

4.12 First Year of Application of the GDPR in France: Plans to Rewrite Entirely the 1978 Informatique et Libertés Law, Exceptionally High Number of Complaints, and Substantial Cooperation with Other Authorities Protecting Personal Data in the European Union

First of all, after the GDPR started to be applied in France, the French government has still been empowered to put forward a future ordinance that would rewrite entirely the Informatique et Libertés law of 1978. This ordinance—presented by the Minister of Justice Nicole Belloubet and highlighting a "formal corrections" and "necessary adaptations" due to the GDPR—was released on 13 December 2018[59] after an opinion of the CNIL which considered this text "not very readable".[60] Thus, it can be expected that the French law will be rewritten entirely sometime in the future, within the framework of the GDPR, for better readability.

When the GDPR entered into force on 25 May 2018, the issue of protection of personal data was not a new one for France. As seen previously, the country already had lengthy experience and high levels of awareness since the passage of the Informatique et Libertés law of 1978. This new obligation to ask explicitly for consent to collect his or her personal data is consolidated with the European framework.

Media coverage in May 2018 increased the awareness of French citizens regarding their right to access, modify, and remove their personal data collected by a public or private organization. The CNIL received 30% more complaints during this first year of application of the GDPR against companies which did not respect these requests[61] (in 2000, the CNIL received 3000 complaints; in 2018, it received 11,000 complaints).[62] Although several French companies have received sanctions, the CNIL did not publish the names of those companies which quickly corrected GDPR

[59]Legifrance (2018) Ordonnance n° 2018-1125 du 12 décembre 2018 prise en application de l'article 32 de la loi n° 2018-493 du 20 juin 2018 relative à la protection des données personnelles et portant modification de la loi n° 78-17 du 6 janvier 1978 relative à l'informatique, aux fichiers et aux libertés et diverses dispositions concernant la protection des données à caractère personnel [Ordinance No. 2018-1125 of 12 December 2018 taken pursuant to article 32 of Law No. 2018-493 of 20 June 2018 relating to the protection of personal data and amending Law No. 78-17 of 6 January 1978 relating to data processing, files and freedoms and various provisions relating to the protection of personal data]. https://www.legifrance.gouv.fr/affichTexte.do?cidTexte=JORFTEXT000037800506&dateTexte=&categorieLien=id. Accessed 13 August 2019.

[60]Commission Nationale Informatique et Libertés 2018c.

[61]Dancer M, La Croix (2019) Thomas Dautieu : «Les citoyens ont redécouvert leur droit d'accès à leurs informations personnelles» [Thomas Dautieu: "Citizens have rediscovered their right to access their personal information"]. https://www.la-croix.com/Debats/Forum-et-debats/Thomas-Dautieu-citoyens-redecouvert-leur-droit-dacces-informations-personnelles-2019-05-26-1201024540. Accessed 13 August 2019.

[62]Gastaud F, Les Echos (2019) RGPD: un an après, des objectifs non atteints [GDPR: one year later, objectives not met]. https://www.lesechos.fr/idees-debats/cercle/rgpd-un-an-apres-des-objectifs-non-atteints-1017223. Accessed 13 August 2019.

infringements. In 2018, Google was fined 50 million euros for not obtaining the consent of persons on Android and for the lack of information given to users.[63]

According to a survey by IFOP[64] conducted in April 2019 for the CNIL, 70% of the French population is said to be more informed about the protection of personal data and 62% have heard about the GDPR.[65] Most of the complaints involved the following issues: the sharing of personal data on the Internet (35.7%); the Marketing/Commercial sector (21%); Human Resources (16.5%); the Banking/Credit sector (8.9%); and the Healthcare/Social sector (4.2%).[66]

The CNIL has noticed some emerging issues: remote viewing; the installation of cameras in care units; the desire by clients of online banks and online service providers to use their right to the portability of their personal data; informed citizens' concerns about the security of their personal data in all sectors; and worries by smartphone users about the personal data to which their applications may have access.[67]

Since the decree of 1 August 2018, the principle of direct exercise of rights for some files has been in effect. Therefore, the CNIL is no longer the first interlocutor for most of the files. However, the CNIL remains the main interlocutor for the TAJ[68] and FICOBA[69] files (4264 requests in 2018).[70] In terms of the role of advisor for the executive and legislative powers in France, the CNIL also provided 120 opinions on projects of law to the French government on personal data or creating new databases, provided 110 authorizations, and participated in approximately 30 parliamentary hearings.[71]

Companies also became aware that even if collecting clients' personal data was very important for their activities, the trust of their users of the digital services was a priority in terms of their competitive status in the marketplace. A total of 18,000 Data Protection Officers were designated internally within the first year since the GDPR entered into force in France (a third of them were public organizations). This is still an insufficient number, given the number of companies legally obligated to

[63]In 2018, Uber was fined 400,000 euros, Bouygues Telecom 250,000 euros and Optical Center 250,000 euros by the CNIL.

[64]Institut Français d'Opinion Publique 2019.

[65]Commission Nationale Informatique et Libertés 2019d.

[66]Commission Nationale Informatique et Libertés 2018d.

[67]Ibid.

[68]Traitement d'antécédents judiciaires [Processing of Judicial Records]. The conditions of removing from the TAJ before the term of the period of conservation are defined by Article 230-8 of the Code of Criminal Procedure. Article 230-8 allows now the convicted persons to make a request of removal to the Public Prosecutor who has 2 months to answer.

[69]Fichier national des comptes bancaires et assimilés [National database of bank account and assimilated].

[70]Commission Nationale Informatique et Libertés 2018d.

[71]Ibid.

respect the GDPR in France.[72] Very small companies are often those which are not yet in compliance with the GDPR. A lot of work remains to be done on the clarity of the GDPR forms provided by the companies to their clients. The CNIL's role is to support this effort in order to avoid subsequent judiciary complaints. In 2018, the CNIL received 22% more calls, had 80% more visits on its website, and performed 310 controls (204 on site, 51 online, 51 on documents, and 4 hearings).[73]

A review of the cases where the CNIL had to intervene reveals that, most of the time, the companies and the public administration continued to: make copies of personal identity documents (ID) or collect more information on the client than necessary for pursuing the goal of a commercial activity; or be careless in removing the personal data from their database after the client's request or after the end of the declared period of collection of these data, often kept in archives by the company. The CNIL provides a reminder of a GDPR framework in a warning to the organization; and, in the large majority of cases, the data or the copies of the data are deleted after notification by the CNIL.[74]

The main criticism is that the sanctions have not yet proven to be sufficient deterrent for the largest companies operating in France.[75] The CNIL issued 49 formal notices primarily to two sectors: insurance companies; and companies specializing in target marketing using SDK technology installed in mobile applications. A total of 11 sanctions have been decided (10 with a fine, nine of which were publicly announced and one non-public warning).[76]

The European (and international) cooperation also has to be improved after the important increase of exchange between the CNIL and the other authorities of protection of personal data in the European Union. With the federal authority of Canada and the authority of the province of Ontario, the CNIL co-wrote a resolution on online educative platforms, which was adopted in October 2018 by the International Conference of authorities of protection of personal data. The CNIL also contributed to various programmes and education campaigns with the European Commission (especially the Cybersecurity Unit of the JRC Research Center) and the Council of Europe for the creation of a "toolbox" for informing youth about protection of their personal data.[77] The CNIL and other authorities of the EU Member States cooperate mainly on treating cases of companies established in France and abroad or for activities affecting persons having residences in several European countries. The cooperation takes place in English, which pushed the CNIL to carry out a deep review

[72] Dowling E, Journal du Net (2019) RGPD, un an après: une avancée majeure pour l'Europe [GDPR, a year later: a major step forward for Europe]. https://www.journaldunet.com/management/expert/71227/rgpd--un-an-apres---une-avancee-majeure-pour-l-europe.shtml. Accessed 13 August 2019.

[73] Commission Nationale Informatique et Libertés 2018d.

[74] Ibid.

[75] Gastaud 2019, see n 62.

[76] Commission Nationale Informatique et Libertés 2018d.

[77] Ibid.

of its procedures. Between 25 May and 31 December 2018, a total of 257 procedures of European cooperation have been introduced by the authorities of protection of personal data. The CNIL has been «chef de file» on 24 cases and involved in 132 other cases.[78]

References

Banck A, Bensoussan-Brulé V, Chaussier N (2018) Le Data Protection Officer: Une nouvelle fonction dans l'entreprise [The Data Protection Officer: A new function in the company]. Bruylant, Brussels

Boucher P (1974) Safari ou la chasse aux Français [Safari or the hunt for the French]. Le Monde

Centre Européen des Consommateurs France (2018) Contenus numériques et géoblocage [Digital content and geoblocking]. https://www.europe-consommateurs.eu/fr/quels-sont-vos-droits/achats-sur-internet/contenus-numeriques-et-geoblocage/. Accessed 12 June 2019

Commission Nationale Informatique et Libertés (1988) 9e rapport d'activité 1988 [9th Activity Report 1988]. https://www.cnil.fr/sites/default/files/atoms/files/20171116_rapport_annuel_cnil_-_rapport_dactivite_1988_vd.pdf. Accessed 12 August 2019

Commission Nationale Informatique et Libertés (2015) Délibération n°80-18 du 3 juin 1980 Interpol [Deliberation n ° 80-18 of 3 June 1980 Interpol]. https://www.legifrance.gouv.fr/affichCnil.do?id=CNILTEXT000017654262. Accessed 12 August 2019

Commission Nationale Informatique et Libertés (2017a) Délibération n° 2017-299 du 30 novembre 2017 portant avis sur un projet de loi d'adaptation au droit de l'Union européenne de la loi n°78-17 du janvier 1978 [Deliberation n ° 2017-299 of November 30, 2017 bearing opinion on a bill of adaptation to the law of the European Union of law n ° 78-17 of 6 January 1978]. https://www.cnil.fr/sites/default/files/atoms/files/projet_davis_cnil.pdf. Accessed 11 August 2019

Commission Nationale Informatique et Libertés (2017b) Le droit à la portabilité en questions. [The right to portability in questions]. https://www.cnil.fr/fr/le-droit-la-portabilite-en-questions. Accessed 12 August 2019

Commission Nationale Informatique et Libertés (2018a) Comment se passe un contrôle de la CNIL [How is a CNIL control carried out]. https://www.cnil.fr/fr/comment-se-passe-un-controle-de-la-cnil. Accessed 12 August 2019

Commission Nationale Informatique et Libertés (2018b) Conformité RGPD: comment recueillir le consentement des personnes? [GDPR compliance: how to obtain people's consent?]. https://www.cnil.fr/en/node/24679. Accessed 12 August 2018

Commission Nationale Informatique et Libertés (2018c) Délibération n 2018-349 du 15 novembre 2018 portant avis sur un projet d'ordonnance prise en application de l'article 32 de la loi n 2018-493 du 20 juin 2018 relative a la protection des données personnelles et portant modification de la loi n 78-17 du 6 janvier 1978 relative a l'informatique, aux fichiers et aux libertés et diverses dispositions concernant la protection des données à caractère personnel [Deliberation n 2018-349 of November 15, 2018 relating to an opinion on a draft order taken in application of article 32 of law n 2018-493 of 20 June 2018 relating to the protection of personal data and amending law n 78-17 of 6 January 1978 relating to data processing, files and freedoms and various provisions concerning the protection of personal data]. https://cdn2.nextinpact.com/medias/d2018-349-ordonnance-vs.pdf. Accessed 13 August 2019

Commission Nationale Informatique et Libertés (2018d) Rapport d'activité 2018 [2018 Activity Report]. https://www.cnil.fr/sites/default/files/atoms/files/cnil-39e_rapport_annuel_2018.pdf. Accessed 13 August 2019

[78]Ibid.

Commission Nationale Informatique et Libertés (2018e) Règlement européen sur la protection des données: ce qui change pour les professionnels [European data protection regulation: what is changing for professionals]. https://www.cnil.fr/fr/reglement-europeen-sur-la-protection-des-donnees-ce-qui-change-pour-les-professionnels. Accessed 11 August 2019

Commission Nationale Informatique et Libertés (2018f) Le RGPD, c'est maintenant: les changements à retenir et les outils pour bien se préparer [The GDPR, it's now: the changes to remember and the tools to prepare well]. https://www.cnil.fr/fr/le-rgpd-cest-maintenant-les-changements-retenir-et-les-outils-pour-bien-se-preparer. Accessed 11 August 2019

Commission Nationale Informatique et Libertés (2019a) La loi «Informatique et Libertés» [Law «Computing and Freedom»]. https://www.cnil.fr/fr/la-loi-informatique-et-Libertés. Accessed 12 August 2019

Commission Nationale Informatique et Libertés (2019b) Les listes d'opposition [Opposition Lists]. https://www.cnil.fr/fr/les-listes-dopposition. Accessed 12 August 2019

Commission Nationale Informatique et Libertés (2019c) Mission (4): Contrôler et sanctionner [Control and sanction]. https://www.cnil.fr/fr/mission-4-controler-et-sanctionner Accessed 12 August 2019

Commission Nationale Informatique et Libertés (2019d) Rapport d'activité 2018 et enjeux 2019 [2018 Activity Report and 2019 challenges]. https://www.cnil.fr/sites/default/files/atoms/files/dossier_de_presse_cnil_bilan_2018_et_enjeux_2019.pdf. Accessed 13 August 2019

Conseil des Ministres du Gouvernement (2017) Compte rendu du Conseil des ministres du 13 décembre 2017 Protection des données personnelles [Report of the Council of Ministers of December 13, 2017 Protection of personal data]. https://www.gouvernement.fr/conseil-des-ministres/2017-12-13/protection-des-donnees-personnelles. Accessed 12 August 2019

Custers B, Sears A, Deschesne F (2019) EU personal data protection in policy and practice. Springer, New York

Gonzalez Fuster G (2014) The emergence of personal data protection as a fundamental right of the EU. Springer, New York

Gouvernement.fr, Archives (1978) Création de la Commission nationale de l'informatique et des libertés (CNIL) [Creation of the National Commission for Data Protection]. https://www.gouvernement.fr/partage/9870-creation-de-la-commission-nationale-de-l-informatique-et-des-libertes-cnil. Accessed 12 August 2019

Guillemain M (2019) L'application du RGPD par les organisations [Application of the GDPR by organizations]. Editions EMS, Caen

INSEE (2019) Exploitation des données du service de la donnée et des études statistiques (Sit@del) [Use of data from the data service and statistical studies] https://www.insee.fr/fr/information/3897381. Accessed 12 August 2018

Institut supérieur d'électronique de Paris (2019) Mastère Spécialisé Management et protection des données a caractère personnel [Specialized Master in Management and Protection of Personal Data]. https://formation-continue.isep.fr/management-et-protection-des-donnees-a-caractere-personnel/. Accessed 12 August 2019

Kosta E (2013) Consent in European data protection law. Martinus Nijhoff Publishers, Leiden

Lebrun M (1997) Interpol. Presses Universitaires de France, Paris

Sénat (2010) Proposition de loi Droit à la vie privée a l'heure du numérique [Proposition of the law on the right to privacy in the digital age]. http://www.senat.fr/amendements/2009-2010/331/Amdt_30.html. Accessed 12 August 2019

Sénat (2019a) Comptes rendus de l'office parlementaire d'évaluation des choix scientifiques et technologiques [Reports of the parliamentary office for the evaluation of scientific and technological choices]. http://www.senat.fr/compte-rendu-commissions/20190121/opecst.html. Accessed 12 August 2019

Sénat (2019b) Projet de loi relatif à la protection des données personnelles [Draft law on the protection of personal data]. https://www.senat.fr/rap/l17-350/l17-3504.html. Accessed 11 August 2019

Tribalat M (2016) Statistiques ethniques, une polémique bien française [Ethnic statistics, a very French controversy]. Social Science, L'Artilleur, Paris.
Vie Public, Direction de l'information légale et administrative (2018) Protection des données personnelles: que contient la loi du 20 juin 2018? [Protection of personal data: what does the law of 20 June 2018 contain?]. https://www.vie-publique.fr/actualite/dossier/securite-internet/protection-donnees-personnelles-que-contient-loi-du-20-juin-2018.html. Accessed 11 August 2019
Villani C (2018) Longuet Gérard, Office parlementaire d'évaluation des choix scientifiques et technologiques, Les algorithmes au service de l'action publique: le cas du portail admission post-bac [Algorithms at the service of public action: the case of the post-baccalaureate admission portal] Assemblée Nationale, Paris

Aurelien Lorange Senior Lecturer at The Hague University of Applied Sciences, International and European Law Program.

Chapter 5
Current Data Protection Regulations and Case Law in Greece: Cash as Personal Data, Lengthy Procedures, and Technologies Subjected to Courts' Interpretations

Georgios Bouchagiar and Nikos Koutras

Contents

Supported by the Luxembourg National Research Fund (FNR) (PRIDE17/12251371).

G. Bouchagiar (✉)
Faculty of Law, Economics and Finance, University of Luxembourg, 4 rue Alphonse Weicker, L-2721 Luxembourg-Kirchberg, Luxembourg
e-mail: georgios.bouchagiar@uni.lu

G. Bouchagiar
Law, Science, Technology & Society, Free University of Brussels, 2 Pleinlaan, 1050 Brussels, Belgium

N. Koutras
School of Business and Law, Edith Cowan University, JO2317, 270 Joondalup Drive, Joondalup, WA 6027, Australia
e-mail: n.koutras@ecu.edu.au

E. Kiesow Cortez (ed.), *Data Protection Around the World*, Information Technology and Law Series 33,
https://doi.org/10.1007/978-94-6265-407-5_5

Abstract This chapter addresses data protection in Greece. Section 5.1 provides an overview of case law of the Supreme Administrative Court and the Supreme Civil and Criminal Court, but also national laws and the Constitution of Greece. Section 5.2 studies core concepts, such as "control" and "consent", to detect similarities and differences between the General Data Protection Regulation and Greek law. Section 5.3 examines risks emerging from new technologies to highlight ignorance and confusion with which people may experience their everyday privacy. Section 5.4 addresses data portability as a trust-enhancing tool that could strengthen controllership and promote transparency in the interests of the data subjects. Greek regulations treat the right to the protection of personal data as a fundamental one, while national courts have repeatedly interpreted this right in relation to constitutional principles, under which attention is drawn to the data subject rather than the data processor. However, lengthy administrative and judicial procedures could become an obstacle, while exercising such constitutional rights. Hence, individuals may need to wait for a more-than-a-ten-year-period to get vindicated after severe violations of their sensitive information. Even though the right to the protection of personal data is an aspect of the traditional "offline" right to privacy, today's digital technologies have also "become subject" to courts' interpretations. In this chapter, personal data case law is examined, and, simultaneously, references are made to current national laws and the Constitution of Greece. By providing a general image of present-day regulations, this chapter aims to detect ways in which national courts interpret some crucial provisions.

Keywords Greece · *Symvoulio Tis Epikrateias* · *Areios Pagos* · Personal data · Privacy · GDPR · Consent · Control · Portability

5.1 Introduction

Under the Greek regime, the protection of individuals with regard to the processing of personal data is guaranteed under Nomos 2472/1997,[1] which transposed Directive 95/46/EC of the European Parliament and of the Council.[2] Moreover, Article 9A of the Constitution of Greece treats the right to be protected from the processing of such data as a fundamental one.

Very recently, in response to challenges posed by the Regulation (EU) 2016/679 of the European Parliament and of the Council,[3] the Minister of Justice, Transparency and Human Rights, Stavros Kodonis, carried out a public consultation[4]—between 20 February and 5 March 2018—on the draft law, or as the Minister put it on the "*legislative initiative*", under the heading "*Introducing legislative measures for the purposes of the Regulation (EU) 2016/679 of the European Parliament and of the Council of 27 April 2016 on the protection of natural persons with regard to the processing of personal data and on the free movement of such data, and repealing Directive 95/46/EC (General Data Protection Regulation), and the transposition of the Directive (EU) 2016/680 of the European Parliament and of the Council of 27 April 2016 on the protection of natural persons with regard to the processing of personal data by competent authorities for the purposes of the prevention, investigation, detection or prosecution of criminal offences or the execution of criminal*

[1]Nomos 2472/1997 was amended by Nomos 3471/2006, which transposed Directive 2002/58/EC of the European Parliament and of the Council of 12 July 2002 concerning the processing of personal data and the protection of privacy in the electronic communications sector (Directive on privacy and electronic communications), and by Nomos 3917/2011, which transposed Directive 2006/24/EC of the European Parliament and of the Council of 15 March 2006 on the retention of data generated or processed in connection with the provision of publicly available electronic communications services or of public communications networks and amending Directive 2002/58/EC. The latter (Directive 2006/24/EC) is no longer in force (date of end of validity: 8 April 2014), albeit, Nomos 3917/2011 is still valid. It is also worth mentioning that, under Article 9(1) of national Nomos 4225/2014, the National Actuarial Authority (NAA) is exempt from provisions of the above Nomos 2472/1997, with regard to personal data that the NAA collects and processes, in the exercise of its powers.

[2]Directive 95/46/EC of the European Parliament and of the Council of 24 October 1995 on the protection of individuals with regard to the processing of personal data and on the free movement of such data, hereinafter referred to as "DPD" (for Data Protection Directive).

[3]Regulation (EU) 2016/679 of the European Parliament and of the Council of 27 April 2016 on the protection of natural persons with regard to the processing of personal data and on the free movement of such data and repealing Directive 95/46/EC (General Data Protection Regulation), hereinafter referred to as "GDPR" (for General Data Protection Regulation).

[4]Greek Ministry of Justice, Transparency and Human Rights (2018, February 20) Νόμος για την Προστασία Δεδομένων Προσωπικού Χαρακτήρα σε εφαρμογή του Κανονισμού (ΕΕ) 2016/679 [Law on the Protection of Personal Data in Application of the Regulation]. http://www.opengov.gr/ministryofjustice/?p=9331. Accessed 20 September 2019.

penalties, and on the free movement of such data, and repealing Council Framework Decision 2008/977/JHA and supplementary provisions".[5]

Given previous national experience,[6] such timely response by the Greek legislator is more than welcome. However, one would wonder why a new law is needed, since the GDPR applies from 25 May 2018, regardless of national provisions. Perhaps, the transposition of the Directive (EU) 2016/680 could be an answer to this. Since Greece is drafting a new law concerning personal data protection, why not include the GDPR?

In fact, by scrutinizing provisions of the above "*legislative initiative*", one could claim that they are very similar to those of the GDPR. However, amendments might emerge during this short two-week-period from 20 February to 5 March 2018. Therefore, no one is to ensure that the final text will be exactly the same as the initial version of the above "initiative".

In this section, personal data case law is examined, while, at the same time, references are made to current provisions of Nomos 2472/1997 and the Constitution of Greece. The purpose of this section is not only to provide an image of the current regime and regulations, but also to detect the way in which national courts interpret certain crucial provisions. Thus, the most recent case law of the two highest courts in the nation,[7] i.e. the Supreme Administrative Court of Greece (The State Council of Greece or, in Greek, *Symvoulio Tis Epikrateias*) and the Supreme Civil and Criminal Court (*Areios Pagos*), will be studied.

[5]National laws may include the term "*and supplementary provisions*" in their headings to amend, for instance, statutes, which can refer to other irrelevant issues. As one could claim, this is a "pain" for lawyers, who have to scrutinize each new law to detect potential amendments of other previous provisions. For instance, Article 79 of Nomos 4509/2017 ("*Measures for treatment of individuals, who are exempted from punishment, due to mental disorder and supplementary provisions*") refers, not to mentally ill, but to Collective Management Organizations (with regard to intellectual property issues).

[6]For instance, Nomos 4481/2017, which transposed the Directive 2014/26/EU of the European Parliament and of the Council of 26 February 2014 on collective management of copyright and related rights and multi-territorial licensing of rights in musical works for online use in the internal market, was brought into force on 20 July 2017. That is more than a year after the deadline set by the European Parliament and the Council (10 April 2016, under Article 43(1) of the above Directive 2014/26/EU).

[7]The Council of State (*Symvoulio Tis Epikrateias*), the Supreme Civil and Criminal Court (*Areios Pagos*) and the Court of Audit are the highest courts in the nation.

5.1.1 Cash as Personal Data (And Several "Errors with Manifest Impact" on the System)

With its Ruling No. 2649/2017 (Full Court), *Symvoulio Tis Epikrateias* annulled No. 1846/13.10.2016 joint decision of the Minister of Justice, Transparency and Human Rights and the Minister of Finance, with regard to the form and content of the Declaration of Finances and Assets (DFA), the Declaration of Financial Interests (DFI) and the electronic submission of these declarations. *Symvoulio Tis Epikrateias* held that the creation of asset registry is contrary to provisions that protect privacy, as there is a risk of leakage of personal data, and that the failure to appoint periods of retention of electronic files is unconstitutional.

The applicants, i.e. bodies representing judges and prosecutors, claimed—amongst others—that the provisions of Article 2(1)(a)(v, vi) of Nomos 3213/2003, under which DFAs shall include, as assets, inter alia, cash (apart from deposits), the amounts of which exceed EUR 15,000, and other movable objects, whose value exceeds EUR 30,000 (per object) and which are retained either in bank counters or in debtors' homes, are contrary to Article 5(1), Article 9(1) and Article 9A of the Constitution of Greece and infringe the principle of proportionality (Article 25(1)(d) of the Constitution), since they breach in a disproportionate and inappropriate way the right to the protection of personal data and private life of debtors and their families.

In accordance with Article 5 of the Constitution of Greece, everyone shall have the right to develop freely their personality and to participate in the social, economic and political life of the country, insofar as they do not infringe the rights of others or violate the Constitution and the good usages. Moreover, under Article 9(1) of the Constitution, every person's home is a sanctuary and the private and family life of the individual is inviolable. No home search shall be made, except when and as specified by law and always in the presence of representatives of the judicial power. Finally, Article 9A of the Constitution provides that all persons have the right to be protected from the collection, processing and use, especially by electronic means, of their personal data, as specified by law. The protection of personal data is ensured by an independent authority, which is constituted and operates as specified by law.

Symvoulio Tis Epikrateias took into consideration not only the above constitutional provisions, but also Article 8 and Article 52 of the Charter of Fundamental

Rights of the European Union (2016/C 202/02),[8] Nomos 2472/1997, which transposed DPD,[9] and settled jurisprudence[10] of the CJEU (including the latter's judgment in case C-131/12).[11]

---

[8]Article 8 of the Charter of Fundamental Rights of the European Union ("[...] *1. Everyone has the right to the protection of personal data concerning him or her. 2. Such data must be processed fairly for specified purposes and on the basis of the consent of the person concerned or some other legitimate basis laid down by law. Everyone has the right of access to data which has been collected concerning him or her, and the right to have it rectified. 3. Compliance with these rules shall be subject to control by an independent authority* [...]"). Article 52(1) of the Charter of Fundamental Rights of the European Union with regard to the scope and interpretation of rights and principles ("[...] *Any limitation on the exercise of the rights and freedoms recognized by this Charter must be provided for by law and respect the essence of those rights and freedoms. Subject to the principle of proportionality, limitations may be made only if they are necessary and genuinely meet objectives of general interest recognised by the Union or the need to protect the rights and freedoms of others.* [...]").

[9]More precisely, *Symvoulio Tis Epikrateias* took into account Article 6(1)(b, c, e) of DPD ("[...] *1. Member States shall provide that personal data must be:* [...] *(b) collected for specified, explicit and legitimate purposes and not further processed in a way incompatible with those purposes. Further processing of data for historical, statistical or scientific purposes shall not be considered as incompatible provided that Member States provide appropriate safeguards; (c) adequate, relevant and not excessive in relation to the purposes for which they are collected and/or further processed;* [...] *(e) kept in a form which permits identification of data subjects for no longer than is necessary for the purposes for which the data were collected or for which they are further processed. Member States shall lay down appropriate safeguards for personal data stored for longer periods for historical, statistical or scientific use* [...]"), Article 7(c, e) of DPD ("[...] *Member States shall provide that personal data may be processed only if:* [...] *(c) processing is necessary for compliance with a legal obligation to which the controller is subject;* [...] *(e) processing is necessary for the performance of a task carried out in the public interest or in the exercise of official authority vested in the controller or in a third party to whom the data are disclosed* [...]") and Article 13(1)(e, f) of DPD ("[...] *1. Member States may adopt legislative measures to restrict the scope of the obligations and rights provided for in Articles 6 (1), 10, 11 (1), 12 and 21 when such a restriction constitutes a necessary measures to safeguard:* [...] *(e) an important economic or financial interest of a Member State or of the European Union, including monetary, budgetary and taxation matters;* [...] *(f) a monitoring, inspection or regulatory function connected, even occasionally, with the exercise of official authority in cases referred to in (c), (d) and (e)* [...]").

[10]CJEU. (2003b). Joined Cases C-465/00, C-138/01 and C-139/01. *Rechnungshof* (C-465/00) *and Österreichischer Rundfunk, Wirtschaftskammer Steiermark, Marktgemeinde Kaltenleutgeben, Land Niederösterreich, Österreichische Nationalbank, Stadt Wiener Neustadt, Austrian Airlines, Österreichische Luftverkehrs-AG, and between Christa Neukomm* (C-138/01), *Joseph Lauermann* (C-139/01) *and Österreichischer Rundfunk*. paras 65–68; CJEU. (2014a). Joined Cases C-293/12 and C-594/12. *Digital Rights Ireland Ltd* (C-293/12) *v Minister for Communications, Marine and Natural Resources, Minister for Justice, Equality and Law Reform, Commissioner of the Garda Síochána, Ireland, The Attorney General, intervener: Irish Human Rights Commission, and Kärntner Landesregierung* (C-594/12), *Michael Seitlinger, Christof Tschohl and others*. paras 38–44.

[11]CJEU. (2014b). Case C-131/12. *Google Spain SL and Google Inc. v Agencia Española de Protección de Datos (AEPD) and Mario Costeja González*. para 66 ("[...] *it should be remembered that, as is apparent from Article 1 and recital 10 in the preamble, Directive 95/46 seeks to ensure a high level of protection of the fundamental rights and freedoms of natural persons, in particular their right to privacy, with respect to the processing of personal data* [...]").

With regard to national provisions, under Article 2(a) of Nomos 2472/1997, personal data shall mean any information relating to a natural person,[12] while in accordance with Article 2(d) of the above law 'processing of personal data' shall mean any operation or set of operations which is performed upon personal data and which is undertaken by the State, or a body governed by public or private law, or an association of persons, or a natural person, whether or not by automatic means, such as collection, recording, organization, conservation or storage, alteration, extraction, use, transmission, dissemination or otherwise making available.[13] Moreover, under Article 2(e) of national Nomos 2472/1997, 'personal data filing system' ('filing system') shall mean any structured set of personal data, which are accessible according to specific criteria.

Concerning lawfulness of processing, under Greek law,[14] personal data shall be collected fairly and lawfully for specified, explicit and legitimate purposes and shall be processed fairly and lawfully in a way compatible with those purposes; shall be adequate, relevant and not excessive in relation to the purposes for which it is processed; shall be accurate and, where necessary, kept up to date; shall be kept in a form which permits identification of data subjects for no longer than, in the judgment of the Data Protection Authority,[15] is necessary for the purposes for which the data was collected or for which it is further processed. Moreover, the DPA may, by reasoned decision, allow storage of personal data for historical, scientific or statistical purposes, where it considers that, in each specific case, data subjects' or third parties' rights are not violated. It is for the controller to ensure that the above provisions are complied with. Personal data that has been collected or processed in violation of the above are destroyed under the responsibility of the controller. If the DPA, ex officio or after complaint, verifies violation of the above, it terminates collection or processing and imposes duty to destroy the data collected or processed.

After having taken into consideration the above national and European provisions, *Symvoulio Tis Epikrateias* held that assets, which debtors must, under Article 2(1)(a)(v, vi) of Nomos 3213/2003 (as amended by Article 173(1) of Nomos 4389/2016), include in their DFAs, meaning cash (apart from deposits), the amounts of which exceed EUR 15,000, and other movable objects, whose value exceeds EUR

---

[12]Under Article 2(a) of Nomos 2472/1997, statistical aggregated information, from which data subjects can no longer be identified, shall not be regarded as personal data. The above Article 2(a) does not provide the full definition of Article 2(a) of DPD ("[…] *'personal data' shall mean any information relating to an identified or identifiable natural person ('data subject'); an identifiable person is one who can be identified, directly or indirectly, in particular by reference to an identification number or to one or more factors specific to his physical, physiological, mental, economic, cultural or social identity* […]").

[13]The term "processing", as defined in Article 2(d) of the above Nomos 2472/1997, does not include the full definition of DPD. See Article 2(b) of DPD, under which "[…] *'processing of personal data' ('processing') shall mean any operation or set of operations which is performed upon personal data, whether or not by automatic means, such as collection, recording, organization, storage, adaptation or alteration, retrieval, consultation, use, disclosure by transmission, dissemination or otherwise making available, alignment or combination, blocking, erasure or destruction;* […]".

[14]Article 4(1, 2) of Nomos 2472/1997.

[15]Data Protection Authority, hereinafter referred to as "DPA".

30,000 (per object) and which are retained either in bank counters or in debtors' homes, not only fall within the bound of debtors' private and family life but also constitute personal data, given that they are information relating to an identified or identifiable natural person.[16]

Thereafter, *Symvoulio Tis Epikrateias* found that, by imposing the duty to submit the above DFAs and DFIs, the legislator aims to promote transparency and to prevent and combat any cases of corruption. This is achieved—mainly—by controlling the change (increase) of debtors' assets for periods during which they have the status, due to which they have the obligation to submit the above declarations. Thus, the creation of asset registry, by recording any asset and its value, with regard to multiple groups of people and innumerable Greek citizens, including judges and prosecutors, and by verifying the accuracy, on pain of heavy criminal and administrative sanctions (provided in Articles 6 and 9 of Nomos 3213/2003), is not subject to the above provisions. Besides, the—alleged—public purpose, at which the creation of asset registry aims, is not incurred. Hence, as *Symvoulio Tis Epikrateias* ruled, the duty to include cash and movable objects not only violates debtors' right to the protection of their personal data, but also breaches their right to freely develop their personality and their right to private life, given that debtors are invited to reveal items of information that relate to their personality and their private and family life.[17]

For the above reasons, joint decision No. 1846/13.10.2016 of the Minister of Justice, Transparency and Human Rights and the Minister of Finance was annulled. However, despite the precedent that *Symvoulio Tis Epikrateias*—one of the highest courts in the nation—produced, after a few months, the same Ministries issued No. 1069/19-10-2017 joint decision with regard to the exact same issues (i.e. the form and content of the DFA and DFI, as well as the electronic submission of these declarations), introducing once again—and in violation of the court's precedent—an administration system, based on the same national laws, which *Symvoulio Tis Epikrateias* had found unconstitutional.

Several bodies, representing judges and prosecutors, reacted immediately and applied before *Symvoulio Tis Epikrateias*. The latter, with its Ruling No. 3312/2017 (Full Court), annulled No. 1069/19-10-2017 joint decision of the Minister of Justice, Transparency and Human Rights and the Minister of Finance. In particular—and interestingly—*Symvoulio Tis Epikrateias* "spoke" of "*errors with manifest impact*" on the whole structure and full function of the (declaration) system and held that numerous provisions—and failures to provide—were unlawful.[18]

---

[16] Ruling No. 2649/2017 (Full Court) of *Symvoulio Tis Epikrateias*, para 25.

[17] Ruling No. 2649/2017 (Full Court) of *Symvoulio Tis Epikrateias*, para 26–27.

[18] Ruling No. 3312/2017 (Full Court) of *Symvoulio Tis Epikrateias*, para 23 (mentioning as unlawful: the duty to declare cash (except for deposits), the amounts of which exceed EUR 15,000, and other movable objects, whose value exceeds EUR 30,000 (per object); the failure to provide periods of time with regard not only to completion of control but also to debtors' personal data retention; the duty to include in annual declarations all assets, regardless of whether there was a change during the previous year; the lack of provisions, with regard to assets acquired during past uses, that relate to non-inclusion of some data (e.g. value, price paid, source of money and amounts that correspond to each source) in the first electronic declaration; the duty to declare assets that belong to the debtor's

In our opinion, the seriousness of the above two cases focused the attention on the unlawfulness and unconstitutionality of the above provisions; and this is where we believe that attention should be drawn to. However, did anyone, actually, realize that *Symvoulio Tis Epikrateias* held that "*cash* […] *constitutes personal data*"?[19]

5.1.2 Balancing Interests: It Might Take a Long Time

Ruling No. 150/2017 of *Symvoulio Tis Epikrateias* concerned a fine imposed by the Greek Data Protection Authority (DPA), due to breaching provisions of Nomos 2472/1997. The applicant, a fund management company, transmitted personal data, which was delivered to an address other than the one declared. Thus, the recipient, a divorced wife, became aware of the data subject's information and used it against him in a judicial act for the payment of maintenance. This processing of data, relating to the subject's address, was found unlawful.

In particular, the applicant claimed that the DPAs' decision No. 104/2012 (which imposed the fine) was unlawful, given that it did not mention names and opinions of the minority. However, *Symvoulio Tis Epikrateias* rejected this claim, given that, under Article 19(2, 3) of Nomos 2472/1997, Article 6 and 7(2, 4) of Rules of Procedure of the DPA (6/1997) and Articles 1 and 15 of Administrative Procedure Code (Nomos 2690/1999), and as *Symvoulio Tis Epikrateias* has already held in other cases,[20] the DPA is not required to mention whether the latter was taken unanimously, or considered minority opinions[21] in its decision.

With regard to facts of the case, the data subject had declared his address and the company, while providing its services, was sending the client briefing notes. However, the firm sent the subject financial data, relating to the last three months of 2000, and delivered it to another address, which was the address of his former wife's firm. On the 29 November 2004, the data subject submitted a complaint to the national DPA, arguing that there had been an unlawful transmission of his personal information, due to which the divorced wife became aware of such data and used it against him in a judicial act for the payment of maintenance (concerning their minors). With its No. 41/2006 decision, the DPA imposed a EUR 5000 fine, albeit the

---

partner (in civil partnership); with regard to bank accounts, the duty to aggregate amounts, deriving from any source, and the duty to mention sources, from which what is left—in a bank account—on the 31st of December derives, and the precise amount that corresponds to each source).

[19]Ruling No. 2649/2017 of *Symvoulio Tis Epikrateias*, para 25. The exact wording in Greek is "*τα επίμαχα περιουσιακά στοιχεία που οφείλουν οι υπόχρεοι* […] *να συμπεριλάβουν στη δήλωση περιουσιακής κατάστασης που υποβάλλουν, δηλαδή, τα μετρητά χρήματα* […] *και τα κινητά περιουσιακά στοιχεία μεγάλης αξίας* […] *εμπίπτουν στην σφαίρα του ιδιωτικού και οικογενειακού βίου των υποχρέων* […] *συνιστούν δε και δεδομένα προσωπικού χαρακτήρα* […]".

[20]Ruling No. 1662/2009 (Full Court) of *Symvoulio Tis Epikrateias*.

[21]Ruling No. 150/2017 of *Symvoulio Tis Epikrateias*, paras 4 and 5.

decision was withdrawn—five years later, by decision No. 120/2011 of the DPA—due to bad composition of the authority. Thus, the latter, after having heard the company, issued the above decision No. 104/2012, imposing a fine (EUR 5000). The DPA found—amongst others—that, regardless of whether or not there had been a data subject's mandate to "hold mail" concerning briefing notes, there had been no declaration with regard to the address, to which financial information was actually delivered. Furthermore, as held by the DPA, the company, as data controller, failed to implement appropriate technical and organizational measures and, hence, unlawfully transmitted personal data to a third party (i.e. the divorced wife).[22]

The company applied before *Symvoulio Tis Epikrateias* and claimed—inter alia—that the data subject had not been harmed, given that the former wife had the right to request his financial information to use it in the judicial act for the payment of maintenance, concerning their minors. Besides, as alleged by the applicant, the legitimate interest of the former wife and the minors overrode data subject's interest to conceal his assets. Thus, the company argued that the processing was lawful, under Article 5(2)(e) of Nomos 2472/1997.[23]

However, *Symvoulio Tis Epikrateias* rejected the above arguments and held that the applicant, as data controller, was liable for unlawful processing of personal data, meaning registration, use, retention, and transmission of such data and failure to implement appropriate technical and organizational measures for the security of this information and its protection against unlawful processing. Moreover, as ruled by the court, regardless of the fact that data subjects' harm is not required in determining whether or not an infringement of Nomos 2742/1997 has been committed,[24] however, in this case, data subject's financial information was not delivered upon request from the former wife and, thus, the fact that this person might have had the right to become aware of such data does not negate unlawfulness of processing.[25]

With regard to this case, it is worth noticing that both administrative and judicial procedures may take a long time: complaint before the DPA in 2004; decision of the DPA in 2006; decision of the DPA withdrawn (by the DPA) in 2011; another decision of the DPA in 2012; final decision of *Symvoulio Tis Epikrateias* in 2017. Hopefully, the same fate has not befallen the judicial procedures, with regard to the payment of maintenance, which may have been completed before the minors' entry into adulthood.

[22] Ruling No. 150/2017 of *Symvoulio Tis Epikrateias*, para 7–8.

[23] Ruling No. 150/2017 of *Symvoulio Tis Epikrateias*, para 9.

[24] See also Ruling No. 1622/2012 (Full Court) of *Symvoulio Tis Epikrateias*.

[25] Ruling No. 150/2017 of *Symvoulio Tis Epikrateias*, para 10.

5.1.3 Exercising the Right to Access (Might Take a Long Time Too)

Ruling No. 1662/2017 of *Symvoulio Tis Epikrateias* concerned the data subject's right to access items of information, which relate to him and which have been processed. As held by *Symvoulio Tis Epikrateias*, the data controller has a special duty to diligent preservation, with regard to the relevant filing system. In this case, the applicant was a bank, which—partially and late—provided access to personal data, which was important for the data subject's career in grade. Some items of personal information had been lost in violation of the above duty of diligence.

More precisely, under Article 12 of Nomos 2472/1997, everyone has the right to know whether personal data, relating to him or her, are or have been processed.[26] The data controller has the duty to reply in writing and the data subject has the right to request and obtain from the controller, without undue delay and in a way that is unambiguous and easy to understand—amongst others—all personal data, relating to him or her, and its origin. This right can be exercised by submitting an application. If the data controller does not reply within fifteen days or in case the controller's answer is not satisfactory, the data subject has the right to appeal before the DPA. Besides, under Article 10 of Nomos 2472/1997 (with regard to confidentiality and data security), the controller shall implement appropriate technical and organizational measures for the security of such data and its protection against accidental or unauthorized destruction, accidental loss, alteration, unauthorized disclosure or access or any other unlawful processing.[27] Finally, under Article 21 of Nomos 2472/1997, in case of violation of the above provisions, the DPA has the power to impose a fine (EUR 880-146,735)[28] on the controller and order—amongst others—permanent or temporal withdrawal of authorization and destruction of the filing system.

In this case,[29] in 2004 (November, 3) the bank's employee exercised the above right to access and submitted an application, requesting copies of all documents that concerned his personal file. On 2 December 2004, the employee applied before the DPA claiming that the bank had not replied to his request (within fifteen days). On 10 February 2005, the employee received fifty-six copies of documents, relating to his personal file, and noted upon the relevant acknowledgement of receipt that his evaluation records, with regard to years 2000, 2001 and 2004 were not included. As claimed by the employee, these documents were extremely important for reasoning his career in grade. The bank argued that the above records, concerning years 2000 and 2001, were

[26]Article 12 of Nomos 2472/1997 establishes the right to access personal data, in accordance with which the data controller has the duty to ensure and provide access. See also Ruling No. 1851/2016 of *Symvoulio Tis Epikrateias*.

[27]In accordance with Article 10 of Nomos 2472/1997, the data controller has a special duty to diligent preservation, with regard to the relevant filing system for specified, explicit and legitimate purposes and for such authorized and lawful data processing. Ruling No. 1662/2017 of *Symvoulio Tis Epikrateias*, para 4; Ruling No. 749/2005 of *Symvoulio Tis Epikrateias*.

[28]Nomos mentions "*GRD 300,000–50,000,000*", which equals to approximately EUR 880-146,735.

[29]Ruling No. 1662/2017 of *Symvoulio Tis Epikrateias*, para 5.

not delivered, because they had not been found, while the records of year 2004 had not been sent, since the very directorate of the bank had not yet received them. The DPA issued its decision No. 61/2005, holding that the relevant records had probably been lost or deducted from the employee's personal file and, thus, given the importance of these documents, the bank was liable for not—fully—satisfying the employee's right to access, in violation of Article 12 of Nomos 2472/1997. Moreover, the DPA held that the bank did not prove that it, as the data controller, had implemented appropriate technical and organizational measures for the security of personal data and its protection against accidental or unauthorized destruction, given that Article 10(3) of Nomos 2472/1997 establishes the principle of due diligence, even in case of accidental loss. Hence, with its decision No. 61/2005, the DPA imposed a fine (EUR 60,000) on the bank due to violation of Articles 10(3) and 12(1) of Nomos 2472/1997. Moreover, on 23 September 2005, the employee again exercised his right to access, by submitting two applications requesting further documents, relating to his personal file. On 18 November 2005, a table of two hundred thirty documents was delivered, in which—as claimed by the bank—, owing to a clerical error, three documents had not been included. The latter were finally delivered on 24 November 2005.

The above decision No. 61/2005 of the DPA was withdrawn due to the bad composition of the authority. Hence, the DPA, after having heard both the employee and the controller, issued its decision No. 170/2014, imposing a fine (EUR 50,000) on the controller, of which EUR 10,000 were due to the violation of Article 10(3) of Nomos 2472/1997 and EUR 40,000 for the infringement of Article 12 of the above law. In particular, the DPA held that the bank did not reply to the employee's request within fifteen days, albeit the bank responded on February 2005 and only partially satisfied his right to access, which was—more comprehensively—satisfied after the employee's second application in September 2005.

The bank applied before *Symvoulio Tis Epikrateias*, which rejected the relevant application. *Symvoulio Tis Epikrateias* held that the applicant did not deny the fact that the relevant records had been lost. This loss was due to the bank's failure to diligently preserve the relevant files, in violation of Article 10(3) of Nomos 2472/1997. Furthermore, as ruled by *Symvoulio Tis Epikrateias*, the DPA had no obligation to mention which appropriate technical and organizational measures would be necessary for the security of personal data and its protection against accidental loss[30] in detail (in its decision). These measures should have been selected and implemented by the very bank. Hence, *Symvoulio Tis Epikrateias* concluded that there was a breach of Articles 10(3) and 12 of Nomos 2472/1997.

Taking into account the above Ruling No. 150/2017 of *Symvoulio Tis Epikrateias*, one might be concerned about several issues. First, it would be reasonable to question whether bad composition of the DPA occurs frequently. However, to answer this, one would need to further scrutinize the DPA's precedent, which falls outside the purposes of this section. Second, after having withdrawn its decision No. 61/2005, what took the DPA nine years to issue decision No. 170/2014? Finally, it is worth repeating that national administrative and judicial procedures do, indeed, take a long time.

[30]Ruling No. 1662/2017 of *Symvoulio Tis Epikrateias*, para 6.

5.1.4 Smart Phones as Filing Systems

In another case, *Areios Pagos* (the Supreme Court of Greece, Criminal Procedure) had to determine whether smart phones constitute filing systems. In its decision No. 474/2016, after having examined sensitive data and finding that it may include information relating to the data subject's sex life, *Areios Pagos* held that a present-day smart phone constitutes a filing system, given that its software is capable of recording videos, e-mails, etc.

Under Article 22(4) of Nomos 2472/1997 the person, who intervenes—without the right to do so and by any means—with regard to a filing system or becomes aware of this system's data, or deducts it, alters it, damages it, destroys it, processes it, transmits it, or makes it accessible to unauthorized persons, or allows these persons to become aware of such data, or exploits it—by any means—, is punished, in case of sensitive personal data, with imprisonment (minimum of one year) and a fine (minimum of GDR 1,000,000, i.e. EUR 2934, and maximum of GDR 10,000,000, i.e. EUR 29,347).

Areios Pagos held that the objective substantiation of the above crime is fulfilled, if there are data in the filing system, i.e. in any structured set of personal data, which is accessible according to specific criteria;[31] there is a data subject and; data is personal (and sensitive). Hence, in case a person uses information and has become aware of this information without having researched a filing system or without having received the information from a third party (i.e. the person who intervened with regard to the filing system), the objective substantiation of the crime is not fulfilled, due to lack of the very—element of substantiation, i.e. the—"filing system". However, this was not the case here. The court had to deal with an infringer, who stole a video, which concerned sex activities between the plaintiff and her schoolmate and which was stored in the plaintiff's mobile phone, copied it to a personal computer and made the above sensitive data accessible to third parties (his two friends) by further copying the file to other devices.

As ruled by *Areios Pagos*, a smart phone constitutes a filing system given that its software enables a person to record in separate files her personal data that relate to her contacts, images, videos, e-mails, etc. Such data is, indeed, organized in a structured set and is accessible according to specific criteria and, thus, it may be processed. Thereafter, *Areios Pagos* set aside Decision No. 237/9-6-2015 of Kalamata Court of Appeal (Chamber of three Judges), which had held that videos recorded and archived in a mobile phone do not constitute a filing system.

[31] Article 2(e) of Nomos 2472/1997.

5.1.5 Conclusions

So far, we have "witnessed" cash being treated as personal data. To gain some more insight into ways, in which national courts interpret concepts and regulations, it is worth mentioning Decision No. 3428/2016 of Athens Court (Chamber of one Judge—Board of Appeal), where the court, while interpreting "consent", held that standard terms that are included in any contract and constitute a "result" of consumer's accession, rather than a negotiated compromise, are not sufficient to establish "consent" as any freely given, specific and informed indication of the data subject's wishes, by which he or she signifies his or her agreement to personal data relating to him or her being processed.

Moreover, lengthy administrative and judicial procedures, with regard to balancing interests or to exercising the right to access, were pointed out. A similar case, where one can observe the above issues of bad composition of the DPA and, thus, withdrawal of its own decision, can be found in Ruling No. 1774/2016 of *Symvoulio Tis Epikrateias*. In this case, the court held that an insurance company, in violation of Article 10(3) of Nomos 2472/1997, sent the data subject a letter, including sensitive personal data, relating to health. The firm had not used a proper "stamped" envelop to enclose data and the document had been delivered by affixing. Hence, sensitive personal data could have been lost, destroyed, or unlawfully processed.

Finally, "technology is subject" to courts' interpretations and smart devices have been treated as personal data filing systems. Similar to such findings was Ruling No. 1306/2016 of *Areios Pagos* (Criminal Procedure), where it held that present-day cameras, which have software, where personal data—i.e. the information captured in a video—is recorded in separated files, constitute "filing systems".[32]

Before moving on to the next section, where ways, in which the GDPR interacts with national jurisdiction, are examined, two final comments, with regard to national case law, should be mentioned: online access to Greek courts' decisions is only allowed (after subscription and only) to legal "experts",[33] via Intrasoft International's database ("NOMOS");[34] and, while courts' decisions are disclosed in the above database, the names of the litigants are not. Therefore, it would be "fair" to claim that, in Greece, personal data (at least the litigants') is, indeed, protected (perhaps, in violation of the right to access information).

[32]In this case, the accused was capturing plaintiffs' movements by using a portable camera.

[33]By "legal experts" we mean those who practice legal professions, such as attorneys-at-law etc.

[34]Intrasoft International (2019) Nomos. https://lawdb.intrasoftnet.com/nomos/nomos_frame.html. Accessed 20 September 2019.

5.2 Ways in Which the GDPR Interacts with the Greek Jurisdiction: Towards an Agreement on the Basics?

5.2.1 Introduction

Since the 2001 revision of the Constitution of Greece, the right to the protection of personal data has been treated as a fundamental one.[35] The above right is an aspect of the right to privacy,[36] which has been protected since the 1975 Constitution.[37] To better understand the concept of the right to the protection of personal data, as viewed in Greece, the notion of general principles, on which it is based,[38] shall be examined.

In accordance with Article 2(1) of the Constitution, the respect for and the protection of the value of the human being constitute the primary obligations of the State. The above value refers to one's physical, mental and social status[39] and relates to human dignity.[40] An unambiguous identifier and a key element of dignity is self-determination, in accordance with which the individual shall freely make decisions on his or her attitude to life.[41] This means that one shall not be based on ignorance, superstition, bias or any addiction, but he or she shall count on his or her inner being and beliefs. In this context, human value demands that legislative provisions must not

[35]Article 9A of the Constitution of Greece. National courts rarely refer to Article 9A of the Constitution. The State Council of Greece (*Symvoulio Tis Epikrateias*) refers to Article 9A mainly regarding powers of the Hellenic Data Protection Authority. See also Decisions No. 3212/2003 and 4241/2010; Mitrou, L. (2017). Article 9A of the Constitution. In Spiropoulos et al., 2017, p. 229.

[36]Bottis 2009, p. 809. The very notion of privacy is difficult to define; put simply, privacy serves a range of interests, including personal autonomy, integrity and dignity, which, in turn, have a broader societal significance. See Bygrave 2014, p. 119.

[37]Article 9(1) of the Constitution of Greece.

[38]Some authors argue that the right to the protection of personal data derives from Article 9(1) of the Constitution—as an aspect of the right to privacy–, while others claim that it is based on Article 2(1) of the Constitution, which protects human value, and Article 5(1) of the Constitution, which protects the right to freely develop one's personality and participate in social, economic and political life of the country. Mitrou 2017, pp. 215–216. Before the introduction of Article 9A, *Symvoulio Tis Epikrateias* had subjected the concept and the system of protection of personal data to the notion of privacy, while recitals of Nomos 2472/1997 had regarded Articles 9, 2(1), 5(1) and 19 of the Constitution as the foundations of the protection of personal data. Mitrou 2004, p. 347. With regard to the right to the protection of personal data, in both civil and criminal cases, the Supreme Court of Greece (*Areios Pagos*) has repeatedly referred to Articles 2(1), 5(1), 9 and 19 of the Constitution, under which respect and protection of the value of the human being constitute the primary obligations of the State, anyone shall have the right to freely develop his or her personality, and private and family life and confidentiality of communications shall be protected. See Decisions Nos. 499/2013, 10/2011 (Criminal) and 1567/2010 of *Areios Pagos*.

[39]Demitropoulos 2008, p. 272.

[40]Pararas 2010, p. 194.

[41]Ziamou 2017, pp. 22–23.

be framed in ways that violate fundamental freedoms of conscience, thought, religion, information and speech.[42] Thus, a waiver of such rights shall not be allowed, since it would constitute a complete denial of human nature. The capacity and the right to self-determination demands that the State must provide appropriate and favorable socio-political measures to guarantee basic living conditions and ensure social security, communication infrastructure, health service, environmental protection, progress of science, research and cultural life, education and so forth for both today's and future generations.[43]

Based on the above principles, the protection of individuals with regard to the processing of personal data was guaranteed under Nomos 2472/1997, which transposed the Directive 95/46/EC of the European Parliament and of the Council.[44] An independent Authority (i.e. the Hellenic Data Protection Authority, HDPA) was given the task to supervise the proper application of the above law.[45]

Having regarded the right to the protection of personal data as a fundamental one, the Greek legislator responded in a timely fashion to obligations under the Regulation (EU) 2016/679 of the European Parliament and of the Council[46] by carrying out a public consultation[47] on the draft law to introduce legislative measures for the purposes of the GDPR and the transposition of the Directive (EU) 2016/680.[48]

---

[42] Tassopoulos 2001, pp. 233–234.

[43] Tassopoulos 2001, p. 209.

[44] Directive 95/46/EC of the European Parliament and of the Council of 24 October 1995 on the protection of individuals with regard to the processing of personal data and on the free movement of such data, hereinafter referred to as "DPD" (for Data Protection Directive).

[45] More precisely, the mission of the HDPA is the protection of personal data and the privacy of individuals in Greece, and its primary goal is the protection of citizens from the unlawful processing of their personal data and their assistance in case it is established that their rights have been violated in any sector (such as financial, health, insurance, education, public administration, transport, mass media, etc.). Moreover, another goal of the HDPA is to support and guide controllers in their effort to comply with their obligations vis-a-vis the law, while taking into consideration the needs of the services in the Greek society and the growing use of modern digital communications and networks. Hence, the HDPA focuses, amongst others, on the identification and development of solutions relating to problems that emerge from the advancements of new technologies and their applications. Hellenic Data Protection Authority (2019a) HDPA. http://www.dpa.gr/. Accessed 20 September 2019.

[46] Regulation (EU) 2016/679 of the European Parliament and of the Council of 27 April 2016 on the protection of natural persons with regard to the processing of personal data and on the free movement of such data, and repealing Directive 95/46/EC (General Data Protection Regulation), hereinafter referred to as the "GDPR" (for General Data Protection Regulation).

[47] Greek Ministry of Justice, Transparency and Human Rights (2018, February 20) Νόμος για την Προστασία Δεδομένων Προσωπικού Χαρακτήρα σε εφαρμογή του Κανονισμού (ΕΕ) 2016/679 [Law on the Protection of Personal Data in Application of the Regulation]. http://www.opengov.gr/ministryofjustice/?p=9331. Accessed 20 September 2019.

[48] Directive (EU) 2016/680 of the European Parliament and of the Council of 27 April 2016 on the protection of natural persons with regard to the processing of personal data by competent authorities for the purposes of the prevention, investigation, detection or prosecution of criminal offences or the execution of criminal penalties, and on the free movement of such data, and repealing Council Framework Decision 2008/977/JHA.

Before examining ways in which the GDPR interacts with the Greek national jurisdiction, it should be noted that the former—as provided by its title—aims to strike a fair balance between the protection of natural persons with regard to the processing of personal data and the free movement of such data. It should also be mentioned that the above draft law (whose provisions are very similar to those of GDPR) has not yet come into force and, thus, interaction between national and European provisions and aspects will be examined in accordance with existing national laws and norms.

In this section, we focus on the interaction between the GDPR and the Greek provisions with regard to the crucial concepts of the data subject's control and consent, as well as the free flow of personal data. Given that Nomos 2472/1997 seems to focus on the protection of the individuals with regard to the processing of their data, rather than the free movement of such data, current technologies and national norms will be studied to detect further similarities and differences between the GDPR and national regulations.

5.2.2 Control and Consent Versus the Free Flow

One of the fundamental principles of information law is respect for personal autonomy.[49] Legal provisions, which govern personal data—and form part of information law and are, thus, governed by the above principle—, protect, amongst others, interests in informational self-determination.[50] Hence, it has been consistently held by authors that the right to the protection of personal data refers to the data subject's control over the processing of his or her data.[51] Furthermore, as academics argue, the key tool for successfully exercising control is the subject's consent[52] to the processing of personal data.

Indeed, the GDPR takes into consideration the above opinions on control[53] and considers data subject's consent as a prerequisite that is necessary for the lawfulness of processing.[54] Thus, processing and collecting[55] of personal data shall be lawful

[49]Bottis 2014, p. 148.

[50]Kang et al. 2011, p. 820.

[51]Oostveen and Irion 2018; Rengel 2014; Cavoukian and Tapscott 1996; Richards and King 2016, p. 8.

[52]Tene and Polonetsky 2012; Solove 2012, p. 1894; Article 29 Data Protection Working Party (2011) Opinion 15/2011 on the definition of consent. https://ec.europa.eu/justice/article-29/documentation/opinion-recommendation/index_en.htm. Accessed 20 September 2019 ("[…] *If it is correctly used, consent is a tool giving the data subject control over the processing of his data. If incorrectly used, the data subject's control becomes illusory and consent constitutes an inappropriate basis for processing* […]").

[53]See, for instance, recitals (7) and (68) of the GDPR.

[54]See Article 6(1)(a) of GDPR. Consent comes first in the list of the six prerequisites mentioned in Article 6 of GDPR.

[55]Under Article 4(2) of GDPR, "processing" includes—amongst others—the collection of data.

if the data subject has given her consent[56] to the processing of his or her personal data for one or more specific purposes.[57] Moreover, "consent" of the data subject means any freely given,[58] specific, informed[59] and unambiguous indication of the data subject's wishes by which he or she signifies agreement to the processing of personal data relating to him or her,[60] by a statement or by a clear affirmative action,. Although the above provide a strict definition of data subject's consent, the main tool to effectively exercise control, albeit, under recital (32) of the GDPR, consent can also be given by (a single-mouse-click, i.e. by) "*ticking a box when visiting an internet website*".[61]

In accordance with national provisions, consent not only comes first in the "list of prerequisites", mentioned in Article 5 of Greek Law No. 2472/1997 with regard to lawfulness of processing, but also constitutes the main and general rule that governs the processing.[62] It is regarded as the most important prerequisite and the main condition,[63] meaning that the very processing of personal data is regarded as an unlawful and unfair behavior, which threatens individual rights and which, thus, needs an "exemption clause" to "become lawful".[64]

---

[56] Where processing is based on the data subject's consent, the controller should be able to demonstrate that the data subject has given consent to the processing operation (recital (42) of GDPR). Moreover, in accordance with Directive 93/13/EEC of 5 April 1993 on unfair terms in consumer contracts, a declaration of consent pre-formulated by the controller should be provided in an intelligible and easily accessible form, using clear and plain language and it should not contain unfair terms (recital (42) of GDPR).

[57] Article 6(1)(a) of GDPR. Under GDPR, when the processing has multiple purposes, consent should be given for all of them (recital (32) of GDPR).

[58] Consent should not be regarded as freely given, if the data subject has no genuine or free choice or is unable to refuse or withdraw consent without detriment (recital (42) of GDPR). In order to ensure that consent is freely given, consent should not provide a valid legal ground for the processing of personal data in a specific case where there is a clear imbalance between the data subject and the controller (recital (43) of GDPR). Besides, consent is presumed not to be freely given, if it does not allow separate consent to be given to different personal data processing operations (recital (43) of GDPR). Furthermore, when assessing whether consent is freely given, utmost account shall be taken of whether, inter alia, the performance of a contract, including the provision of a service, is conditional on consent to the processing of personal data that is not necessary for the performance of that contract (Article 7(4) of GDPR).

[59] For consent to be informed, the data subject should at least be aware of the identity of the controller and the purposes of the processing for which the personal data are intended (recital (42) of GDPR).

[60] Article 4(11) of GDPR. Article 2(h) of DPD contains similar wording. The only addition of GDPR is the term "*unambiguous*" (that refers to "*indication of the data subject's wishes*") and the phrase "*by a statement or by a clear affirmative action*" (which relates the way individual signifies his or her agreement to the processing).

[61] It should be noted that, although DPD uses similar wording to define "consent", it makes no mention of the capacity (provided by recital (32) of GDPR) to give consent simply by ticking a box.

[62] Consent is mentioned in Article 5(1) of Nomos 2472/1997, while the other five prerequisites are mentioned in the next paragraph, Article 5(2)(a-e) of Nomos 2472/1997.

[63] Bottis 2009, pp. 811–813.

[64] In its Ruling No. 3545/2002, *Symvoulio Tis Epikrateias* regarded "processing of personal data" as a violation of human value and privacy and held that provisions of Nomos 2472/1997 impose

However, despite the above differences, concerning consent and, hence, control, between national and international provisions, it would be fair to argue that the European legislator's wishes and efforts to guarantee and safeguard the data subject's control can be found in the provisions of the GDPR.[65]

Besides, as mentioned above, the latter aims to strike a fair balance between the protection of natural persons with regard to the processing of personal data and the free movement of such data. In particular, under the GDPR, the right to the protection of personal data must be considered in relation to its function in society and be balanced against other fundamental rights.[66] Indeed, the GDPR respects all fundamental rights, including—amongst others—freedom of expression and information[67] and freedom to conduct a business.[68] The former is essential to a functioning democracy and indispensable for progress of arts, science, law and politics, while the latter is essential to free market ideas, which underpin present-day economic models.[69] By striking a fair balance between fundamental rights, it is true that the GDPR aims not only to protect individuals' rights with regard to processing of their personal information, but also to ensure the free flow of such data. The latter is, actually, needed so that individuals may successfully exercise the above fundamental rights, i.e. freedom of expression and information and freedom to conduct a business.

On the contrary, national law seems to focus on individual control,[70] rather than free flow of personal data. For instance, with regard to sensitive personal data,

---

restrictions with regard to personal data processing so as to guarantee protection of human values that are mentioned in Articles 2(1) and 9(1) of the Constitution.

[65]See, for instance, recitals (7) and (68) of the GDPR.

[66]See Recital 4 of GDPR.

[67]Under Article 11 of the Charter of Fundamental Rights of the European Union, everyone has the right to freedom of expression, which includes freedom to hold opinions and to receive and impart information and ideas without interference by public authority and regardless of frontiers. This right is not an absolute right; "[…] *The exercise of these freedoms, since it carries with it duties and responsibilities, may be subject to such formalities, conditions, restrictions or penalties as are prescribed by law and are necessary in a democratic society, in the interests of national security, territorial integrity or public safety, for the prevention of disorder or crime, for the protection of health or morals, for the protection of the reputation or rights of others, for preventing the disclosure of information received in confidence, or for maintaining the authority and impartiality of the judiciary* […]", see Article 10(2) of the European Convention for the Protection of Human Rights and Fundamental Freedoms.

[68]Under Article 16 of the Charter of Fundamental Rights of the European Union "[…] *The freedom to conduct a business in accordance with Union law and national laws and practices is recognised* […]".

[69]Taylor (2014) A critical analysis of the EU right to erasure as it applies to internet search engine results. MS thesis. https://www.duo.uio.no/bitstream/handle/10852/43102/1/8019.pdf. Accessed 20 September 2019.

[70]It should be noted that the HDPA also focuses on data subject's control, not only by issuing guidelines, concerning, for instance, the duties of data controllers or the role of data protection officers, but also by providing opinions on important issues or conducting annual reports etc. See for example: Hellenic Data Protection Authority (2019b) Γνωμοδοτήσεις της Αρχής [Opinions of the Authority]. http://www.dpa.gr/portal/page?_pageid=33,120923&_dad=portal&_schema=PORTAL. Accessed 20 September 2019. In its English version the HDPA's official website does not provide full information of its content.

processing is prohibited and may be allowed only in case there is an authorization of the HDPA and if several criteria are met.[71] Furthermore, under Article 14 of Greek Law No. 2472/1997, everybody has the right to apply before court, in case he or she is harmed due to automated processing of personal data, if such processing aims to evaluate the individual's personality, and, in particular, a natural person's performance in work, financial solvency, trustworthiness, and behavior. With regard to this provision, the HDPA issued its guidelines concerning personal data protection in fields of employment relationship,[72] under which decisions relating to employees' personality, such as behavior or performance, shall not be taken ("*solely*") on the basis of automated processing of personal data, given that such a procedure would turn employees into "*items of information*" and would further harm their personality.[73]

With regard to automated individual decision-making, it is worth mentioning that, under Article 22(1) of the GDPR, the data subject shall have the right not to be subject to a decision based solely on automated processing, including profiling, which produces legal effects concerning him or her or similarly significantly affects him or her. However, this provision shall not apply if the decision is based on the data subject's explicit consent,[74] which may be—validly—given by a "single-mouse-click".[75]

So far, we have observed that the national law No. 2472/1997 focuses on the protection of individuals with regard to processing of their personal data, rather than the free flow of such data. However, the latter is strongly supported by new emerging technologies. Thus, to better understand ways in which the GDPR interacts with national reality, current national norms that deal with information technology[76] should be studied.

5.2.3 Emerging Technologies: A Need to Agree on the Basics?

In both the public and private sector, Greece is moving away from traditional service channels, where, for instance, in-person services are provided, and is—slowly, but steadily—heading towards self-service technologies,[77] where interfaces enable

[71] Article 7 of Nomos 2472/1997.

[72] Directive No. 115/2001 of the HDPA.

[73] See para 7 of chapter C and para 4 of chapter H of Directive No. 115/2001 of the HDPA.

[74] Article 22(2)(c) of GDPR.

[75] Recital (32) of GDPR.

[76] Information technology can be understood as any equipment or system that is used in the automatic acquisition, storage, manipulation, management, movement, control, display, switching, interchange, transmission, or reception of data or information. Government of Canada (2019) Directive on management of information technology. https://www.tbs-sct.gc.ca/pol/doc-eng.aspx?id=15249#appA. Accessed 20 September 2019.

[77] Meuter et al. 2000.

people to receive a service without any employee involvement. Such self-service delivery may be found not only in private sector, but also in the public area and, hence, citizens may access government services without direct assistance from its personnel.[78]

Indeed, these technologies have been encouraged by the State and, thus, one may receive, for instance, tax services via the Ministry's website,[79] without the need to visit traditional tax offices or wait in queues. Of course, self-service technologies are not fully adopted, meaning that there are occasions, in which citizens and customers may "partly" receive self-service, where the relevant (public or private) personnel facilitates service and assists individuals. For example, a private firm's personnel may guide the consumer to a computer to complete the service delivery (e.g. pay a mobile telephone bill). In other cases, traditional and digital services may be provided simultaneously and, for instance, citizens are enabled to pay court fees during a procedure, where part of the service is self-service (e.g. online application) and the rest is traditional (by visiting the relevant cashier of a court or a bank). Fully or partly provided, the above technologies have minimized in-person service and have guaranteed 24/7 access.

Furthermore, contrary to computers that are tied in a specific location, smart mobile devices, e.g. phones or tablets, facilitate access to self-service technologies. In fact, the State offers access to many of its mobile-friendly websites, while more and more private companies provide remote access, thanks to which no physical presence is needed. While one may access many private or State's websites anywhere and anytime, get a personalized experience, or save costs, there are nevertheless, several risks emerging, such as identity theft or loss, authentication and individuals' security threats.

While examining such technologies, one should also take into consideration both the Open Data[80] and Big Data[81] environment. With regard to the Open Data movement, the national government and Greek firms make their datasets available and, hence, citizens and consumers may access them on a self-service basis. For instance, Chambers offer several services through their websites, and citizens may, for instance, request a certificate or register their firm via an "one-stop" service.[82] In such ways, not only transparency is promoted but also bureaucratic procedures are reduced and simplified. Moreover, concerning the Big Data environment and given the decline in cost of data processing, improved services can be provided and evidence-based decision-making may be achieved.

[78] See, for example, Nomos 3979/2011 with regard to eGovernment.

[79] Greek Ministry of e-Governance (2019a) myTAXISnet. https://www.gsis.gr/en. Accessed 20 September 2019.

[80] Baack 2015.

[81] Big Data refers to the exponential growth and availability of data in an environment where three "v" characteristics are identified: volume of data that is collected and processed; velocity with which data is being produced and processed; variety of sources, where data comes from. King and Forder 2016, p. 698.

[82] See, for example: Chamber of Corfu (2019) Chamber of Corfu. http://www.corfucci.gr/kerkyra/shared/index.jsp?context=101. Accessed 20 September 2019.

And how does the GDPR interact with this reality?

The above norms indicate that consumers' and citizens' ordinary life may contain innumerable digital activities, during which personal data is not only produced but also collected and processed.[83] For example, while accepting a tax service,[84] a citizen will very likely provide his or her Tax Identification Number, or while undertaking online transactions the consumer will probably provide his or her credit card information. Given that, under the GDPR, "personal data" means any information relating to a natural person, who can be identified, directly or indirectly,[85] one could claim that the criterion that has to be met and that makes the data personal is, not the actual identification but, the capacity to identify one person.[86] Thus, it would be fair to argue that the meaning of personal data—as defined by the GDPR—is very wide,[87] since an individual can indeed be identified by several means.[88]

Similarly, under Article 2(a) of Greek Law No. 2472/1997, 'personal data' means any information relating to the data subject, while, under Article 2(c) of the above national law, 'data subject' means the natural person to whom personal data relates and who is or can be identified.

---

[83]As many authors observe, by data processing, any private company may know the preferences of the transacting user inside and out. Tene and Polonetsky 2012.

[84]With regard to processing of personal data by public authorities, *Symvoulio Tis Epikrateias* has expressed a crucial principle: by rejecting perceptions that treat processing of personal data as a means and a supported action undertaken by the administration, the court held that when the processing is undertaken by a public authority, this must be provided by a specific law that has to comply with the Constitution, otherwise processing is unlawful and shall be terminated regardless of any Data Protection Authority's intervention. Ruling No. 2285/2001 (Full Court) of *Symvoulio Tis Epikrateias.*

[85]"Personal data" means "[…] *any information relating to an identified or identifiable natural person ('data subject'); an identifiable natural person is one who can be identified, directly or indirectly, in particular by reference to an identifier such as a name, an identification number, location data, an online identifier or to one or more factors specific to the physical, physiological, genetic, mental, economic, cultural or social identity of that natural person* […]". Article 4(1) of GDPR.

[86]Tene 2008.

[87]Bottis 2013, p. 273.

[88]CJEU (2003a) Case C-101/01. Criminal proceedings against *Bodil Lindqvist.* para 27. ("[…] *the act of referring, on an internet page, to various persons and identifying them by name or by other means, for instance by giving their telephone number or information regarding their working conditions and hobbies, constitutes the processing of personal data wholly or partly by automatic means* […]"). IP or cookies may constitute personal data. Article 29 Data Protection Working Party (2007) Opinion 4/2007 on the concept of personal data. Retrieved from https://ec.europa.eu/justice/article-29/documentation/opinion-recommendation/index_en.htm. ("[…] *So, unless the Internet Service Provider is in a position to distinguish with absolute certainty that the data correspond to users that cannot be identified, it will have to treat all IP information as personal data, to be on the safe side* […]"); Article 29 Data Protection Working Party (2008) Opinion 1/2008 on data protection issues related to search engines. Retrieved from https://ec.europa.eu/justice/article-29/documentation/opinion-recommendation/index_en.htm. ("[…] *Persistent cookies containing a unique user ID are personal data and therefore subject to applicable data protection legislation* […]").

To detect some differences between the national law and the GDPR, with regard to the very main concepts and definitions of terms, let us mention an example. Let us assume that a consumer visits a firm's website, "ticks the relevant box" and, hence, accepts terms of use and privacy policies, and that the firm processes her data (e.g. name, credit card number etc.).

Under both Greek Law and the GDPR, the above data is personal, since the consumer can be identified. But was consent validly given, and, thus, was processing lawfully undertaken?

As noted above, under recital (32) of the GDPR, consent can be given by ticking a box when visiting a website, and, hence, one could claim that the above consumer validly gave her consent and her personal data was lawfully processed.

Article 2(k) of the Greek Law No. 2472/1997 provides similar wording and defines 'consent' as any freely given, specific, and informed indication of the data subject's wishes by which he or she signifies his or her agreement to personal data relating to him or her being processed. It further demands that the individual must be informed, meaning that the data subject shall be aware of (at least) the purpose of processing, the data or categories of data that relates to processing, the recipients or categories of recipients of such data, the name and address of the data controller, or the latter's representative. Moreover, Greek Law does not mention that consent can be given by ticking a box, and, hence, one could claim that the above consumer, under Greek Law, never gave her consent and her personal data was, thus, unlawfully processed. Besides, no one really reads terms of use and privacy policies.[89] Thus, it would be fair to argue that individuals are in no way informed when they—generously—tick boxes.

5.2.4 Conclusions

Under the Greek and the European regime, the right to the protection of personal data is regarded as a fundamental one and is treated, amongst others, as an aspect of the right to privacy, which relates to the concepts of dignity, honor, and personal respect.

Although national law focuses on individuals' control over personal data, rather than the free movement of such data, emerging technologies, which the State has already adopted, call for the need to pay attention to circulation of such items of information. In such a way, crucial socially and economically useful purposes could be achieved, while individuals' fundamental rights, such as the freedom of expression and information and freedom to conduct a business, could be guaranteed.

Given the recent public consultation on the national draft law to introduce legislative measures, this fair balance—between the above fundamental rights—seems to be the direction, towards which the Greek legislator wishes to move. If this is the

[89] Pingo and Narayan 2016, p. 4; Gindin 2009.

case, harmonization could be achieved, which could then resolve current uncertainties that deal with the very crucial notions of consent, control, and the free flow of our information.

Giving consent by ticking boxes may not be the safest way to provide authorization, since terms of use are rarely read. However, it is a flexible mechanism that can allow free flow of personal information. Besides, if signing a contract was needed before each "movement of our data", many purposes, including those in fields of healthcare, would never have been achieved. If people realized that consent can be validly given by ticking boxes, they could get informed and free flow of information could be achieved. This might also be a good reason to start reading terms of use and, perhaps, stop generously ticking boxes.

5.3 Most Prominent Issues in Greek Jurisdiction Regarding Data Protection Regulations: Ignorance, Confusion and Misleading

5.3.1 Introduction

Some years ago, Greeks used to communicate using fixed line telephones, visit libraries or book travel tickets via agencies. Music used to be delivered in vinyl and people had to wait for a week for new TV episodes. Although some still prefer traditional ways, emerging technologies have entered our lives. We may have not yet become fully "transparent citizens, subject to profile and commodification",[90] however, our ordinary lives include a smart new world, where privacy is challenged.

The Greek legislator's initiative to meet the new standards, which the Regulation (EU) 2016/679 of the European Parliament and of the Council[91] put, was very extensive, but its consultation only lasted two weeks.[92] One may observe that plenty of the GDPR's provisions were copied and pasted into the new national law proposal, while several procedural issues remain unresolved. Namely, lengthy administrative and judicial procedures might remain, as in some cases[93] an individual may apply before the Hellenic Data Protection Authority, which can—in due time—issue its

[90] Brin 1999.

[91] Regulation (EU) 2016/679 of the European Parliament and of the Council of 27 April 2016 on the protection of natural persons with regard to the processing of personal data and on the free movement of such data, and repealing Directive 95/46/EC (General Data Protection Regulation), hereinafter referred to as "GDPR" (for General Data Protection Regulation).

[92] Greek Ministry of Justice, Transparency and Human Rights (2018, February 20) Νόμος για την Προστασία Δεδομένων Προσωπικού Χαρακτήρα σε εφαρμογή του Κανονισμού (ΕΕ) 2016/679 [Law on the Protection of Personal Data in Application of the Regulation]. http://www.opengov.gr/ministryofjustice/?p=9331. Accessed 20 September 2019.

[93] See Rulings Nos. 150/2017 and 1662/2017 of the Hellenic Council of State (*Symvoulio Tis Epikrateias*).

ruling, albeit it might, later on, withdraw it and, thus, take more than ten years to come to an end.

In this section, new technologies are examined to highlight people's ignorance with regard to risks and dangers introduced by the current "e-reality".[94] Moreover, uncertainties relating to applications of law will be regarded as a major and prominent issue with regard to national jurisdiction. Finally, attention will be drawn to some "unique" practices of misleading audiences in favor of private interests.

5.3.2 *E-Reality at Stake*

National legal provisions that govern personal data aim at staying closely related to technology.[95] However, it seems that the latter has overtaken the former and, hence, the current framework is attached to old notions of privacy. Indeed, crucial concepts, including the very "personal data", are still based on ideas developed many years ago.[96] Although it would be abnormal to regard the Internet as a new means these days, many of its features and applications need to be treated as "something new". Part of the unprecedented e-reality, which we are experiencing today, can—for the sake of brevity—be summarized in the fields of cloud computing, targeting and analytics.[97]

A fundamental feature of cloud computing[98] technologies is that the consumer, who may be a firm or an individual, entrusts his or her—or third parties'—information to the provider and uses this technology to create data.[99] For instance, an attorney-at-law, after having stored all her documents in the Cloud, can modify an older document that has already been uploaded. This new modified document is produced due to technologies that the firm provides. Thus, the above procedure happens online by using technology controlled by the firm.[100] Since data constitutes a major source

[94]This term is used to include all ordinary activities, which were once delivered offline, albeit, are today undertaken via the Internet (such as e-commerce, e-government etc.).

[95]It is worth noting that—as some have aptly put it—the alleged absolutely necessary connection between information and technology may be misleading with regard to both nature and regulation of information. Bottis 2014, p. XIX.

[96]As "ideas developed many years ago" we refer to the Directive 95/46/EC of the European Parliament and of the Council of 24 October 1995 on the protection of individuals with regard to the processing of personal data and on the free movement of such data, hereinafter referred to as DPD (for Data Protection Directive). In fact, DPD was based on a striking different technology landscape.

[97]Internet of things, biometrics, personalized services, smart mobile devices or robotics could also be mentioned as fields of current e-reality.

[98]Given that authors have been discussing Cloud technologies since 2008, one could argue that they constitute a "quite" old subject of legal discussion. See, for instance, Cavoukian 2008.

[99]For examples of datafication and its difference with digitization, see Mayer-Schönberger and Cukier 2013, pp. 73–97.

[100]Reed (2010) Information 'ownership' in the Cloud (SSRN Paper No. 45/2010). https://ssrn.com/abstract=1562461. Accessed 20 September 2019.

of income,[101] the above information must be kept in a safe place. Hence, firms have built their own datacenters, the function and operation of which not only cost large sums of money but also have a major impact on the environment.[102]

In the field of targeting, individuals' activities are tracked to deliver tailored advertising.[103] In particular, today's "free" internet is paid for by (amongst others) advertising,[104] during which personal data is collected,[105] Processing of the latter, with some "help" of cookies,[106] enables controllers to identify the user and detect his or her online—or even offline[107]—activities.[108] Thereafter, the user's data is used to profile[109] the former or to create target groups, to which the collector will address personalized ads.[110] Profiling or sorting consumers into groups may—in the Big Data[111] environment—be extremely "effective", albeit the line between sorting and

[101] Pasquale 2015, p. 141.

[102] Morozov 2012, p. 286.

[103] Indeed, the more finely tailored the ad, the higher the revenues of advertisers and various intermediaries. See also Article 29 Data Protection Working Party (2010) Opinion 2/2010 on online behavioral advertising. https://ec.europa.eu/justice/article-29/documentation/opinion-recommendation/index_en.htm. Accessed 20 September 2019.

[104] Behavioral advertising is based on the observation of the behavior of individuals over time and seeks to study the characteristics of this behavior through their actions. By examining repeated site visits, interactions, keywords, online content production, etc., it aims to develop a specific profile and, hence, provide data subjects with advertisements tailored to match their inferred interests. See Article 29 Data Protection Working Party (2010) Opinion 2/2010 on online behavioral advertising. https://ec.europa.eu/justice/article-29/documentation/opinion-recommendation/index_en.htm. Accessed 20 September 2019.

[105] Richards and King 2016.

[106] Persistent cookies remain on the device after the user closes her browser and may be used again the next time she accesses the platform. Moreover, "web beacons" technologies let the company know whether the user has opened a certain message or accessed a certain link. See for instance: Airbnb 2019a Airbnb privacy policy. https://www.airbnb.gr/terms/privacy_policy. Accessed 20 September 2019; Airbnb 2019b Airbnb cookie policy. https://www.airbnb.gr/terms/cookie_policy. Accessed 20 September 2019.

[107] See, for example, Google's "Store Sales Measurement", a program that aims at matching goods, which are purchased in physical stores, to the "clicking" of online ads ("Bricks to Clicks"). This enables the firm to know whether a consumer bought the product, on the ad of which she clicked. Lam B and Larose C (25 September 2017) United States: FTC asked to investigate Googles matching of bricks to clicks. http://www.mondaq.com/article.asp?articleid=630914&email_access=on&chk=2167746&q=1536832. Accessed 20 September 2019.

[108] Snyder 2011.

[109] Under Article 4(4) of GDPR "[…] *'profiling' means any form of automated processing of personal data consisting of the use of personal data to evaluate certain personal aspects relating to a natural person, in particular to analyse or predict aspects concerning that natural person's performance at work, economic situation, health, personal preferences, interests, reliability, behaviour, location or movements* […]".

[110] Förster and Weish 2017, p. 19.

[111] Big Data refers to the exponential growth and availability of data in an environment where three "v" characteristics are identified: volume of data that is collected and processed; velocity with which data is being produced and processed; variety of sources, where data comes from. King and Forder 2016, p. 698.

profiling in favor of private interests and discrimination, based on personal data collected,[112] is extremely blurry.[113] This—already blurry—distinguishing line is alarmingly disappearing, since users may be discriminated against on grounds of their sensitive data, not only with regard to advertising, but also while firms just operate by analyzing[114] users' data[115] or "training their machines".[116] Since the environment of Big Data enforces and promotes the correlating of information,[117] any firm that knows, for instance, an individual's gender may discriminate against him or her, on the grounds of the above-mentioned sensitive information or of other multiple personal data, which the firm may draw as conclusions by combining a huge volume of information[118] (such as the address, where the user lives, or the information that a consumer is the mother of two minors).[119] To put it simply, a private company is, for instance, capable of using such data to create a system, which will sort people into lists, put the most promising candidates on top, and pick the best to fill the vacant posts in the company.[120] In this context, users are rarely—or most probably never—aware of data collection processes and the uses or identity of the actors involved.[121]

Finally, as we have shifted from atoms to bits,[122] information is measured in teras or even zetas, rather than bytes. Thus, firms seek new innovative practices to analyze

[112]Under Article 21(1) of Charter of Fundamental Rights of the European Union "[…] *Any discrimination based on any ground such as sex, race, colour, ethnic or social origin, genetic features, language, religion or belief, political or any other opinion, membership of a national minority, property, birth, disability, age or sexual orientation shall be prohibited* […]".

[113]Gandy 2010.

[114]Mantelero 2016, pp. 239–40.

[115]There have been cases, in which firms have in fact created personal data. Namely, Target produced personal data, meaning the information that a consumer was pregnant, which not only was true but also the very consumer had not known. Crawford and Schultz 2014, pp. 94–95, 98.

[116]Some propose that machine learning systems could be designed to limit discrimination without processing personal data. Veale and Binns 2017.

[117]As some authors have put it, "[...] *Big Data is notable not because of its size, but because of its relationality to other data* […]". Boyd and Crawford (2011) Six provocations for Big Data (SSRN Scholarly Paper No. ID 1926431). https://papers.ssrn.com/abstract=1926431. Accessed 20 September 2019.

[118]Rubinstein (2012) Big Data: The end of privacy or a new beginning? (SSRN Scholarly Paper No. ID 2157659). https://papers.ssrn.com/abstract=2157659. Accessed 20 September 2019.

[119]O'Neil 2016, pp. 3–5, 130–134, 151.

[120]Such systems are numerous. For instance, IMPACT was created in 2009 by Michelle Rhee to evaluate teachers, while Cataphora was created in 2008 by the homonymous company in San Francisco. These systems are being used by multiple firms. O'Neil 2016.

[121]For the use of 'notice and consent' with regard to privacy concerns in online behavioral advertising, see Barocas and Nissenbaum (2009) On notice: The trouble with notice and consent (SSRN Scholarly Paper No. ID 2567409). https://papers.ssrn.com/abstract=2567409. Accessed 20 September 2019.

[122]Mayer-Schönberger and Cukier. 2013, pp. 78–79.

this data deluge,[123] while efforts are undertaken to prevent identification of individuals. However, failure to anonymize personal data has not only been empirically proven[124] but also widely criticized by scholars.[125] Hence, it would be fair to claim that our personal information is either useful or truly anonymous.

At national level, the above developments came to stay, however, they were not, nor are they, accompanied by information on and awareness of risks and dangers. At the same time, regulations are hard to apply given confusions that may occur.

5.3.3 What Do People Know?

In Greece, both professionals—such as attorneys-at-law or physicians—and ordinary people very often use cloud computing to ensure the preservation and successful management of their files or to avoid potential deletion of their documents, due to e.g. malware/virus attacks, wastage of their personal computers' storage space or use of external devices. Moreover, Greek digital natives make wide use of the above "clouds", where they store their favorite songs, videos or personal images and so forth. Hence, it is an ordinary practice to entrust cloud providers, while storing information that deals with personal and professional life of the individual.

Furthermore, at national level and with regard to tailored advertising, common people are rarely aware of targeting practices, which innumerable firms follow to safeguard their economic interests. Although new technologies are widely used by people, the latter are not that much informed with regard to risks that may threaten their privacy. Generous ticking on boxes, in conjunction with beliefs that regard surveillance and other threats as a science fiction scenario or as an isolated symptom that might have happened once on the other side of the Atlantic, seems to be the image concerning the majority. Not to mention anonymization techniques—and failures–, which are known to a few, mainly experts, who deal with law and technology.

In other words, while the GDPR is probably the hottest topic in the EU, in Greece, there can be some lack of awareness, which further blurs the picture. The above developments and practices challenge or disrupt the very definition of the data controller and the processor and the very notion of data transfer and subject's consent.

---

[123] Faniel and Zimmerman 2011.

[124] See—amongst others—Ohm 2010; Sweeney 2000.

[125] As many authors argue, in the age of Big Data, there is no manner in which to render personal data anonymous, due to the fact that the ("anonymized") data subject is in any case identifiable. Scholz 2017, p. 35; Schneier 2015, pp. 50–53; Golle 2006; Bohannon 2013; Narayanan and Shmatikov 2008. Inability to anonymize personal data in Big Data environment is due to collection and correlation of huge volumes of data, derived from multiple sources, and, thus, due to capacity to draw countless conclusions with regard to an individual, who may be identified. Some scholars argue that anonymized or de-identified data is a "temporary state". Tene and Polonetsky 2012, p. 257. Others question the very distinction between personal and "anonymized" data. Viola De Azevedo Cunha 2012. It is argued that anonymization can only be achieved in "Small Data" environments, given that volume and variety of data, which is processed in the world of Big Data, facilitate and encourage (re-)identification of any individual. Mayer-Schönberger and Cukier 2013, p. 154.

Are people (professionals included) truly aware of the risks and can regulations be applied without confusion and uncertainties?

Let us assume that a Greek citizen ticks the terms of use of a website, which is managed by a German firm that, jointly with a French company, determines the purposes and means of the data processing.[126] Let us also assume that data is processed, on behalf of the above German firm, by an Italian company, which is the processor.[127] Moreover, the same data could be disclosed to a legal person in Belgium, who would be the recipient.[128] and further shared with third parties[129] in a non-European country. Let us, finally, assume that the above Greek citizen accessed the website via his smart phone that was made in China and operated by Japan, while using an application developed in the United Kingdom, which also processes information in Brazil, transmitting to the U.S.A.

Somewhere between the above procedures a violation of privacy could occur. Although it may be true that regulations are provided to resolve such complex issues,[130] would they be applicable in real practice, and—more importantly—would

---

[126]In this case, the above firm would be the 'controller' that means "[…] *the natural or legal person, public authority, agency or other body which, alone or jointly with others, determines the purposes and means of the processing of personal data; where the purposes and means of such processing are determined by Union or Member State law, the controller or the specific criteria for its nomination may be provided for by Union or Member State law* […]". See Article 4(7) of GDPR.

[127]'Processor' means a natural or legal person, public authority, agency or other body which processes personal data on behalf of the controller. Article 4(8) of GDPR.

[128]'Recipient' means a natural or legal person, public authority, agency or another body, to which the personal data are disclosed, whether a third party or not. Article 4(9) of GDPR.

[129]'Third party' means a natural or legal person, public authority, agency or body other than the data subject, controller, processor and persons who, under the direct authority of the controller or processor, are authorised to process personal data. Article 4(10) of GDPR.

[130]It should be noted that in cases, where things (or regulations) are not very clear, guidelines and opinions can be very helpful. For instance, see Article 29 Data Protection Working Party (2017a) Guidelines on automated individual decision-making and profiling for the purposes of regulation 2016/679. https://ec.europa.eu/newsroom/article29/item-detail.cfm?item_id=612053. Accessed 20 September 2019 ("[…] *Profiling can be opaque. Often it relies upon data that is derived or inferred from other data, rather than data directly provided by the data subject. Controllers seeking to rely upon consent as a basis for profiling will need to show that data subjects understand exactly what they are consenting to. In all cases, data subjects should have enough relevant information about the envisaged use and consequences of the processing to ensure that any consent they provide represents an informed choice. Where the data subject has no choice, for example, in situations where consent to profiling is a precondition of accessing the controller's services; or where there is an imbalance of power such as in an employer/employee relationship, consent is not an appropriate basis for the processing* […]"); Article 29 Data Protection Working Party (2017b) Opinion on some key issues of the Law Enforcement Directive (EU 2016/680). https://ec.europa.eu/newsroom/article29/item-detail.cfm?item_id=610178. 15 Accessed 20 September 2019 ("[…] *The general prohibition on "solely automated individual decision", including profiling, having an "adverse legal effect" or "significantly affecting" the data subject should be respected. National laws providing exceptions to this prohibition under Article 11(1) must provide suitable safeguards for the rights and freedoms of data subjects, including the right to obtain human intervention, in particular to express his or her point of view, to obtain an explanation of the decision reached after such assessment or to challenge the decision. 2. National law may not, under any circumstance, authorise profiling that results in discrimination if based on the processing of sensitive data (Article 11.3). Automated*

the data subject be aware—not of provisions that could apply but—of the very violation that would have occurred?

The above confusion and uncertainties may be understood as a broader phenomenon that does not relate solely to Greek jurisdiction. However, it is of great importance, since it may in fact constitute an ordinary practice and everyday experience, which people ignore, and to which laws are hard to apply. In what follows, we peruse issues of same significant importance, which appear in Greek jurisdiction.

5.3.4 Intentions to Mislead

In contrast to individuals' ignorance, with regard to the protection of their data, some firms have been well "aware" of regulations that govern privacy and the protection of personal data, and have undertaken significant efforts to "inform" interested parties—and make sums out of this "information service".

More precisely, under Article 37(5) of the GDPR, the data protection officer (DPO) shall be designated on the basis of professional qualities and, in particular, expert knowledge of data protection law and practices and the ability to fulfil the tasks referred to in Article 39.[131] The GDPR demands no certification for those to

decision making based on sensitive data can be carried out only in the presence of a legal basis under EU or national law which provides for the safeguards mentioned hereinafter (see Article 11(1) and (2)). 3. National legislators are recommended to place an obligation on controllers to carry out a DPIA in connection with automated decisions. 4. Member States (without prejudice to the possible measures restricting the provision of information to the data subject according to Article 13(3)) must require the obligation of controllers to provide appropriate information to the data subject in particular where the personal data are collected without his/her knowledge (Article 13(2)(d)), which can be often the case when profiling and automated decisions are carried out [...]"); Article 29 Data Protection Working Party (2016a) Guidelines for identifying a controller or processor's lead supervisory authority. http://ec.europa.eu/information_society/newsroom/image/document/2016-51/wp244_en_40857.pdf. 3. Accessed 20 September 2019 ("[...] *Identifying a lead supervisory authority is only relevant where a controller or processor is carrying out the cross-border processing of personal data.* [...] *This means that where an organisation has establishments in France and Romania, for example, and the processing of personal data takes place in the context of their activities, then this will constitute cross-border processing* [...]").

[131] Under Article 39 of GDPR "[...] *The data protection officer shall have at least the following tasks: (a) to inform and advise the controller or the processor and the employees who carry out processing of their obligations pursuant to this Regulation and to other Union or Member State data protection provisions; (b) to monitor compliance with this Regulation, with other Union or Member State data protection provisions and with the policies of the controller or processor in relation to the protection of personal data, including the assignment of responsibilities, awareness-raising and training of staff involved in processing operations, and the related audits; (c) to provide advice where requested as regards the data protection impact assessment and monitor its performance pursuant to Article 35; (d) to cooperate with the supervisory authority; (e) to act as the contact point for the supervisory authority on issues relating to processing, including the prior consultation referred to in Article 36, and to consult, where appropriate, with regard to any other matter. 2. The data protection officer shall in the performance of his or her tasks have due regard to the risk associated with processing operations, taking into account the nature, scope, context and purposes of processing* [...]".

be appointed as data protection officers, whose choice is clearly undertaken under the controller's responsibility that has to estimate their professional skills.

However, this is not the case in Greece, where certification is not only "needed" but also highly paid. In particular, after having taken advantage of the "GDPR pandemonium", multiple entities[132] organize "DPO seminars", which not only promise "certification" but also cost vast sums. Paying EUR 1800 for a five-day-seminar and another EUR 250 for examinations[133] may not be a fair deal, when the certification promised is actually not needed.

Luckily, the Hellenic Data Protection Authority took notice of such practices and condemned them, after having held[134] that such market practices may be welcome, since they enforce information on GDPR issues, albeit having to be put in their right place to avoid false impressions of the regulation's requirements. As the Hellenic Data Protection Authority concluded, the GDPR does not demand (and does not encourage) certification on a (non-)compulsory basis.[135]

Another example, where the Hellenic Data Protection Authority intervened to avoid having firms misrepresenting facts, can be found in its recent Decision No. 26/2019 (Γ/ΕΞ/5230/26-07-2019). The Accountants and Auditors Association of Attica submitted a complaint to the Hellenic Data Protection Authority claiming that a firm (PWC) had been unlawfully processing its employees' data. According to the complaint, employees were asked to fill out and sign a form by which they gave their consent to the processing, including sharing of their personal data with third parties, such as PWC's clients, or camera-surveillance in the workplace. To the Authority, the requirement of Article 5(1)(a) of the GDPR demands that controllers choose consent as a legitimate basis, under Article 6(1)(a) of the GDPR, only if the other grounds of Article 6(1) cannot apply.

Here, the Authority held that consent was inappropriately chosen as the legitimate basis, since the purposes of the processing were related to Article 6(1)(b, c, f) of the GDPR and, in particular, to performance of the contract, compliance with legal obligations, as well as legitimate interests pursued by the controller. To the Authority, the controller misrepresented the legitimate basis of the processing (alleged consent), failed to demonstrate compliance with the processing principles, but also placed the burden of compliance on the shoulders of employees. The Authority imposed on PWC, whose annual net turnover was EUR 41,936,426.00, an administrative fine of EUR 150,000.00.

---

[132]Enter "*πιστοποίηση DPO*" (the Greek term for "*certification DPO*") as a keyword in a search engine query and multiple firms' websites will appear.

[133]See DPO Academy (2018) The data protection officer course. https://www.dpoacademy.gr/el/the-dpo-course/. Accessed 20 September 2019; Priority (2018) DPO certification master class. https://www.priority.com.gr/page/gdpr-dpo-training/. Accessed 20 September 2019.

[134]Lawspot. (11 August 2017). Data Protection Officers. Retrieved from https://www.lawspot.gr/nomika-nea/data-protection-officers-kanenas-foreas-stin-ellada-den-ehei-diapisteythei-mehri-simera.

[135]Lawspot. (11 August 2017). Data Protection Officers. Retrieved from https://www.lawspot.gr/nomika-nea/data-protection-officers-kanenas-foreas-stin-ellada-den-ehei-diapisteythei-mehri-simera.

5.3.5 *Some Ethical Conclusions*

What is hotly debated in Greece is the economic and financial crisis, through which the country is going, rather than the GDPR. When one fails to pay rent or meet basic and standard living conditions, it is hard to speak of privacy issues. However, this crisis has been an old subject of political discussion and—most probably—its nature is ethical, rather than economical.

In an era where science fiction has turned into science of facts, confusions that could mislead crowds and draw attention towards wrong directions may emerge. In a country, where authors used to write thousands of books, albeit now minors are authors of thousands of "twits", it may be hard to consider what matters most. E-reality may offer great opportunities, however, relationships are changing, since networks have turned neighbors, lovers, partners or even strangers into "friends", sorted in the very same group, and, hence, no one is to tell for sure what these digital natives will look like when they become old.[136]

Europeans argue that data is the new oil, the model for the years to come and the fuel that drives our economy. However, we can surely do better than what we did with fuel. Since there is no time for wars, basic concepts of privacy, the notion of which was built on an offline landscape, could be re-shaped to enforce transparency, accountability and trustworthiness. The very notions, the basic principles and concepts that deal with personal data, could be revised to resolve current uncertainties and to avoid misleading practices.

Could such scenarios become realities under the GDPR? In the next section, we will be discussing ways in which the Regulation could be applied and deal with the above issues.

5.4 The GDPR's Potential in Greece: Data Portability as a Means to Enhance Transparency, Accountability, and Trustworthiness

5.4.1 *Introduction*

After having gained some insight[137] into ways, in which Greek case law treats personal data, and manners that national courts follow to interpret privacy concepts and regulations, lengthy administrative and judicial procedures, with regard to balancing interests or to exercising the relevant rights, were detected. Moreover,

[136] Palfrey and Gasser 2010.

[137] See Sect. 5.1.1.

examining ways in which the GDPR interacts with national jurisdiction[138] revealed that national law seems to focus on the protection of the individuals with regard to the processing of their data, rather than the free movement of such data. However, as previously studied,[139] emerging technologies that the State has already adopted call for the need to pay attention to the circulation of personal data. Besides, it has already been argued that a fair balance -between protection and flow- seems to be the direction, towards which the Greek legislator wishes to move. In such a scenario, harmonization could be achieved and could, in turn, resolve current uncertainties that deal with the very crucial notions of consent, control, and free flow of our information.[140] People's ignorance, with regard to risks and dangers introduced by current "e-reality", was highlighted in our previous discussion,[141] where uncertainties relating to applications of law were regarded as a major and prominent issue with regard to national jurisdiction.

Ignorance, confusion and misleading practices were detected and, hence, it is now time to draw attention to ways, in which the GDPR's application could solve the above issues and enforce transparency, accountability and trustworthiness. It is true that the GDPR cannot (and of course, the European legislator is not "obliged" to) resolve all national issues, as these were studied in our previous discussions. However, in this section, we examine data portability as a great challenge and a new important right, which will very likely not only enforce market competition but also enhance controllership and transparency and turn data subjects into active re-users of their information, who will, then, be able to share the wealth that new technologies create. Thereafter, the application of the GDPR in current national reality will be studied to highlight ways in which emerging issues may be resolved. After examining the GDPR's potential in both the public and private sector, we will conclude that the Regulation could, indeed, be the answer to many current uncertainties, which have already been discussed in previous sections.

5.4.1.1 Data Portability: A Brave New Right

One of the most important rights that the GDPR introduces is the right to data portability.[142] In particular, the data subject shall have the right to receive the personal

---

[138] See Sect. 5.1.2.

[139] See Sect. 5.1.2.

[140] See Sect. 5.1.2.

[141] See Sect. 5.1.3.

[142] The term "portability" can be found in previous provisions. For instance, Article 30 of the Directive 2002/22/EC of the European Parliament and of the Council of 7 March 2002 on universal service and users' rights relating to electronic communications networks and services (Universal Service Directive) mentions the "number portability", which relates to the right of all subscribers of

data concerning him or her, which he or she has provided[143] to a controller, in a structured, commonly used and machine-readable format[144] and have the right to transmit those data to another controller without hindrance[145] from the controller to which the personal data have been provided, where the processing is based on consent or on a contract, and where the processing is carried out by automated means.[146] While data subjects exercise their right to data portability, they should

---

publicly available telephone services to retain their number(s). See also Recital (31) of the Directive 2002/21/EC of the European Parliament and of the Council of 7 March 2002 on a common regulatory framework for electronic communications networks and services (Framework Directive), where it is mentioned that "[...] *Interoperability of digital interactive television services and enhanced digital television equipment, at the level of the consumer, should be encouraged in order to ensure the free flow of information, media pluralism and cultural diversity.* [...] *Open APIs facilitate interoperability, i.e. the portability of interactive content between delivery mechanisms, and full functionality of this content on enhanced digital television equipment* [...]".

[143]Data "provided by" an individual includes personal data that relates to a person's activity or that comes as a result from observation. Article 29 Data Protection Working Party (2016b) Guidelines on the right to data portability. https://ec.europa.eu/newsroom/article29/item-detail.cfm?item_id=611233. 9-10. Accessed 20 September 2019 ("[...] *There are many examples of personal data, which will be knowingly and actively "provided by" the data subject such as account data (e.g. mailing address, user name, age) submitted* via *online forms. Nevertheless, data "provided by" the data subject also result from the observation of his activity. As a consequence, the WP29 considers that to give its full value to this new right, "provided by" should also include the personal data that are observed from the activities of users such as raw data processed by a smart meter or other types of connected objects, activity logs, history of website usage or search activities. This latter category of data does not include data that are created by the data controller (using the data observed or directly provided as input) such as a user profile created by analysis of the raw smart metering data collected* [...]").

[144]Under Recital (21) of the Directive 2013/37/EU of the European Parliament and of the Council of 26 June 2013 amending Directive 2003/98/EC on the re-use of public sector information "[...] *A document should be considered to be in a machine-readable format if it is in a file format that is structured in such a way that software applications can easily identify, recognise and extract specific data from it. Data encoded in files that are structured in a machine-readable format are machine-readable data. Machine readable formats can be open or proprietary; they can be formal standards or not. Documents encoded in a file format that limits automatic processing, because the data cannot, or cannot easily, be extracted from them, should not be considered to be in a machine-readable format.* [...]".

[145]Such "hindrance" can be characterised "*as any legal, technical or financial obstacles placed by data controller in order to refrain or slow down access, transmission or reuse by the data subject or by another data controller*". See Article 29 Data Protection Working Party (2016b) Guidelines on the right to data portability. https://ec.europa.eu/newsroom/article29/item-detail.cfm?item_id=611233. 15 Accessed 20 September 2019 ("[...] *such hindrance could be: fees asked for delivering data, lack of interoperability or access to a data format or API or the provided format, excessive delay or complexity to retrieve the full dataset, deliberate obfuscation of the dataset, or specific and undue or excessive sectorial standardization or accreditation demands* [...]").

[146]See Article 20(1) of the GDPR. See also Recital (68) of the GDPR, which mentions that "[...] *That right should apply where the data subject provided the personal data on the basis of his or her consent or the processing is necessary for the performance of a contract. It should not apply where processing is based on a legal ground other than consent or contract. By its very nature, that right should not be exercised against controllers processing personal data in the exercise of their public duties. It should therefore not apply where the processing of the personal data is necessary*

have the right to have the personal data transmitted directly from one controller to another, where technically feasible.[147]

The right to data portability[148] can be regarded as an economic right, which aims to let individuals "share wealth" created by Big Data[149] or benefit from digital services. Thus, one of its purposes is to create a competitive market environment, in which consumers will be capable of switching providers.[150] However, the above right aims not only to enforce competition and consumer protection, but also to promote interconnection of services and interoperability.[151] Thus, user-centric platforms can

---

for compliance with a legal obligation to which the controller is subject or for the performance of a task carried out in the public interest or in the exercise of an official authority vested in the controller [...]".

[147]See Article 20(2) of the GDPR. Under Article 20(3-4) of the GDPR "[...] *The exercise of the right referred to in paragraph 1 of this Article shall be without prejudice to Article 17. That right shall not apply to processing necessary for the performance of a task carried out in the public interest or in the exercise of official authority vested in the controller.* [...] *The right referred to in paragraph 1 shall not adversely affect the rights and freedoms of others* [...]". See also Recital (68) of the GDPR ("[...] *The data subject's right to transmit or receive personal data concerning him or her should not create an obligation for the controllers to adopt or maintain processing systems which are technically compatible. Where, in a certain set of personal data, more than one data subject is concerned, the right to receive the personal data should be without prejudice to the rights and freedoms of other data subjects in accordance with this Regulation. Furthermore, that right should not prejudice the right of the data subject to obtain the erasure of personal data and the limitations of that right as set out in this Regulation and should, in particular, not imply the erasure of personal data concerning the data subject which have been provided by him or her for the performance of a contract to the extent that and for as long as the personal data are necessary for the performance of that contract. Where technically feasible, the data subject should have the right to have the personal data transmitted directly from one controller to another* [...]").

[148]The discussion with regard to data portability originated with the internet users' need to transfer data that they had been building up, such as e-mail, friends' lists or address books from one service to another. Van der Auwermeulen 2017.

[149]See Article 29 Data Protection Working Party (2014) Opinion 06/2014 on the notion of legitimate interests of the data controller, under Article 7 of Directive 95/46/EC. https://ec.europa.eu/justice/article-29/documentation/opinion-recommendation/index_en.htm. 47 Accessed 20 September 2019 ("[...] *It would also let individuals 'share the wealth' created by big data and incentivise developers to offer additional features and applications to their users* [...]").

[150]See Article 29 Data Protection Working Party (2014) Opinion 06/2014 on the notion of legitimate interests of the data controller, under Article 7 of Directive 95/46/EC. https://ec.europa.eu/justice/article-29/documentation/opinion-recommendation/index_en.htm. 48 Accessed 20 September 2019 ("[...] *it can also contribute to the development of additional value-added services by third parties who may be able to access the customers' data at the request and based on the consent of the customers. In this perspective, data portability is therefore not only good for data protection, but also for competition and consumer protection* [...]").

[151]See Article 29 Data Protection Working Party (2016b) Guidelines on the right to data portability. https://ec.europa.eu/newsroom/article29/item-detail.cfm?item_id=611233. 3 Accessed 20 September 2019 ("[...] *the right to data portability is also an important tool that will support the free flow of personal data in the EU and foster competition between controllers. It will facilitate switching between different service providers, and will therefore foster the development of new services in the context of the digital single market strategy* [...]").

very well be developed in favor of individuals' rights and interests.[152] In this context, the right to data portability, being not just an economic right, aims to strengthen control of the data subject over his or her personal information,[153] while it also promotes transparency and minimization of unfair and discriminatory practices.[154]

In fact, data portability constitutes a unique challenge with regard to competition law[155] and business practices,[156] while, simultaneously, it provides opportunities to

---

[152]See Article 29 Data Protection Working Party (2016b) Guidelines on the right to data portability. https://ec.europa.eu/newsroom/article29/item-detail.cfm?item_id=611233. 3 Accessed 20 September 2019 ("[…] *As a good practice, data controllers should start developing the means that will contribute to answer data portability requests, such as download tools and Application Programming Interfaces* […]").

[153]See Recital (68) of the GDPR ("[…] *To further strengthen the control over his or her own data, where the processing of personal data is carried out by automated means, the data subject should also be allowed to receive personal data concerning him or her which he or she has provided to a controller in a structured, commonly used, machine-readable and interoperable format, and to transmit it to another controller. Data controllers should be encouraged to develop interoperable formats that enable data portability* […]"). Interestingly, the use of the wording "*his or her own data*", instead of "*data relating to him or her*" (which was normally used in previous provisions of the Directive 95/46/EC of the European Parliament and of the Council of 24 October 1995 on the protection of individuals with regard to the processing of personal data and on the free movement of such data), indicates that a person's ownership of (and control over) "her own" personal data could be regarded as the default.

[154]See Article 29 Data Protection Working Party (2013) Opinion 03/2013 on purpose limitation. https://ec.europa.eu/justice/article-29/documentation/opinion-recommendation/index_en.htm. 47 Accessed 20 September 2019 ("[…] *Allowing data portability could enable businesses and data-subjects/consumers to maximize the benefits of big data in a more balanced and transparent way. It can also help minimize unfair or discriminatory practices and reduce the risks of using inaccurate data for decision making purposes, which would benefit both businesses and data-subjects/consumers* […]").

[155]Graef et al. 2013.

[156]Geradin and Kuschewsky 2013. The authors regard portability as the key to market entry and further mention that "[…] *this right of data portability is seen as a mere extension of the principle that it is "your" data, not the controllers'* […]".

increase trust[157] and transparency,[158] avoid monopolies,[159] promote innovation,[160] and turn passive data subjects into active re-users,[161] who will, indeed, share the wealth that new technologies create.[162]

By fostering competition amongst digital services and interoperability between platforms, data portability can be regarded as a strategic feature that enhances controllership.[163] This element could very well solve prominent issues of ignorance, confusion and misleading and at the same time enforce transparency, accountability and trustworthiness.

---

[157] Bizannes E (nd) Tag: Data portability project. http://social.techcrunch.com/tag/data-portability-project/. Accessed 2 September 2019 ("[…] *Site owners have an economic interest to support the portability of people's data* […] *sites and their users have a relationship, and the relationship is stronger if the user can trust the website to protect their domain over their data* […]").

[158] See also European Data Protection Supervisor (2016) Opinion 9/2016, Opinion on personal information management systems. https://edps.europa.eu/sites/edp/files/publication/16-10-20_pims_opinion_en.pdf. Accessed 20 September 2019 para 55 ("[…] *The new GDPR, including rules on increased transparency, and powerful rights of access and data portability, should help give individuals more control over their data, and may also contribute to more efficient markets for personal data, to the benefit of consumers and businesses alike* […]"); Article 29 Data Protection Working Party (2016b) Guidelines on the right to data portability. https://ec.europa.eu/newsroom/article29/item-detail.cfm?item_id=611233. 15 Accessed 20 September 2019 ("[…] *Data controllers must respect the obligation to respond within the given terms, even if it concerns a refusal. In other words, the data controller cannot remain silent when it is asked to answer a data portability request* […]").

[159] See also European Data Protection Supervisor (2014) Preliminary Opinion of the European Data Protection Supervisor: Privacy and competitiveness in the age of big data: The interplay between data protection, competition law and consumer protection in the Digital Economy. https://edps.europa.eu/sites/edp/files/publication/14-03-26_competitition_law_big_data_en.pdf. Accessed 20 September 2019 para 83 ("[…] *Data portability could release synergies between competition law and data protection law in at least two ways. First, it could prevent abuse of dominance, whether exclusionary or exploitative, and consumers being locked into certain services through the limitation of production, markets or technical development to the prejudice of consumers. It would emulate the benefits of number portability provided for in telecommunications law. Second, data portability could empower consumers to take advantage of value-added services from third parties while facilitating greater access to the market by competitors, for example through the use of product comparison sites or of companies offering energy advice based on smart metering data* […]").

[160] See Article 29 Data Protection Working Party (2016b) Guidelines on the right to data portability. https://ec.europa.eu/newsroom/article29/item-detail.cfm?item_id=611233. 5 Accessed 20 September 2019 ("[…] *the right to data portability is expected to foster opportunities for innovation and sharing of personal data between data controllers in a safe and secure manner, under the data subject's control* […]").

[161] Custers and Uršič 2016, p. 9.

[162] See Article 29 Data Protection Working Party (2014) Opinion 06/2014 on the notion of legitimate interests of the data controller, under Article 7 of Directive 95/46/EC. https://ec.europa.eu/justice/article-29/documentation/opinion-recommendation/index_en.htm. 47 Accessed 20 September 2019.

[163] See European Data Protection Supervisor (2015) Recommendations on the EU's options for data protection reform. https://edps.europa.eu/sites/edp/files/publication/15-07-27_gdpr_summary_en_0.pdf. para 3.2 Accessed 20 September 2019 ("[…] *Data portability is the gateway in the digital environment to the user control which individuals are now realising they lack* […]").

5.4.2 User-Centric Platforms to Enforce Transparency, Accountability, and Trustworthiness

As previously discussed,[164] in both the public and private sector, Greece is heading towards self-service technologies, where interfaces enable people to receive a service without direct assistance from any personnel. So, how could data portability promote transparency, accountability, and trustworthiness while delivering the above services?

With regard to the public sector, citizens need to access their own digital lives from different platforms.[165] For instance, one may use the Ministry's platform to receive—fully online—numerous tax services.[166] However, when time to pay social security contributions comes, citizens have to register via a different website that is managed by a limited liability company ("H.ΔΙ.Κ.Α. A.E.").[167] The advantage here is that people may use the same username and password to enter the above two different platforms and receive "dissimilar" services (tax and social security ones), albeit substantial differences, with regard to the very nature and status of each of the above websites' managers (i.e. the Ministry, in case of tax services, and a company, in case of social security contributions), seem to cloud the picture. On one hand, it is obvious that the terms of use that a public entity provides cannot be -and are not- the same as those, which the above limited liability company provides.[168] On the other hand, are tax and social security services so different that they actually need to be managed and provided by two dissimilar entities via two dissimilar platforms? Portability of content and data could, in this case, be achieved by guaranteeing the same safeguards with regard to terms of use and privacy policies and, perhaps, by providing both tax and social security services via a single platform (and by a single entity). At the same time, other e-government services could be delivered via

---

[164] See Sect. 5.1.2.

[165] The European Council in October 2013 committed to 'complete the Digital Single Market' by 2015 including 'the right framework conditions for a single market for Big Data and Cloud computing', by developing e-government, e-health, e-invoicing and e-procurement, by the acceleration of e-identification and trust services, e-invoicing and payment services, and by the portability of content and data. European Council (2013) Conclusions—24/25 October 2013. http://www.consilium.europa.eu/uedocs/cms_data/docs/pressdata/en/ec/139197.pdf. Accessed 20 September 2019 para 7 ("[…] *There is also a need to address the bottlenecks in accessing one's "digital life" from different platforms which persist due to a lack of interoperability or lack of portability of content and data. This hampers the use of digital services and competition. An open and non-discriminatory framework must therefore be put in place to ensure such interoperability and portability without hindering development of the fast moving digital sphere and avoiding unnecessary administrative burden* […]").

[166] Greek Ministry of e-Governance (2019a) myTAXISnet. https://www.gsis.gr/en. Accessed 20 September 2019.

[167] E-Governance Social Security (2019a) e-Governance Social Security. www.idika.gr. Accessed 20 September 2019.

[168] See Greek Ministry of e-Governance (2019b) Terms and conditions of use of the website. https://www.gsis.gr/en/terms-and-conditions-use-website. Accessed 20 September 2019; E-Governance Social Security (2019b) Terms and conditions of use. http://www.idika.gr/oroi.Accessed 20 September 2019.

ministries' platforms, while citizens could use the same usernames and passwords and, thus, benefit from an open and non-discriminatory framework that would ensure interoperability and portability. Fostering such practices would let citizens participate in "digital decision-making" and, thus, set the foundations upon which democracy can be built.

Concerning the private sector, value added services could be offered to guarantee that citizens would enjoy benefits from Big Data and enrich their experience. In particular, users could transfer between online services, change providers, but keep their existing data.[169] Interconnection of services and interoperability could lead to the development of user-centric platforms, where the data subject would be the controller of his or her information and a dynamic competition would emerge as to which provider would offer more and of better quality innovative services. This way passive data subjects could not only become active re-users of their information but also share the wealth that new technologies create. Namely, consumers could very well download their personal information with regard to insurance services that they are already receiving and be, then, advised by third parties whether alternative insurance companies could provide a better deal. Third parties could offer such advisory services by processing and examining existing patterns and ground truth data. Data portability could also engage in fields of quantified self and the Internet of Things industries to deliver a more complete picture of an individual's life, albeit drawing the appropriate attention to transparency to avoid relevant risks.[170]

To sum up, both the public and private sector could focus on the development of user-centric platforms and, thus, transparency, accountability, and trustworthiness could, actually, be enhanced. In this context, users could bring their identities, files and histories with them, without the need to manually add them to each new service. Thereafter, each service could draw on data relevant to the context. While individuals

[169]See European Data Protection Supervisor (2014) Preliminary opinion of the European Data Protection Supervisor: Privacy and competitiveness in the age of big data: The interplay between data protection, competition law and consumer protection in the Digital Economy. https://edps.europa.eu/sites/edp/files/publication/14-03-26_competitition_law_big_data_en.pdf. Accessed 20 September 2019 para 26 ("[…] *This right to data portability would allow users to transfer between online services in a similar way that users of telephone services may change providers but keep their telephone numbers. In addition, data portability would allow users to give their data to third parties offering different value-added services. By way of illustration, if applied to smart metering it would enable customers to download data on their energy usage from their existing electricity supplier and then to hire a third party able to advise them whether an alternative supplier could offer a better price, based on their patterns of electricity consumption. Such transparency enables individuals to exercise their other data protection rights and may be seen to mirror the objective of rules on the provision of clear and accurate information to the consumer* […]").

[170]See Article 29 Data Protection Working Party (2016b) Guidelines on the right to data portability. https://ec.europa.eu/newsroom/article29/item-detail.cfm?item_id=611233. Accessed 20 September 2019 5 ("[…] *Data portability can promote the controlled and limited sharing by users of personal data between organisations and thus enrich services and customer experiences* […]" and "[…] *The so-called quantified self and IoT industries have shown the benefit (and risks) of linking personal data from different aspects of an individual's life such as fitness, activity and calorie intake to deliver a more complete picture of an individual's life in a single file* […]").

would add or change their information, this would be updated on other services—if data subjects permitted so—without the need to visit other platforms to re-enter it. Moreover, service providers would "welcome" such data and there would be no need to "fill out forms", a factor that could drive people away. Simultaneously, while individuals would browse services and share their experiences, their data could be automatically updated on a provider's service, in case the data subject permitted this. Hence, relationship between users and providers would remain up-to-date and services could, indeed, be adapted even in those cases that the individuals would not visit the relevant website or platform. This way, mutual benefit could be achieved and relationships could encourage continuous usage.[171]

5.4.3 Conclusion

It is true that happiness is not an algorithm, but in an environment where people can even touch their personal data by using innovative interfaces, platforms and devices, the above user-friendly and user-centric systems could be implemented to safeguard individuals' interests and guarantee controllership. We certainly cannot solely allow algorithms to define what matters, even though it is important to grab this chance that allows us to share the promised benefits, which were, actually, created by new technologies. Big Data may bring the very concept of privacy to the discussion table and challenge the very notion of a human being, who may today, as a tech-junkie, measure and quantify every pattern of his or her digital self and life.[172]

In a state, where attention seems to have been drawn to the protection of the individuals with regard to the processing of their personal data, rather than the free movement of our information, data portability could be the answer that would very likely enforce transparency of procedures and practices, which people now ignore,

---

[171] Indeed, some authors regard the right to data portability as one of the most important novelties within the EU General Data Protection Regulation, both in terms of warranting control rights to data subjects and in terms of being found at the intersection between data protection and other fields of law. De Hert et al. 2018. For a discussion on APIs for Cloud application development with regard to portability, see Petcu et al. 2013, p. 1417 ("[…] *Open application programming interfaces, standards and protocols, as well as their early integration in the software stack of the new technological offers, are the key elements towards a widely accepted solution and the basic requirements for the further development of Cloud applications* […]"). As others argue, a disadvantage of data portability is that it increases the complexity of control and processing of personal data. Since the procedures are often not clear to the users and only minimal privacy settings are in place, this is not sufficient to effectively protect the user's privacy. Van der Auwermeulen 2017, p. 60. For potential threats to an individual's privacy, see Weiss 2009, p. 252 ("[…] *Even if the individual would live as a hermit without an Internet and phone connection, there are potential threats to this person's privacy if, for example, other people would start invading the hermit's space for whatever reason. In order to preserve the hermit's privacy, it is important to understand what constitutes a privacy invasion for the hermit (his own privacy preference), how likely it is to stumble on his piece of land without even recognizing it (public accessibility), and what degree of self-defense he has built up for himself (self-control)* […]").

[172] Mayer-Schönberger and Cukier 2013, p. 94.

promote relevant parties' accountability and guarantee trustworthiness of public and private personnel.

We believe that the GDPR will, in practice, enable individuals to re-shape old notions and basic principles, which deal with our personal information, and, hence, move towards a new direction, where many of today's uncertainties could be resolved.

Maybe, the time to put our personal information into the appropriate context has come,[173] and perhaps this is the right moment to speak of consent—the key tool to successfully and effectively exercise control—as a truly informed indication of the data subject's wish based on trust, rather than consent as a "*freely given, specific, informed and unambiguous indication of the data subject's wishes by which he or she, by a statement or by a clear affirmative action, signifies agreement to the processing of personal data relating to him or her*", which may, however, be validly given by a "single-mouse-click" on terms of use and privacy policies[174] that nobody reads.

References

Airbnb (2019a) Airbnb privacy policy. https://www.airbnb.gr/terms/privacy_policy. Accessed 20 September 2019

Airbnb (2019b) Airbnb cookie policy. https://www.airbnb.gr/terms/cookie_policy. Accessed 20 September 2019

Baack S (2015) Datafication and empowerment: How the open data movement re-articulates notions of democracy, participation, and journalism. Big Data Soc https://doi.org/10.1177/2053951715594634

Barocas S, Nissenbaum H (2009) On notice: The trouble with notice and consent. https://papers.ssrn.com/abstract=2567409. Accessed 20 September 2019

Bizannes E (nd) Tag: Data portability project. http://social.techcrunch.com/tag/data-portability-project/. Accessed 2 September 2019

Bohannon J (2013) Genetics. Genealogy databases enable naming of anonymous DNA donors. Science https://doi.org/10.1126/science.339.6117.262

Bottis M (2009) The protection of private life and the European Legislation with regard to Personal data: Thoughts on the protection of private life in the USA. In: Stathopoulos M (ed) Honorary volume. Sakkoulas, Greece, pp 809–823

Bottis M (2013) Surveillance, data protection and libraries in Europe and the US-notes on an empirical data case study on surveillance and Greek academic libraries. In: Bottis M (ed) Privacy and surveillance: Current aspects and future perspectives. Nomiki Bibliothiki, Greece, pp. 272–282

Bottis M (2014) The history of information: From papyrus to the electronic document. Nomiki Bibliothiki, Greece

Boyd D, Crawford K (2011) Six provocations for big data. https://papers.ssrn.com/abstract=1926431

Brin D (1999) The transparent society: Will technology force us to choose between privacy and freedom? Hachette UK, London

Bygrave L A (2014) Data privacy law: An international perspective. Oxford University Press, Oxford

Cavoukian A (2008) Privacy in the clouds. Identity Inform Soc https://doi.org/10.1007/s12394-008-0005-z

[173] Nissenbaum 2009.

[174] See Recital (32) of GDPR.

Cavoukian A, Tapscott D (1996) Who knows: Safeguarding your privacy in a networked world. McGraw-Hill Professional, New York

Chamber of Corfu (2019) Chamber of Corfu. http://www.corfucci.gr/kerkyra/shared/index.jsp?context=101. Accessed 20 September 2019

Crawford K, Schultz J (2014) Big data and due process: Toward a framework to redress predictive privacy harms. Boston Coll Law Rev 55:93–128

Custers B, Uršič H (2016) Big data and data reuse: A taxonomy of data reuse for balancing big data benefits and personal data protection. Int Data Privacy Law https://doi.org/10.1093/idpl/ipv028

De Hert P, Papakonstantinou V, Malgieri G, Beslay L, Sanchez I (2018) The right to data portability in the GDPR: Towards user-centric interoperability of digital services. Comput Law Secur Rev https://doi.org/10.1016/j.clsr.2017.10.003

Demitropoulos A (2008) Constitutional rights, 2nd edn. Constitutional Law, vol. 3. Sakkoulas, Greece

DPO Academy (2018) The data protection officer course. https://www.dpoacademy.gr/el/the-dpo-course/. Accessed 20 September 2019

E-Governance Social Security (2019a) e-Governance Social Security. www.idika.gr. Accessed 20 September 2019

E-Governance Social Security (2019b) Terms and conditions of use. http://www.idika.gr/oroi. Accessed 20 September 2019

European Council (2013) Conclusions - 24/25 October 2013. http://www.consilium.europa.eu/uedocs/cms_data/docs/pressdata/en/ec/139197.pdf. Accessed 20 September 2019

European Data Protection Supervisor (2014) Preliminary opinion of the European Data Protection Supervisor: Privacy and competitiveness in the age of big data: The interplay between data protection, competition law and consumer protection in the digital economy. https://edps.europa.eu/sites/edp/files/publication/14-03-26_competitition_law_big_data_en.pdf. Accessed 20 September 2019

European Data Protection Supervisor (2015) Recommendations on the EU's options for data protection reform. https://edps.europa.eu/sites/edp/files/publication/15-07-27_gdpr_summary_en_0.pdf. Accessed 20 September 2019

European Data Protection Supervisor (2016) Opinion 9/2016, Opinion on personal information management systems. https://edps.europa.eu/sites/edp/files/publication/16-10-20_pims_opinion_en.pdf. Accessed 20 September 2019

Faniel I M, Zimmerman A (2011) Beyond the data deluge: A research agenda for large-scale data sharing and reuse. IJDC 6:58–69

Förster K, Weish U (2017) Advertising critique: Themes, actors and challenges in a digital age. In: Commercial communication in the digital age: Information or disinformation? Walter de Gruyter GmbH & Co KG, Berlin, pp 15–35

Gandy O H (2010) Engaging rational discrimination: Exploring reasons for placing regulatory constraints on decision support systems. Ethics Inf Technol https://doi.org/10.1007/s10676-009-9198-6

Geradin D, Kuschewsky M (2013) Competition law and personal data: Preliminary thoughts on a complex issue. Concurrences https://research.tilburguniversity.edu/en/publications/competition-law-and-personal-data-preliminary-thoughts-on-a-compl. Accessed 20 September 2019

Gindin S E (2009) Nobody reads your privacy policy or online contract: Lessons learned and questions raised by the FTC's action against Sears. Nw J Technol Intellect Property 1:1–37

Golle P (2006) Revisiting the uniqueness of simple demographics in the US population. ACM https://doi.org/10.1145/1179601.1179615

Graef I, Verschakelen J, Valcke P (2013) Putting the right to data portability into a competition law perspective. Law. The Journal of the Higher School of Economics, 53–63.

Greek Ministry of e-Governance (2019a) myTAXISnet. https://www.gsis.gr/en. Accessed 20 September 2019

Greek Ministry of e-Governance (2019b) Terms and conditions of use of the website. https://www.gsis.gr/en/terms-and-conditions-use-website. Accessed 20 September 2019

Hellenic Data Protection Authority (2019a) HDPA. http://www.dpa.gr/. Accessed 20 September 2019

Hellenic Data Protection Authority (2019b) Γνωμοδοτήσεις της Αρχής [Opinions of the Authority]. http://www.dpa.gr/portal/page?_pageid=33,120923&_dad=portal&_schema=PORTAL. Accessed 20 September 2019

Intrasoft International (2019) Nomos. https://lawdb.intrasoftnet.com/nomos/nomos_frame.html. Accessed 20 September 2019

Kang J, Shilton K, Estrin D, Burke J (2011) Self-surveillance privacy. Iowa Law Rev (3:809–848

King NJ, Forder J (2016) Data analytics and consumer profiling: Finding appropriate privacy principles for discovered data. Comput Law Secur Rev https://doi.org/10.1016/j.clsr.2016.05.002

Lawspot (2017) Data protection officers (date publication: 11 August 2017) https://www.lawspot.gr/nomika-nea/data-protection-officers-kanenas-foreas-stin-ellada-den-ehei-diapisteythei-mehri-simera. Accessed 20 September 2019

Mantelero A (2016) Personal data for decisional purposes in the age of analytics: From an individual to a collective dimension of data protection. Comput Law Secur Rev https://doi.org/10.1016/j.clsr.2016.01.014

Mayer-Schönberger V, Cukier K (2013) Big data: A revolution that will transform how we live, work, and think. Houghton Mifflin Harcourt, Boston

Meuter M L, Ostrom A L, Roundtree R I, Bitner M J (2000) Self-service technologies: Understanding customer satisfaction with technology-based service encounters. J Mark https://doi.org/10.1509/jmkg.64.3.50.18024

Mitrou L (2004) The protection of personal data and case law of Symvoulio Tis Epikrateias. In: Honorable volume of Symvoulio Tis Epikrateias (75 years). Sakkoulas, Greece

Mitrou L (2017) Article 9A of the constitution. In: Spiropoulos F, Kontiadis K, Anthopoulos C, Gerapetritis G (eds) Interpretation of the constitution. Sakkoulas, Greece, pp 214–233

Morozov E (2012) The Net Delusion: The Dark Side of Internet Freedom (reprint). PublicAffairs, New York

Narayanan A, Shmatikov V (2006) How to break anonymity of the Netflix prize dataset. http://arxiv.org/abs/cs/0610105. Accessed 20 September 2019

Narayanan A, Shmatikov V (2008) Robust de-anonymization of large sparse datasets. IEEE https://doi.org/10.1109/SP.2008.33

Nissenbaum H (2009) Privacy in context: Technology, policy, and the integrity of social life. Stanford University Press, Palo Alto

Ohm P (2010) Broken promises of privacy: Responding to the surprising failure of anonymization. UCLA Law Rev 57:1701–1777

O'Neil C (2016) Weapons of math destruction: How big data increases inequality and threatens democracy. Crown, New York

Oostveen M, Irion K (2018) The golden age of personal data: How to regulate an enabling fundamental right? Springer https://doi.org/10.1007/978-3-662-57646-5_2

Palfrey J, Gasser U (2010) Born digital: Understanding the first generation of digital natives (reprint). Basic Books, New York

Pararas P (2010) The Constitution – Corpus I (articles 1–4). Sakkoulas, Greece

Pasquale F (2015) The Black Box Society: The secret algorithms that control money and information. Harvard University Press, Cambridge

Petcu D, Macariu G, Panica S, Crciun C (2013) Portable Cloud applications – From theory to practice. Future Gener Comput Syst https://doi.org/10.1016/j.future.2012.01.009

Pingo Z, Narayan B (2016) When personal data becomes open data: An exploration of lifelogging, user privacy, and implications for privacy literacy. In: Morishima A, Rauber A, Liew C L (eds) Digital libraries: Knowledge, information, and data in an open access society. Springer International Publishing, New York, pp 3–9

Priority (2018) DPO certification master class. https://www.priority.com.gr/page/gdpr-dpo-training/. Accessed 20 September 2019

Reed C (2010) Information 'ownership' in the Cloud https://ssrn.com/abstract=1562461. Accessed 20 September 2019

Rengel A (2014) Privacy as an international human right and the right to obscurity in cyberspace. Gr J Int Law https://papers.ssrn.com/abstract=2599271. Accessed 20 September 2019

Richards N M, King J H (2016) Big data and the future for privacy. In: Research handbook on digital transformations. Edward Elgar Publishing, Northampton

Rubinstein I (2012) Big data: The end of privacy or a new beginning? https://papers.ssrn.com/abstract=2157659. Accessed 20 September 2019

Schneier B (2015) Data and Goliath: The hidden battles to collect your data and control your world. W W Norton & Company, New York

Scholz T M (2017) Big data in organizations and the role of human resource management: A complex systems theory-based conceptualization. Peter Lang, New York

Snyder W (2011) Making the case for enhanced advertising ethics: How a new way of thinking about advertising ethics may build consumer trust. J Advertising Res 51:477–483

Solove D J (2012) Introduction: Privacy self-management and the consent dilemma symposium: Privacy and technology. Harv Law Rev 7:1880–1903

Sweeney L (2000) Simple demographics often identify people uniquely. https://doi.org/10.1184/R1/6625769.v1

Tassopoulos G (2001) Moral and political foundations of the Constitution. Sakkoulas, Greece

Taylor S J (2014) A critical analysis of the EU right to erasure as it applies to internet search engine results. MS thesis. https://www.duo.uio.no/bitstream/handle/10852/43102/1/8019.pdf. Accessed 20 September 2019

Tene O (2008) What Google knows: Privacy and Internet search engines. Utah Law Rev 4:1433–1492

Tene O, Polonetsky J (2012) Big data for all: Privacy and user control in the age of analytics. Nw J Technol Intellect Property 5:239–274

van der Auwermeulen B (2017) How to attribute the right to data portability in Europe: A comparative analysis of legislations. Comput Law Secur Rev https://doi.org/10.1016/j.clsr.2016.11.012

Veale M, Binns R (2017) Fairer machine learning in the real world: Mitigating discrimination without collecting sensitive data. Big Data Soc https://doi.org/10.1177/2053951717743530

Viola De Azevedo Cunha M (2012) Review of the data protection directive: Is there need (and room) for a new concept of personal data? Springer https://doi.org/10.1007/978-94-007-2903-2_13

Weiss S (2009) Privacy threat model for data portability in social network applications. Int J Inf Manag https://doi.org/10.1016/j.ijinfomgt.2009.03.007

Ziamou T (2017) Article 2 of the Constitution. In: Spiropoulos F, Kontiadis K, Anthopoulos C, Gerapetritis G (eds) Interpretation of the Constitution. Sakkoulas, Greece, pp 20–34

Mr. Georgios Bouchagiar Doctoral researcher, Faculty of Law, Economics and Finance, University of Luxembourg, 4 rue Alphonse Weicker, L-2721 Luxembourg-Kirchberg, Luxembourg; Law, Science, Technology & Society, Free University of Brussels, 2 Pleinlaan, 1050 Brussels, Belgium. Supported by the Luxembourg National Research Fund (FNR) (PRIDE17/12251371).

Dr. Nikos Koutras Lecturer in Law, School of Business and Law, Edith Cowan University, JO2317, 270 Joondalup Drive, Joondalup WA 6027, Australia.

Chapter 6
Privacy and Personal Data Protection in Indonesia: The Hybrid Paradigm of the Subjective and Objective Approach

Edmon Makarim

Contents

Abstract Recently, the Indonesian media has raised certain issues related to privacy and personal data in the country; in particular, there are concerns about the implications of European Regulation 679/2016 on General Personal Data Protection for Indonesians. Coupled with the case of Facebook and Cambridge Analytica, the news has seized public attention in Indonesia. Since 2008, Indonesia has regulated personal data protection in Article 26 of the Law No. 11 on 2008 concerning electronic information and transaction. This, in turn, was derived from Article 15 of the Government Regulation on e-System Operating and Transaction and then implemented by

E. Makarim (✉)
Faculty of Law, University of Indonesia, Jl. Prof. Mr. Djokosoetono, Kampus Universitas Indonesia Depok, 16424 Depok, Indonesia
e-mail: edmon_makarim@yahoo.com; edmonmakarim@gmail.com

E. Kiesow Cortez (ed.), *Data Protection Around the World*, Information Technology and Law Series 33,
https://doi.org/10.1007/978-94-6265-407-5_6

the Communication and Informatics Ministry Regulation No. 20 on 2016 about Personal Data Protection in e-System. In the meantime, the Government had also drafted the Bill for Personal Data Protection, a single omnibus law designed to more comprehensively regulate and consolidate those issues; the objective was to prevent the complexity and potential disharmony of various levels of laws in the Indonesian national legal system from being a legal barrier to implementation. To bring clarity to the understanding and protection mechanisms, the authors were called upon to straighten out any existing confusion relating to Indonesian telematics laws or the legal convergence of the country's information and communication law.

Keywords Indonesian data protection law · GDPR · Indonesian privacy law · Bill for personal data protection · e-System · Right to privacy

6.1 Introduction

It is well known that privacy actually refers to human rights, in particular, protecting individuals' dignity as human beings. The right to privacy refers to their security and quality of life and actions in their private life (private spheres) as well as to what happens to them in the public areas of life (public spheres). The definition of privacy has two aspects:

(i) the internal scope which includes everything that would be treated as an offence against someone's personal life (namely, intrusion or interference from outside influences); and
(ii) the external scope which includes anything that affects one's quality of life in the society (namely, exposure of one's personal, opinion, and intentional data to another party).

Most legal experts define privacy narrowly as the right of every person not to be disturbed by others (the right to be let alone, secrecy, and security); in other words, everyone should feel safe in their personal life, body, property, and personal communications. In a broad sense, privacy is not just about the safety of every person but also proper touch to comfort them in the social interaction. It would be understood as referring to anonymity, the confidentiality of personal data, protection from others' actions solely intended to humiliate, and so forth. This line of thought is a logical consequence of the meaning of human values as contained in Article 2 of the Universal Declaration of Human Rights (UDHR) and also Article 17 of the International Covenant on Civil and Political Rights (ICCPR).

More recently, the scope of privacy includes personal data such as regulated in the European Convention on Human Rights and the ASEAN Declaration of Human Rights.

Charter of Fundamental Rights of the European Union (2000/C 364/01)

Article 7

Respect for private and family life: Everyone has the right to respect for his or her private and family life, home and communications.

Article 8: Protection of personal data

1. Everyone has the right to the protection of personal data concerning him or her.
2. Such data must be processed fairly for specified purposes and on the basis of the consent of the person concerned or some other legitimate basis laid down by law. Everyone has the right of access to data which has been collected concerning him or her, and the right to have it rectified.
3. Compliance with these rules shall be subject to control by an independent authority.

ASEAN Human Rights Declaration

Article 21: Every person has the right to be free from arbitrary interference with his or her privacy, family, home or correspondence including personal data, or to attacks upon that person's honor and reputation. Every person has the right to the protection of the law against such interference or attacks.

6.2 Global Discussion of Privacy Laws and Lessons Learned for Indonesia

Extensive research on global discussion, as well as many literature reviews, have revealed two different paradigms and regimes of privacy law and personal data protection: the Subjective Approach and the Objective Approach.

In the subjective approach, the paradigm of regulation focuses on individual rights in one's private life, and protection is limited to a reasonable expectation of privacy in which there is an assumption of risk to consider in the implementation of that legitimate interest. Because this is regarded as an individual right, the government does not have too much power to interfere and it prefers to implement the self-regulation regime based on market forces. This is the approach of most U.S. experts who, in principle, believe that the State should not interfere deeply in privacy protection mechanisms. They believe that self-regulatory rules result in making the economic cost efficient and effective.

Conversely, in the objective approach (developed in Europe), the legal thinking objectively looks at personal data protection as a necessary measure to protect privacy rights. In other words, personal data would be treated as an intangible property attached or linked to someone's subject data. It is widely believed that any activities related to personal data could potentially infringe someone's privacy. Consequently, the Data Subject has a right to control their personal data, particularly any usage of the personal data by any parties who have obtained and processed the personal data (Controller and Processor), and any parties who received the personal data (recipient and third party).

From the objective approach, personal data is also viewed as a strategic resource to the State. Therefore, the Government—through its Supervisory Authority—can interfere and has the power to ensure that any processing of personal data implements the principles and mechanism of personal data protection regulations. Any infringement of those regulations would result in some form of sanction. Therefore, any party seeking to collect personal data of others must obtain the necessary licensing and/or approval; furthermore, this process should be supervised by the state agencies to ensure that every person's security and quality of life are maintained.

It should be noted that when commercial communication activities are carried out electronically, both paradigms also have different derivative regulatory mechanisms.

- The Out Option ("Opt-out") mechanism derives from the application of the subjective approach. Each person is considered have a legitimate interest to call or to initiate communication with others, unless there is an objection or an opposition to those activities. In a message sent via electronic communication, the sender must provide the means to express disapproval (unsubscribe). If, after a recipient has rejected a message by unsubscribing and the sender sends another message, such an action by the sender would be considered as a privacy violation. For example, in the context of telephone communication, there is a policy whereby businesses must provide a Do-Not-Call-Registry ("DNCR"), which allows anyone to register themselves in order not to be bothered by telemarketing. Although at first glance it looks like a protection for consumers (the user of the operators), it actually poses a burden on consumers because they have to make an effort to ensure their privacy rights by registering to the DNCR.
- Meanwhile, the Option-in ("Opt-in") mechanism derives from the objective approach. Here, each person should get the recipient's approval to ensure the basic legal right to communicate with others. The sender has an obligation to ensure that their communication does not violate the privacy of others. In practice, the sender must obtain the explicit consent of the parties or guarantee that the personal data will be lawfully obtained. In other words, any initiation of communication should prevent harm to anybody who will receive the communication.

In the global context, both of these different paradigms are then articulated and mediated by the OECD Guidelines and the APEC global Privacy Framework regarding the Cross Border Privacy Rules and Accountability Agent for implementing the privacy's regulation. The Accountability Agent could also be called a Privacy Trustmark Provider. In the latest development, European regionally has regulation no. 679/2016 on General Data Protection Regulation (GDPR) which might have implications for other states outside of the European territory.

Pursuant to the global discussions, there are some lessons-learned for Indonesia that might result in combining those two perspective and paradigms to the country's national legal system. The global discussion basically focuses on how to ensure transparency and accountability in processing personal data.

Similar to the global dynamics, Indonesia also has some laws and regulations concerning privacy and personal data. In general, these issues were regulated under the following three measures: the Law of Electronic Information and Transaction Act (UU-ITE); the Government Regulation on Electronic System Operating and Transaction (PP-PSTE); and the Ministry Regulation on personal data protection in the electronic system (Permen PDP).[1] Those regulations were implemented and adjusted by other government authorities of other sectors according to their laws and regulations.

The Indonesian legal system accommodates self-regulation and self-enforcement by providing the Privacy Trustmark, but it also has the government authority to supervise the implementation of personal data protection and facilitate the panel for alternative dispute resolution.

In the latest development, the government has also drafted the Bill of Law for Personal Data Protection Act since 2008 ["Rancangan Undang-Undang Perlindungan Data Pribadi" (RUU-PDP)]. Even though a special law has not yet been enacted, in general it had already been adopted in some existing laws and regulation. Therefore, it is important to explain the Indonesian Legal Framework on Privacy and Personal Data Protection according to the Indonesian Law Hierarchy.

6.3 Legal Framework

The legal framework, as discussed in the previous section, put forward the Law of EIT and its implementing regulation (Minister of Communication and Informatics Regulation Number 20 of 2016 about Private Protection in Electronic System) as the core text regarding other regulations on personal data protection, and other related laws and regulation, such as Human Rights, Citizen Administration, Consumer Protection, Health.

Regulations related to Personal Data in the Legislation in Indonesia

- Indonesian Constitution, the Undang-Undang Dasar Negara Republik Indonesia 1945 ("UUD-1945"), Preamble and Body of Text (Article 28).

Human Rights

- Criminal Code ("KUHP"), Articles 430–434
- Law No. 39/1999 on Human Rights ("UU-HAM"), Articles 21 and 31 Privacy to property, communication, and profiling
- Indonesian Law No. 21/2007 on Eradication of Criminal Acts of Human Trafficking ("UU TPPO"), Article 33 Confidentiality of the reporter's identity.

[1] In 2019, the government introduced two implementing regulations that also govern the personal data protection, namely Government Regulation No. 71 of 2019 on the Implementation of e-System and Transactions (GR 71/2019) and Government Regulation No. 80 of 2019 on E-Commerce (GR 80/2019).

Media and Telecommunications

- Law Number 36 of 1999 on Telecommunications ("UU Telekomunikasi"), Articles 40–42(1)
- Law No.19/2016 revising the Law 11/2008 on Electronic Information and Transaction ("UU-ITE"), Articles 26(1), 31(1)-(2) and 43(2)
- Law No. 14/2008, on Public Information Openness ("UU KIP"), Articles 6(3) (c), 17(g)-(h) and 19.

Defence and Security

- Law Number 5/2018 on Amendment to Law Number 15/2003 on the Establishment of Government Regulation in lieu of Law Number 1 of 2002 on Eradication of Crime of Terrorism into Law ("UU Anti-Terorisme")
- Law No. 17/2011 on State Intelligence ("UU Intelijen Negara")
- Law No. 9/2013 on Prevention and Eradication of Criminal Funding for Terrorism ("UU Pendanaan Terorisme"), Article 9(1).

Judicial

- Criminal Code Procedure ("KUHAP"), Article 48(2)-(3)
- Law No. 20/2001 on Amendments to Law No. 31/1999 on Eradication of Corruption ("UU Tipikor")
- Law No. 30/2002 on the commission to eradicate corruption ("UU KPK")
- Law No. 18/2003 on Advocates ("UU Advokat"), Article 19 (1)-(2)
- Law No. 18/2011 on Amendments to Law No. 22/2004 on Judicial Commissions ("UU KY"), Article 20A(1) (c).

Archival and Demography

- Law No. 26/2006 on Citizen Administration ("UU-Adminduk"), Article 1(22), 2(c) and 84–86
- Law No. 43/2009, on Archives ("UU Kearsipan"), Articles 5, 6(5), 7(g), 9, 34–35, 40, 44, 49, (b), 51–52, 66(2), (5)-(6).

Health

- Law No. 29/2004 on Medical Practice ("UU Praktik Kedokteran"), Article 46, 47, 48(1), 51(c), and 52(e)
- Law No. 35/2009 on Narcotics ("UU Narkotika")
- Indonesian Law No. 36/2009 on Health ("UU Kesehatan"), Article 8, 57(1) and 189(2) (c)
- Law No. 44/2009 on Hospitals ("UU Rumah Sakit"), Article 29(1) (h), (l), (m), 32 (i), 38 (1) and 44
- Law No. 18/2014 on Mental Health ("UU Kesehatan Jiwa"), Article 68(d) and 70(1) (e)

- Law No. 36/2014 on Health Workers ("UU Tenaga Kesehatan"), Article 58(1) (c) and 70–73(1).

Finance and Banking

- Law No. 10/1998 on Amendments to Law No. 7/1992 on Banking ("UU Perbankan"), Article 1(28), 40(1)
- Law No. 23/1999 on Bank Indonesia ("UU BI")
- Law No. 21/2008 on Sharia Banking ("UU Perbankan Syariah"), Article 41
- Law No. 8/2010 on Prevention and Eradication of Money Laundering Action ("UU TPPU"), Article 11 (1), 40 (b), 42, 54 (2) and 83 (1)
- Law No. 21/2011 on the Financial Services Authority ("UU OJK"), Article 33(1)-(3).

Trade and Industry

- Law No. 08/1997 on Company Documents ("UU Dokumen Perusahaan"), Article 4 and 11(3)-(4)
- Law No. 8/1999 on Consumer Protection ("UUPK")
- Law No. 7/2014 on Trade ("UU Perdagangan"),[2] Article 65 (3).

Other Regulations

- Government Regulation No. 82/2012 on Electronic System and Transaction Provider ("PP-PSTE"),[3] Article 1, 15(2)
- Communication and Informatics Ministry Regulation No. 20/2016 on Personal Data Protection ("Permenkominfo Data Pribadi"), Article 2, 3.

6.3.1 Indonesian Constitution and Privacy

Uniquely in Indonesia, the principle of privacy had already been included in the grundnorms as the second values of Pancasila, *"Kemanusiaan Yang Adil dan Beradab"* (Fair and Civilized Humanity), which is articulated in the 4th paragraph of the Preamble of the Constitution. Even though most Indonesian people live according to community values that put community interest as a higher value than individual interest, it does not mean interfering with individual rights. Humanity is the second value of Pancasila, reminding everybody that they have a responsibility to be fair and

[2]The government introduced government regulations on e-commerce (GR 80/2019) as an implementing regulation of Law No. 7/2014 on Trade governing the e-commerce sector both domestic and overseas businesses. It regulates personal data protection under Chapter XI (arts. 58–59).

[3]PP-PSTE was then amended by GR 71/2019 in 2019. It regulates personal data under arts. 14–18.

proper in their actions. This sila teaches us not to intrude on anyone in the community. Commonly called "*perilaku yang ajeg*", it means to not act improperly in a way that would injure anyone.

In the reformation age, there are four amendments to 1945s Constitution of the Republic of Indonesia. Although the Constitution does not explicitly use the terms "privacy and personal data protection," these terms are generally perceived as being included as an integral part of the Article on the protection of dignity and personal life in Article 28G and 28H of the 1945 Constitution. It should be noted that Article 28 J balances Freedom and Privacy when someone's freedom limits the freedom of others. In other words, everybody has a duty and responsibility to respect other people's rights including their privacy; therefore, they should act properly without interfering other people's privacy.

It should be noted, from 10 (nine) Articles to protect the human rights (Article 28, 28a-h) only one article contained a clause states the duty of every person to respect the rights of others. This is also reinforced by Article 27 of the Constitution that requires each person to respect the rule of law and without exception. Indeed, the Constitution should balance individual rights with the public interest or national interest.

6.3.2 Privacy in Indonesian Human Rights Law

To carry out the obligations stipulated in the 1945 Constitution, the People's Consultative Assembly of the Republic of Indonesia with the Decree of the People's Consultative Assembly of the Republic of Indonesia Number XVII/MPR/1998 concerning Human Rights assigns the Higher Institutions of the State and all Government Apparatus to:

- respect, enforce, and disseminate the knowledge of human rights to the entire community; and
- immediately ratify various United Nations instruments on Human Rights as the sources of law, provided they are not contrary to Pancasila and the 1945 Constitution.

The regulation on human rights is basically contained in various laws and regulations, including the law that ratifies various international conventions on human rights. To cover all existing laws and regulations, a Law on Human Rights is needed. The rationale for the establishment of this Law is as follows:

a. God Almighty is the creator of the universe with all its contents;
b. basically, humans are endowed with the soul, form, structure, ability, willingness and convenience of the Creator, to guarantee the continuation of their lives;

c. to protect, maintain and enhance human dignity, it requires recognition and protection of human rights, because without this humanity will lose its nature and dignity, so as to encourage humans to become wolves to other humans (homo homini lupus);
d. because humans are social beings, human rights are limited by other human rights, so freedom or human rights are not without limits;
e. human rights must not be eliminated by anyone and under any circumstances;
f. every human right contains the obligation to respect the human rights of others, so that in human rights there is a basic obligation;
g. human rights must be truly respected, protected, and enforced, and for that the government, state apparatus and other public officials have obligations and responsibilities to guarantee the implementation of respect, protection and enforcement of human rights.

In this Law, the regulation of human rights is determined by referring to the United Nations Declaration of Human Rights, the United Nations Convention on the Elimination of All Forms of Discrimination against Women, the United Nations Convention on the Rights of the Child, and various instruments and other international regulations concerning human rights. The material of this Law is also adjusted to the legal needs of the community and the development of national law based on Pancasila and the 1945 Constitution.

This law specifically regulates the right to life and the right not to be removed and/or not eliminated, the right to have a family and continue with the offspring, the right to develop themselves, the right to justice, the right to personal freedom, the right to security, the right to welfare, the right to participate in government, women's rights, children's rights, and the right to freedom of religion. In addition to regulating human rights, the Law also regulates basic obligations, as well as the duties and responsibilities of the government in the enforcement of human rights.

In addition, this Act regulates the establishment of the National Human Rights Commission as an independent institution that has the functions, duties, authorities, and responsibilities to carry out studies, research, counselling, monitoring, and mediation on human rights.

This Law also regulates public participation in the form of complaints and/or claims for human rights violations, teaching proposals regarding policy formulation relating to human rights to the National Human Rights Commission, research, education, and dissemination of information on human rights.

This Law on Human Rights is an "umbrella law" which encompasses all laws and regulations concerning human rights. Therefore, direct and indirect violations of human rights are subject to criminal, civil and/or administrative sanctions in accordance with the provisions of the legislation.

Privacy rights, as part of human rights, have been regulated in some Articles of Law No. 39 of 1999 on Human Rights. In this law, despite the freedom of information and communication, everybody also has duties and responsibilities with regard to rights. Each person should respect the other person's right. Every person must respect the human rights of others, as well as the morals, ethics, and order of life in society, nation, and state.

It should be noted that trespassing and profiling would be treated as infringing on human rights from the elucidation of Articles 21 and 31.

Human Rights Law

Article 14

(1) *Everyone has the right to communicate and obtain information necessary to develop the personal and social environment.*

Everyone has the right to seek, obtain, possess, store, process and convey information by using all the means available.

Article 21

Every person is entitled to a personal unity, both spiritual and material, and therefore should not be the object of research without his consent.

Here, "being the object of research" means the activity of placing a person as a party to be asked for comments, opinions, or information concerning their personal life, personal data, and recorded images and sound.

Article 31

(1) *The residence of any person shall not be disturbed.*
(2) *Stepping on or entering a yard of residence or entering a house contrary to the will of the person inhabiting it, is permissible only in matters established by law.*

Paragraph (1) Referred to as "not to be disturbed" as a right related to private life (privacy) within its residence.

Article 69

Every person must respect the human rights of others, morals, ethics and order of life in society, nation and state. Every person's human rights give rise to basic obligations and responsibilities to respect the human rights of others as well as the duty of the Government to respect, protect, enforce and promote it.

6.3.3 *Privacy as Secrecy of Personal Life Excluding Public Information for Public Interest*

Quite often, media interest invades and exposes an individual's private life. For the sake of the public interest, the media can publish someone's private information even though, according to Article 7 of the EU Charter of Fundamental Rights, everyone has the right to be respected with regard to their personal life. However, "public interest" itself can be interpreted as two things, namely: (i) the public interest to access information; and (ii) the public interest to restrict access to the information itself in the context of confidentiality. Both issues, the opening (disclosing) and the closing (withholding) of information, are actually protected by law. This legal principle has been recognized in Law No. 14 Years 2008 on Public Information ("UU-KIP") as Maximum Access Limited Exemption.

On the other hand, the Public Information Law excludes any information that might have a legitimate interest as confidential, such as privacy law (secrecy of personal life), trade secrets, and confidential information by the State categorized as Excluded Information.

Furthermore, Government Regulation No. 61/2010 on the Implementation of Freedom of Information Law ("PP-KIP") also stipulates where the term of protection accords with the provisions of applicable legislation. This implies the existence of the legal recognition of that special arrangement that exists in other laws.

UU-KIP

Article 2 (4)

Public Information is exempt confidential in accordance with the Law, decency, and common interests based on the examination of the consequences if the information given to the public, and after carefully considering the closing of Public Information to protect the interests of greater than open or otherwise.

In this context, "the consequences" refer to the consequence that harm the interests protected by this Act if the information is disclosed. Classified information should be open or closed based on the public interest. If the larger public interest can be protected by withholding the information, the information must be kept secret or closed and/or vice versa.

Article 8

(1) *Exclusion Period Public Information when opened to reveal the contents of an authentic act of a personal nature and will last one's will or determined under the provisions of the legislation.*
(2) *Exemption Period when opened Public Information and Public Information given to the applicant to reveal personal secrets established over a period of time required for the protection of one's personal secrets.*
(3) *Public Information referred to in paragraph (1) and (2) can be opened if:*

   a. *revealed the secret party gives written consent, and/or*
   b. *disclosure relates to a person's position in the public offices in accordance with the provisions of the legislation.*

Paragraph (1)

This section explains what is meant by "the provisions of legislation" such as legislation on archives.

Paragraph (2)

The term "public information which, if opened and given to the Public Information Applicant may reveal personal secrets" includes:

1. history and condition of a family member;
2. history, condition and treatment, treatment of physical health, and psychological one;
3. financial condition, assets, income, and bank account of a person;
4. evaluation results with respect to the capability, intellect, abilities and recommendations, and/or
5. Records relating to an individual's personal unit activities related to formal and non-formal education unit.

Paragraph (3) (a)

Self-explanatory.

(1)(3) (b)

This section explains what is meant by "the provisions of legislation" such as legislation regarding the eradication of corruption and legislation on the combating corruption commission.

Relevant with the theory of justice, in the context of public information and mass communication, distributive justice would be implemented as the positive freedom for anybody in order to have access to public information as being a public good for the people. However, for private information, it should be different. Private information covered by privacy norms should be approached by the interactive justice theory. Interactive justice implements the negative freedom to anybody to respect other rights. Instead of the positive freedom protected by law, there is also a negative freedom, because every person must also have an internal awareness (virtue) to respect the rights of others. In the context of electronic communications, it must take into account the effect of mass communication on someone's privacy that has been predicted by the communicator. It is important to note that the pretext of public interest can also be misused to attack others in public spaces. In these instances, a good legal system should continue to provide equilibrium to every person to be able to recover their rights if they are violated by any person, whether by individuals, corporations, communities, and law enforcement in an arbitrary or unlawful manner.

In the context of mass communication, there is also a fallacy in the media with regard to implementing the Freedom of the Press; often, this is equated as the Legal Privilege of Journalist and Media Company to explore someone's privacy on behalf of the public right to know. However, the media should treat this as a qualified privilege; it is not an absolute privilege. Absolute privilege only works in the context of disclosure of information in the court or parliamentary session where the ultimate truth is revealed based on the evidence found. The media must respect qualified privilege, because the media is in fact never value-free or free from the influence of existing subjective values. Therefore, the media are provided with the code of ethics of high value to avoid betraying the mandate of developing of public itself to meet the right of people to know. Media power it looks like the control of authorities to the parties that perform governmental functions. Unfortunately based on the Indonesian Law No. 40/1999 on the Press, the formulation the privacy defined by Press Council from their own perspective to facilitate their legal interest.

6.3.3.1 Personal Data in Electronic Information and Transaction Act

Based on the elucidation of Article 26 UU-ITE, privacy has been defined in a wider sense, namely: (i) privacy in your body; (ii) privacy in your property; and (iii) privacy in your communication. UU-ITE provides certainty that the delivery and retrieval of personal data will have the consent from the subject of the data. Furthermore, it is also related to the prohibition regarding illegal content on secrecy in Article 32 UU-ITE with the threat of punishment in Article 48 UU-ITE. Instead of the civil suit, there is also a criminal sanction for the acquisition and disclosure of secrecy (including someone's privacy). In addition, it has a criminal weighting if those infringements are committed by a corporation.

UU-ITE

Article 26:

(1) *Unless otherwise stipulated by law and regulation, the use of any information through electronic media concerning personal data of a person must be carried out with the approval of the person concerned.*
(2) *Any person violated by his rights as referred to in paragraph (1) may file a claim for losses incurred under this Law.*
(3) *Every Electronic System Operator must delete irrelevant Electronic Information and/or Electronic Documents which are under its control at the request of the person concerned based on a court decision.*
(4) *Every Electronic System Operator must provide a mechanism for the elimination of Electronic Information and/or Electronic Documents that are not relevant in accordance with the provisions of the legislation.*
(5) *Provisions concerning procedures for the elimination of Electronic Information and/or Electronic Documents as referred to in paragraph (3) and paragraph (4) shall be regulated in government regulations.*

Article 32 UU ITE:

Any person intentionally and without right or unlawful in any way modify, add, subtract, transmitting, damaging, removing, moving, hiding an electronic information and/or electronic documents belonging to another person or public property;

In the use of Information Technology, the protection of personal data is one part of privacy rights. Personal rights contain the following meanings:

a. Personal rights are the right to enjoy personal life and are free from all kinds of interference.
b. Personal rights are the right to be able to communicate with other people without spying.
c. Personal rights are the right to monitor access to information about one's personal life and data.

The derivative regulation from Article 26 UU-ITE is Article 15 of PP-PSTE which accommodates a few principles and best practices in Personal Data Protection regulation.

PP-PSTE[4]

(1) The Electronic System Operator must:

  (a) maintain the confidentiality, integrity and availability of the Personal Data that it manages;
  (b) guarantee that the acquisition, use and utilization of Personal Data is based on the approval of the owner of Personal Data, unless otherwise stipulated by the legislation; and
  (c) guarantee the use or disclosure of data is carried out based on the approval of the owner of the Personal Data and in accordance with the objectives submitted to the owner of Personal Data at the time of data acquisition.
  (2) If a failure occurs in the confidential protection of the Personal Data that it manages, the Electronic System Operator must notify the owner of the Personal Data in writing.

Further provisions concerning the guidelines for the protection of Personal Data in the Electronic System as referred to in paragraph (2) shall be regulated in a Ministerial Regulation.

Later on, as the implementing regulation of UU- ITE and PP-PSTE, the Government c.q. the Ministry of Communication and Informatics has issued Ministry Regulation No. 20/2016 concerning the Protection of Personal Data in Electronic Systems ("Permen PDP"). This regulation had accommodated some basic principles of the Personal Data regulation. This regulation applied to the e-system operator and/or provider and does not differ any legal subject as a controller, processor, recipient, or third party. The jurisdiction of Article 2 UU-ITE also covers extra-territorial jurisdiction based on the national interest.

---

[4]The amendment of PP-PSTE by GR 71/2019 incorporates core principles of personal data protection laid down by Infocom Ministry Regulation No. 20/2016. The amendment also provides the right to erasure to personal data owners.

In summary, there are some important points from Permen PDP which were basically rooted in the approval principles:

- **Definition**: Definition of the Personal Data is certain personal data that is stored, maintained, and maintained by the truth and protected by confidentiality, and the Certain Individual Data defined as any information that is true and real that is inherent and can be identified, directly or indirectly, in each individual whose utilization is in accordance with the provisions of the legislation. The parties in this regulation are the Owners (subject data),[5] e-System Operators[6] and its Users.[7]
- **Basic policy** for processing determined by the Approval of the Owner of Personal Data. The Approval of the Owner of Personal Data, hereinafter referred to as Approval, is a written statement, both manually and/or electronically, provided by the Owner of Personal Data after obtaining a complete explanation of acquisition, collection, processing, analysis, storage, appearance, announcement, delivery and dissemination and confidentiality or confidentiality of Personal Data.
- **Scope of the Personal Data Protection in Electronic Systems** includes protection against acquisition, collection, processing, analyzing, storing, displaying, announcing, sending, disseminating, and destroying Personal Data.
- **The principle of good personal data protection**, which includes: (a) respect for Personal Data as privacy; (b) Confidential Personal Data in accordance with the Agreement and/or based on the provisions of the legislation; (c) based on Agreement; (d) relevance with the aim of acquiring, collecting, processing, analyzing, storing, displaying, announcing, sending, and disseminating; (e) Electronic system feasibility used; (f) good faith to immediately notify the Owner of Personal Data in writing of any failure to protect Personal Data; (g) availability of internal rules for managing Personal Data; (h) responsibility for Personal Data that is under User control; (i) easy access and correction of Personal Data by the Owner of Personal Data; and (j) integrity, accuracy and validity and up-to-date status of Personal Data. The Privacy is the freedom of the Owner of Personal Data to declare confidential or not to state the confidentiality of his Personal Data, unless otherwise specified in accordance with the provisions of the legislation. The Approval would be given after the Owner of Personal Data states confirmation of the truth, confidentiality status and purpose of managing Personal Data. The validity is the legality in obtaining, collecting, processing, analyzing, storing, displaying, announcing, sending, disseminating, and destroying Personal Data.

[5]Owners of Personal Data are individuals who are attached to Certain Individual Data.

[6]Definition of the Electronic System is a series of electronic devices and procedures that function to prepare, collect, process, analyze, store, display, announce, transmit, and/or disseminate electronic information. Meanwhile the definition of Electronic System Operator is any Person, state operator, Business Entity, and community that provides, manages, and/or operates Electronic Systems individually or jointly to Electronic System Users for the needs of themselves and/or other parties.

[7]Article 1(7): Users of Electronic Systems, hereinafter referred to as Users, are every Person, state organizer, Business Entity, and community that utilizes goods, services, facilities, or information provided by the Electronic System Operator.

- **Personal Data Protection in Electronic Systems is carried out in the process**: (a) acquisition and collection; (b) processing and analyzing; (c) storage; (d) appearance/viewing, announcement, delivery, dissemination and/or opening of access; and, (e) deleting/destruction.
- **Requirements**: The Electronic System used for the process personal data must be certified in accordance with the provisions of the legislation. Every Electronic System Operator must have (i) internal rules for the protection of Personal Data to carry out the process, (ii) must prepare internal rules for the protection of Personal Data as a form of preventive action to avoid failures in the protection of Personal Data that it manages. The preparation of internal rules must consider aspects of the application of technology, human resources, methods, and costs and refer to the provisions in this Ministerial Regulation and other relevant legislation. Other precautionary measures to avoid failure in the protection of Personal Data managed by each e-System Operator, at least in the form of activities: (a) increasing awareness of human resources in their environment to provide protection of Personal Data in the Electronic System they manage; and (b) conduct failure prevention training for the protection of Personal Data in the Electronic System that it manages for human resources in its environment. The e-System Operator that carries out the process must provide an approval form in the Indonesian Language to request approval from the Owner of the Personal Data in question.
- **Acquisition and Collection of Personal Data**: (i) must be limited to information that is relevant and in accordance with its objectives and must be carried out accurately; (ii) The Supervisory and Sector Supervisory Agency can determine relevant and appropriate information.
- **In obtaining and collecting Personal Data,** the e-System Operator must respect the Owner of Personal Data for the privacy of the Personal Data is carried out through the provision of options in the Electronic System for the Owner of Personal Data against: (a) confidentiality or confidentiality of Personal Data; and (b) changes, additions, or updates to Personal Data. Choice for the Owner of Personal Data on the confidentiality or confidentiality of Personal Data does not apply if the laws and regulations have expressly stated Personal Data specifically for some of its elements declared confidential. Choice for the Owner of Personal Data should have the right to make changes, additions, or renewal of Personal Data provided that an opportunity for the Owner of Personal Data if he wishes to change his Certain Personal Data.
- **The acquisition and collection of Personal Data** by the e-System Operator must be based on the Agreement or based on the provisions of the legislation. The owner of the Personal Data who gives the Agreement may declare that the specific Individual Data owned by him is confidential. In case the Agreement does not include the approval of the disclosure of the confidentiality of Personal Data then: (a) every Person who obtains and collects Personal Data; and (b) Electronic System Operator; must maintain the confidentiality of the Personal Data. Provisions to maintain the confidentiality of Personal Data for every Person and Operator of the Electronic System also applies to Personal Data declared confidential in accordance with the provisions of the legislation.

- **Personal data obtained and collected directly must be verified to the Owner of Personal Data.** Personal data obtained and collected indirectly must be verified based on the results of various data sources. Data sources in the acquisition and collection of Personal Data must have a legal basis.
- **The Electronic System used to accommodate the acquisition and collection of Personal Data must**: (a) have the ability of interoperability and compatibility; and (b) use legal software. Interoperability is the ability of different Electronic Systems to work in an integrated manner. Compatibility is the suitability of one Electronic System with another Electronic System.
- **Processing and Analyzing Personal Data**: Personal data can only be processed and analyzed according to the needs of the Electronic System Operator that has been clearly stated when obtaining and collecting it, it's carried out based on the Agreement. It does not apply if the Personal Data processed and analyzed comes from Personal Data that has been displayed or announced openly by the Electronic System for public services. Personal data that is processed and analyzed must be Personal Data that has been verified for accuracy.
- **Storage Personal data**: Personal data stored in the Electronic System must be Personal Data whose accuracy has been verified and must be in the form of encrypted data. It must be stored in the Electronic System: (a) in accordance with the provisions of the legislation governing the obligation of the period of storage of Personal Data in each Sector Supervisory and Regulating Agency; or (b) no later than 5 (five) years, if there is no provision of legislation specifically regulating it. If the Owner of Personal Data is no longer a User, the e-System Operator must keep the Personal Data within the time limit from the last date the Owner of Personal Data becomes User.
- **The Data Center** (Data Center) and Disaster Recovery Center (Electronic Recovery Center) for public services used for the protection of Personal Data must be placed in the territory of the Republic of Indonesia. The Data Center is a facility used to place Electronic Systems and their related components for the purposes of data placement, storage and processing. Disaster Recovery Center is a facility that is used to recover data or information and important functions of Electronic Systems that are disrupted or damaged by natural and/or human-caused disasters. Further provisions concerning the obligation to place Data Centers and Disaster Recovery Centers in the territory of Indonesia shall be regulated by relevant Sector Supervisory and Regulatory Agencies in accordance with the provisions of the legislation after coordinating with the Minister. Storage of Personal Data in an Electronic System must be carried out in accordance with the provisions concerning the procedures and means of securing the Electronic System. Procedures and means of securing the Electronic System must be in accordance with the provisions of the legislation. If the storage time of Personal Data has exceeded the time limit, Personal Data in the Electronic System can be written-off unless the Personal Data will still be used or utilized in accordance with the initial purpose of the acquisition and collection. If the Owner of Personal Data requests the removal of certain Individual Data, the request for removal is carried out in accordance with the provisions of the legislation.

- **Displaying (showing/viewing), Announcement, Delivery, Dissemination, and/or Opening of Personal Data Access**: Showing, announcing, sending, distributing, and/or opening access to Personal Data in an Electronic System can only be done: (a) for approval unless otherwise stipulated by the provisions of the legislation; and (b) after verification of accuracy and conformity with the purpose of obtaining and collecting the Personal Data. Displaying, announcing, sending, disseminating, and/or opening access to Personal Data in the Electronic System including those carried out between Electronic System Operators, between Electronic System Organizers and Users, or between Users. Delivery of Personal Data managed by e-System Providers to government agencies and regional governments as well as the public or private domiciled in the territory of the Republic of Indonesia, outside the territory of the Republic of Indonesia must: (a) coordinate with the Minister or officials/institutions that are authorized to do so; and (b) apply statutory provisions concerning the exchange of Personal Data across national borders. The coordination is in the form of: (a) report on the implementation plan for sending Personal Data, at least containing the clear name of the destination country, the clear name of the recipient's subject, the date of implementation, and the reason/purpose of delivery; (b) ask for advocacy, if needed; and (c) report the results of the implementation of activities. For the purposes of the law enforcement process, the Electronic System Operator must provide Personal Data contained in the Electronic System or Personal Data produced by the Electronic System at the legitimate request of law enforcement officers based on the provisions of the legislation. Personal Data should be relevant and in accordance with the needs of law enforcement. The usage and utilization of Personal Data displayed, announced, accepted and distributed by the Electronic System Operator must be based on the Agreement that must be in accordance with the objectives of obtaining, collecting, processing and/or analyzing the Personal Data.
- **Destruction of Personal Data**: Destruction of Personal Data in an Electronic System can only be done: (a) if the provisions for the period of storage of Personal Data in the Electronic System based on this Ministerial Regulation or in accordance with the provisions of other laws and regulations which specifically regulate each Sector Supervisory and Regulating Agency for that have expired; or (b) at the request of the Owner of Personal Data, unless otherwise determined by the provisions of the legislation. The Destruction must eliminate some or all of the documents related to Personal Data, including electronic or non-electronic ones that are managed by Electronic System Operators and/or Users so that the Personal Data cannot be displayed again in Electronic Systems except Data Owners Personally provides new personal data. The removal of some or all of the files shall be carried out based on the Agreement or in accordance with the provisions of other laws and regulations which specifically regulate each sector for that.
- **Personal data owners' rights**: Owner of Personal Data has the right: (a) for the confidentiality of his Personal Data; (b) submit a complaint in order to resolve the Personal Data dispute over the failure of the protection of the confidentiality of his Personal Data by the Electronic System Operator to the Minister; (c) get access or opportunity to change or update their Personal Data without disturbing

the Personal Data management system, unless otherwise determined by the provisions of the legislation; (d) get access or opportunity to obtain historical Personal Data that has been submitted to the Electronic System Operator as long as it is in accordance with the provisions of the legislation; and (e) request the destruction of Specific Individual Data owned in Electronic Systems managed by Electronic System Operators, unless otherwise determined by the provisions of the legislation.

- **User liability**: Mandatory users: (a) maintain the confidentiality of Personal Data obtained, collected, processed and analyzed; (b) use Personal Data according to the user's needs only; (c) protect Personal Data along with documents containing the Personal Data from acts of abuse; and (d) are responsible for the Personal Data contained in its control, both in the control of the organization that is its authority and individually, if there is an act of abuse.
- **Obligation of electronic system providers**: Each Electronic System Operator must: (a) certify the Electronic System that it manages in accordance with the provisions of the legislation; (b) maintain the truth, validity, confidentiality, accuracy and relevance as well as conformity with the purpose of obtaining, collecting, processing, analyzing, storing, displaying, announcing, sending, disseminating, and destroying Personal Data; (c) notify the Owner of Personal Data in writing if there is a failure of confidential protection of Personal Data in the Electronic System under its management, with the following notification: (i) must be accompanied by reasons or causes of failure of confidential protection of Personal Data; (ii) can be done electronically if the Personal Data Owner has given an Agreement for that stated at the time of obtaining and collecting his Personal Data; (iii) must be ascertained to have been received by the Owner of Personal Data if the failure contains a potential loss for the person concerned; and (iv) written notification is sent to the Owner of Personal Data no later than 14 (fourteen) days after the failure is known; (d) have internal rules related to the protection of Personal Data in accordance with the provisions of the legislation; (e) provide an audit track record of all the activities of the Electronic System that it manages; (f) provide options to the Owner of Personal Data regarding the Personal Data that he manages can/or cannot be used and/or displayed by/to third parties for the Agreement as long as it is related to the purpose of obtaining and collecting Personal Data; (g) provide access or opportunity to the Owner of Personal Data to change or update his or her Personal Data without disturbing the Personal Data management system, unless otherwise specified by the provisions of the legislation; (h) destroying Personal Data in accordance with the provisions in this Ministerial Regulation or other provisions of legislation that specifically regulate each Sector Supervisory and Regulating Agency for that; and (i) provide a contact person who is easily contacted by the Owner of Personal Data regarding the management of his or her Personal Data.
- **Dispute resolution**: Every Owner of Personal Data and Electronic System Operator can submit a complaint to the Minister for failure of privacy protection of Personal Data. Complaints are intended as an effort to resolve disputes in consultation or through other alternative solutions. Complaints shall be made based on

reasons: (a) no written notification of failure of confidential protection of Personal Data by the Operator of Electronic Systems to the Owner of Personal Data or other Electronic System Operator related to the Personal Data, whether potential or not potentially causing losses; or (b) there has been a loss for the Owner of Personal Data or other Electronic System Operator related to the failure of the confidential protection of the Personal Data, even though written notification has been made for the failure of confidential Personal Data protection but the late notification time. The Minister can coordinate with the leaders of the Supervisory and Sector Regulatory Agencies to follow up on complaints. The Minister delegates the authority to resolve the Personal Data to the Director General. The Director General may form a Personal Data dispute settlement panel. Complaints and handling of complaints are based on the following procedures: (a) a complaint is made no later than 30 (thirty) working days after the complainant knows the information; (b) the complaint is submitted in writing containing: (i) name and address of the complainant; (ii) reasons or basis of complaints; (iii) the request for resolution of the problem being complained; and (iv) the place of complaint, the time of submission of the complaint, and the signature of the complainant; (c) complaints must be accompanied by supporting evidence; (d) officials/Personal Data dispute resolution team for failure of confidentiality protection of Personal Data must respond to complaints no later than 14 (fourteen) working days after the complaint is received which at least contains a complete or incomplete complaint; (e) incomplete complaints must be completed by the complainant no later than 30 (thirty) working days after the complainant receives the response as referred to in letter d and if it exceeds the time limit, the complaint is deemed cancelled; (f) Personal Data official/institution for dispute resolution for failure of confidentiality protection of Personal Data must handle settlement of complaints starting 14 (fourteen) working days after the complaint is received completely; (g) settlement of disputes on the basis of complete complaints is carried out in consultation or through other alternative solutions in accordance with the provisions of the legislation; and (h) Personal Data dispute officials/institutions for failure of confidentiality protection of Personal Data that handles complaints can provide recommendations to the Minister for administrative sanctions for Electronic System Administrators even though complaints can or cannot be resolved through deliberation or through other alternative solutions.

If an effort to resolve disputes by deliberation or through other alternative resolution efforts have not been able to resolve the dispute over the failure of privacy protection of Personal Data, each Owner of Personal Data and Electronic System Operator may file a lawsuit over the failure of confidential protection of Personal Data. The lawsuit is only in the form of a civil claim and is filed in accordance with the provisions of the legislation. If in the process of law enforcement by law enforcement officers in accordance with the provisions of the legislation that has the authority to make confiscation, then only the Personal Data related to a legal case can be confiscated without having to confiscate the entire Electronic System. Electronic System Providers who provide, store and/or manage confiscated Personal Data are prohibited from taking any action that may result in changes or loss of the Personal Data and still be required to maintain security or provide confidential Personal Data protection in the Electronic System that it manages.

- **Government and community role**: To facilitate the implementation of Personal Data protection in the Electronic System and to empower community participation, the Director General educates the public regarding: (a) understanding of Personal Data; (b) the nature of privacy data; (c) understanding of the Agreement and its consequences; (d) understanding of the Electronic System and its mechanism; (e) the right of the Owner of Personal Data, User obligations, and obligations of the Electronic System Operator; (f) provisions concerning the settlement of disputes in the event of a failure of confidential protection of Personal Data by the Electronic System Operator; and (g) other provisions of legislation related to the protection of Personal Data in Electronic Systems. The community can participate in the implementation of education. It can be done through education and/or training, advocacy, technical guidance, and socialization using various media.
- **Supervision**: Supervision of the implementation of this Ministerial Regulation is carried out by the Minister and/or the head of the Sector Inspection and Regulatory Authority. Supervision carried out by the Minister as referred to in paragraph (1) includes direct or indirect supervision. (2) The Minister has the authority to request data and information from the Electronic System Operator in the context of protecting Personal Data. (3) Requests for data and information can be carried out periodically or at any time if necessary. The Minister delegates the authority of supervision to the Director General.
- **Administrative sanctions:** Everyone who obtains, collects, processes, analyzes, stores, displays, announces, sends, and/or disseminates Personal Data without rights or does not comply with the provisions in this Ministerial Regulation or other statutory regulations subject to administrative sanctions in accordance with provisions of legislation in the form of: (a) verbal warning; (b) written warning; (c) temporary suspension of activities; and/or (d) announcements on sites on the network (online website). (2) Provisions concerning the procedure for implementing administrative sanctions shall be regulated by a Ministerial Regulation. The Administrative sanctions are given by the minister or the head of the relevant sector supervisory and regulatory agencies in accordance with the provisions of the legislation. The Imposition of sanctions by the leaders of the relevant sector supervisory and regulatory agencies is carried out after coordinating with the Minister.
- **Other provisions:** If the Owner of Personal Data is a person who belongs to the category of children in accordance with the provisions of the legislation, the granting of the Agreement referred to in this Ministerial Regulation is carried out by the parent or guardian of the child concerned. Parents are the biological father or mother of the child concerned in accordance with the provisions of the legislation. The guardian is a person who has the obligation to take care of the child concerned before the child is adult in accordance with the provisions of the legislation.

- **Transitional provisions:** Electronic System Providers who have provided, stored and managed Personal Data before this Ministerial Regulation applies must maintain the confidentiality of Personal Data they manage and adjust to this Ministerial Regulation no later than 2 (two) years.

The implementation agency is the Ministry which delegated the following two tasks to the Directorate General: supervising the implementation of this Regulation; and facilitating the Alternative Dispute Resolution by creating a panel to do that.

It should be noted that according to Permen PDP, an electronic system that can be used in the process of protecting personal data should be certified and have internal rules regarding the protection of personal data that must pay attention to aspects of the application of technology, human resources, methods, and costs. This regulation indirectly requires a data protection officer for each e-system operator to implement this regulation and have a function as a contact point to the Ministry. When compared to the GDPR, one important point not yet covered in this regulation is the Right to Data Portability which has the potential to contradict/conflict with the *Citizen Administration Act* that implements the Information System of Citizen Administration (Sistem Informasi Administrasi Kependudukan/"SIAK") with their National e-ID Card (KTP-el) according to their sectoral laws and regulation.

6.3.3.2 Privacy as a Right of the Consumer

Subject to Article 4 of the Consumer Law, any subject of data that becomes the user of the electronic system shall be protected by their rights as a Customer in its electronic and non-electronic transaction, specifically:

(i) the right to comfort, safety, and safety in consuming goods and/or services;
(ii) the right to choose goods and/or services and obtain the goods and/or services in accordance with the exchange rates and the conditions and promised warranties; and
(iii) the right to true, clear, and truthful information about the condition and guarantee of goods and/or services.

In fact, by using electronic systems and electronic transactions, consumers not only have paid the price of goods and/or services used, but they have also provided identity and personal data to the e-System Provider. However, in fact, the value is not yet counted in the transacted exchange rate. Therefore, consumers should obtain correct, clear, and honest information about the conditions and guarantees as stated in the Privacy Statement presented by the e-System Operator. Pursuant to Article 7 of the Consumer Law, Business Actors are obliged to: (i) provide true, clear, and honest information regarding the conditions and warranties of goods and/or services and provide explanations of use, repair, and maintenance; (ii) guarantee the quality of goods and/or services produced and/or traded under the provisions of the applicable quality standards of goods and/or services; and (iii) compensate, indemnify, and/or reimburse consumers for losses arising from the use, use and use of traded goods and/or services; In addition, pursuant to Article 15 of the Consumer Law, Business Parties are also prohibited from using coercion or other means to offer goods and/or services that may cause both physical and psychological disturbance to the psyches of consumers. Thus, the Business Actor has an obligation not to compel or to manipulate the consumer. As the owner of personal data, every consumer may request the Business Actor as Data Controller to remove the consumer's personal data as well the Business Owner's right to the data, in order to guarantee the security of the consumer's personal data usage accordingly.

Consumer Protection Act[8]

Article 4: Consumer rights are:

1. the right to comfort, security and safety in consuming goods and/or services;
2. the right to choose goods and/or services and get the goods and/or services in accordance with the exchange rate and the conditions and guarantees promised;
3. the right to correct, clear and honest information regarding the condition and guarantee of goods and/or services;
4. the right to hear opinions and complaints about the goods and/or services used;
5. the right to get proper advocacy, protection and efforts to resolve consumer protection disputes;
6. the right to get consumer guidance and education;
7. download rights are treated or served correctly and honestly and are not discriminatory;
8. the right to get compensation, compensation and/or replacement, if the goods and/or services received are not in accordance with the agreement or not as they should be;
9. rights regulated in other statutory provisions.

[8]Consumer protection is also governed by GR 80/2019 on E-Commerce. The regulation expressly stated the treatment of personal data as ownership rights (art. 58). It contains the obligation of e-commerce business to store personal data in accordance with the 'standard of personal data protection' or 'developing ordinary business practice' to the extent these standards and practices conform with the principles laid down under art. 59. The principles of personal data protection under art. 59(2) are as follows: a) legitimate collection; b) purpose limitation; c) data adequacy and relevancy (elaboration of purpose limitation); d) accuracy; e) temporal limitation; f) lawfulness; g) confidentiality, security, and integrity; h) no cross-border personal data transfer shall be made unless the target country declared has an adequate level of protection by the Minister. The relationship between the GR 71/2019 and GR 80/2019 is unique. Although the two regulations are within the same level of the regulatory hierarchy, GR 80/2019 only regulates the e-commerce sector, whereas GR 71/2019 is applicable for all e-system operators. Therefore, GR 80/2019 is only applicable as *lex specialis* for the e-commerce sector. Consequently, the e-commerce sector shall secure compliance with both regulations. The supervisory authority for GR 80/2019 is the Minister of Trade. Thus enforcement and sanction of personal data violation under this regulation are administered by the Trade Ministry. These non-compliance measures include warning, priority watchlist, blacklist, temporary service blockage, or revocation of permit (art. 80(2)).

Article 15

Business actors in offering goods and/or services are prohibited from using coercion or other means that can cause physical and psychological disturbances to consumers.

Article 62: Threat of violation ⇒ imprisonment for a maximum of 5 years or a fine of 2 billion rupiahs.

6.3.3.3 Personal Data in the *Citizen Administration Act*

In the context of the *Citizen Administration Act*, UU-Adminduk:

- Article 1 number (22): Personal Data is defined as certain personal data which is stored, maintained, and kept true; as well, its confidentiality is protected. Article 84 paragraph (1) states that the Personal Data of Population to be protected contains: (a) description of physical and/or mental disabilities; (b) fingerprint; (c) iris eyes; (d) signature; and (e) other data elements that are a person's disgrace.
- Article 2: Every Resident has the right to: (c) obtain protection of Personal Data; (d) legal certainty over ownership of documents; (e) information concerning data on the results of the Population Registry and the Civil Registry of her and/or her family; and (f) redress and restitution as a result of errors in the Registration of Population and Civil Registration as well as the misuse of Personal Data by the Implementing Agencies (municipal government).

However, based on Article 87, Users of Personal Data from Residents (both public and private bodies) can obtain and use Personal Data from officers at Organizers and Implementers who have access rights. This shows that the Government acts alone in the delivery of personal data to private parties without the approval of the Data Subject. In the context of identity, the government applies an electronic ID card (KTP-el), which is a Citizenship Card with a chip that is the official identity of the population as a proof of self-issued by the Implementing Agency. Each resident shall have a permanent and long-life Citizen Identity Number (Nomor Induk Kependudukan/"NIK") granted by the Government and issued by the Implementing Authority to each resident after the registration of the personal data (Article 13). Unfortunately, the syntax of number can be predicted easily because it represents the consequential of the government administration code. Therefore, it could be classified to the lower level in expectation to privacy.

Based on the *Citizen Administration Act*, the Indonesian government (Ministry of Home Affairs) implements the single credential policy. NIK should act as a prerequisite to the other citizen documents. The Citizen Document, KTP-el, shall be used as the basis of issuance for other public documents such as passport, driver's license, taxpayer's principal number, insurance policy, land title certificate, and issuance of other identity documents. Every Indonesian citizen and foreigner who has a permanent residence, 17 years old whether married or married, shall have a National e-ID card (Article 63 of the Law on Adminduk). The National e-ID card or Indonesia

Citizen Card called in abbreviation as Kartu Tanda Penduduk Elektronik ("KTP-el"). This card is embedded with RFID chips containing electronic records of the personal data (Article 64 paragraph (6)). As described in the general explanation of the revision of the UU Adminduk with regard to the application of ID cards, every resident can have only one National ID card; previously, it was possible for residents to have more than one such card because the Information System of the Citizen Administration (Sistem Administrasi Kependudukan) was not centralized. The KTP-el has loaded the security code and the e-recording of the residents' personal data, including: some attribute data (such as NIK, address, blood group, citizenship, religion, marital status); and some biometric data (such as iris eyes, signature, and fingerprints).

After the revision of the UU-Adminduk, the period of validity of the applicable 5 (five) year ID cards is now a lifetime, insofar as there is no change in the elements of the Population data and the changing of the resident's domicile (Article 64 paragraph (4)). This needs to be done in order to allow the smooth operation of the public service in various sectors either by government or private sector and also to obtain information on the financial savings of the country every 5 (five) years. In line with the establishment of the demographic database, Adminduk Law is expected to clarify the regulation of access rights for the use of Population Data either for officers at the Operator, Implementing Agency, and User. The term "users" includes state institutions, ministries/non-ministerial government institutions, and/or Indonesian legal entities (explanation section 79 paragraph (2)).

According to Article 64 of the Adminduk Law, it can be said that Indonesia is implementing a centralized model in which all other identity and/or identity documents must refer to the existence of the Identity Number (NIK) as a Single Identity Number valid as an official identity for access to all public services. To carry out all public services, the Government will integrate existing identity numbers and be used for public services no later than 5 (five) years after the ratification of the Act. The KTP-el function is to be stepped up gradually into a multipurpose KTP into which individual data is loaded in the chip, thereby adapting it to the stated needs (explanation of Paragraph (6)). In practice, however, the multipurpose KTP cannot be used at this time; this is because the KTP could not be equipped with Digital Signatures and Digital Certificates as planned, due to the space in the chip being relatively small.

6.4 Comparative Study of the European GDPR with the Indonesian Legal System

As mentioned above, the GDPR and the Indonesian system have some similarities, but are not fully identical.

GDPR

1. General Provisions
2. Principles

3. Rights of The Data Subject
4. Controller and Processor
5. Transfer of Personal Data to Third Countries or International Organizations
6. Independent Supervisory Authorities
7. Co-Operation and Consistency
8. Remedies, Liability and Penalties
9. Provisions Relating to Specific Processing Situations
10. Delegated Acts and Implementing Acts
11. Final Provisions

Indonesian

1. General Provision
2. Protection
3. Rights of Personal Data Owners
4. Obligation of Users
5. Obligations of Electronic System Providers
6. Dispute Settlement
7. Government and Community Role
8. Supervision
9. Administrative Sanctions
10. Other Provisions
11. Transitional Provisions
12. Closing Provisions

Bill of Personal Data Protection (RUU-PDP)

1. General Provisions
2. Types of Personal Data
3. Processing of Personal Data
4. Rights of Personal Data Owners
5. Control and Personal Data Processing
6. Personal Data Transfer
7. Direct Marketing
8. Formation of Personal Data Control Guidelines
9. Participation of The Community
10. Commission
11. Dispute Settlement
12. Criminal Provisions
13. Transitional Provisions
14. Closing Provisions

When compared to the GDPR, Indonesia has some unique legal provisions, as follows:

- Regarding the Material Scope and Territorial Scope, based on article 2 UU-ITE, the Indonesian regulation is extraterritorial jurisdiction.

- Indonesia defines the legal subject as Owner of Personal Data (Data Subject), e-System Operator and User (Controller and Processor).
- Regarding the Principles, Indonesia had already adopted the principles of the European GDPR, but with different legal provisions.
- Regarding the Right to Erasure, Indonesia does not implement the principles "without undue delay," but makes the Data Subject ask the court to approve the deletion order to the operator.
- Regarding the Right to Data Portability, Indonesia does not have a particular provision concerning Data Portability but does have a regulation.

6.5 Prominent Issues Regarding Personal Data Protection and Online Digital Identity in Indonesia

Based on the presentation and the ideas mentioned above, the effort to have a special law for comprehensive Personal Data Protection is still in progress, but its development has been affected by the country's political situation. Therefore, the first thing that should be done is optimizing, synchronizing, and harmonizing the existing legal conditions. To provide redress for the losses suffered by each owner of the data, sufficient instruments are needed to allow a modest recovery. In addition, alternative dispute resolution for personal data infringement would be more useful than the civil action, administrative sanctions, or criminal sanctions for some violations of Privacy and Personal Data in Indonesia.

In practice, there are many cases regarding the personal data infringement, such as Spamming, Interception, and Misuse of personal data of the Operator (Controller and Processor) that could not be solved until now. Even though the Facebook and Cambridge Analytical cases also received public attention, this issue was not solved properly and the public received no explanation of the case details and how a settlement in the public interest would require that Facebook be made accountable and subject to administrative sanctions. There is no information regarding the panel or the administration sanctions from the Ministry based on Permen PDP.

6.5.1 Spamming or Commercial Promotion

Almost daily, every user receives a commercial promotion of business from e-System Operators/Providers. The issue of credit theft by operators began some time ago and resulted in many protests from consumer protection agencies. Unfortunately, however, the rules of the Indonesian Telecommunications Regulatory Body ("BRTI") are more in favor of the telecommunications industry; as a result, they are more focused on non-detrimental implementation through the use of pulses and the provision of ways to exit the system (unsubscribe). This is the case despite the lack of a mechanism that would allow operators to send commercial information to their customers without approval. Generally, they have renewed their standard usage contracts by giving a check on the agreement on the use of services to customers.

Meanwhile, the handling of complaints against the spamming problem is still an ongoing effort, despite the fact that this problem is relatively easy to resolve, namely by implementing PP-PSTE on telecommunications networks and telecommunications services in Indonesia. Spamming happens because the operator is negligent in registering and administering tasks for the application of behavior and airworthiness that are used together with the Content Provider Operator. The problem can be clearly seen when there are consumer complaints. Consumers file personal and class actions against unlawful acts committed, and request the judge to issue a temporary decision to suspend temporary services and confiscate an application system used to clarify the extent to which employers' promises to consumers in ongoing electronic system are fulfilled. This issue will be resolved immediately when the judge gives a verdict and gives a claim for full material and immaterial compensation submitted. Only then will a misbehaving businessperson think twice about doing mischief that has seemed understandable because of our customers' permissive culture.

6.5.2 *Regarding the Right to Erasure Versus Freedom of the Press*

A debate among the media about the planned revision of the ITE Law contributed to the development of a new right in the regulation on Personal Data, namely the right to ask for removal (better known as the "Right to be Forgotten"). The media assume that it will be contrary to the freedom of the press to preach someone. In order to accommodate these aspirations, the government and the House of Representatives finally decided that the Data Deletion Request must accompany an application to the court. However, this is clearly not in accordance with the principle of protecting personal data, because it should be done immediately and without delay (without undue delay) unless there is a valid reason. As a result, business people are very happy because this complex, costly, and lengthy process enables them to continue to have the right to store and use the personal data which is still relevant to their business affairs. However, for the data owner, the process required to ask for deletion takes time and entails costs.[9]

[9]GR 71/2019 specifies two different rights, these are the right to erasure and the right to delisting. The right to erasure is only granted should: a) the data have been obtained without consent; b) the consent have been revoked; c) the data have been unlawfully obtained; d) the data obtained no longer be relevant to the initial purpose; e) the data stored has exceeded the retention period; f) disclosure of data by the e-system operator that injured the personal data owners. In contrast, the exercise of the right to delisting from the search engine requires a court decree.

6.5.3 Personal Data Protection Versus Citizen Administration

One of the contradictions that might arise in the protection of personal data is the enactment of the Adminduk Law which gives absolute power to the Ministry of Internal Affairs over the personal data that it controls. Although it can be said that the management of personal data in the Population Administration System does not adhere to the principles of good personal data protection, the Ministry has the power to do so under the pretext of *lex specialis*.

6.5.4 Authentication of GSM Card Number on Population Data

The Public objected when the government imposed mandatory GSM card registration for cell phones. The registration system for GSM SIM-Card cards uses an authentication system to the Population Administration Information System ("SIAK") through the Operator System. Each customer is required to register by sending an SMS containing the National ID Number ("NIK") and the Family Card Number ("KK") to a specific Number 4444. The community then becomes restless and feels it is too excessive because the government—via the Operator—confirms whether the NIK is in accordance with the KK Number, resulting in the Operator also obtaining the KK number. While the information related to the KK number is NIK and the names of family members of that person. On the other hand, updating the data in SIAK is not always well maintained; as a result, someone who has purchased the card cannot use it even though the error occurred because there was no data update on SIAK.

The public was also worried when it was discovered that personal information was available on the Internet; this happened because registering a cell phone number required the provision of a person's identity. The government avoided taking the blame because it happened not because of the data leakage on the SIAK system. The government explained that SIAK only confirmed but did not provide any data to the operator. This happened precisely because of the mistakes of the people themselves and the existence of irresponsible parties using the situation and asking the police to investigate the matter. Under the pretext of fighting terrorism, the government has retained its policies and rules.

6.5.5 Searching for Someone's Financial Information in the Context of Tax Search Interests

Recently, in line with Tax Amnesty regulations, the government issued a regulation concerning the authority given to tax officers to conduct information tracing of people for tax purposes. Along with this, the tax director general is developing a new electronic identity system (Kartin1) in addition to the Tax ID number ("NPWP") which is expected to be a platform for the use of other identities. The government argued that it was forced to develop these tools because the data in SIAK and e-KTP turned out to be out of sync with the NPWP data.

Although the community is actually quite worried about this, it cannot do much because they do not know how far it works technically. Under the pretext of overseeing the public's obligation to pay taxes and the government's need to prevent money laundering and terrorism funding, the government retains its policies and rules.

6.5.6 Fintech Misuse of Contact Number for Harassment Because of Bad Debt

Recently, there was a case of misuse of registered mobile contact data by FinTech organizers who charged someone's debt payment obligations to their friends.[10] Using information provided on individuals' loan applications to the application store, the FinTech organizers are interested in the right to be able to access the applicants' contact data; however, these applicants do not know that they will be treated like that, with their information being used in this manner. Recorded in January 2018 to June 2018, it is a consumer complaint against peer-to-peer landing technology financial institutions (FinTech) with the initial name RP. This RP offers the convenience of online loans for users by accessing applications that have been downloaded and activated in the user's mobile. This includes company requests, access permits, short messages, and telephone records to the user's phone camera that must be installed. Problems arise when the user cannot return or repay the loan on time. When this happens, RP contacts users and threatens them if they cannot repay the owed money. Then other users will be charged a very high interest, and RP will contact all contacts on the user's cellphone to inform them that the user is in debt and has not paid what is owed. This case is still in the news and it is not known if the aggrieved party has taken RP/Fintech to court.

This action not only violates consumer protection, but also disrupts the privacy of other people who are not related to the loan. RP indicated violating the rules, namely: (i) UU ITE article 26 concerning personal data, Articles 27 to 26; (ii) Financial Services Authority Regulation ("OJK") Number 1 of 2013 concerning Protection of Financial Services Consumer Data; and (iii) Ministerial Regulation of Communication and Informatics Technology Number 20 of 2016 concerning the protection of personal data in electronic systems. The OJK regulation stated that when Financial Service Providers uses the data and/or information to carry out their activities, Financial Service Providers must have a written statement that the other party has obtained written approval from someone and/or a group of people to provide this data. So it can be said that the company has collected debt illegally against people or parties that have absolutely no connection to the debt.

[10] Agustinus 2018.

Currently, OJK limits (but does not forbid completely) the access of customers' personal digital data to FinTech lending or online loans, especially as there are no Indonesian laws that specifically regulate the protection of personal data with strict sanctions. Under the OJK's limits, FinTech is only able to access data on three features—the camera, the microphone, and the location—in the borrower's device. These limits will remain in place until the emergence of personal data protection laws. Unfortunately, this arrangement only applies to legal FinTech lending companies; many illegal FinTech companies continue to freely access the user's personal data.

All of the aforementioned cases show that despite the regulation of PDP, it seems that the Minister has not implemented and enforced it properly. Currently, officials are still making improvements to the Ministry's organizational structure. Based on the new Ministerial Regulation, there will be one directorate to supervise the governance of personal data protection under the Directorate General of Informatics Applications ("APTIKA"). After completing the reorganization of the Organization and Work Procedure, the Ministry may soon implement the provisions of the PDP Regulation.

Based on the presentation and ideas mentioned above, the effort to have a special law for comprehensive Personal Data Protection is still underway, but it will depend on the political situation; as a result, such a law might not be developed in the coming years. Therefore, the focus and effort should first be put on optimizing, synchronizing, and harmonizing the existing legal conditions. Redress for the loss is owned by each owner of the data; it can be said to have enough modest recovery instruments. In addition, it would be useful to have alternative dispute resolution for personal data infringement instead of the civil action, administrative sanctions for criminal violations of privacy and personal data in Indonesia.

On the other hand, the criticisms being made by people, business, and media do not highlight to what extent the government has implemented Permen PDP in the business sector. Ironically, although the government's ambition is to promote and boost the digital economy by promoting e-commerce, it actually needs to clarify the implementation of personal data protection in e-IDAS in Indonesia and ASEAN. It should be noted that implementing the highest level of standard protection would be a barrier to regional e-commerce, but the lower-level standard would also be dangerous to the security of e-transaction.

6.6 Implication of GDPR Implementation for Indonesia

Regarding the influence of the GDPR to Indonesia, there are at least two important points: the Right to Erase; and the Right to Portability in the e-system provider. Indonesia has also revised the Law No. 11 of 2008 on Information and Electronic Transactions into Law No. 19 Years 2016 which contains the Right to be Forgotten; unfortunately, however, it does not yet have provisions on the Right to Portability. As one of the big users of data to the public, Indonesia needs to review its legal provisions on: the interoperability of the e-identity (e-ID) and the e-Authentication System in Indonesia; and its duties and responsibilities with regard to the protection of such personal data. Therefore, legal research is required to clarify the legal framework associated with e-Identification and Authentication systems (e-IDAS) that use the online digital identities and its personal data of Indonesian citizens. Compared to European Regulation 910/2014 on e-IDAS, the provisions of Indonesia's law on personal data and online identity are still relatively underdeveloped. Currently, these provisions are spread over various laws and regulations; reform is needed to facilitate cross-border electronic transactions, especially in the ASEAN Economic Community.

In the past decades, both regionally and globally, the issue of cyber security in e-commerce cannot be separated from the legal issues of privacy and personal data protection in an electronic transaction, not only for commercial activities but also for accessing public services. Many countries realize the urgency of the need to protect their citizens' personal data and to recognize this data as invaluable national assets; this includes the right of citizens to be aware of not being exploited or being the object of profiling by others. For the sake of global e-commerce, the e-transaction process needs an interoperability of the various e-identity systems in the market as well as guarantees of personal data protection compliance.

Related to the interoperability of the identity system, the GDPR explicitly provides for the clarity of the rights of everyone (subject data) against any use of their personal data. This includes: (i) the right to be informed; (ii) the right to access; (iii) the right to verify; (iv) the right to data portability; (v) the right to object; and (vi) rights in relation to automated decision making and profiling. [The term "profiling" means any form of automated processing of personal data relating to a natural person, in particular to analyze or predict aspects of natural personality at work, economic situation, health, personal preferences, interests, reliability, behaviour, location, or movements.]

Furthermore, in the Guidelines on the Right to Data Portability made by the Working Party of the Article 29 Data Protection, they are concerned with several important elements, namely: (i) the right to obtain data; (ii) the right to transmit personal data; and (iii) means of data portability and controllership. They describe the terms of applying the right to portability, namely: (i) such personal data must be processed automatically; (ii) personal data shall be subject to the data subject and on the basis of consent; and (iii) not prejudicing the rights and freedoms of third parties or the relying party. In the case of obtaining data, any subject of data which has provided data to the providers of electronic systems shall have the right to obtain electronic data that is commonly used to access the system of others in a machine-readable format. Technically, the "commonly used" is in the form of Application Programming Interface (API) as a set of subroutine definitions, protocols, and tools for building software and applications. It refers to the interfaces of applications or web services made available by data controllers, so that other systems or applications can link and work with their systems. Furthermore, after the data is obtained, the subject of data then can use it by transmitting data directly to other parties or transmitting it directly from one system to another system "without hindrance." It also provides empowerment to the subject of data as consumers to be unlocked (lock-in) to the company. On the other hand, the policy also encourages the growth of service industries to facilitate mediation for it.

Based on the Working Group Report, on the technical level, the interoperability of the data will pay attention to several conditions, namely:

- **First condition**: personal data concerning the data subject: Only personal data is in scope of a data portability request. Therefore, any data which is anonymous or does not concern the data subject will not be in scope.
- **Second condition**: data provided by the data subject: Data actively and knowingly provided by the data subject is included in the scope of the right to data portability (for example, mailing address, user name, age). Observed data are "provided" by the data subject by virtue of the use of the service or the device. For example, they may include a person's search history, data traffic, and location data as well as other data such as heartbeats tracked by fitness or health trackers. In contrast, inferred data and derived data provided by the data subject do not fall within the scope of the right to data portability. In general, given the policy objectives of the right to data portability, the terms "provided by data subject" must be interpreted broadly, excluding only a service provider's "inferred data" and "derived data" (for example, algorithmic results).
- **Third condition**: The third condition is designed to avoid retrieval and transmission of data containing the personal data of other (non-consenting) data subjects to a new data control (Article 20 (4) of the GDPR). Such an adverse effect would occur, for example, if the transmission of data from one data controller to another, under the right to data portability, would prevent third parties from exercising their rights as data subjects under the GDPR (such as the right to information, access, etc.). The data subject initiating the transmission of his or her data to another data controller, must either consent to the new data controller for processing or enter into a contract with them. Where the data is set, another ground for unlawful processing must be identified. For example, a legitimate interest under Article 6(1) (f) may be pursued by the data controller to whom the data is transmitted, in particular when the subject of the data controller is to provide a service to the data subject that allows the latter to process personal data for a purely personal or household activity.

The existence of the rights to data portability and data deletion makes it mandatory for the provider to inform prior (informed) owners of the data on how they perform the obligation. Basically, they must act quickly (without undue delay), should give a response, and answer the Data Subject's request for the right of data portability. Conversely, there are opposing views regarding the right to be forgotten and the right to data portability. Entrepreneurs of freedom of rights believe that the Right to Be Forgotten contradicts the Freedom of the Press because it is counterproductive to the right to convey news about a person. Similarly, with regard to the Right to Data Portability, some business actors in the United States believe that it will conflict with a conducive competition climate, especially as it relates to the commercial value of customer data protected with Intellectual Property Rights as company secrets.

In 2016–2017, UNCITRAL also established a Working Group to discuss the Legal Issues of Digital Identity and Trust Services. As reported in March 2017, the Working Group states that, in general, the legal principles in ID Management and Trust services are: (i) Party Autonomy; (ii) technological neutrality; (iii) functional equivalence; and (iv) non-discrimination. It is further agreed that the Identification process requires several steps, namely: (a) verification of the validity and accuracy of the identity document; (b) verification of whether the person presenting the document was the person identified in that document; and (c) correctness of the steps undertaken and judgment used in identifying the person. It is realized that the use of ID-Management does not by itself answer the threat of forgery, hacking, and good faith guarantee of the relying party. The Working Group recognizes that the determinants are Level of Assurances and Risk Management as well as transparency mechanisms in the use of personal data of such identity that must accord with its objectives and become a determinant of interoperability between ID Management. They have not succeeded in furthering the 2017 research, and agree to explore further in the next year's session.

It is important to note that in the interest of the Cross Border issue, the Working Group is not authorized to determine its technical standards; rather, it is tasked to focus only on its policy aspect. Given that interactions between countries continue to rely on paper-based identities, the existence of Digital Identity should meet the functional equivalence requirement so that it can be equated with written evidence. References are also made to the Intra-ASEAN Secure Transaction Framework, applicable to the public and private sectors based on ISO 29115 standards. It is explained that the objective of non-regulatory schemes in ASEAN is to promote legal recognition of identification and authentication across ASEAN countries. But there are many challenges to be faced in this regard, and UNCITRAL is a good place to deal with these challenges by developing harmonization of provisions for global consensus. The UNCITRAL expert team on ID-Management and trust services does not impose specific solutions on the commercial side; rather, it provides a set of options to meet the needs of risk management. Commercial parties should be free to link various securities to different levels of assurance. However, it is important to note that the value of ensuring a common understanding of identity affirmation in the ID-Management scheme against a set of trust levels should not be questioned. Thus, the availability of a common frame of reference in which the ID-Management system can be mapped is considered essential for international trade.

Looking closely at the dynamics, it is clear that the global legal trend towards Identity Management, particularly in the use of identification and authenticity systems, appears to lead to an open system policy; however, relatively high levels of security must be maintained. Mutual Recognition is based on the principle of registration and examination of the level of security quality. In the interoperability of e-IDAS systems, it is done with legal compliance with Personal Data Protection, especially regarding the existence of the Right to Data Portability and the Right to Erasure. Both rights are basically prioritized on the certainty of the response to data subject requests that must be followed up quickly "without undue delay." The linkage of personal data protection law related to the implementation of e-IDAS is absolute because the right of deletion and the right to portability of personal data will be highly dependent on the guarantee of the implementation of legal compliance with general data protection law principles.

Related to personal data violations carried out by Facebook, the Ministry of Communication and Informatics has asked the National Police Chief to investigate the possibility that companies or individuals could violate Indonesia's privacy law, a day after Facebook stated that the personal data of more than one million Indonesians might be used by Cambridge Analytica's political consulting firm. The Ministry said Facebook's representatives in Indonesia might face up to 12 years in jail and 871.000 dollars in fines if found guilty. The Ministry of Communication and Informatics asked Facebook to submit the results of the company's audit to find out how this personal information was used by Cambridge Analytica.[11]

The most recent case, in March 2019, involved a violation of personal data that can be categorized as a cyber incident, where a hacker hacked several sites to retrieve user data. One of the hacked sites is Bukalapak, which is one of the largest online shopping sites in Indonesia. The hacker claimed to have succeeded in harvesting 13 million pieces of data from Bukalapak users. The hacker then sells each database hacked individually on the Dream Market with a total value of 1.2431 Bitcoin, equivalent to USD 5000. However, Bukalapak stated that even though there were cyber incidents, hackers did not collect user personal data such as user passwords and financial data.[12]

Sales of personal data in the financial sector are still rampant in Indonesia, with personal data being sold freely for the purpose of marketing banking products. Credit card marketing workers and bank employees are involved. Information on the personal data that is bought and sold for free only contains the name, address, and telephone number on behalf of the biological mother, but also financial ability. Certain types of information can only be accessed from official institutions. The data is then sold online. Buying and selling data online is easily found in the market on online sites. Every piece of data sold is very cheap, starting from IDR 0.1 to IDR 16 per data. Personal data is sold in large quantities at once, and partly divided by several criteria, one of which is a priority credit card. For example, personal sales data is sold at the site www.temanmarketing.com, where requests are made via a conversation on Whatsapp. This site has been investigated by the police because it has been proven to sell personal data. In April 2018, IS—as the site's owner—was arrested by the Metro Jaya Regional Police.[13]

In the Indonesian context, the setting of online digital identity and the protection of personal data is still strongly perceived in the government-centric paradigm in which the Ministry of Home Affairs has its own rules as a lex specialist in the area of personal data protection. Meanwhile, instituting the right to delete personal data will

[11]UH 2018 Facebook Hadapi Penyelidikan di Indonesia terkait Pelanggaran Privasi [Facebook Face Investigation in Indonesia on Privacy Violation]. https://www.voaindonesia.com/a/facebook-hadapi-penyelidikan-di-indonesia-terkait-pelanggaran-privasi/4335493.html. Accessed 13 July 2019.

[12]Rahman 2019 Hacker Klaim Curi dan Jual 13 Juta Akun Bukalapak [Hackers Claimed to Steal and Sell 13 Million Bukalapak Accounts]. https://inet.detik.com/security/d-4472166/hacker-klaim-curi--dan-jual-13-juta-akun-bukalapak. Accessed 13 July 2019.

[13]Khaerudin (Ed.) 2019 Data Pribadi Dijual Bebas [Personal Data for Free]. https://kompas.id/baca/premium_promo/data-pribadi-dijual-bebas/. Accessed 17 July 2019.

be difficult because it depends on the process of appealing to the courts; in the legal world, business actors can be protected by claiming that—for various reasons—the personal data they retain is still relevant to their business. The related rights of Portability of Data can also be said to be relatively unfavourable and unknown because the legislation does not make these rights explicit. There is no arrangement that makes it mandatory for business operators of electronic system providers to respond to requests for data subjects on the basis of rights to the portability of such data.

6.7 Conclusion

- Based on the explanation above, it would be interesting if, in developing a new domestic law, Indonesia implemented a hybrid paradigm of the U.S. and EU perspective, by combining those two principles. The existence of the UU-ITE, PP-PSTE, and Permen PDP basically follows the privacy and protection rules of EU-style and U.S.-style expectations. In implementation, it is also consistent with the APEC Privacy Framework where protection can be optimized with involvement of a professional independent actor (accountability agent or Privacy Trustmark Provider). One of the categories found in Trustmark Provider is privacy protection reliability (Privacy Trustmark), which is a fifth category in PP-PSTE. It indirectly follows the recommendation of APEC to implement more flexible privacy to support the empowerment of professionals in the field of ICT for issuing the Privacy Trust Mark.
- In the waiting period for the long-term process of promulgating the Bill of Privacy and Personal Data Protection Act (RUU-PDP), the existing problems of many cases related to the PDP could be resolved by optimizing the UU-ITE, PP-PSTE, and Permen PDP. The influence of the GDPR should have a positive impact on Indonesian people's awareness and the more comprehensive revision of the Laws and Regulations. It also would be very useful to learn from the European Regulation 910/2014 how the Europeans are implementing e-IDAS and GDPR. Although Indonesia has implemented the Government Centric with Centralized Identity, in practice it cannot deny the existence of Soft-Identity Providers. Therefore, it would be useful to accommodate the policy of federated identity management (open identity) so that it also shows openness to interoperability with other Digital Identity systems. This could be initiated by the Minister of Communications and Informatics Regulation, which could implement an Online Digital Identity that incorporates electronic signatures and Electronic Certificates, in an effort to build a good Identity Ecosystem.
- It was detrimental to Indonesia when European declared that the level of data protection in Indonesia was at a lower value and thus Europe would not allow Indonesia to obtain personal data from Europeans. Ironically, Indonesia's personal data can still be used by Europeans. This position is clearly an unfair condition for Indonesia's national interests. Of course, in responding to this, Indonesia must

seek alternative ways, based on article 2 UU-ITE, to develop a balanced position such as the Corporate Binding Rules. In order to safeguard national interests, the government should be more active in monitoring the use of personal data abroad. It is possible for the government agency to trace or audit, prohibit, or request the removal of personal data abroad if it is detrimental to Indonesia's interests or if it threatens national security.

6.8 Recommendations

- To formulate Privacy policy, the developers should refer to the APEC Privacy Framework as an important source, rather than the policy of the OECD which represents the developed countries. At a minimum, the rules need to absorb the following 5 (five) norms in Fair Information Practices Principles, namely: (i) Notice; (ii) Choice; (iii) Access; (iv) Security; and (v) Enforcement. Indonesia must improve its personal data protection law if it does not want to be regarded as having lower personal data protection standards than those in Europe, particularly concerning the Right to Data Portability. This will affect e-commerce relations between Indonesia and Europe.
- Addressing the grievances against Spamming issues can be accomplished by applying PP-PSTE to the telecommunications network and telecommunications services in Indonesia. These issues occurred because Operators were negligent in performing registration duties and examining the trustworthiness of applications that were used together with a Content Provider Operator. The problem can be clearly seen when there is a consumer lawsuit. The Consumer files a class action suit against unlawful acts committed and requests the judge to issue a temporary decision to suspend temporary services and confiscate the application system used in order to clarify the extent to which the entrepreneur has violated its promise to consumers in an ongoing electronic system. Hypothetically, the issue will be completed when the judge issues the verdict and grants the full compensation claim, both materially and immaterially filed. This should force the rogue businesses to think twice before repeating the mischievous actions that had been impressed understandable because the permissive culture of our customers.
- Even though Indonesia has implemented Government Centric with Centralized Identity Affairs, it should also show openness to interoperability with other Digital Identity systems. This can be facilitated by the Minister of Communications and Informatics Regulation concerning the implementation of Digital Identity and the operation of electronic signatures and Electronic Certificates with reference to international dynamics in an effort to build the Trusted Identity Ecosystem.

References

Agustinus (2018) Cara RupiahPlus Menagih Utang Berbahaya dan Mengganggu Privasi [The Way RupiahPlus Collect Dangerous and Disturbing Privacy Debt]. https://kumparan.com/@kumparanbisnis/cara-rupiahplus-menagih-utang-berbahaya-dan-mengganggu-privasi-27431110790536672. Accessed 16 August 2018

Further Reading

Djafar W, Fadhli M, Setianti BL (2016) Perlindungan Data Pribadi: Usulan Pelembagaan Kebijakan dari Perspektif Hak Asasi Manusia [Protection of Personal Data: Proposed Institutionalization of Policies from a Human Rights Perspective]. Seri Internet dan Hak Asasi Manusia, pp. 1–66

Djafar W, Fadhli M, Setianti BL, Sumigar BRF (2016) Melembagakan Pengaturan Internet Berbasis Hak Asasi Manusia: Masukan Naskah Akademik RUU Perubahan UU No. 11 Tahun 2008 tentang Informasi dan Transaksi Elektronik [Institutionalizing Human Rights-Based Internet Arrangements: Academic Text Input Bill Amendment to Law No. 11 of 2008 concerning Electronic Information and Transactions]. Policy paper UU ITE, pp. 1–73

ELSAM (2016) Policy Brief Hak Atas Penghapusan Informasi (Right to be Forgotten) dan Kebebasan Berekspresi: Pertarungan Wacana. Rekomendasi bagi Perubahan UU No. 11/2008 tentang Informasi dan Transaksi Elektronik [Policy Brief Right to Be Forgotten and Freedom of Expression: Discourse. Recommendations for Amendment to Law No. 11/2008 concerning Information and Electronic Transactions], May 2016. Seri Internet dan HAM, pp. 1–6

Ferrera GR, Lichtenstein SD, Reder MEK, August R, Schiano WT (2001) Cyberlaw: Text and Cases. South-Western College Publishing, Ohio

Hildebrandt M, Gutwirth S (eds) (2008). Profiling the European citizen: Cross-disciplinary perspectives. Springer Publishing Company, New York

Kozyris PJ (ed) (2007) Regulating Internet abuses: Invasion of privacy. Kluwer Law International, The Netherlands

Luwarso L (ed) (2003) Mengatur Kebebasan Pers [Regulating Press Freedom]. Dewan Pers, Jakarta

Makarim E (2005) Pengantar Hukum Telematika: Suatu Kompilasi Kajian [Introduction to Telematics Law: A Compilation of Studies]. PT. Raja Grafindo Persada, Jakarta

Rannenberg K, Royer D, Deuker A (eds) (2009) The future of identity in the information society: Challenges and opportunities. Springer Publishing Company, New York

Surowidjojo AT (2003) Hukum, Demokrasi, & Etika: Lentera Menuju Perubahan [Law, Democracy & Ethics: Lanterns for Change]. Masyarakat Transparansi Indonesia, Jakarta

Dr. Edmon Makarim, Dean of Faculty of Law, University of Indonesia, Jakarta/Depok, Indonesia.

Chapter 7
Data Protection Regulation in the Netherlands

Godelieve Alkemade and Joeri Toet

Contents

Abstract In the first section of this chapter, the authors will discuss the existing generic personal data protection regime in the Netherlands and recent or expected legislative changes in and related to this regime in the foreseeable future. The authors will complement this with a high-level overview of sector-specific personal data protection legislation. In Sect. 7.4 they will summarize the changes that the EU General Data Protection Regulation ("GDPR") has introduced to this regime in the Netherlands. In Sect. 7.5 they will discuss key distinguishing elements of the Dutch personal data protection environment while focusing specifically on the latitude that the GDPR provides Member States for implementation or deviation. In Sect. 7.6 the

G. Alkemade (✉)
The Hague University of Applied Sciences, The Hague, The Netherlands
e-mail: G.O.M.Alkemade@hhs.nl

J. Toet
Vrije Universiteit Amsterdam, Amsterdam, The Netherlands

E. Kiesow Cortez (ed.), *Data Protection Around the World*,
Information Technology and Law Series 33,
https://doi.org/10.1007/978-94-6265-407-5_7

authors will refer back to Sect. 7.5 by sharing their expectations on how they expect the EU General Data Protection Regulations to affect these prominent issues.

Keywords Dutch Data Protection Law · EU General Data Protection Regulation · GDPR · Right to privacy · AVG · Dutch law

7.1 Introduction

In the Netherlands, the fundamental right to privacy is included in the Constitution,[1] which states that everyone has the right to privacy, including thc privacy of mail and telephone correspondence. Furthermore, there are various laws in the Netherlands that (in) directly aim to protect the privacy in the broad sense. In this chapter, we will focus on one aspect of privacy, i.e. the protection of personal data. Some of the more important personal data protection privacy laws are based on legislation of the European Union, which means that the level of data protection within the European Union ("**EU**") is similar in these areas.

In the Netherlands—and many other jurisdictions—one should distinguish between comprehensive personal data protection laws and sector specific data protection laws. The first apply throughout the private and public sectors while the latter only apply to specific defined segments such as the electronic communications sector, criminal law, the financial sector, tax authorities, freedom of information laws and the medical sector.

In the Netherlands, several supervisors have been designated and have been provided with duties and powers to ensure compliance with these laws. As in the other EU Member States the most important supervisor for compliance with the General Data Protection Regulation is the national data protection authority[2] but we advise you to check the designated supervisor for a specific law.

The Netherlands is a Member State of the European Union and as such is bound to implement and uphold the European directives and regulations. Hence like in other EU Member States also, significant Dutch laws regulating the protection of personal data are directly or indirectly influenced by and adapted to EU rules and case law. An important recent EU legislation that influenced the Netherlands data protection laws is the General Data Protection Regulation ("**GDPR**")[3]—which is applicable since 25 May 2018 and which replaces the Data Protection Directive (95/46/EC)—and the European Directive for the Police and Judicial Authorities Directive ("the

[1] The Constitution of the Kingdom of the Netherlands 2008 Articles 10, 13. https://www.government.nl/documents/regulations/2012/10/18/the-constitution-of-the-kingdom-of-the-netherlands-2008.

[2] Autoriteit 2019 EDPB annual report 2018. https://autoriteitpersoonsgegevens.nl/en.

[3] Regulation (EU) 2016/679 of the European Parliament and of the Council of 27 April 2016 on the protection of natural persons with regard to the processing of personal data and on the free movement of such data, and repealing Directive 95/46/EC (General Data Protection Regulation).

data protection law enforcement directive")[4] which had to be incorporated by EU Member States into their national law by 6 May 2018. Another important piece of EU legislation is the Directive on privacy and electronic communications also known as the "E-privacy Directive".[5] EU Member States had to implement the necessary provisions to comply with this Directive before 31 October 2003. Implementation in The Netherlands has taken place in the Dutch Telecommunications Act.[6] This has subsequently been modified amongst other things to accommodate the so-called 'cookie directive',[7] which embodies a 2009 amendment to the E-privacy directive. The E-privacy directive is expected to be replaced by a regulation in the (near) future[8] to better accommodate today's technical reality and to ensure direct and uniform application in all EU-member States.

In Sect. 7.2 we will give a high-level overview of the Dutch Implementation Act ("*Uitvoeringswet AVG*").[9] In Sect. 7.3 we will look at the European Directive for the Police and Judicial Authorities Directive as implemented in the Netherlands in the Police Data Act and the Judicial and Criminal Data Act, after which we will discuss the e-privacy directive and the Dutch Telecommunications Act. Finally, we will take a look at the Dutch Personal Records Database Act[10] which defines the rules regarding the personal data processed in the Personal Records Database. In the next sections (Sects. 7.4–7.6) we will restrict ourselves to the GDPR.

7.2 General Comprehensive Personal Data Protection

As of 25 May 2018, the General Data Protection Regulation is directly applicable in the Netherlands as it is in the other EU Member States. The title of the regulation reveals the comprehensive nature of its rules regarding the processing of personal

[4]Directive (EU) 2016/680—protecting individuals with regard to the processing of their personal data by police and criminal justice authorities, and on the free movement of such data.

[5]Directive 2002/58/EC of the European Parliament and of the Council of 12 July 2002 concerning the processing of personal data and the protection of privacy in the electronic communications sector.

[6]Dutch Telecommunications Act, available at wetten.nl—Regeling—Telecommunicatiewet—BWBR0009950.

[7]Directive 2009/136/EC of the European Parliament and of the Council of 25 November 2009 amending Directive 2002/22/EC on universal service and users' rights relating to electronic communications networks and services, Directive 2002/58/EC concerning the processing of personal data and the protection of privacy in the electronic communications sector and Regulation (EC) No 2006/2004 on cooperation between national authorities responsible for the enforcement of consumer protection laws (Text with EEA relevance).

[8]European Commission 2019 Proposal for an ePrivacy regulation. https://ec.europa.eu/digital-single-market/en/proposal-eprivacy-regulation.

[9]Uitvoeringswet Algemene verordening gegevensbescherming [Dutch Implementation Act]. Available at https://wetten.overheid.nl/BWBR0040940/2018-05-25.

[10]Wet Basis Registratie Personen. [Dutch Personal Records Database Act]. http://wetten.overheid.nl/BWBR0033715/.

data. The fact that it is a regulation means that it directly addresses individuals and companies in the Member States throughout the European Union and that its provisions apply without (a need for) implementation into national law.

Notwithstanding the GDPR's direct effect, it also addresses Member States of the European Union in several respects and allows—and in some areas requires—Member States to deviate from or to supplement parts of the GDPR in their national legislation. Topics that (have been deemed to) require implementation into national law have been addressed and implemented by means of the Dutch Implementation Act.[11] In this act you will not find the GDPR provisions that are not affected, which means that you have to read both the GDPR and the Netherlands GDPR implementation act to get a complete overview of this piece of legislation in the Netherlands. The Netherlands have chosen for a so-called 'policy-neutral execution' meaning that the GDPR Implementation Act respects as much as possible the requirements that applied under the Dutch Data Protection Act ("**DDPA**"),[12] which applied prior to the GDPR and implemented the EU Data Protection Directive 95/46/EC.

7.3 Sector Specific Requirements

7.3.1 The Data Protection Law Enforcement Directive

Being both part of a more comprehensive EU personal data protection package, the European Union published the text of the European Directive for the Police and Judicial Authorities Directive protecting individuals with regard to the processing of their personal data by police and criminal justice authorities, and on the free movement of such data a.k.a. "the data protection law enforcement directive"[13] at the same day as it published the text of the GDPR. Both had to be incorporated in the EU Member States legislation in May 2018. The GDPR does not apply directly to law enforcement agencies. See Recital 19 of the GDPR.[14] While the GDPR—being a

[11] Ibid.

[12] Wet bescherming persoonsgegevens [Dutch Data Protection Act]. http://wetten.overheid.nl/BWBR0011468/2018-05-01.

[13] Directive (EU) 2016/680 of the European Parliament and of the Council of 27 April 2016 on the protection of natural persons with regard to the processing of personal data by competent authorities for the purposes of the prevention, investigation, detection or prosecution of criminal offences or the execution of criminal penalties, and on the free movement of such data, and repealing Council Framework Decision 2008/977/.

[14] The protection of natural persons with regard to the processing of personal data by competent authorities for the purposes of the prevention, investigation, detection or prosecution of criminal offences or the execution of criminal penalties, including the safeguarding against and the prevention of threats to public security and the free movement of such data, is the subject of a specific Union legal act. This Regulation should not, therefore, apply to processing activities for those purposes. However, personal data processed by public authorities under this Regulation should, when used for those purposes, be governed by a more specific Union legal act, namely Directive (EU) 2016/680

regulation—does not require transposition into the local laws of EU Member States, the law enforcement directive—being a directive- does. In the Netherlands the implementation of this piece of European legislation on—as the text of the directive reads: "*... the protection of natural persons with regard to the processing of personal data by competent authorities for the purposes of the prevention, investigation, detection or prosecution of criminal offences or the execution of criminal penalties, and on the free movement of such data...*", has been accomplished by changing both the Netherlands Police Data Act and the Judicial and Criminal Data Act.[15] The first act prescribes the conditions for the processing of personal data (not only of the criminals or suspects but also of other involved individuals such as witnesses) necessary for carrying out their duties by the police, the special investigation service, the Royal Netherlands Marechaussee and the Dutch national department of criminal investigation. The second act, the Judicial and Criminal Data Act, addresses the judicial authorities collecting personal data for investigating, prosecuting and settling criminal offenses and for issuing Certificates of Good Behaviour. The aim of the directive is to find a balance between better protecting the citizens' right of data protection when their data is processed by the above-mentioned authorities and better cooperation between these authorities in the EU Member States to protect individuals against crime and terrorism.[16]

---

of the European Parliament and of the Council. Member States may entrust competent authorities within the meaning of Directive (EU) 2016/680 with tasks which are not necessarily carried out for the purposes of the prevention, investigation, detection or prosecution of criminal offences or the execution of criminal penalties, including the safeguarding against and prevention of threats to public security, so that the processing of personal data for those other purposes, in so far as it is within the scope of Union law, falls within the scope of this Regulation. Such provisions may determine more precisely specific requirements for the processing of personal data by those competent authorities for those other purposes, taking into account the constitutional, organisational and administrative structure of the respective Member State. When the processing of personal data by private bodies falls within the scope of this Regulation, this Regulation should provide for the possibility for Member States under specific conditions to restrict by law certain obligations and rights when such a restriction constitutes a necessary and proportionate measure in a democratic society to safeguard specific important interests including public security and the prevention, investigation, detection or prosecution of criminal offences or the execution of criminal penalties, including the safeguarding against and the prevention of threats to public security. This is relevant for instance in the framework of anti-money laundering or the activities of forensic laboratories.

[15] Wijziging van de Wet politiegegevens en de Wet justitiële en strafvorderlijke gegevens ter implementatie van Europese regelgeving over de verwerking van persoonsgegevens met het oog op de voorkoming, het onderzoek, de opsporing en vervolging van strafbare feiten of de tenuitvoerlegging van straffen [Amendments to the Police Data Act and the Judicial and Criminal Data Act to implement European regulations on the processing of personal data with a view to the prevention, investigation, detection and prosecution of criminal offenses or the execution of sentences]. Available at https://zoek.officielebekendmakingen.nl/kst-34889-6.html.

[16] European Commission 2018 Data protection in the EU. https://ec.europa.eu/info/law/law-topic/data-protection/data-protection-eu_en.

7.3.2 The E-Privacy Directive

Another important piece of EU legislation is the Directive on privacy and electronic communications also known as the e-privacy directive.[17] For multiple reasons as explained later in this section, the e-privacy directive is expected to be replaced by an e-privacy regulation in the near future.[18] As the title suggests the e-privacy directive covers publicly available electronic communication services such as email and telecommunications. The e-privacy directive is a so-called 'lex specialis' with regard to the GDPR. If an electronic communication service is not offered to the public then this directive does not apply although general data privacy principles do. Considering the fast pace of developments in this area it should be no surprise that this directive has been adapted several times since its adoption. Worth mentioning in relation to the Netherlands are the introduction of mandatory notification of personal data breaches and of course the 'cookie' provision.[19] EU Member States had to implement the necessary provisions to comply with this directive including the amendments. For the Netherlands please refer in this respect to the Dutch Telecommunications Act.[20] The Telecommunications Act reflects the aim of the directive—including its amendments—to protect the privacy and the security of the personal data in electronic communications by the electronic communication service providers.

As mentioned before the e-privacy directive is expected to be replaced by an e-privacy regulation in the (near) future.[21] The reasons for this change are several. Think again at the fast developments and challenges in this field—such as WhatsApp and Skype—requiring a broader scope and an adaption to the technical reality of today. A regulation being immediately applicable and enforceable in the EU Member States is expected to create a level playing field for both consumers and service providers. And last but not least the aim is to simplify the e-privacy rules also by ensuring consistency with the GDPR including the consequences for non-compliance. We should not, however, close our eyes to recent developments in this field. Amongst other things

[17]Directive 2002/58/EC of the European Parliament and of the Council of 12 July 2002 concerning the processing of personal data and the protection of privacy in the electronic communications sector.

[18]European Commission 2019 Proposal for an ePrivacy regulation. https://ec.europa.eu/digital-single-market/en/proposal-eprivacy-regulation.

[19]Directive 2009/136/EC of the European Parliament and of the Council of 25 November 2009 amending Directive 2002/22/EC on universal service and users' rights relating to electronic communications networks and services, Directive 2002/58/EC concerning the processing of personal data and the protection of privacy in the electronic communications sector and Regulation (EC) No 2006/2004 on cooperation between national authorities responsible for the enforcement of consumer protection laws (Text with EEA relevance).

[20]Dutch Telecommunications Act, available at wetten.nl—Regeling—Telecommunicatiewet—BWBR0009950.

[21]European Commission 2019 Proposal for an ePrivacy regulation. https://ec.europa.eu/digital-single-market/en/proposal-eprivacy-regulation.

the political developments after the elections for the European Parliament in May 2019 and a revised proposal for the e-privacy regulation by the Finnish government in November 2019—including amendments concerning the further processing of (meta)data—have led to delays and uncertainty on the final text and timing of the adoption process.

7.3.3 *The Dutch Personal Records Database Act*[22]

Finally, we want to mention the Dutch Personal Records Database Act which defines the rules regarding the personal data processed by Netherlands municipalities in the so-called Personal Records Database.[23] This act is a 'lex specialis' with regard to the GDPR so the GDPR and the Dutch GDPR implementation act apply to topics not covered by this Act. In this database, the personal data of Dutch residents, former Dutch residents and non-residents such as temporary students and workers are being processed. The data that is being processed includes the social service number, nationality, residence permit, travel documents, parents and contact data but also information on life events such as relocation, marriage, child birth and decease. Data in this database can only be provided to and used by authorized third parties (and the municipality itself) as defined in the Personal Records Database Act if and to the extent they need it for carrying out their task. Depending on the personal situation of an individual examples of such organisations are social security organisations, the pension fund of the data subject, the ministry of education and the public register registering the property of real estate.

7.4 On the Interaction of the GDPR with National Legislation in the Netherlands

As highlighted in Sect. 7.2 above, the provisions of the GDPR have direct effect in The Netherlands and the majority of substantive requirements apply without further need or possibility of national deviation. Requirements that require national implementation have been implemented into the national legal context by means of the Dutch Implementation Act ("*Uitvoeringswet AVG*"). As mentioned, a leading principle for the implementation of the GDPR into the national legal context in The Netherlands has been that the implementation was to respect policy choices made under the Dutch Personal Data Protection Act and align with the provisions of the GDPR in as much as possible. Although the Netherlands maintains several specific policy choices from

[22] Wet Basis Registratie Personen. [Dutch Personal Records Database Act]. http://wetten.overheid.nl/BWBR0033715/.

[23] Personal Records Database, available at https://www.rijksoverheid.nl/onderwerpen/privacy-en-persoonsgegevens/basisregistratie-personen-brp.

the past that stand out in the international context, deviations from the GDPR overall are limited. In Chapter 3 (Articles 22–39) of the Dutch Implementation Act we find provisions for implementing the GDPR and in Chapter 4 (Articles 40–47) exceptions and restrictions. The relevant articles are referred to in Table 7.1. Without claiming to provide a complete overview the following table sums up the most noteworthy implementation provisions that are specific to The Netherlands. Please consult the full text of the Dutch Implementation Act for a complete overview.

Update of the Dutch implementation act

The GDPR has been in force for some time now and a fair amount of experience has been gained to allow for reflection on its operational impact. At the time of writing, the Dutch Ministry of Safety and Justice ("*Ministerie van Veiligheid en Justitie*") has in fact just published its first evaluation of the GDPR and the national implementation act in particular along with its intentions to address known challenges.

The Dutch Ministry of Safety and Justice recognizes several challenges with the original Dutch Implementation Act. It has expressed the intention to amend the implementation act to address several challenges that arise primarily around the processing of sensitive personal data in specific situations. Changes are envisaged in respect of the processing of sensitive personal data by accountants when performing statutory duties, by patient interest groups for their membership administration, by the national body for whistle blowers ("*Huis voor Klokkenluiders*") for statutory supervisory and enforcement activities and by controllers generally for authentication purposes (biometric data).

The Ministry recognizes a number of other areas where challenges currently exist, but where it is still exploring different possible solutions together with stakeholders involved. These include topics such as the ability of financial institutions to process medical data to meet due diligence requirements in respect of vulnerable customer groups, the ability to pass on privacy related damages to processors, the use of consent for the (re)use of existing datasets for scientific research and possibilities to reduce the administrative burdens around the treatment of "standard" processing activities.

7.5 Key Challenges and Developments in Relation to Data Protection Legislation in the Netherlands

7.5.1 Use of Data Subject Access Rights as Supplemental e-Discovery Instruments

Many legal systems feature a form of pre-trial discovery. This enables parties to a pending dispute to obtain access to evidence that a counterparty or other third party may hold to assess and develop their legal position prior to further court proceedings. While the legal system in The Netherlands does not feature a general discovery procedure as best known from the United States of America, there are several specific

Table 7.1 Chapters 3 and 4 Articles

Articles Dutch Implementation Act	Background
23	Article 23 establishes reasons of substantial public interest that may lift the prohibition to process special categories of personal data pursuant to Article 9.2 sub g GDPR
24	Article 24 establishes the reasons of scientific or historical research or statistical purposes in order to be able to lift the prohibition to process special categories of personal data pursuant to Article 9.2 sub j GDPR
25/26/27/28/29/30/31/32/33	The prohibition to process certain types of sensitive personal data is furthermore lifted for certain types of processing activities: • 25: racial information where the processing is necessary to safeguard equal treatment ("positive" discrimination) and the data subject did not object in writing to such processing • 26: political information where the processing seeks to fulfil requirements for performing certain public duties • 27: religious data or data on philosophical belief where processing is necessary for spiritual care and the data subject did not object in writing to such processing • 28,29,30: genetic, biometric and health data where the processing is allowed by the purposes mentioned in these articles. Biometric data processing is allowed where necessary for authentication or security purposes; health data where the processing takes place for certain employment related situations • 31,32,33: criminal data where the data is processed by bodies permitted by legislation to apply criminal law or by bodies permitted by the Netherlands Police Data Act Judicial and Criminal Data Act to process such data, where processing is necessary to assess a request from the person concerned to make a decision on him or to deliver a performance to him and where this is related to personnel and processed in accordance with the Dutch Works Council Act ("*Wet op de Ondernemingsraden*")
38	The Dutch Data Protection Authority may not collect an imposed administrative fine during administrative or judicial appeal
39	The Data Privacy Officer has a statutory confidentiality duty in respect of all matters known to him pursuant to this capacity
40	The limitations to automated individual decision making—other than based on profiling—do not apply in so far as this is necessary to comply with a legal obligation or to perform a task in the public interest in which case suitable measures must be taken to protect the interest of the data subject

(continued)

Table 7.1 (continued)

Articles Dutch Implementation Act	Background
42	The breach notification duty of the GDPR does not apply to parties that are subject to similar notification obligations pursuant to the Dutch Financial Supervision Act ("*Wet Financieel Toezicht*")
44	A data controller may deny data subjects the exercise of the right to access, rectification or restriction where processing activities take place solely for scientific or historical research purposes, or statistical purposes
46	National identification numbers—commonly assumed to refer to the national Citizen Identification Number ("*Burger Service Nummer*") but arguably also passport and drivers' license numbers—may only be processed if and in so far such processing is provided for explicitly by law

Source Alkemade & Toet

mechanisms through which parties to a dispute may seek access to evidence they do not themselves hold. The use of subject access requests appears to be complementing these procedures.

The two traditional procedures available to obtain evidence in The Netherlands are:

- The Dutch Act on Transparent Governance ("*Wet Openbaarheid Bestuur*") provides grounds for members of the public to obtain access to documents produced by government bodies and institutions as well as private parties carrying out activities in a public capacity. This mechanism is intended to ensure transparency and accountability over matters of public administration, and unsurprisingly so information obtained pursuant to this act is commonly relied on as evidence in both civil and administrative proceedings. There are few formalities a requesting party needs to abide by. While the requested organisation may charge the requestor a nominal fee to cover the direct expenses of the production of information, this is often neglected in practice. More importantly, the indirect costs of handling the request and responding to this remain with the addressee. Overall this makes for a broad and low threshold discovery mechanism in matters involving government counterparties.
- The Dutch Code of Civil Procedure ("DCCP") provides parties to a dispute in civil litigation a potential right of access to evidence held by third parties (the "*exhibitieplicht*" of Article 843a DCCP). This right is not absolute or unconditional. A key requirement that determines the scope of this mechanism is that the requesting party must have a legitimate interest to the requested information; information requested must be directly and specifically relevant to the dispute. A balance of interest (proportionality) test weighs the interests of parties and prevents parties from having to disclose evidence that unjustifiably impacts the interests of others. A subsidiarity test prevents disclosure in the event that a judge

would be able to come to an appropriate decision in respect of the underlying dispute without this information. It is worth noting that the costs of the procedure are borne by the requesting party. Overall exercising this right can thus be costly and complex, which additionally limits the use of this mechanism to matters where the pursued outcome of proceedings warrants the cost and effort.

These procedures—and especially the procedure under the DCCP—remain comparatively specific in their use when compared to the more general discovery instruments available in some jurisdictions. In this light, it is interesting that the EU Data Protection Directive, and the implementing provisions of the Dutch Data Protection Act, have provided individuals with an additional transparency and recourse mechanism where information is processed in respect of them. A key right is the right of individuals to request a data controller to confirm whether the data controller processes data relating to an individual, and—where applicable—the obligation of the data controller to provide a comprehensive overview of the categories of data involved in processing, the purposes for which these are processed and the origins as well as the recipients of this data (Article 35 DDPA).

While data controllers were able to request a nominal fee for responding to such requests and select exceptions existed to limit manifest abuse, information access rights under the DDPA nevertheless appear to have developed into a low-cost and low-risk addition to the more limited discovery and transparency mechanisms mentioned above. Subject access rights now appear to be used quite routinely (in attempt) to obtain information in preparation of, or as a part of, proceedings in cases where one or more individuals feature as a party (e.g. employment cases, damage litigation).

In our experience where the information requested is provided, subject access requests are only occasionally followed by the exercise of rights relating to the affected processing activity. In the vast majority of cases a follow-up action appears to be connected to an underlying grievance and the actions appears to be aimed at strengthening the individual's position in the respective dispute rather than being aimed at righting a wrong in the processing activity itself. The evolving practice naturally has led to questions regarding the objective and permissibility of using this instrument in support of legal proceedings generally. In this light it is interesting to note that the Dutch Supreme Court ruled that the use of data subject access rights—even for the purpose of obtaining evidence in a court case that does not directly concern the processing activity per se—is presumed to be based on a legitimate interest of the individual and their use in general cannot be dismissed as an abuse of law.[24] While we do not share the opinion that the purpose of the request has no bearing on the exercise of the right at all, it is clear that the grounds to resist access requests despite remote connection to the core of the dispute are very limited.

A natural follow-up question is what the scope of a response to a subject access request should entail. Several cases have been heard and referred to the Court of Justice of the European Union. In the case leading to the CJEU's judgement of M & S, a district court in The Netherlands was called on to rule on this in several

[24] Hoge Raad 29 June 2007, LJN AZ4663 and Hoge Raad HR 29 June 2007 LJN AZ4664 (Dexia and UHB).

cases in which—following a change of policy—the national immigration service refused to provide copies of the legal analyses in respect of immigration requests. The CJEU held that it is up to Member States to determine the form in which data subjects are to be provided with information regarding the personal data undergoing processing, and conversely whether and to what extent this requires disclosure of the documents in which personal data is contained. Communication of personal data may take place in the form of a summary of personal data or a redacted version of the document in which this is contained as long as the personal data is intelligible.[25] In the same proceedings as referred to above, the Supreme Court also ruled that data controllers cannot satisfy the right to access personal data simply by providing a general overview of information held, but rather will need to provide all relevant information relating to the individual. The Court expressly argues for an extensive interpretation of the right access one's information.[26]

Data subject access rights are just one of several types of rights provided to individuals under data privacy legislation. Managing the response to individual rights requests generally can be a significant challenge to companies: they are not always clearly identifiable, their scope is not always easily delineated and responding to them timely can prove to be a serious logistical challenge. At the same time, the grounds to resist even unreasonable requests are limited and ambiguous. In many cases, significant time and effort is required to comply with these requests, which makes for time-consuming and costly exercises. It turns out that on top of this, they frequently appear to accompany other disputes, which makes that the impact of the response is not always straightforward. It is often challenged and serves as ground for further action. It follows that parties processing large amounts of personal data generally do well to consider subject rights proactively and in light of the overall relation they (wish to) maintain with individuals, such as by designing their customer experience, request handling procedures and supporting information systems hand-in-hand to easily accommodate these to minimize cost, legal risk and disruption to their activities.

7.5.2 Data Transfers Outside the EU

The Netherlands are a small country in which international economic flows and multinationals such as Shell, AkzoNobel, Philips, Heineken, ABN AMRO, DSM, ING bank, Rabobank and Unilever play a crucial role in the economy. Exchanging information—including personal data on personnel, clients and business relations—is essential for doing business in such an international environment, not only within the EU but also on a global scale. Within the EU (or actually the European Economic

[25]CJEU Joined Cases C-141/12 and C-372/12 (M and S).

[26]Ibid.

Area ("EEA")[27] such transfer of personal data is normally not a problem due to harmonization in this field of law, however exporting personal data to, or importing personal data from other so-called third countries or international organizations, is subject to stringent rules.

Because this chapter is written from a Dutch (the Netherlands being an EU Member State),[28,29] legal perspective we will focus on data transfers from the Netherlands to jurisdictions outside the EU. We will leave aside compliance with foreign data export restrictions in respect of data transfers to the Netherlands.

The GDPR restricts the transfer of personal data to third countries and international organizations. Such transfers are possible provided one of a number of possible conditions is met that each seek to ensure the data is processed taking into account similar safeguards in the receiving jurisdiction as in the EU. According to chapter V, the GDPR recognizes the following mechanisms for such transfer of personal data:

1. 'adequacy decision' for countries, territories, sectors and international organizations by the European Commission[30] in which case the same regime is applicable to the transfers as to a transfer within the EEA (Article 45) or
2. in the absence thereof 'appropriate safeguards' offered by third countries or international organizations. These include amongst others the so-called standard contractual clauses, approved codes of conduct and certification mechanisms, ad hoc contractual clauses approved by the competent data protection authority[31] (Article 46) and Binding Corporate Rules (Article 47) being a set of binding rules demonstrating adequate safeguards allowing multinationals to transfer personal data within a corporate group while
3. 'derogations for specific situations' such as amongst others explicit consent, performance of a contract, non-repetitive limited transfers based upon the legitimate interest of the controller, are described as an export solution in Article 49 in case neither an adequacy decision nor appropriate safeguards apply.

Some prominent issues in the Netherlands regarding data transfer outside the EU are the following. In Sect. 7.6.2 we shall take a closer look at these issues.

(i) In the absence of an adequacy decision, adequate safeguards and one of the exhaustively listed derogations, Article 77.2 of the Dutch Data Protection Act ("DDPA") that was valid until 25 May 2018, allowed the Dutch Minister of

[27] EFTA 2018 Incorporation of the GDPR into the EEA Agreement. http://www.efta.int/EEA/news/Incorporation-GDPR-EEA-Agreement-508041.

[28] The Kingdom of the Netherlands consists of four countries (the Netherlands, Aruba, Curaçao and Sint Maarten) and three public bodies (Bonaire, St. Eustatius and Saba). Only the Netherlands is located within the EU. Transfer of personal data from the Netherlands to the other parts of the Kingdom is considered to be a transfer to a third country.

[29] Explanatory Memorandum of Implementation Act, General Data Protection Regulation page 50 par 5.2.8 Available at https://www.rijksoverheid.nl/documenten/kamerstukken/2017/12/13/memorie-van-toelichting-uitvoeringswet-algemene-verordening-gegevensbescherming.

[30] European Commission (nd) Adequacy decisions. https://ec.europa.eu/info/law/law-topic/data-protection/data-transfers-outside-eu/adequacy-protection-personal-data-non-eu-countries_en.

[31] Data protection authority refers to the supervisory authority as defined in the GDPR.

Justice to grant a licence with appropriate provisos for a transfer of personal data to a third country without an appropriate level of protection. The minister did so after having taken into account the advice of the data protection authority. This created a lot of administrative burden, which in turn made for a fairly time-consuming process that often delayed the start of processing activities.[32] Since this process is not in line with the GDPR this provision has now been eliminated.

(ii) Another issue—that has been addressed by the GDPR—is the fact that before the GDPR became applicable draft Binding Corporate Rules first had to be approved by the data protection authority in the main jurisdiction of establishment of a multinational in the EU.[33] After approval by the 'lead authority', this authority managed a process through which the comments and approvals of the data protection authorities in other relevant Member States were collected to ensure that the Binding Corporate Rules would also apply to transfers of personal data from those jurisdictions. This process led to a compounding of different requirements into Binding Corporate Rules. Overall it proved to be fairly bureaucratic, drawn-out and costly. One can imagine that the more countries a multinational had establishments in, the more authorities were required to approve the Binding Corporate Rules and the more challenging the process thus became. Another point is that Binding Corporate Rules require measures that exceed the requirements of applicable law if and to the extent they provide more protection than such law. A multination will need to weigh the benefit of having a common baseline versus extra requirements in the target jurisdiction since Binding Corporate Rules might effectively raise the bar for global privacy compliance to a level comparable to EU law with a similar effect on liabilities for privacy claims.

(iii) Although not specific for the EU or the Netherlands, we want to mention that international companies are frequently presented with conflicting requirements from different jurisdictions. They are for instance on the one hand required to cooperate in a US pre-trial discovery procedure by sending personal data to the US while on the other hand the European data protection laws prohibit them to do so.[34]

---

[32] http://wetten.overheid.nl/BWBR0011468/2018-05-01 Wet bescherming persoonsgegevens Article 77.2.

[33] Article 29 Data Protection Working Party (2005) Working document setting forth a co-operation procedure for issuing common opinions on adequate safeguards resulting from "binding corporate rules." http://ec.europa.eu/justice/article-29/documentation/opinion-recommendation/files/2005/wp107_en.pdf.

[34] Moerel, Jansen and Koëter 2009 U.S. subpoenas and European data protection legislation. https://pure.uvt.nl/portal/files/5651143/U.S._Subpoenas_and_European_Data_Protection_Legislation_juli_2009.pdf.

7.5.3 Processing Employee Data Works Council

Dealing with employee data is complex for the employer not least as legal obligations regarding the processing of such data may arise from different—local and EU—laws such as the GDPR, employment and collective agreement laws. Noteworthy in this context is that while right to privacy is generally speaking an individual right, in some EU jurisdictions we find a collective right to privacy provided for in local Works Councils legislation.[35] The Netherlands is such country. In this chapter, we will focus on this 'collective right on privacy' as prescribed for in the Netherlands Works Council Act ("WCA").[36] Compliance with the WCA can take a considerable amount of time.

Article 2.1 of the WCA reads:

> Any entrepreneur carrying on an enterprise in which normally at least 50 persons are working shall, in the interests of the proper functioning of the enterprise (…), establish a Works Council in order to ensure the proper consultation and representation of the persons working in the enterprise.

Article 27 of the WCA reads:

> 1 The endorsement of the Works Council shall be required for every proposed decision on the part of the entrepreneur to lay down, amend or withdraw: (…)[37]
>
> k) Regulations relating to the handling and protection of personal information of persons working in the enterprise;
>
> l) Regulations relating to measures aimed at or suitable for monitoring or checking the attendance, behaviour or performance of persons working in the enterprise; (…)
>
> 2. The entrepreneur shall submit his proposed decision in writing to the Works Council. In addition, he shall present a summary of his reasons for the decision, as well as the consequences that the decision is expected to have for persons working in the enterprise.

Reading the broad wording of these articles, one should realize how comprehensive this requirement of endorsement is, the more so as it not only covers the processing of personal data of staff or processes aimed at monitoring staff but also measures suitable to do so. The latter would mean that in principle every electronic

[35]According to the directive 2009/38/EC on European Works Councils EU Member States are to provide for the right to establish European Works Councils in certain companies. However, the powers of the European Works Council have been limited to the provision of information and consultation, Directive 2009/38/EC of the European Parliament and of the Council of 6 May 2009 on the establishment of a European Works Council or a procedure in Community-scale undertakings and Community-scale groups of undertakings for the purposes of informing and consulting employees. Available at https://eur-lex.europa.eu/legal-content/EN/ALL/?uri=CELEX%3A32009L0038.

[36]Netherlands Works Council Act Available at https://www.ser.nl/-/media/ser/downloads/engels/2013/works-councils-act.pdf.

[37]Paragraph 3 of Article 27 reads: "The obligation mentioned in paragraph (1) shall not apply if and insofar as the matter in question has already been regulated for the enterprise in a collective labour agreement or in an arrangement relating to terms of employment laid down by a body under public law."

device such as security camera surveillance, access control, or even software assisting the employee in the recovery and prevention of Repetitive Strain Injury could fall within the scope of Article 27.

The Works Council can—if needed—go to court to enforce compliance with the WCA by the employer. The employer on the other hand can go to court if the Works Council refuses endorsement and try to substantiate why the court should give approval for the proposed decision instead of the Works Council. For an example of the latter refer to the case of the KLM vs the KLM's Works Council[38] regarding the KLM works council refusing to endorse a proposed decision to use an automated time registration system to register employee activities in parts of the company. This case is also interesting because when the works council invoked the then applicable Dutch Data Protection Act ("DDPA"), the court remarked that it was up to the individual employee to turn to the KLM in case of non-compliance with the DDPA.[39]

Again, one should realize first that not all countries within the EU do have (similar national) Works Councils laws as in the Netherlands so the situation may differ throughout the EU. Finally, endorsement for an employee data processing by the Works Council does *not* deprive the individual employee from his individual rights to data protection. However, endorsement by the Works Council might suggest that the various interests and the fundamental rights and freedoms of the data subject have been weighted carefully and that these interests have not been found overriding by the Works Council.

7.6 The GDPR and the Dutch National Jurisdiction Insights

At the time of writing, regulatory enforcement in The Netherlands under GDPR is still limited. We would like to start this chapter with some recent Dutch data protection authority decisions.

---

[38]Decision:NL:RBAMS:2008:BD6534. Available at https://uitspraken.rechtspraak.nl/inziendocument?id=ECLI:NL:RBAMS:2008:BD6534.

[39]Decision sub 6.8.: "De OR stelt voorts dat de Wet Bescherming Persoonsgegevens bijzondere regels kent omtrent het doorgeven van persoonsgegevens naar derde landen en in het bijzonder naar landen buiten de Europese Unie. KLM heeft op dit punt volgens de OR nog onvoldoende duidelijkheid verschaft. Wat de OR beoogt met deze stelling is onduidelijk. De Wet Bescherming Persoonsgegevens biedt - zoals de naam doet vermoeden - bescherming tegen ongeoorloofd gebruik van persoonsgegevens. Daar waar KLM handelt in strijd met deze wet, staat het de individuele medewerker vrij om naleving te vragen." The Works Council also states that the Dutch Data Protection Act has specific rules regarding the transfer of personal data to third countries and in particular to countries outside the European Union. According to the Works Council, KLM has not provided sufficient clarity on this point. It is unclear what the Works Council intends with this statement. The Dutch Data Protection Act offers—as the name suggests—protection against unauthorized use of personal data. Where KLM acts contrary to this law, the individual employee is free to request compliance. Available at https://uitspraken.rechtspraak.nl/inziendocument?id=ECLI:NL:RBAMS:2008:BD6534.

According to Article 57.1 preamble, a and f GDPR: "… *each supervisory authority shall on its territory* (…) *monitor and enforce the application of this Regulation* (…) *handle complaints lodged by a data subject, or by a body, organisation or association* (…) and *investigate, to the extent appropriate, the subject matter of the complaint* (…). In Article 58 of the GDPR you can find the investigative, corrective, authorisation and advisory powers given to the supervisory authorities to perform the tasks referred to in Article 57.1.

As we can read on page 19 of the 2018 annual report of the Dutch data protection authority[40] the authority has in 2018 emphasized informing and advising more than investigating and imposing fines. On the website of the Dutch data protection authority[41] we can nevertheless observe that in November 2018: "*The Dutch Data Protection Authority (Dutch DPA) imposes a fine of €600.000 upon Uber B.V. and Uber Technologies, Inc. (UTI) for violating the Dutch data breach regulation. In 2016, a data breach occurred at the Uber concern in the form of unauthorised access to personal data of customers and drivers. The Uber concern is fined because it did not report the data breach to the Dutch DPA and the data subjects within 72 h after the discovery of the breach.*" While the date of this decision lies after the entry into force of the GDPR, according to Article 48.8 of the Netherlands GDPR implementation Act—explaining the transitional arrangements[42]—legal procedures and cases involving the Dutch data protection authority prior to the entry into force of the GDPR are subject to the law as it applied prior to the entry into force of the GDPR, hence the Dutch Data Protection Act ("DDPA").[43] Worth mentioning is that the standards regarding data breach notification under the DDPA and the GDPR are broadly the same. It is to be seen whether this decision will be appealed and whether it will hold up to judicial scrutiny, but the authority's decision follows an interesting display of supervisory initiative during such a pivotal change of law.

Another interesting case is a decision of the Dutch data protection authority of 30 October to issue the Netherlands Employee Insurance Agency (UWV) with an order subject to a penalty payment.[44] If the UWV has not provided for a sufficient level of protection on their employers' portal by 31 October 2019, the UWV will have to pay a penalty payment of 150,000 Euro per month with a maximum of 900,000 Euro. Interesting is that the investigation started under the regime of the DDPA (infringement of Article 13 i.e. the UWV in its capacity of controller failing to implement appropriate technical and organisational measures to ensure a level of security appropriate to the risk) but—as the Dutch data protection authority remarked

[40] 2018 annual report of the Dutch data protection authority. Available at https://autoriteitpersoonsgegevens.nl/sites/default/files/atoms/files/ap_jaarverslag_2018.pdf.

[41] Dutch Data Protection Authority decision on Uber B.V. Available at https://autoriteitpersoonsgegevens.nl/sites/default/files/atoms/files/boetebesluit_uber.pdf and at https://autoriteitpersoonsgegevens.nl/en/news/dutch-dpa-fine-data-breach-uber.

[42] Netherlands GDPR implementation Act, available at https://wetten.overheid.nl/BWBR0040940/2018-05-25.

[43] Dutch Data Protection Act, available at https://wetten.overheid.nl/BWBR0011468/2018-05-01.

[44] 2018 Annual report of the Dutch data protection authority, p. 47, available at https://autoriteitpersoonsgegevens.nl/sites/default/files/atoms/files/ap_jaarverslag_2018.pdf.

in its report—because the breach continued after 25 May 2018 the UWV as from 25 May 2018 failed to comply with Article 32.1 of the GDPR imposing the same obligation. At the end of 2019, the Dutch data protection authority granted the UWV a postponement of the term to comply with the requirements until 1 March 2020 and in June 2020 decided after an investigation that the UWV has improved the level of security and that it is not required to pay a penalty.

The last case we want to mention is a decision of the Dutch data protection authority of 18 July 2019. It concerns the requirements as in Article 32, paragraph 1 GDPR: "*… the controller and the processor shall implement appropriate technical and organisational measures to ensure a level of security appropriate to the risk, …*" In the Haga hospital in The Hague many hospital employees looked at the medical records of a Dutch celebrity without any medical or other valid reason. After an investigation, the Dutch data protection authority concluded that the technical and organizational measures taken by the hospital to secure patient information were not appropriate, because the hospital did not (routinely) validate accesses medical files and could as a result not take action against unauthorised access. Further, it determined that access to medical files should have been secured using (at least) two factor authentication of users. The Dutch data protection authority imposed an administrative fine of € 460,000 on the hospital (subject to an additional penalty payment).

7.6.1 Data Subject Access Rights as Extrajudicial E-Discovery Instruments

While data subjects had conceptually similar rights under the EU Privacy Directive and its implementation in the Dutch Data Protection Act ("**DDPA**"), the GDPR strengthens data individuals' rights in several respects and complements these with an explicit right to erasure and right to data portability.[45] As such data subject rights appear to provide individuals with additional litigation tooling in what is generally already considered a comparatively favourable regime for class action lawsuits in Europe.[46]

Where the EU Data Protection Directive and the Dutch Data Protection Act provided that data subjects had the right to access the personal data a data controller held in their respect, neither explicitly provided that this right entailed the right to receive a copy of this personal data. In fact, the Court of Justice for the European Union expressly allowed Member States the ability to determine the form in which data controllers were to respond to data subject access requests.[47] This room for deviation appears to be more limited under the GDPR as this now expressly provides

[45] Chapter III GDPR on the Rights of the Data Subject.

[46] Meerdink 2019_ Class actions regime broadened in the Netherlands. https://www.debrauw.com/alert/class-actions-regime-broadened-in-the-netherlands/. Accessed 28 December 2019.

[47] CJEU Joined Cases C-141/12 and C-372/12 (M and S).

that data subjects must receive a copy of their personal data (Article 15.3 GDPR). The key question that remains is whether this right to a copy of personal data applies only to information directly relating to the individual, or whether it also extends to the context in which personal data is processed (i.e. the full document or record in which it is contained). The verdict is still out at the time of writing with some case law appearing to favour a more extensive interpretation[48] and other judgements appearing to support a more restrictive interpretation.[49] The ultimate scope of interpretation will have an evident impact on the ability to obtain evidence for potential use in civil proceedings outside of the traditional court proceedings.

The ability to easily make a data subject access request has always been intended to be low-threshold. Requests could be made by individuals in any form (e.g. written or oral), did not need to be motivated by requesting individuals and were not dependent on judicial proceedings (they also do not require mandatory legal representation). Where the Dutch Data Protection Act allowed data controllers to charge data subjects a nominal fee for complying with their request (Article 39), the GDPR provides as a matter of principle that data controllers must respond to access requests free of charge (Article 12.5) and thereby further lowers the barriers to making such access requests and reduces the timelines to responding to such requests.

The GDPR maintains several measures that seek to facilitate data controllers in complying with these and to limit the possibility of abusive or frivolous subject access requests. A controller that processes significant amounts of personal data in respect of an individual may request the individual to specify the information to which the individual seeks access, including by specifying the processing activity, before responding. Data controllers may refuse to respond to requests that are "manifestly unfounded or excessive", or charge a reasonable fee reflecting the administrative cost of taking the requested action in respect of such requests (Article 12-5). Data controllers however carry the burden of proof in this respect. Important questions in practice will be what will qualify as manifestly unfounded or excessive requests; and how data controllers balance the increasing costs and risks of subject access requests versus potential regulatory interference—especially where likely connected to litigation—and potential non-compliance with the GDPR.

7.6.2 Data Transfers Outside the EU

The provisions of the GDPR are directly applicable and binding on individual EU Member States but frequently the GDPR requires such Member States to implement measures or it allows them to derogate from it. In the Netherlands, the general rules

[48]Rechtbank Midden-Nederland 25 juli 2018, ECLI:NL:RBMNE:2018:3624 and Rechtbank Den Haag. 31 Augustus 2018, ECLI:NL:RBDHA:2018:10910; Appeals Court of The Hague, 17 September 2019, ECLI:NL:GHDHA:2019:2398.

[49]District Court of North Holland, 23 May 2019, nr. C/15/282075/HA RK 18-215; District Court of Amsterdam, 20 June 2019, nr. C/13/654823/HA RK 18-315.

for the implementation of the GDPR including derogations have been laid down in the GDPR implementation act.[50] This implementation act is subject to renewal as has been explained in Sect. 7.4.

Chapter 5 (Articles 44–50) of the GDPR covers the transfer of personal data to third countries or international organizations. See also Sect. 7.5.2. Such transfer is possible on the basis of (i) an adequacy decision (Article 45 GDPR), (ii) appropriate safeguards including the so-called standard contractual clauses (Articles 46, 47) or (iii) derogations for specific situations (Article 49 GDPR). Article 49.5 of the GDPR allows Member States—in the absence of an adequacy decision—to limit the transfer of specific categories of personal data for 'important reasons of public interest'. The Netherlands chose not to use the possibility to set limits as offered by Article 49.5 in its GDPR implementation act, but refers in this respect to possible sector specific laws.[51] For instance data transfer from public registers, as referred to in Article 49.1.sub g GDPR has been regulated in specific Dutch legislation. This is in line with the choice by the Netherlands for a 'minimalistic' and 'policy-neutral' approach, i.e. making only a limited use of the right to deviate from the GDPR and to align the implementation of the GDPR as much as possible with current Netherlands law.[52]

As said above the European Commission can take a so-called 'adequacy decision' for countries, territories, sectors and international organizations. The European Commission do not consider the US to be an adequate country unless recipients are adhering to so-called Privacy Shield Framework. This Framework replaced the previous EU-US Safe Harbour Framework after Mr. Schrems in 2015 successfully challenged the adequacy of it before the Court of Justice of the European Union in the so-called 'Schrems case'.[53,54] Another consequence of this 'Schrems case' ruling is that the national data protection authority must be able to get an independent opinion on such adequacy decisions and must have access to a court if a concerned person files a complaint on unjustified transfer outside the EU while this transfer has been based upon an adequacy decision of the European Commission. Article 20 of the Netherlands GDPR implementation act has been added to observe this requirement and allows the Dutch data protection authority to bring an application before the administrative jurisdiction division of the Council of State in such a case. After this ruling (also referred to as 'Schrems I') Mr. Schrems challenged personal data transfers to the US on the basis the so-called standard contractual clauses (this case is referred to as 'Schrems II'). According to the opinion of the Advocate General at

[50] Uitvoeringswet Algemene verordening gegevensbescherming [Dutch Implementation Act], available at https://wetten.overheid.nl/BWBR0040940/2018-05-25.

[51] Explanatory Memorandum of Implementation Act on the General Data Protection Regulation p. 74, Available at https://www.rijksoverheid.nl/documenten/kamerstukken/2017/12/13/memorie-van-toelichting-uitvoeringswet-algemene-verordening-gegevensbescherming.

[52] See also Sect. 7.2 of this chapter.

[53] Case C-362/14,Available at https://eur-lex.europa.eu/legal-content/EN/TXT/HTML/?uri=CELEX:62014CJ0362&from=NL.

[54] In addition to this since 2017 the US Judicial Redress Act has extended the benefits of the US Privacy Act to Europeans and given them access to US courts.

the Court of Justice of the European Union of 19 December 2019, we quote: "... *Commission Decision 2010/87/EU on standard contractual clauses for the transfer of personal data to processors established in third countries is valid* ...". On 16 July 2020, the Court of Justice of the EU (CJEU) issued its decision in the Schrems II case. The court confirmed the validity of the standard contractual clauses as a personal data transfer mechanism on the proviso that EU data protection authorities should suspend or prohibit such transfers if they are of the opinion that the clauses cannot be complied with or if the level of protection cannot be ensured otherwise. Breaking news was however that the Court in the same ruling limited the possibilities to transfer personal data from the EU to the US by invalidating the Privacy Shield Framework. The latter having enormous regulatory and commercial implications.

In general, we can conclude that for such an international orientated country as the Netherlands the GDPR provides for more options if it comes to data transfers outside the EU because it provides additional options and flexibility for exporting (and importing) personal data to third countries. Some administrative burdens have been reduced such as the abolishment of authorization for standard contractual clauses as approved by the European Commission or a data protection authority.[55] However as mentioned before the potential risks for companies transferring personal data to third countries or international organizations have increased because of the increased fines. Of course, only time will tell how authorities and judges will interpret the GDPR and what the actual impact of the GDPR will be. To what extent will its high standards be enforced and to what extent new options as approved codes of conducts, certification mechanism and ad hoc transfers will be used for transfer of personal data to 'third counties'?

Referring back to the specific problems mentioned in Sect. 7.5.2:

(i) The provision as described in Article 77.2 of the DDPA allowing the Dutch Minister of Justice to grant a license for transfer in circumstances as described above is not in line with the GDPR in which the role of the data protection authority in this area is strengthened. The elimination of this provision is a welcome removal of an administrative burden.
(ii) It is helpful that the GDPR has officially acknowledged and defined Binding Corporate Rules as an export solution for both processors and controllers and that it has simplified the approval process by introducing in Article 47.1 the so-called one "stop shop", meaning that the competent data protection authority shall validate the Binding Corporate Rules in accordance with the consistency mechanism as described Article 63 of the GDPR. This was intended to simplify the Binding Corporate Rules approval and implementation procedures. However, as it stands numerous companies are complaining about the lack of progress in the processing of their Binding Corporate Rules requests. The intended efficiency gains have so far been elusive.
(iii) The question is whether the GDPR offers an adequate solution for the issue that international companies have to deal with conflicting requirements from

[55]The Dutch Data Protection Act ("DDPA") was amended in 2012 in order to add model contracts as approved by the European Commission to the list of permitted derogations.

different jurisdictions. Unfortunately, this is not the case. Article 48 of the GPDR prohibits the transfer of personal data from the EEA to 'third countries' if required by a court, tribunal or administrative authority unless: (i) it is authorized by an international agreement between the third country and the EU or the Member State or (ii) if any other ground for the international transfer of personal data can be relied upon. This means that the position of EU companies has not fundamentally changed in this respect after the introduction of the GDPR while the position has deteriorated in that the potential risks have increased dramatically due to the increased penalties. We will learn in due course whether the European Data Protection Board will give some guidance to respond to these concerns or whether the courts will to interpret Article 48 in a practical way.

(iv) The controller should be aware of a new obligation under the GDPR. Article 13.1.sub e and Article 14.1. sub f obliges the controller to inform the data subject on the intention to transfer personal data to a third country or international organization and on which legal basis they intend to do so. This might be considered by some controllers as the GDPR creating an additional layer of red tape.

N.B. An organization should be aware that if and to the extent the above mechanisms involve the processing of personal data of employees the Works Council might need to be involved according to Dutch law. See Sects. 7.5.3 and 7.6.3 of this chapter.

7.6.3 Processing Employee Data Works Council

As mentioned before, the rights of the Works Council regarding the privacy within its enterprise are complementary to and not a replacement for those that already exist on the basis of the GDPR. In the GDPR you will not find the word 'works council'. This does not alter the fact that in recital 155 and Article 88 of the GDPR[56] the right of EU Member States to provide specific rules for the protection of the personal

[56] Article 88: Processing in the context of employment. (1) Member States may, by law or by collective agreements, provide for more specific rules to ensure the protection of the rights and freedoms in respect of the processing of employees' personal data in the employment context, in particular for the purposes of the recruitment, the performance of the contract of employment, including discharge of obligations laid down by law or by collective agreements, management, planning and organisation of work, equality and diversity in the workplace, health and safety at work, protection of employer's or customer's property and for the purposes of the exercise and enjoyment, on an individual or collective basis, of rights and benefits related to employment, and for the purpose of the termination of the employment relationship. (2) Those rules shall include suitable and specific measures to safeguard the data subject's human dignity, legitimate interests and fundamental rights, with particular regard to the transparency of processing, the transfer of personal data within a group of undertakings, or a group of enterprises engaged in a joint economic activity and monitoring systems at the work place. (3) Each Member State shall notify to the Commission those provisions of its law which it adopts pursuant to paragraph 1, by 25 May 2018 and, without delay, any subsequent amendment affecting them.

data of employees has been explicitly acknowledged. However, the implementation table in the memorandum of the Dutch GDPR implementation act[57] states that the Netherlands will not use the amount of scope provided for in Article 88 of the GDPR.

Does this mean that nothing changes for the Works Council? If you just look at the text of the law you might think this is not the case. But on the other hand, we think it does. Typically, organizations have to introduce, amend of withdraw data privacy regulations to be and stay compliant with the GDPR. Many of these shall be related to the personal data of employees and thus covered by the broad Article 27 of the WCA. Just think of the impact of introducing codes of conduct, certification mechanisms, seals and marks, mandatory data protection impact assessments, new rules regarding data transfers outside the EU and the consequences of the obligation to record every personal data processing.

Indeed, this and other important changes in this space will considerable increase the workload on both the Works Council and the enterprise. To be able to perform their respective duties it is important that both the company and the Works Council adopt a professional and cooperative attitude and ensure mutual involvement in these GDPR implementation processes. Further the Works Council—if and to the extent needed—can consider also to exercise the other competencies attributed to it such as the right to information, the right to be trained in this subject and the right to hire an expert.

References

Dutch Data Protection Authority (2018) Besluit tot het opleggen van een bestuurlijke boete (6 November 2018) [Decision to impose an administrative fine]. https://autoriteitpersoonsgegevens.nl/sites/default/files/atoms/files/boetebesluit_uber.pdf. Accessed 28 December 2019

Dutch Data Protection Authority (2019) Annual report 2018 (4 April 2019). https://autoriteitpersoonsgegevens.nl/sites/default/files/atoms/files/ap_jaarverslag_2018.pdf. Accessed 28 December 2019

European Commission (nd) Data protection in the EU. https://ec.europa.eu/info/law/law-topic/data-protection/data-protection-eu_en. Accessed 28 December 2019

European Commission (nd) Adequacy decisions. How the EU determines if a non-EU country has an adequate level of data protection. https://ec.europa.eu/info/law/law-topic/data-protection/data-transfers-outside-eu/adequacy-protection-personal-data-non-eu-countries_en. Accessed 28 December 2019

European Free Trade Association (2018) Incorporation of the GDPR into the EEA Agreement (13 April 2018). http://www.efta.int/EEA/news/Incorporation-GDPR-EEA-Agreement-508041. Accessed 28 December 2019

Government of the Netherlands (nd) Basisregistratie Personen (BRP) [Basic registration of persons]. https://www.rijksoverheid.nl/onderwerpen/privacy-en-persoonsgegevens/basisregistratie-personen-brp. Accessed 28 December 2019

[57]Explanatory Memorandum of Implementation Act on the General Data Protection Regulation, 2017, https://www.rijksoverheid.nl/documenten/kamerstukken/2017/12/13/memorie-van-toelichting-uitvoeringswet-algemene-verordening-gegevensbescherming, p. 77.

Moerel E M L, Jansen N, Koëter J (2009) U.S. subpoenas and European data protection legislation. https://research.tilburguniversity.edu/en/publications/us-subpoenas-and-european-data-protection-legislation-on-conflict. Accessed 28 December 2019

Statista (2019) KOF globalization index – 100 most globalized countries 2018 (29 April 2019). https://www.statista.com/statistics/268168/globalization-index-by-country/. Accessed 28 December 2019

Godelieve Alkemade, Lecturer, Business Economics Program, The Hague University of Applied Sciences, The Netherlands.

Joeri Toet, Lecturer at the Faculty of Law, Vrije University Amsterdam, The Netherlands.

Chapter 8
The GDPR Influence on the Tanzanian Data Privacy Law and Practice

Alex B. Makulilo

Contents

Abstract The recent adoption of the General Data Protection Regulation (GDPR) in the European Union has a worldwide effect on international transfer of personal data. The fact that the GDPR restricts transfer of personal data outside the European Union unless a third country has adequate level of protection of such data, has sparked law and policy reform in third countries in compliance with the GDPR. This chapter provides an overview of the influence the GDPR on the Tanzanian data privacy law and practice.

Keywords GDPR · Personal data · Tanzania · Data protection law · Practice · Law reform

[1]Regulation (EU) 2016/679 of the European Parliament and of the Council of 27 April 2016 on the protection of natural persons with regard to the processing of personal data and on the free movement of such data, and repealing Directive 95/46/EC (General Data Protection Regulation).

A. B. Makulilo (✉)
Open University of Tanzania, P.O. Box 23409, Dar es Salaam, Tanzania
e-mail: alex.makulilo@out.ac.tz

E. Kiesow Cortez (ed.), *Data Protection Around the World*,
Information Technology and Law Series 33,
https://doi.org/10.1007/978-94-6265-407-5_8

8.1 Introduction

The General Data Protection Regulation (GDPR)[1] is the current data protection regime in the European Union. The law reform process leading to the adoption of the GDPR was officially announced on 25 January 2012 and the Regulation was set to come into force two years after its publication. However, this was not possible due to lengthy discussions and negotiations between the European Union institutions, namely the European Commission, the European Parliament and the Council of the European Union. Such deliberations took four years. Finally, the GDPR was adopted on 8 April 2016. Subsequently, it was published in the Official Journal of the European Union on 4 May 2016 and came into force 20 days later. However, the GDPR's effective date was postponed until 25 May 2018. The transition was meant to give EU member states time to align their laws and practices with the GDPR.[2]

The GDPR replaces Directive 95/46/EC and 28 national laws of EU member states. Although the review process that culminated to its adoption was officially launched in 2009, in reality the foundation of such process goes as far back as to numerous discussions, commissioned and non-commissioned reports, conference proceedings, commentaries by researchers, academics and practitioners, case law of the European Court of Justice, practices of national data supervisory authorities, etc. between 1995 and 2009.[3] These sources provided clear signals that the Directive's revision was inevitable.

It is imperative to note that revision of the EU Directive came about after two decades of its adoption. Viviane Reding, the then Vice-President of the European Commission, responsible for Justice, Fundamental rights and Citizenship, had specifically pointed out three main trends as catalysts for EU data protection regulatory reforms: modern technologies, globalized data flows and access to personal data by law enforcement authorities.[4] Modern technologies including the growth in mobile Internet devices, web-user generated contents, the outburst of social networking sites and above all the cloud computing technologies have been identified as new trends which postdate the Directive 95/46/EC. Because the latter law was adopted while the internet was in its embryonic stages in the 1990s, the recent technological developments especially in what have become known as the Internet of Things, cloud computing and Big Data analytics, have strained its operation. The modern technological developments have in turn increased globalised data flows at a 'rocketing' rate. Accordingly, globalization of technology has seen an increased role of third countries relating to data protection, and has also led to a steady increase in

[2]GDPR, Recital 171; Article 99.

[3]See various decisions, reports, and surveys of the European Commission at http://ec.europa.eu/justice/data-protection/document/index_en.htm. Accessed 4 December 2019; see also 1st–13th annual reports of the Article 29 Working Party on Data Protection http://ec.europa.eu/justice/data-protection/article-29/documentation/annual-report/index_en.htm. Accessed 4 December 2018; Article 29 Working Party on Data Protection's Opinions, Working Documents and Recommendations (1997–2011), http://ec.europa.eu/justice/data-protection/article-29/documentation/opinion-recommendation/index_en.htm. Accessed 4 December 2019.

[4]Reding 2011.

the processing of personal data of Europeans by companies and public authorities outside the European Union.[5] As a result, it has been difficult to precisely allocate responsibility, liability and accountability of various parties notably data controllers, processors as well as joint data controllers and processors. The cross-border flows of data to third countries have also posed great challenges on how Europeans can enforce their data protection rights in non-EU jurisdictions. Besides these two trends, the growing appetite for personal data for reasons of public interest, in particular for public security matters, is also an important challenge for data protection.[6] While 'the collection and processing of personal information can be very valuable in order to secure important and legitimate public and public interests—if done in a way which fully respects the requirements of legality, necessity, and proportionality its reverse may be disastrous to individuals'[7] control of their personal data.

The totality of the above trends exerted pressure to the need for revising the Directive. Such revision aimed at achieving the following objectives: strengthening the rights of data subjects; enhancing the internal market dimension; reinforcing data controllers' responsibility; revising the rules on police and judicial cooperation in criminal matters; improving, strengthening and streamline the current procedures for international transfers in the context of global dimension of data protection and providing better enforcement of data protection rules.[8]

8.2 Approach and Main Features of the GDPR

As a Regulation, the GDPR has a binding force upon EU/EEA member states and has direct effect upon them. The rationale for adopting a Regulation instead of a Directive (which has to be implemented or transposed by each member) is to achieve harmonization of the rules and practices. However, it is important to note that the GDPR permits member states to transpose many aspects into their domestic laws thereby questioning the overall aim of the Regulation of harmonisation and consistency in the law and practice.

Unlike the Directive, the structure of the EU General Data Protection Regulation is highly complex. It is a longer and more detailed text than the Directive. The GDPR has a preamble containing one hundred and sixty-nine recitals as well as eleven chapters with ninety-nine articles.

However, like its predecessor, the EU General Data Protection Regulation is grounded on the same philosophical basis and objectives as the Directive. The philosophical underpinning of the GDPR is human rights and accordingly the twin objectives of the Regulation are to protect fundamental rights and freedoms of natural

[5] Ibid.

[6] Ibid.

[7] Ibid.

[8] Ibid., pp. 3–5; see also European Commission 2010.

persons particularly their rights to protection of personal data and to ensure free flow of information within the European Union.[9]

Indeed, the scope of the Regulation is much broader than the Directive. Like its predecessor, the Regulation applies to the processing of personal data wholly or partly by automated means and to the processing other than by automated means of personal data which form part of a filing system or are intended to form part of a filing system. As its initial point, therefore, the GDPR applies to processing of personal data of natural person in both public and private sector regardless of the technology employed. This means both manual and automatic processing of personal data are covered by the Regulation. However, the GDPR does not apply to the processing of personal data in the course of an activity which falls outside the scope of the Union law; by a natural person in the course of a purely personal or household activity; and in the realm of national security and criminal law enforcement.[10] By contrast to the Directive, the GDPR does not only apply to all EU nations but every company holding data on EU citizens regardless of its geographical location.

Some definitions in the Directive have been left out from the Regulation. Others have been retained by being complemented with additional elements in order to broaden their scope or to clarify them. For example, the definition of "personal data" has been expanded to include a wider range of consumer data. In the Directive "personal data" is limited to information used to identify an individual while the GDPR has gone far to include online identification markers, location data, genetic information and more, in the definition of "personal data". In some instances, completely new definitions not part of the Directive have been introduced in the Regulation. Most of these definitions have been dealt with in such ways that they address the challenges of modern technologies.

The General Data Protection Regulation has retained most basic principles of data protection, in Directive 95/46/EC. However, to make the GDPR stronger, additional elements have been introduced notably the transparency principle, clarification of the data minimization principle and establishment of a comprehensive responsibility and liability of the data controller.[11] Similarly, the criteria of lawful processing have remained the same as in the Directive, only that the balance of interest criterion has to be applied. Also the Regulation clarifies conditions regarding re-purposing of the processing as well as conditions of consent with regard to processing of personal data.

Likewise, the GDPR retains almost the same data subject rights as the Directive, with few additional rights. The old rights have their scope been far clarified. The principle of transparency is at the root of the exercise of such rights. It is interesting to note in this regard that one of the new right introduced in the Regulation is 'the right to be forgotten' which simply mandates a data subject to direct the controller or processor, as the case may be, to erase and destroy completely any information relating to him or her, especially when its purpose or period required has expired or

[9]GDPR, Article 1.

[10]GDPR, Article 2.

[11]Explanatory Memorandum to the First Draft Proposal of the Regulation, p. 8.

consent has been withdrawn.[12] The Court of Justice of the European Union (CJEU) had considered the right to be forgotten in *Google Spain SL, Google Inc. v Agencia Española de Protección de Datos, Mario Costeja González*[13] prior to the adoption of the GDPR. The court held that an Internet search engine operator is responsible for the processing that it carries out of personal information which appears on web pages published by third parties. Accordingly, an Internet search engine must consider requests from individuals to remove links to freely accessible web pages resulting from a search on their name on the ground that the search results appear to be inadequate, irrelevant or no longer relevant or excessive in the light of the time that had elapsed.

The other right introduced by the GDPR is data portability which allows individuals to obtain and reuse their personal data for their own purposes across different services. It allows them to move, copy or transfer personal data easily from one IT environment to another in a safe and secure way, without hindrance to usability.[14]

As far as obligations are concerned, the GDPR clarifies issues of controller and processor's obligations in the data processing. Joint data controllers are also clarified in the GDPR. It is noteworthy that the Regulation introduces in clear terms the 'principle of accountability' as an obligation on the part of data controllers and processors. Controllers and processors are also obliged to carry out a data protection impact assessment prior to risky processing operation.[15] Also important to note is that the Regulation puts obligation on data controllers and processors to employ Data Protection Officers (DPO) whom will be required to possess knowledge on issues of data protection law and regulations.[16] The officer is required to discharge his or her duties with some levels of independence. There is also a requirement of data breach notification. The GDPR introduces a security breach communication framework for all data controllers regardless of the sector in which they operate. Notification obligations (to supervisory authorities and to data subjects) are triggered by accidental or unlawful destruction, loss, alteration, unauthorised disclosure of, or access to, personal data.[17]

The general principles of transfer of personal data to third countries and international organizations are still maintained by the Regulation. The criteria and procedures for the adoption of an 'adequacy' decision by the Commission are based on Articles 25 and 26 of the Directive: rule of law, judicial redress and independent supervisory authority. However, the Regulation makes it clear that there is a possibility for the Commission to assess the level of protection afforded by a territory or a processing sector within a third country. Also, binding corporate rules and standard contractual clauses are clearly spelt as means to be considered in the 'adequacy' assessment of data protection levels in third countries. It is also interesting to note

[12]GDPR, Article 17.

[13]Case C-131/12, Judgment of the Court (Grand Chamber), 13 May 2014.

[14]GDPR, Article 20.

[15]GDPR, Article 35.

[16]GDPR, Article 37.

[17]GDPR, Articles 33, 34.

that in assessing the level of adequacy of protection, EU will take into account the third country's accession to the Council of Europe Convention of 28 January 1981 for the Automatic Processing of Personal Data and its Additional Protocol.[18]

Choice of law and jurisdiction rules have been radically changed in the Regulation. While in the Directive, these were based upon the 'territoriality principle' in the Regulation, such rules are based upon the 'country of origin' principle.

The Regulation clarifies a number of enforcement measures to be available for data subjects to enforce their rights. Sanctions and compensations have been enhanced. Previously the Directive did not clarify these issues as they were only left to the member states to provide them in their national data protection legislation.

The GDPR has also introduced a new concept not addressed in the Directive 95/46/EC. This is privacy by design and by default. It is noteworthy that privacy is not only regulated by legislation. There are other means that may help to protect privacy. Privacy by design and by default is one such other means. In this regulatory approach, privacy is considered as a fundamental component in the design and maintenance of information systems and mode of operation for each organisation. According to Article 25 of the GDPR, the data controller is required to implement appropriate technical and organisational measures for ensuring that, by default, only personal data which is necessary for each specific purpose of the processing are processed. This obligation relates to the amount of personal data collected, the extent of their processing, the period of their storage and their accessibility.

In terms of governance structure, the GDPR has replaced the Article 29 Working Party with the European Data Protection Board. Yet the Board is similarly composed of representatives (i.e. heads) of national supervisory authorities of each member state. Members of the Commission are no longer part of the Board, although they may attend its meetings, etc. The Regulation clarifies the independence of the Board, and describes its responsibilities and roles. Data protection regulators are provided just as in the Directive. A single lead supervisory authority located in the Member State in which an organisation has its main establishment regulates that organisation's compliance with the GDPR.

8.3 The Tanzanian Data Protection Law Landscape

8.3.1 The Context

Tanzania is a United Republic of the defunct sovereign state called Tanganyika (now mainland Tanzania) and Zanzibar. The two entities united on 26 April 1964. The Union resulted in two governments, the government of the United Republic of Tanzania and the Revolutionary Government of Zanzibar. The government of the United Republic of Tanzania has dual mandates. It caters for union matters between

[18] GDPR, Recital 106.

mainland Tanzania and Zanzibar. The United Republic also caters for non-union matters for mainland Tanzania.[19] On the other hand, the Revolutionary Government of Zanzibar caters for non-union matters for Zanzibar.

The Constitution of United Republic of Tanzania (URT) 1977 is the supreme law. Any law or conduct that contravenes the Constitution becomes invalid.[20] There is a similar provision in the Constitution of Zanzibar 1984.[21] The executive powers in the United Republic are vested in the President of the United Republic while for Zanzibar, the President of the Revolutionary Government of Zanzibar.[22] Legislative powers are vested in the Parliament of the United Republic of Tanzania and Zanzibar House of Representatives.[23] In both cases the legislature consists of the President and National Assembly. The latter is largely composed of elected representative of the people. The legal system in the United Republic of Tanzania and Zanzibar follows the English common law. The latter is based on case law and precedents.

The Tanzanian socialism based on *Ujamaa* ideology used to be the major determinant of the Tanzanian socio-economic and political context until 1990s. Today most of socio-economic and political context is based upon liberalism, although the Constitution still mentions in its preamble *Ujamaa* as the national ideology. The political system prevailing today in Tanzania is multi-partyism.

Technologically, Tanzania has come far. As pointed out, after independence, particularly in 1974, Tanzania banned the importation of computers and related equipment in the country.[24] This was done through the Government Gazette.[25] However, in the late 1980s the ban was lifted and by 1990s, there was proliferation of computers in the country and their increasing usage in the public and private sectors.[26] The importation of the mobile phone technology in 1990s as well as the Internet particularly around 2000s, has seen significant penetration of ICTs in Tanzania. A survey conducted by the Tanzania Regulatory Communications Authority (TCRA) reveals that by June 2010, Tanzania had an estimated number of 4.8 million internet users.[27] Out of this number, only 5% used internet services from cyber cafes, 55% used internet from organisations or institutions, and 40% from households.[28] In terms of penetration, the survey reveals that only 11% of Tanzanians were accessing and

[19]Non-union matters refer to all the matters that are not listed in the First Schedule of the Tanzanian Constitution.

[20]URT Constitution 1977, Articles 30(5), 64(5).

[21]Katiba ya Zanzibar ya 1984, Ibara ya 4.

[22]URT Constitution 1977, Article 4(1) and Katiba ya Zanzibar ya 1984, Ibara ya 26.

[23]Ibid., Article 64 and Ibara ya 78 respectively.

[24]Mgaya 1994.

[25]Ibid.

[26]Makulilo 2006.

[27]Tanzania Communications Regulatory Authority 2010 Report on internet and data services in Tanzania: A supply-side survey. http://www.tcra.go.tz/publications/InternetDataSurveyScd.pdf. Accessed 4 December 2019.

[28]Ibid.

using internet services.[29] On the other hand, by March 2010, there were more than 17 mobile phone users in Tanzania.[30]

8.4 The Regime of Data Protection Law

8.4.1 The Constitutional Right to Privacy

Tanzania has no general data protection legislation. However, the Constitution of the United Republic of Tanzania provides for constitutional protection of an individual privacy. Article 16(1) of the Constitution states that every person is entitled to respect and protection of his person, the privacy of his own person, his family and of his matrimonial life, and respect and protection of his residence and private communications. Yet the right to privacy stated in the Tanzanian Constitution is not absolute. It is limited in a number of ways. Article 16(2) of the Constitution states that for the purpose of preserving the person's right in accordance with this Article, the state authority shall lay down legal procedures regarding the circumstances, manner and extent to which the right to privacy, security of his person, his property and residence may be encroached upon without prejudice to the provisions of this Article.

In addition to the above specific restrictions of the right to privacy in the URT Constitution, there are restrictions of general nature of the right to privacy as provided in Article 30(2) of the Constitution.[31] Interpreting this clause, the Court of Appeal of Tanzania (the highest court) has generally laid down the legal standards against which any law which seeks to limit or derogate from the basic right of individual has

---

[29]Ibid.

[30]The Citizen 2010 Mobile Phone Users now top 17 million. Tanzania Communications Regulatory Authority 2010 Report on internet and data services in Tanzania: A supply-side survey. http://www.tcra.go.tz/publications/InternetDataSurveyScd.pdf. Accessed 4 December 2019.

[31]This provision states as follows:

"It is hereby declared that the provisions contained in this Part (Bill of Rights) of this Constitution which set out the principles of rights, freedom and duties, do not render unlawful any existing law or prohibit the enactment of any law or the doing of any lawful act in accordance with such law for the purposes of: (a) ensuring that the rights and freedoms of other people or of the interests of the public are not prejudiced by the wrongful exercise of the freedoms and rights of individuals; (b) ensuring the defence, public safety, public peace, public morality, public health, rural and urban development planning, the exploitation and utilisation of minerals or the increase and development of property of any other interests for the purposes of enhancing the public benefit; (c) ensuring the execution of a judgement or order of a court given or made in civil or criminal matter; (d) protecting the reputation, rights and freedoms of others or the privacy of persons involved in any court proceedings, prohibiting the disclosure of confidential information or safeguarding the dignity, authority and independence of the courts; (e) imposing restrictions, supervising and controlling the information, management and activities of private societies and organisations in the country; or (f) enabling any other thing to be done which promotes or preserves the national interest in general.

to meet. In *Kukutia Ole Pumbuni and Another v Attorney General and Another*,[32] the Court held that any act which restricts fundamental rights of the individual must strike a balance between the interests of the individual and those of the society of which the individual is a component. Moreover, such law must not be arbitrary and the limitations imposed by it must not be more than is reasonably necessary to achieve the legitimate objective.

So far there is little case law interpreting Article 16 on the constitutional right to privacy. The High Court missed an opportunity to interpret the scope of the constitutional right to privacy in the case of Irene *Uwoya v Global Publishers Ltd and Others*,[33] where Irene Uwoya claimed for violation of her right to privacy due to the defendants' act of publishing of photographs, videos and articles revealing her sexual life. This case was not decided on merit. It was dismissed due to the plaintiff's lack of appearance in court. Similarly, in *Jebra Kambole v The Attorney General*,[34] the petitioner abandoned his constitutional claim of the right to privacy in the course of submission. Accordingly, the court did not have an opportunity to interpret Article 16 of the Tanzanian Constitution. The only case, up to present, in which the High Court has offered interpretation of the right to privacy under Article 16 of the URT Constitution, is *Jamii Media Company Ltd v The Attorney General and Inspector General of Police*[35] where the court construed the scope of the "disclosure orders" in relation to the law enforcement under the Cybercrimes Act 2015.

In *Jamii Media* the High Court of Tanzania considered the constitutionality of the "disclosure orders" under the Cybercrimes Act. In this case, *Jamii Media* filed a petition against the Tanzanian police force, alleging that the police force's power to demand personal information of individuals suspected of crimes was unconstitutional. *Jamii Media* challenged the constitutionality of Sections 32 and 38 of the Cybercrimes Act in order to protect the privacy of information of its subscribers who registered in the Jamii Forums and engaged in various topics critical to the government.

In its submission, *Jamii Media* argued that the provision of Section 32 of the Act is arbitrary as it does not require the police to disclose the criminal case under investigation when they issue "disclosure orders". Also, it argued that there were no regulations made by the responsible Minister as required under Section 39 of the Cybercrimes Act to prescribe procedures for interfering with the basic right. Lack of regulations was a breach of Article 16(2) of the Constitution which requires such procedures. The other argument advanced by the petitioner was that, Section 32 is too

[32] *Kukutia Ole Pumbuni and Another v Attorney General and Another* (1993) TLR 159:167. http://www.jurisafrica.org/docs/ald-mcm/2-constitutional-dev-inafrica/2(vi)%20KUKUTIA+OLE+PUMPUN+AND+ANOTHER+v+ATTORNEY+GENERAL+AND+ANOTHER+1993+TLR+159.pdf. Accessed 4 December 2018.

[33] High Court of Tanzania, Dar es Salaam, *Irene Uwoya v Global Publishers Ltd and Others,* 2013, Civil Case No. 83, (unreported).

[34] High Court of Tanzania, Dar es Salaam (Main Registry), *Jebra Kambole v The Attorney General*, 2015, Miscellaneous Civil Cause No. 35 (unreported).

[35] High Court of Tanzania, Dar es Salaam (Main Registry), *Jamii Media Company Ltd v The Attorney General and Inspector General of Police,* 2016, Miscellaneous Civil Cause No. 9 (unreported).

wide because it requires a person to surrender to the police, information in a form that can be taken away. Accordingly, if the police take away electronic devices such as laptops, mobile phones, Ipads, tablets, etc. in connection with relevant information required by the police, there is no guarantee that the investigator will not access other pieces of information contained in the same device and which is irrelevant to the matter being investigated. Overall, the petitioner argues that Section 32 is unreasonable, arbitrary and lacks safeguards against possible abuse by the police, and for that it violates an individual's right to privacy enshrined under Article 16(1) and (2) of the Constitution. The respondent's case was simply that the Cybercrimes Act was lawfully enacted, therefore the legislation is valid. Moreover, the respondent argued that the provisions challenged are merely investigatory and do not determine the rights of the people conclusively.

In its judgment, the Court found for the respondent holding that Section 32 of the Cybercrimes Act does not empower the police to take away the devices. The court went further to hold that the words "shall be deemed to require the person to produce or give access to it in a form in which it is legible and can be taken away" under this section of the Act are in reference to data not the device.

8.4.2 Statutory Law for Protection of Personal Data

The law on the protection of personal data in Tanzania is undeveloped. The country has no general data protection legislation. The law reform leading to the enactment of such law has not gone far since 2016 when the Tanzanian Law Reform Commission issued a consultation call for public opinion with the view of proposing a law in this field. The status of this process remains unknown to date to the public. Previously in 2014 the Ministry of Communication, Science and Technology law prepared a draft Data Protection Bill. This draft Bill has never been made public except to a limited number of stakeholders.[36]

Like data protection legislation as well as data protection bills in many African countries, the Tanzanian draft Data Protection Bill is based upon the EU Data Protection Directive 95/46/EC. It covers processing of personal data in the public and private sectors by automated and non-automated means. The Bill exempts from its scope processing of personal data by or on behalf of the government and which involves national security, defence or public safety; or the purpose of which is the prevention, investigation or proof of offences.[37]

In addition, the draft Data Protection Bill contains the usual eight data protection principles with restriction of collection of personal data unless the collection is for a lawful purpose, directly related to a function or activity of the data collector and the collection of the data is necessary or incidental for, or directly related to, that

---

[36] For critical comments, see Boshe 2014, 2016.

[37] Draft Data Protection Bill, s. 5(3)(b).

purpose.[38] Likewise, a data controller is prohibited from collecting personal data by unlawful means; or by means that, in the circumstances are unauthorised; or intrude to an unreasonable extent upon the privacy of the data subject concerned.[39] The Bill requires that where a data controller holds personal data that was collected in connection with a particular purpose, it shall not use that data for any other purpose.[40] It also provides that where a data controller holds personal data, it shall not disclose the data to a person, body or agency, other than the data subject concerned unless as authorised under specific circumstances.[41]

Under the draft Data Protection Bill, a data controller is restricted to hold personal data for period longer than it is necessary.[42] The Act also establishes a data protection authority to implement the Act.

If the draft Data Protection Bill is enacted without any significant changes, it will provide minimum information processing principles as well as conditions for such processing. However, with the recent coming in force of the General Data Protection Regulation (GDPR) in Europe, on 25 May 2018, this draft Bill might not fulfil the adequacy requirement of the EU law. The latter restricts transfer of personal data from Europe to non-EU member states (also known as third countries) unless the third country provides an adequate standard of protection of personal data. Since the GDPR has a world-wide effect, the draft law process would benefit from the EU law reform process.

Although Tanzania has no comprehensive data protection legislation, some principles and conditions for processing personal data are available in sector specific legislation. The Electronic and Postal Communications (Consumer Protection) Regulations (the Consumer Protection Regulations)[43] provide for the basic principles and conditions for processing personal data in the communications sector. The Regulations apply on entities which are licenced to provide electronic communication or postal services in the course of their business purposes. Accordingly, the collection and maintenance of personal information is required to comply with six information processing principles.

The first data protection principle is that personal information must be fairly and lawfully collected and processed. Second, collection and processing of personal data must be for identified purposes. Third, the processing of personal data must be based on accurate information. Fourth, personal information must be processed in accordance with the consumer's other rights. The fifth principle is that personal data must be protected against improper or accidental disclosure. Sixth, personal data must not be transferred to any party except as permitted by terms and conditions agreed

[38]Draft Data Protection Bill, s. 6(1).

[39]Draft Data Protection Bill, s. 6(2).

[40]Draft Data Protection Bill, s. 9.

[41]Draft Data Protection Bill, s. 10.

[42]Draft Data Protection Bill, s. 13(1).

[43]Electronic and Postal Communications (Consumer Protection) Regulations, 2018, R.6, https://www.tcra.go.tz/images/documents/regulations/10_GN_61__The_Electronic_and_Postal_Communications_Consumer_Protection__Regulations_2018.pdf.

with consumer, as authorised by the Tanzania Communication Regulatory Authority (TCRA) or otherwise as permitted by other applicable laws and regulations.

The major limitation of the Consumer Protection Regulations is that they are only applicable in the communications sector. This means the processing of personal data in other sectors is beyond the purview of the Regulations. Also, the Regulations fail to provide for the retention period of personal data in the custody of private and public sector entities risking data to be held by service providers for an indefinite period. Consent which is normally one of the pre-conditions for processing personal data is also not provided for in the Consumer Protection Regulations. Similarly, there are no usual rights of data subjects in the Regulations such as the right to be forgotten.

Other statutes which have implication to the protection of the right to privacy include the Regulations and Identification of Persons Act, Cap.36 R.E 2002. In 2011Tanzania commenced to register and issue national identification cards (National IDs) to its citizens and residents. All matters relating to national IDs are provided for under the Regulation and Identification of Persons Act. This Act requires officers working for the agency not to disclose information collected from individuals for purposes of registration except under specific conditions provided by the law itself.

The Human DNA Regulation Act 2009 is another piece of legislation with some provisions relevant to protection of the right to privacy in Tanzania. The DNA Act regulates the collection, packing, transportation, storage, analysis and disposal of sample for human DNA and disclosure of genetic information and research. It incorporates in part IV (ss. 23-37) provisions governing collection and analysis of sample for human DNA. Also, the Act incorporates provisions governing disclosure of information on human DNA in part VIII (ss. 52-65).

Another piece of legislation for protection of privacy in the field of health sector is the HIV and AIDS (Prevention and Control) Act 2008. The latter protects personal data in the context of HIV/Aids. The Act criminalises certain conducts and practices by health practitioners. One of such conducts is subjecting individuals into HIV test without their consent or knowledge.[44] The other principle contained in the HIV Act is about communication of HIV test results. Section 16(1) of the Act states that the results of an HIV test shall be confidential and shall be released only to the person tested. Moreover, the HIV Act very generally places an obligation of confidentiality to medical practitioners in handling all medical information and documents.[45]

8.5 The GDPR Influence on Tanzanian Law Reform

The Tanzanian data protection law reform has not gone far. It has largely been influenced by the Directive 96/45/EC as demonstrated by the 2014 draft Data Protection

[44]See Section 15(7) of the HIV and AIDS (Prevention and Control) Act, which states, 'Any health practitioner who compels any person to undergo HIV testing or procures HIV testing to another person without the knowledge of that other person commits an offence'.

[45]The HIV and AIDS (Prevention and Control) Act, s. 17(1).

Bill. There is currently no new version of the draft law published that reflects the spirit of the GDPR. Accordingly, the influence of the GDPR on Tanzania cannot be fully drawn at this stage. This is because, the impact of a law does not only depend upon the textual analysis but also many other factors-chiefly among them is enough practice of the law. Nonetheless, it is still possible to analyse certain implications of the GDPR at this moment.

First, the GDPR has a worldwide scope. Accordingly, it applies on data controllers and processors in Tanzania much the same as it does in Europe if Tanzanian data controllers and processors have EU 'establishments' where personal data is processed 'in the context of the activities' of such an establishment. The term 'establishment' implies the effective and real exercise of activity through stable arrangements.[46] In *Weltimmo v NAIH*[47] the CJEU observed that the notion of 'establishment' is a broad and flexible concept that should not be confined to legal form. The presence of a single representative may be sufficient. Accordingly, a Tanzanian data controller or processor who processes personal data of a data subject in the European Union under the umbrella of 'establishment' is subject to the ambit of the GDPR. More precisely, data controllers or processors in Tanzania not established in EU may still be subject of the GDPR if they process personal data of EU data subjects in connection with 'the offering of goods or services' or 'monitoring their behaviour'. Factors such as the use of language on websites which offer goods or services or currency generally used in one or more EU member states are relevant in ascertaining whether such a controller or processor which is not established in EU is actually offering goods or services or is monitoring behaviour of EU data subjects.[48] Mere accessibility of the controller's or processor's or intermediary's website in the Union, of an email address or of other contact details, or the use of language generally used in the third country where the controller is established, is not sufficient to ascertain offering of goods or services or monitoring of behaviour.[49] Thus, data controllers and processors in Tanzania must comply with the requirements of the GDPR under those circumstances. Overall, compliance of the Tanzanian data protection controllers and processors to the GDPR is mandatory, short of which heavy fines under the GDPR are likely to be applied.

Second, the GDPR has come up with new legal concepts such as privacy impact assessment, data portability, privacy by design and by default, the right to be forgotten, etc. Most of the concepts as well as new obligations to data controllers and processors in the GDPR which reflect the state of technology are not provided in the draft Data Protection Bill 2014. This is because the draft Bill was prepared prior to the GDPR or the drafters of such Bill did not go too far to ascertain the long-term effect of the GDPR. This means that, law reform may be required to update the 2014 draft Bill.

Third, the provisions on transfer of personal data to third countries incorporated in the GDPR have ramifications on legal reforms to third countries including Tanzania. Generally, the GDPR restricts transfer of personal data from the European Union to

---

[46]GDPR, Recital 22.

[47]C-230/14.

[48]GDPR, Recital 23.

[49]Ibid.

a third country if the latter does not offer an adequate protection of personal data. The regime of transfer of personal data in the GDPR necessarily requires Tanzania to undertake law reform to meet those criteria.

Lastly, it is imperative to note that companies in Tanzania that process EU personal data will have to comply with the GDPR. Breaches of personal data under the GDPR attract huge fines than those which are provided in the Directive. Accordingly, Tanzanian data controllers and processors must as well make sure they comply with the GDPR so that they are not held responsible for data breaches.

8.6 Conclusion

An overview of the above discussion and analysis clearly show that the GDPR has significant influence on law reform on Tanzania. The most of important effect is on cross-border transfer of personal data. This triggers compliance by data controllers and processors in Tanzania to the requirements of the GDPR in the event they process personal data of data subject in the EU in the context of 'establishment' or offer goods and services to EU data subjects or monitor their behaviours. Compliance to EU data protection standards may mean that Tanzania has to reform its laws in line with the Regulation.

References

Boshe P (2014) An evaluation of the Data Protection Bill in Tanzania. PL & BIR 127:25–26

Boshe P (2016) Data privacy law reforms in Tanzania. In: Makulilo A B (ed) African data privacy laws. Springer, Switzerland, pp 161–187

European Commission (nd) Data protection. http://ec.europa.eu/justice/data-protection/document/index_en.htm. Accessed 4 December 2018

European Commission (2010) A comprehensive approach on personal data protection in the European Union. https://docbox.etsi.org/Workshop/2011/201109_CLOUD/01_ToolsAndLegalConcepts/EC_DirectorateGeneralJustice_klabunde.pdf. Accessed 2 December 2019

Makulilo A B (2006) The admissibility of computer printouts in Tanzania: Should it be any different than traditional paper document? LLM thesis. https://www.duo.uio.no/bitstream/handle/10852/20801/temp2-1.pdf?sequence=2. Accessed 2 December 2019

Mgaya K (1994) Development of information technology in Tanzania. In: Drew E P, Foster F G (eds) Information and technology in selected countries: Reports from Ireland, Ethiopia, Nigeria and Tanzania. http://www.tanzaniagateway.org/docs/development_of_information_techno_in_tanzania.pdf. Accessed 4 December 2018

Reding V (2011) The upcoming data protection reform for the European Union. IDPL1:3–5

Tanzania Communications Regulatory Authority (2010) Report on Internet and data services in Tanzania: A supply-side survey. http://www.tcra.go.tz/publications/InternetDataSurveyScd.pdf. Accessed 4 December 2018

Prof. Dr. Alex B. Makulilo, Faculty of Law, The Open University of Tanzania, Dar es Salaam, Tanzania.

Chapter 9
Data Protection Around the World: Turkey

Başak Erdoğan

Contents

Abstract Like elsewhere in the world, data protection law is a popular topic as an emerging branch in the legal world in Turkey. After the adoption of Law no. 6698 on the Protection of Personal Data ("DPL") and the formation of the Turkish Data Protection Authority ("DPA") in 2016, the protection of data subjects' rights with regards to personal data and privacy has become a major subject of discussions both in the academia and in practice. This chapter deals with Turkey's stand concerning personal data protection in comparison with the General Data Protection Regulation ("GDPR"). To that extent, this chapter firstly analyses Turkey's main laws and regulations and case-law with regard to the protection of personal data. This is followed by a comparison of the Turkish DPL with the GDPR, where the strengths and weaknesses of Turkish law in the field of data protection are demonstrated. The chapter concludes with the possible application of the GDPR in Turkey and its impact on the Turkish data protection law.

B. Erdoğan (✉)
MEF University, Ayazağa Cad., No: 4, 34396 Maslak, Sarıyer, Istanbul, Turkey
e-mail: erdoganb@mef.edu.tr

E. Kiesow Cortez (ed.), *Data Protection Around the World*,
Information Technology and Law Series 33,
https://doi.org/10.1007/978-94-6265-407-5_9

Keywords General Data Protection Regulation · GDPR · Turkey · Data protection law · DPL · Data Protection Authority · Harmonisation · Extraterritoriality

9.1 Introduction and an Overview of the Turkish Data Protection Law

9.1.1 Introduction

The rise of massive data collection is one of the most important forces shaping today's society. The ramification of this trend in the legal world is the need for protecting privacy against acts such as profiling and the unauthorized or unlimited collection of data. The legal world could not oversee this trend; hence, many countries developed rules for protecting personal data. One of the very advanced and detailed legislation on this issue is prepared by the European Union ("EU"). The General Data Protection Regulation ("GDPR")[1] which entered into force on 25 May 2018 has also attracted attention in Turkey. Having been a candidate member for over 30 years, Turkey has many reasons to bring its data protection law into line with EU standards.

Turkey has also welcomed a new data protection law namely the Law no. 6698 on the Protection of Personal Data ("DPL")[2] in 2016 and has established a public authority for the surveillance of the protection of personal data, namely the Data Protection Authority ("DPA") the same year. The DPL is the result of long-lasting discussions and draft legislations. Until the DPL came into force, several attempts to enact data protection laws had been initiated. The first preparations date back to 1995 with the establishment of the first commission to prepare a draft code on the protection of personal data. Since the beginning of the 2000s, several other draft codes were prepared, none of which resulted in codification. The final draft of the DPL was rapidly prepared and voted on in the Parliament in 2016, and came into force within the same year.[3]

This long period of preparation points out the depth of the discussion with regard to protection of personal data in Turkey. This chapter focuses on Turkey's data protection regulation and its relationship with the GDPR. In Sect. 9.1, the current data protection laws and regulations is briefly introduced along with current case-law. In Sect. 9.2, the DPL will be analysed in comparison with the GDPR. Section 9.3 addresses important issues concerning data protection law in Turkey. Lastly, Sect. 9.4 examines the possible interactions between the GDPR and Turkish data protection laws.

---

[1] Regulation (EU) 2016/679 of the European Parliament and of the Council of 27 April 2016 on the protection of natural persons with regard to the processing of personal data and on the free movement of such data, and repealing Directive 95/46/EC (General Data Protection Regulation), Official Journal ("OJ") L 119.

[2] Kişisel Verilerin Korunması Kanunu, [Law on the Protection of Personal Data] OJ no. 29677, 24 March 2016.

[3] See Küzeci 2018, pp. 311–314.

9.1.2 Data Protection Legislation in Turkey

Although a specific code on data protection is quite recent, Turkish regulations and case-law concerning data protection rights and privacy are very extensive. Below, first the Turkish data protection regulations, then the relevant case-law will be presented.

Turkey's main legislation regarding data protection is the DPL. The DPL entered into force on 07.10.2016[4] and is based on Directive 95/46/EC on the Protection of Individuals with regard to the Processing of Personal Data and on the Free Movement of such Data[5] ("Directive 95/46/EC"), which was in force before the GDPR.

Due to the lack of specific legislation regarding data protection until 2016, a variety of different regulations and codes include articles concerning the protection of personal data.[6] In addition to these rules, Articles 23–25 in Turkish Civil Code ("TCC")[7] are also applicable to the protection of personal data within the scope of protection of personal rights. On the other hand, with the reform in Turkish Penal Code ("TPC")[8] in 2005, crimes of recording personal data, illegally sharing or collecting personal data, and non-annihilation of personal data were introduced. The DPL also makes specific reference to these rules.[9]

Prior to the DPL, another crucial step was the recognition of the right to data privacy in the Turkish Constitution. Following the referendum in 2010, a new paragraph was added to Article 20 of the Turkish Constitution on the right to privacy. The said paragraph gives a general right on data protection and provides that data processing is only possible upon explicit consent or by law.

Following the enactment of the DPL, supplementing regulations were also adopted. These are: The Regulation on the Erasure, Destruction or Anonymisation of Personal Data,[10] the Regulation on the Working Organisation of the Data Protection

---

[4]However, some articles in the DPL entered into force six months after the publication of the Law in the OJ. These are articles concerning data transfer (Article 8), data transfer to other countries (Article 9), rights of data subjects (Article 11), complaint procedure to data controllers (Article 13), complaint procedure to the DPA (Article 14), the examination procedure by the DPA (Article 15), the registry of data controllers (Article 16), crimes (Article 17) and sanctions (Article 18).

[5]Directive 95/46/EC of the European Parliament and of the Council of 24 October 1995 on the protection of individuals with regard to the processing of personal data and on the free movement of such data, (1995) OJ L 281.

[6]Examples are: Law on the Regulation of Electronic Trade ("ETL")—Elektronik Ticaretin Düzenlenmesi Hakkında Kanun, OJ no. 29166, 5 November 2014; Electronic Communication Law ("ECL")—Elektronik Haberleşme Kanunu, OJ no. 27050 (bis.), 10 November 2008; Banking Law—Bankacılık Kanunu, OJ no. 25983 (bis.), 1 November 2005; Regulation on Patient Rights—Hasta Hakları Yönetmeliği OJ no. 23420, 1 August 1998.

[7]Türk Medeni Kanunu, OJ no. 24607, 08 December 2001 (entered into force 1 January 2002).

[8]Türk Ceza Kanunu, OJ no. 25611, 12 October 2004 (entered into force 1 April 2005).

[9]*See* Sect. 9.2.3.

[10]Kişisel Verilerin Silinmesi, Yok Edilmesi veya Anonim Hale Getirilmesi Hakkında Yönetmelik, OJ no. 30224, 28 October 2017 (entered into force 1 January 2018).

Authority,[11] the Regulation on the Registry of Data Processors,[12] the Regulation on the Data Protection Specialists,[13] the Regulation on the Organisation of the Data Protection Authority,[14] the Regulation on the Promotion of the Employers in the Data Protection Authority,[15] the Regulation on the Disciplinary Chief of the Data Protection Authority,[16] and the Regulation on Personal Health Data.[17]

On the international level, Turkey is party to the 1981 Convention for the Protection of Individuals with Regard to Automatic Processing of Personal Data ("1981 Convention"), which was signed in 1981, but ratified 35 years later in 2016. Turkey also ratified the Additional Protocol to 1981 Convention[18] in 2016 but not yet the Additional Protocol[19] in 2018. On the other hand, Turkey is party to the European Convention on Human Rights and Fundamental Freedoms since 1949.

9.1.3 Case Law

9.1.3.1 Constitutionality of Rules Dealing with Personal Data

During the time between the adoption of Article 20 of the Constitution and that of the DPL, Turkish courts dealt with the constitutionality and legality of several laws and regulations on personal data. For instance, the Council of State (Danıştay), the high court for administrative matters has challenged the constitutionality of a provision in the Public Health Insurance Law ("PHIL")[20] imposing all health institutions to provide the Social Security Institution (Sosyal Güvenlik Kurumu) ("SSI") with data obtained from patients, and authorizing the Ministry of Employment and Social Insurance (Çalışma ve Sosyal Güvenlik Bakanlığı) to determine the legal boundaries of data sharing. The Constitutional Court ("CC") has concluded that data processing by the SSI in this matter is obligatory in order to conduct health services. Nonetheless,

[11] Kişisel Verileri Koruma Kurulu Çalışma Usûl ve Esaslarına Dair Yönetmelik, OJ no. 30242, 16 November 2017.

[12] Veri Sorumluları Sicili Hakkında Yönetmelik, OJ no. 30286, 30 December 2017 (entered into force 1 January 2018).

[13] Kişisel Veri Koruma Uzmanlığı Yönetmeliği, OJ no. 30327, 9 February 2018.

[14] Kişisel Verileri Koruma Kurumu Teşkilat Yönetmeliği, OJ no. 30403, 26 April 2018.

[15] Kişisel Verileri Koruma Kurumu Personeli Görevde Yükselme ve Unvan Değişikliği Yönetmeliği, OJ no. 30412, 5 May 2018.

[16] Kişisel Verileri Koruma Kurumu Disiplin Amirleri Yönetmeliği, OJ no. 30777, 17 May 2019.

[17] Kişisel Sağlık Verileri Hakkında Yönetmelik, OJ no. 30808, 21 June 2019.

[18] Additional Protocol to the Convention for the Protection of Individuals with Regard to Automatic Processing of Personal Data, regarding supervisory authorities and transborder data flows (ETS no. 181).

[19] Protocol amending the Convention for the Protection of Individuals with regard to Automatic Processing of Personal Data (CETS No. 223).

[20] Sosyal Sigortalar ve Genel Sağlık Sigortası Kanunu, OJ no. 26200, 16 June 2006 (entered into force in October 2008).

the CC has annulled the part of the said provision giving the authority to the Ministry on the grounds that the authority to establish rules regarding data protection belongs only to legislative bodies as per Article 20 of the Constitution; hence, governmental bodies do not possess such power.[21] Similarly, in 2014, the CC annulled the relevant Article of the ECL authorising the Information Technologies and Communications Institution (Bilgi Teknolojileri ve İletişim Kurumu) ("BTK") to establish conduct regarding data protection and confidentiality in the electronic communications sector, since it confers legal authority to an executive body and constitutes an excess of power.[22]

The Decree-Law no. 663[23] on the Organization and Powers of the Ministry of Health and Related Institutions had provided the SSI to obtain all personal health data from public and private health institutions. The CC has annulled the said Article on the grounds that fundamental rights and freedoms as well as political rights cannot be subject to and limited by decree-laws.[24] A very similar provision was re-implemented with an omnibus bill[25] in order to circumvent this decision of the CC; however, this provision was challenged, too. This time, the CC has concluded that the interference with the right to data protection was not proportional, especially since the challenged provision envisages collection, processing, and sharing of health data "*by all means*".[26,27] With a similar reasoning, the CC has annulled provisions in other Decree-Laws giving authority to custom officers[28] and Atatürk Higher Institution for Culture, Religion and History (Atatürk Kültür, Dil ve Tarih Yüksek Kurumu)[29] to demand any data or information within their fields.

Lastly, some provisions on penalties concerning crimes on data protection were challenged before the CC. For instance, Article 136 of the TPC was challenged due to its lack of clarity on the definition of the term "personal data". The Court concluded that the term personal data was clearly defined in many court decisions, therefore the relevant articles of the TPC comply with the principle of legality of crimes.[30]

---

[21] E. 2014/74, K. 2014/201, 25.12.2014, OJ no. 29364, 23.05.2015.

[22] E. 2013/122, K. 2014/74, 09.04.2014, OJ no. 29072, 26 July 2014.

[23] Sağlık Alanında Bazı Düzenlemeler Hakkında Kanun Hükmünde Kararname, OJ no. 28103 bis., 2 November 2011.

[24] E. 2011/150, K. 2013/30, 14 February 2013, OJ no. 28688, 26 June 2013.

[25] 6495 sayılı Bazı Kanun ve Kanun Hükmünde Kararnamelerde Değişiklik Yapılmasına Dair Kanun, OJ no. 28726, 2 August 2013.

[26] E. 2013/114, K. 2014/184, 4 December 2014, OJ no. 29418, 16 July 2015.

[27] The DPL included an article (Article 30) amending the annulled provision and stipulating that health data could be processed by health institutions in accordance with the DPL. This provision was recently annulled with the Decree Law no. 703 dated 2 July 2018. 703 Sayılı Anayasada Yapılan Değişikliklere Uyum Sağlanması Amacıyla Bazı Kanun ve Kanun Hükmünde Kararnamelerde Değişiklik Yapılması Hakkında Kanun Hükmünde Kararname, OJ no. 30473 (bis. 3), 9 July 2018.

[28] E. 2011/107, K. 2012/ 184, 22 November 2012, OJ no. 28892, 24 January 2014.

[29] E. 2011/141, K. 2013/10, 10 January 2013, OJ no. 28865, 28 December 2013.

[30] E. 2015/32, K. 2015/102, 12 November 2015, OJ no. 29550, 2 December 2015.

Furthermore, some provisions in the DPL[31] have been brought before the CC. The CC did not consider these articles unconstitutional.[32]

9.1.3.2 Right to Privacy and Interference by Public Authorities

In Turkey, case-law is very rich with regard to data protection and interference with privacy rights. The CC evaluated twice the legality of the obligatory declaration of religion in ID cards, in 1979[33] and in 1995.[34] In both decisions, the CC did not consider this as an oppression to express religious opinions or beliefs. This issue was also evaluated by the European Court of Human Rights ("ECHR")[35] and the Court has decided that this practice is a violation of Article 9 entitled freedom of thought, conscience and religion.[36] Similarly, a provision in the Law on Turkish Statistics[37] assigning real or natural persons, or institutions the duty to provide any data required by the Turkish Statistics Board (Türkiye İstatistik Kurumu) by any means, was declared unconstitutional, since according to the said Law "*the Board is entitled to demand any data regardless of the fact that this constitutes an interference with the fundamental rights and freedoms*".[38] Nevertheless, in another decision, the CC has not annulled another provision in the same Law obliging a random selection of citizens for the requirement to provide statistical information.[39]

As to the processing of sensitive data, the CC has evaluated a provision in the PHIL regarding an obligatory identity verification by means of using biometric data in health institutions and concluded that the interference is proportional, being that it is made in accordance with public interest and that the use of personal data is only limited to the content and duration of the service provided. Interestingly, according

---

[31] The exceptions to the requirement express consent, conditions regarding processing sensitive data, and regulatory authorities given to the DPA were among the challenged provisions.

[32] E. 2016/ 125, K. 2012/143, 28 September 2017, OJ no. 30310, 23 January 2018.

[33] E. 1979/9, K. 1979/44, 27 November 1979, OJ no. 16928, 13 March 1980.

[34] E. 1995/17, K. 1995/16, 21 June 1995, OJ no. 22433, 14 October 1995.

[35] ECHR (Second Section), *Sinan Işık v. Turkey*, no. 21924/05, 2 February 2010.

[36] The Court, however, did not examine the issue from the point of revealing sensitive personal data. ECHR (Second Section), Sinan Işık v. Turkey, no. 21924/05, 2 February 2010, paras. 37–53.

[37] Türkiye İstatistik Kanunu, OJ no. 25997, 18 November 2005.

[38] E. 2006/167, K. 2008/86, 20 March 2008, OJ no. 26917, 25 June 2008.

[39] E. 2010/12, K. 2011/135, 12 October 2011, OJ no. 28156, 28 December 2011.

to the CC, "*biometric data is not as sensitive as the ones mentioned in Article 6 of the 1981 Convention*".[40]

Another issue that the CC has dealt with is the vast surveillance conducted by police or other administrative bodies. For instance, the CC has not annulled a provision in the Identity Declaration Law[41] obliging accommodation providers and private health institutions as well as social service providers to collect data of consumers through computers and provide a network granting access to police and law enforcement officers. According to the CC, the provision aims at protecting the public order.[42] Similarly, the CC decided that the authority given to the National Intelligence Service (Milli İstihbarat Teşkilâtı) ("NIS") to have access to data kept by legal persons or institutions as well as to all records in criminal proceedings is constitutional.[43]

In contrast, the interception of telephone conversations of "all" Turkish nationals by the NIS via a court order has been considered as a violation of Article 8, the right to respect for private and family life, by the ECHR.[44] To that extent, the ECHR has also found violations of Article 8 in two cases where old and inaccurate police reports were used during an investigation conducted by public prosecutors[45] and where telephone interceptions were unlawfully used during a disciplinary investigation against a judge.[46]

The sale of personal data has also been challenged before the CC. In 2014, the CC annulled an article of the Law on Postal Services[47] providing an option to the National Post (Posta ve Telgraf Teşkilatı), a private joint stock company under Turkish Law, to sell the address data of real persons with their consent and of legal persons without such a requirement, given the fact that legal persons are also entitled to data protection.[48]

Turkish case-law also recognized the right to be forgotten. In a constitutional complaint regarding the non-erasure of a fourteen years old news on the Internet, the CC has stated that although the right to be forgotten has not been explicitly provided in any code, "*it belongs to the positive obligations of the State in order to enhance the self-entitlement of persons*".[49] The CC has rejected similar constitutional complaints on the grounds that not enough time has passed over the incident that would legitimize

---

[40] E. 2014/180, K. 2015/30, 19 March 2015, OJ no. 29315, 3 April 2015. This decision was rightfully criticised on the grounds that the mentioned provision did not entail necessary safeguards for the protection of personal data. Akgül 2015, p. 210.

[41] Kimlik Bildirme Kanunu, OJ no. 14591, 11 July 1973.

[42] E. 1996/68, K. 1996/01, 6 January 1999, OJ no. 24292, 19 January 2001.

[43] E. 2014/122, K. 2015/ 123, 30 December 2015, OJ no. 29640, 1 March 2016.

[44] ECHR (Second Section), *Mustafa Sezgin Tanrıkulu v. Turkey*, no. 2473/06, 18 May 2017, paras 62–65.

[45] ECHR (Second Section), *Cemalettin Şanlı v. Turkey*, no. 22427/04, 18 November 2008, paras 41–44.

[46] ECHR (Second Section), *Karabeyoğlu v. Turkey*, no. 30083/10, 7 June 2016, paras 112–121.

[47] Posta Hizmetleri Kanunu, OJ no. 28655, 23 May 2013.

[48] E. 2013/ 84, K. 2014/ 183, 04.12.2014, OJ no. 29294, 13 March 2015.

[49] *N.B.B*, No. 2013/5653, 3 March 2016.

the right to be forgotten.[50] The General Assembly of the Court of Appeal (Yargıtay), the high court for civil and criminal matters, also recognised the right to be forgotten in a case[51] in which the victim's name in a previous crime was fully given in a court decision and later in books mentioning it.

9.2 How Does the GDPR Interact with Turkish Jurisdiction?

As the DPL is based on the Directive 95/46/EC, it is built upon a similar basis with the GDPR. The GDPR, in contrast, has more advanced rules in terms of data protection and the maintenance of data security. Both systems will be assessed below in terms of field of application, principles and exceptions, and rights, duties and remedies.

9.2.1 Field of Application and Terms

Both the DPL and the GDPR set forth rules concerning the protection of personal data. The definition of data in the DPL and the GDPR is also very similar. The DPL has a wide margin regarding what information should be qualified as data. Accordingly, "*any information that is attributed or attributable to a natural person*" is personal data. Like the GDPR, the DPL only applies to the data of natural persons, while legal persons are excluded from its sphere of application.[52]

The DPL is applied to the *processing* of personal data. Following activities are listed as processing: "*collection, recording, storage, keeping, alteration, re-arrangement, disclosure, transferring, taking over, making available, categorisation, or blockage*" (Article 3(1)/e). The list is not exhaustive such as in the GDPR which lists "*collection, recording, organisation, structuring, storage, adaptation or alteration, retrieval, consultation, use, disclosure by transmission, dissemination or otherwise making available alignment or combination, restriction, erasure, or destruction*" as methods of data processing (Article 4(2)). Similar to the GDPR,

---

[50] *Asli Alp ve Şükrü Alp*, No. 2014/18260, 4 October 2017; *Asım Bayar ve Veysel Bayar*, No. 2014/4141, 4 October 2017; *G.D (2)*, No. 2014/1808, 4 October 2017; *Gözde Yiğit*, No. 2017/16026, 5 October 2017; *Fahri Göncü*, No. 2014/17943, 5 October 2017. In the first two cases the passage of time over the published content from the date of application was five and six years respectively, and in the third and fourth case, it was four years. In the last case, 11 years have passed over the published content, but the CC has concluded that the news was still relevant given the specifics of the case at hand.

[51] E. 2014/4-56, K. 2015/1679, 17 June 2015.

[52] As mentioned above, the CC has concluded that legal persons are also entitled to protection concerning personal data. See Sect. 9.1.3.2. Nevertheless, the DPA has decided that legal persons cannot seek protection under the DPL. No. 2018/131, 19 November 2018.

the DPL also recognizes non-automatic means of data processing alongside with automatic ones in case they are part of a filing system.

Like the GDPR, the DPL is applicable to any kind of personal data except anonymized data, but differently, the DPL does not contain a specific provision regarding pseudonymized data. As to sensitive data, Article 6 DPL defines the term as "*data regarding a person's race, ethnic origin, political views, philosophical beliefs, religion, sect or other beliefs, appearance, membership to associations, foundations or trade unions, health, sexual life, imprisonment or security measures as well as biometric and genetic data*". This definition is almost the same in the GDPR with the exception of "*sexual orientation*" being excluded in the DPL. Furthermore, under Article 9(1) GDPR, biometric and genetic data are deemed as sensitive data provided that they are "*processed for the purpose of uniquely identifying a natural person*".[53] Such difference does not exist under the DPL.

The DPL also distinguishes between data controllers and data processors. Data processor is a "*natural or legal person who process personal data on behalf of the data controller upon the authority given by them*" (Article 3(1)/ğ). On the other hand, data controller is a "*natural or legal person who is entitled to determine the purpose and means of data processing, and to operate and manage a data registration system*" (Article 3(1)/ı).

The data transfer to third parties is allowed upon explicit consent of the data subjects. Additionally, the conditions in Articles 5(2) and 6(3) should also be met. As to the data transfer to third countries, the express consent of data subjects is again required. Besides, Article 9 DPL only permits the transfer of data to "approved" third countries. In the absence of such approval, controllers in Turkey and in the third country need to give a written warranty and the DPA needs to approve the transfer of data. In accordance with Article 9(4) DPL, for such decision, the DPA shall consider the international agreements that Turkey has ratified, the reciprocity concerning data transfers between Turkey and the third country, the purpose and duration of data processing, third country's data protection regulations and practice, and the warranted safety measures given by the data controller. The DPA has not yet decided upon which third countries are approved; however, published required criteria to be evaluated.[54] Accordingly, the DPA would evaluate the criteria set out in Article 9(4) in addition to the establishment of an independent data protection authority, international conventions on data protection to which the third country is party of, regional or international organisations to which the third country is party of, and trade volume with the third country. In the absence of approved third countries, the DPA has however concluded in a decision[55] that corporate e-mails using the Google platform would entail the international transfer of data to a third country thus the use is subject to criteria set out in Article 9 DPL. Regarding adequacy decisions for third

[53] *Yücedağ* suggests that biometric and genetic data should be considered as sensitive data on the condition that they are processed for the purpose of identifying natural persons, as the GDPR suggests. Yücedağ 2017, p. 769.

[54] No. 2019/125, 2 May 2019.

[55] No. 2019/157, 31 May 2019.

countries, the GDPR refers to wider and more detailed requirements under Articles 45 and 46. Under the GDPR system, Turkey is not listed as one of the countries providing adequate protection.

9.2.2 *Principles and Exceptions*

In Article 4, the DPL recognizes the following principles: "*lawful and fair processing*", "*accurate and actual processing*", "*processing for specific, explicit and legitimate purposes*", "*processing in accordance with the purpose, as well as limited and proportionate processing*" and "*storing only within the time period envisaged in the law, or necessary for the purpose of processing*". The principles of "*transparency*",[56] "*appropriate security*" and "*accountability*"[57] in Articles 5(1)/a, 5(1)/f and 5(2) GDPR are not explicitly mentioned in the DPL. These principles, as well as the criteria set in Articles 5(2), and 6(2) and (3) determine the scope in which data processing is allowed.[58]

Article 5 DPL provides that processing is possible upon the explicit consent of the data subject. Consent should be "*specific to the content, based on information and given freely*" as per Article 3(1)/a DPL. The GDPR differentiates consent regarding personal data and for sensitive data. In contrast, the DPL requires explicit consent for both types of data in Articles 5(1) and 6(2). The GDPR stipulates the consent given by minors; however, there is no specific provision regarding consent given by minors in the DPL. Issues involving minors would be resolved under the TCC.[59]

The conditions for processing without data subject's express consent is regulated under Article 5(2) DPL. The principles which were based upon the Directive 95/46/EC are similar to those in the GDPR. The express consent is not required if, "*processing is explicitly envisaged in the law; it is necessary to protect the life or physical integrity of the data subject (or another person) who is not able to provide express consent due to practical impossibility, or whose consent is not legally valid; it is necessary for complying a contractual obligation provided that it is directly related to the conclusion or fulfilment of a contract; it is necessary for the fulfilment of a legal obligation by the data controller; it is necessary for the creation, use or protection of a right; it is necessary for legitimate interests of the data controller provided that it does not harm the fundamental rights and freedoms of the data subject*".[60] Differently, the DPL also recognizes the former disclosure of data by data subject as

---

[56] *Develioğlu* suggests that transparency should also be safeguarded as part of lawful and fair processing. Develioğlu 2017, p. 45.

[57] These principles are reflected in the responsibilities of data controllers under Article 12 DPL. Develioğlu 2017, p. 50.

[58] Yücedağ 2019, p. 49; Çekin 2018, pp. 42 and 45.

[59] In this sense, Yücedağ 2017, p. 767.

[60] According to Çekin, harming fundamental rights and freedoms is not an appropriate term and it should be read as "the legitimate interests should not override fundamental rights and freedoms of the data subject". Çekin 2018, pp. 73–74.

an exception to the requirement of explicit consent (Article 5(2)/d). The relationship between these conditions with the requirement for explicit consent is debated. The current tendency in the literature is to not seek a hierarchy between the requirement for express consent and others.[61] Another interpretation to this extent is to give the judge a discretionary power to determine whether data processing without express consent is lawful even if the mentioned conditions are met.[62]

Concerning exceptions to consent to the processing of sensitive data, the DPL makes a distinction between sensitive data regarding health and sexual life and other types of sensitive data. Without explicit consent, health and sexual data can only be processed by authorised bodies and institutions, or persons under the duty of confidentiality for the purposes of protecting public health, preventive medicine, conducting services on medical diagnosis, treatment and care services, planning health services, and their financing in accordance with Article 6(3) DPL.[63] On the other hand, other types of sensitive data may be processed without explicit consent if that is envisaged in the law.[64] In any case, the conditions required under Article 5 should also be met for the processing of sensitive data.[65] The GDPR, in contrast, has a different set of exceptions on processing sensitive data. Here, the manifest disclosure of the data by the data subject is an exception for the requirement of explicit consent (Article 9(2)/e).

Cases to which the DPL is not applied are similar to those in Directive 95/46/EC. The Directive 95/46/EC is not applied to public security, defence, or criminal law issues. Following the Directive 95/46/EC, the DPL has a similar, but wider exception in Article 28. The DPL does not apply to data processing for family purposes, for statistics provided that data is anonymised with public statistics, for art, history, literature or to processing made within the freedom of expression (Article 28(1)/a,b,c). In addition to these, the DPL does not apply to data processing made by public authorities for the purpose of national defence, national security, public security, public policy or economic security, or made by judiciary authorities (Article 28(1)/c and d). On the other hand, the obligation to inform and to register to the processors' registry does not apply in case data processing is necessary for preventing or investigating crimes, the data is already disclosed by the data subject, data processing is made by public authorities and is necessary for auditing or disciplinary actions, and in cases where data processing is necessary for tax or economic purposes.

[61] Dülger 2019, p. 26; Yücedağ 2017, p. 773.

[62] Develioğlu 2017, p. 58.

[63] The DPA has rendered a decision on the measures to be taken while processing sensitive data. *See* Sect. 9.1.3.2.

[64] The wording of Article 6(3) excluding the explicit envisaging consent in law for sensitive data whereas its requirement for normal types of data is criticized. *See* Küzeci 2018, pp. 332–333.

[65] Yücedağ 2017, pp. 772–773.

9.2.3 Rights, Duties and Remedies

The rights of data subjects and duties of controllers in the DPL have a similar nature to those in the GDPR. Nonetheless, rules in the GDPR are more detailed. The DPL recognizes the right to information, right to access, right to rectification, right to erasure, right to data portability, right to object and right to compensation. The DPL does not stipulate the right to be forgotten as envisaged in Article 17, but recognizes a less detailed right to erasure in line with the Directive 95/46/EC. As to the right to object, the DPL recognizes it only in case processing leads to an unfavourable result against the data subject. The wording of the provision seems to be more open to interpretation than the wording of Article 21 GDPR.

Concerning the duties of controllers, the DPL contains fewer comprehensive rules than the GDPR. For instance, the DPL does not provide a general obligation of recording. Neither is there a specific provision regarding data protection by design or by default mechanisms. Article 12 DPL lists general obligations of data controllers regarding data safety. These are: "*to take all technical and administrative measures to ensure data security, to conduct necessary inspections, to refrain from disclosing personal data obtained, and to inform the DPA immediately in case of unlawful acquisition of personal data by third parties*". Data controllers are jointly responsible with data processors in accordance with Article 12(2) DPL. In case of a data breach, controllers are under the obligation to inform the DPA as soon as possible. The DPA, by explicitly referring to the GDPR, concluded that the immediate period for informing data breaches is 72 h.[66]

Data controllers should register in the Data Controllers Registry.[67] The DPA also introduced the Information System on Data Controllers Registry (Veri Sorumluları Sicil Bilgi Sistemi) ("VERBIS"), an online database for the purpose of facilitating registry records. The DPA announced[68] the deadlines for the registration in VERBIS as follows: 01.10.2018–30.09.2019 for real or legal persons having more than 50 employees or a turnover above TRY 25,000,000, and for entities registered abroad; 01.01.2019–31.03.2020 for real and legal persons having less than 50 employees or a turnover under TRY 25,000,000, but processing sensitive data; 01.04.2019–30.06.2020 for public entities. Nevertheless, the deadline for real or legal persons having more than 50 employees or a turnover above TRY 25,000,000, and for entities registered abroad are extended to 31.12.2019.[69] In a former decision,[70] the DPA declared that processors using unautomated processing systems; public notaries; associations, foundations and trade unions that only process personal data concerning

---

[66]No. 2019/10, 24 January 2019.

[67]For an overview of the registration procedure, *see* Sümer 2019 A procrastinator's guide to data controller registration in Turkish data protection law. https://iapp.org/news/a/a-procrastinators-guide-to-data-controller-registration-in-turkish-data-protection-law/. Accessed 23 September 2019.

[68]No. 2018/88, 19 July 2018.

[69]No. 2019/265, 3 September 2019.

[70]No. 2018/32, 2 April 2018.

their employees, members and donators within their field of activity; political parties; lawyers; independent accountants; and certified public accountants are exempted from registration liabilities. In addition to these, customs brokers,[71] mediators,[72] and real or legal persons having less than 50 employees or a turnover under TRY 25,000,000 who do not process sensitive data[73] are exempted from registration liabilities by the DPA as well.

Other important novelties of the GDPR is the appointment of a data protection officer ("DPO") and the requirement to conduct a Data Protection Impact Assessment. These new institutions are not regulated under the DPL.

Article 13 DPL provides a complaint procedure for data subjects: they can file written complaints to data controllers which should be responded to within 30 days. In case of a negative or non-satisfactory response, data subjects could file another complaint before the DPA. The DPA can also act *ex officio* and examine a possible data breach without a prior complaint.

The DPL envisages three types of remedies: administrative sanctions, penal sanctions, and indemnity. Administrative fines are imposed if a data controller does not comply with the duty of transparency or with the requirements regarding data controllers' registry, does breach data security, or does not abide by the decisions of the DPA. The administrative fines range from TRY 5000 to TRY 1,000,000 depending on the severity of the violation. Multiple fines can be enforced by the DPA. In addition to the administrative fines, a disciplinary investigation is available if the violation is caused by public officials. Concerning penal sanctions, the DPL refers to Articles 135–138 TPC. Article 135 establishes an imprisonment sentence from one to three years in case of the recording of personal data. Article 136 imposes an imprisonment sentence from two to four years in case of unlawful acquisition and disclosure of personal data. Last but not least, Article 138 sets an imprisonment sentence for one to two years for not destroying personal data. Lastly, data subjects also have the rights envisaged in Articles 23–25 TCC to prevent infringements to personality rights. Accordingly, data subjects have the right to demand the cessation of the infringement, the prevention of a possible future infringement, the declaration of the infringement, to demand material or non-material indemnity, or to demand transfer of profits obtained from the infringement. The GDPR also holds a variety of different remedies. Depending on the severity of the breach, the GDPR includes very high administrative fines per Article 83. The right to demand indemnity is subject to Member State Law in accordance with Article 82 GDPR. The same holds for penal sanctions that may be applicable as per Member State Law following Article 84 GDPR.

[71]No. 2018/68, 28 June 2018.

[72]No. 2018/75, 5 July 2018.

[73]No. 2018/87, 19 July 2018.

9.3 Prominent Issues

Although Turkey adopted important laws and regulations on the protection of personal data, there are some obstacles on ensuring high protection standards. One of the biggest challenges to that extent is the frequent use of personal data both by public authorities and private companies. The DPA, on the other hand, has shown efforts to prevent the use of personal data especially in the private sector. The activities and relevant decisions of the DPA present a positive development. Nevertheless, the independency of the DPA is also a source of concern. Some of the important aspects of these issues will be reflccted below.

9.3.1 Frequent Use of Personal Data

In Turkey, the collection of personal data by public authorities has always been a problematic issue. Even after the adoption of special regulations on the protection of personal data, Turkish governmental bodies still possess wide authorities concerning processing and collection of personal data.

The digitalisation of public services has added another layer to this problem. For instance, many state institutions offer online documentation services in a portal called *e-State*.[74] The service has been offered to Turkish citizens since 2008. Persons can obtain their residency, civil registry, criminal and health records; they can pay their tax debts or student loans, or monitor court documents online within the portal. There are other online service portals that are run by public institutions as well. To name a few, MERNIS[75] is the database containing civil registry records; UYAP[76] database is used by legal personnel, lawyers and citizens to manage their legal disputes and legal records; lastly, e-Nabız[77] is the database containing health records and allowing citizens to obtain doctor appointments and other health related requests.

Ever since the digitalisation of public services has begun, the online storing of data raised questions about the level of data security offered by the state. Unfortunately, in 2016, a security breach occurred concerning another platform storing electorates' personal data and it was revealed that the data of electorates having the right to vote as of 2010 was hacked and leaked to the Internet. The hacked information consists of ID numbers, names, surnames, registered addresses, dates of birth, fathers' and mothers' names of nearly 50 million Turkish citizens.[78] Again, in 2016, it was revealed that

[74] https://www.turkiye.gov.tr. This website shows that over 44 million users are currently registered in the e-state database. Accessed 16 October 2019.

[75] https://www.nvi.gov.tr. Accessed 16 October 2019.

[76] http://www.uyap.gov.tr. Accessed 16 October 2019.

[77] https://enabiz.gov.tr. Accessed 16 October 2019.

[78] Hern A 2016 Database allegedly containing ID numbers of 50 m Turks posted online. https://www.theguardian.com/technology/2016/apr/04/database-allegedly-containing-id-numbers-of-50m-turks-posted-online. Accessed 16 October 2019; BBC News 2016 Turkish authorities

health data contained in the data system of 33 hospitals in Turkey was hacked.[79] Although access to websites showing both content was banned immediately after the leakage, probably the content can still be found on the Internet.

In 2013, the State Supervisory Council ("SSC") (Devlet Denetleme Kurulu) published an 817-page long report regarding personal data protection in Turkey. This report, which is no longer available online,[80] stresses many issues such as the lack of information of the personnel on the importance of data stored, use of passwords that are easy to crack, storage of same data by different public entities, lack of confidentiality agreements with IT companies and lack of safety measures to protect data, as obstacles for the adequate protection of personal data within public institutions.[81]

The sale of personal data by public authorities is another source of concern. In 2013, news appeared in the media alleging that the Ministry of Social Insurance sold health data within the public health insurance system to a private company.[82] Later on, this fact was confirmed in the reports prepared by the Court of Accounts (Sayıştay) and it was revealed that health data was sold to five different companies for TRY 65,000.[83] It is unfortunately unknown to what extent health data was shared and whether the data was anonymised.

As to the developments after the adoption of the DPL, Turkey has also adopted a new ID card that contains civil registry records, photo and biometric data of data subjects. Accordingly, an "ID sharing system" was introduced which allow a long list of legal persons such as banks, insurance companies, legal persons offering public services, and leasing companies to access civil registry data. The provisions are incorporated into the Law on Civil Registry Services[84] with a recent change in October 2017. Although the Law states that non-compliance would be subject to remedies set out in the DPA, access to civil registry data by such a wide group is a concern about privacy. Therefore, other methods for ensuring adequate protection of personal data is highly necessary,[85] given the unpleasant examples mentioned above.

'probing huge ID data leak'. https://www.bbc.com/news/technology-35978216. Accessed 16 October 2019.

[79] T24 Haber, 2016 Türkiye'deki 33 Hastane Verileri İnternete Sızdırıldı [In Turkey, Data from 33 Hospitals leaked to the Internet]. http://t24.com.tr/haber/anonymous-turkiyedeki-hastane-kayitlarini-hackledi-bilgiler-internete-sizdirildi,341067. Accessed 24 September 2019.

[80] The table of contents and the concluding part of this report are available on the website of Turkish Medical Association (Türk Tabipler Birliği). http://www.ttb.org.tr/images/stories/file/2015/ddk_rapor.pdf. Accessed 16 October 2019. References to the report are made to this available part of the document.

[81] TC Cumhurbaşkanlığı Devlet Denetleme Kurulu 2013, pp. 784–787.

[82] Erbaş Ö 2014 Kişisel Sağlık Verileri Satılamaz, ama SGK sattı [Personal Health Data cannot be sold but Social Security Institution Sold It]. https://m.bianet.org/bianet/saglik/159720-kisisel-saglik-verileri-satilamaz-ama-sgk-satti. Accessed 24 September 2019.

[83] Sayıştay 2014, pp. 49–53.

[84] 7039 sayılı Nüfus Hizmetleri Kanunu ve Bazı Kanunlarda Değişiklik Yapılmasına Dair Kanun, OJ no. 30229, 3 November 2017.

[85] Küzeci 2018, p. 453.

An interesting decision of the DBA shows how much data public authorities can obtain. The DPA rejected the complaint of a former public officer whose investigation records are still available in the personnel archive, on the grounds that the Regulation on Public Archive Services[86] stipulates the maintenance of such data for a period of 101 years.[87] It is clear that there is no public benefit for keeping records for a period that normally exceeds a person's lifetime.

Not only public authorities, but also private persons frequently use personal data. A problematic issue in practice is the use of personal data by private companies as a method of identity verification or security checks. For instance, banks as well as GSM companies make a copy of a person's ID,[88] even copies of previously paid invoices or credit card receipts for some of their operations. The 2013 SSC report states that GSM companies hold ID copies of around 68 million persons in Turkey.[89] Another example is private cargo companies that follow a decision of the BTK namely "Security Measures Concerning Postal Shipping"[90] rendered in 2016. Accordingly, cargo companies are under the obligation to store name, address details, and ID number of both the sender and the receiver. This information is required to be stored for two years within the cargo companies' database. Similarly, companies also require consumers to submit ID numbers from in distance contracts in order to be able to provide this information for shipping. Given that the ID number can only be given once and cannot be subject to change as per Article 46 of the Law on the Civil Registry Services, frequent use of ID numbers makes this information very susceptible to fraud. Unauthorized advertorial calls and SMS from companies are also a source of concern.[91]

Despite these negative experiences, Turkish data protection policies have been improved with the adoption of the DPL and the formation of the DPA. Both public and private institutions have been revising their privacy policies and data protection has gained the care and importance it needed. It is hoped that the consistent application of the DPL will change the outlook of data protection and privacy in Turkey.

---

[86]Devlet Arşiv Hizmetleri Hakkında Yönetmelik, OJ no. 19816, 16 May 1988.

[87]No. 2018/69, 28 June 2018.

[88]In fact, this practice is not allowed in accordance with Article 11(3) of Regulation on the ID Sharing System which states that institutions that have access to the ID sharing system as well as banks cannot demand copies of IDs or any other ID documentation. Kimlik Paylaşımı Sistemi Yönetmeliği, OJ no. 26370, 8 December 2006.

[89]TC Cumhurbaşkanlığı Devlet Denetleme Kurulu 2013, p. 784.

[90]BTK (2016) Posta Gönderilerine Güvenlik Tedbirlerine Yönelik Usul ve Esaslar, 2016/DK-YED/517, 27 December 2016, https://www.btk.gov.tr/uploads/boarddecisions/posta-gonderilerine-iliskin-guvenlik-tedbirlerine-yonelik-usul-ve-esaslar.pdf. Accessed 16 October 2019.

[91]*See* Sect. 9.1.3.2.

9.3.2 Activities of the DPA

The role of DPA as an authority monitoring personal data protection in practice is a welcomed development. Since its foundation with the DPL, the DPA not only deals with complaints from data subjects with regard to breaches concerning personal data, but also announces these through its website. The DPA also plays an active role in sharing knowledge on data protection law, including publishing various guidelines on different topics in data protection law. The DPA also publishes a periodical named "Kişisel Verileri Koruma Dergisi" (Data Protection Law Review) and organizes conferences regularly.

The most important role that the DPA bears is rendering decisions upon complaints from data subjects. The DPA publishes its decisions if the breach is frequent in practice, as per Article 15(6) DPL. Accordingly, the DPA has published various decisions on its website since its foundation. Although these decisions are only legally binding for the data subjects that made the complaint and the real or legal person that caused the breach, they present a very important example for the practice to ensure compliance; thus, they are a valuable asset for the protection of personal data.

The complaints that the DPA has dealt with concern a wide range of data breaches. They can be grouped as follows:

- **Unauthorized reveal of personal data**: The very first decision[92] of the DBA available, establishes a data breach by websites offering telephone directory services where people can access people's names through phone numbers or vice versa. In a subsequent decision,[93] the DPA has decided that companies offering services through counters and desks should organize their internal structure in a manner that prevents third people from collecting personal data of data subjects, so that they would not be able to hear, see, learn or obtain personal data while data subjects disclose them. The DPA has fined a pharmacy revealing a customer's health data to a third person due to absence of express consent,[94] and a lawyer for TRY 50,000 for mistakenly sending an SMS containing personal data to a different client.[95] The DPA has issued a warning to a company who operates online selling through its website and made available the data of customers to other registered customers.[96]
- **Safeguards for adequate protection**: A resolution from the DPA[97] establishes measures that need to be taken by data controllers processing sensitive data. Among them, most important ones are consistent and sustainable procedures, staff trainings, confidentiality agreements, encrypted storage and secure logs to

[92] No. 2017/62, 21 December 2017.
[93] No. 2017/61, 21 December 2017.
[94] No. 2018/143, 5 December 2018.
[95] No. 2019/166, 31 May 2019.
[96] No. 2018/91, 26 July 2018.
[97] No. 2018/10, 31 January 2018.

data, as well as security measures for the physical storage of data. In a different resolution,[98] the DPA has stipulated the duties of controllers' staff, who have access to personal data and reminds them to take all necessary technical and administrative precautions in order to prevent data processing out of purpose.

- **Compliance with the principles in the DPL**: The DPA has concluded in a decision that the use of fingerprint reader (i.e. biometric data) in a gym for establishing customer records as the only way of using the service provided is not in line with principles of processing in accordance with the purpose, as well as limited and proportionate processing.[99] In another decision, the DPA has decided that a company's method of anonymisation is not in line with the DPL, since it still involves personalised advertisement in users' social media accounts.[100] The DPA has sanctioned a cell-phone technical service company for a breakable pseudonymisation of customer data on their website with a fine of TRY 50,000,000[101] and later with TRY 150,000,000 for not enforcing necessary measures to prevent data breach.[102]
- **Unauthorized presentation of advertorial content to data subjects**: The DBA has issued a resolution on the cessation of the unwanted distribution of advertising SMS or e-mails and declared that criminal proceedings would be initiated against those who do not comply.[103] In addition to this, the DPA has also imposed administrative fines on companies who send such advertisement material without complying with the principle of legality.[104]
- **Privacy policy texts**: DPA has decided that clarification of the privacy policy for data subjects and the request for consent should be given in separate texts; hence data subjects should not be obliged to give their consent to the content of a privacy policy text only.[105] The DPA has also warned companies whose privacy policy texts are not in line with the DPL and subsequent regulations.[106] In a decision[107] on the data collected for a loyalty card of a supermarket chain, the DPA has decided that the wording in the privacy policy text allowing the collection of sensitive data should be modified.
- **Online data breaches**: The DPA instructed Mimar Sinan University, a public university in Turkey that published the results of an exam including the names of students publicly on the Internet, to create an exam announcement system that is not open to non-students.[108] In another decision, the DPA has sanctioned

---

[98] No. 2018/63, 31 May 2018.

[99] Nos. 2019/81 and 2019/165, 25 March 2019 and 31 May 2019.

[100] No. 2019/82, 25 March 2019.

[101] No. 2019/52, 5 March 2019.

[102] No. 2019/23, 14 February 2019.

[103] No. 2018/119, 16 October 2018.

[104] Nos. 2019/159, 2019/162 and 2019/204, 31 May 2019 and 8 July 2019.

[105] No. 2018/90, 26 July 2018.

[106] No. 2019/122, 2 May 2019.

[107] No. 2019/82, 25 March 2019.

[108] No. 2019/188, 1 July 2019.

Facebook to a fine of TRY 1,100,000 due to a data breach caused by a photo API bug which allowed third parties to access photos of around 300.000 users in Turkey for 12 days.[109] Another leakage in Facebook caused by a bug in the "*view as*" section allowing third party access to Facebook profiles has been subjected to a fine of TRY 1,600,000.[110] The DPA has decided to impose a fine of TRY 550,000 to Clickbus on the grounds that the company overlooked a data leakage for two months which affected 67.519 persons residing in Turkey.[111] The DPA has imposed a fine of TRY 1,450,000 on Mariott International Inc. because of a data breach in their guest reservation system which continued for four years.[112] Cathay Pacific Airway Limited was also sanctioned with a fine of TRY 550,000 for a data leakage in the customer database for a period of two months.[113] Dubsmash Inc, was fined TRY 730,000 due to a data breach which resulted in the sale of data and affected 679.269 persons from Turkey.[114] A tourism company also faced a fine of TRY 500,000 because of a data leakage following a cyber-attack to their server.[115] A company named S Şans Oyunları A.Ş. running an online betting website was sanctioned with a fine of TRY 180,000 for a leakage of an Excel file containing members information.[116]

- **Exceptions for express consent**: Following a request by a company in the oil sector, the DPA evaluated the lawfulness of an automated system created by the company. The system would allow the company to control the amount of oil sold with the help of licence plates and consequently prevent misuse. The company wanted to operate the system without seeking express consent from data subjects which had already been obtained in accordance with oil market regulations. According to the DPA, the use of the system falls under the exceptions of required express consent (legitimate necessity) provided that data subjects in the system are informed about the new usage of their data.[117]

9.3.3 The Nature of the DPA

Article 21(1) DPL states that the DPA is an independent authority and cannot take orders, instructions or advice from any other person or organisation. Following the recent change towards presidential regime[118] in Turkey, the nature and establishment

[109] No. 2019/104, 11 April 2019.

[110] No. 2019/269, 18 September 2019.

[111] No. 2019/141, 16 May 2019.

[112] No. 2019/143, 16 May 2019.

[113] No. 2019/144, 16 May 2019.

[114] No. 2019/222, 17 July 2019.

[115] No. 2019/255, 27 August 2019.

[116] No. 2019/254, 27 August 2019.

[117] No. 2019/78, 25 March 2019.

[118] Since its foundation in 1923, the Republic of Turkey had been governed under a parliamentary regime. However, in the referendum on 17 April 2017, amendments to the Constitution leading

of the DPA also changed. Consequently, the DPA is now under the authority of the Ministry of Justice as per Presidential Circular no. 1.[119] The Decree Law no. 703 introduced some changes to the DPL regarding the organisation of the DPA. Under the new system, four out of nine members is elected by the President, whereas five members is elected by the Parliament.[120] In addition to this, the DBA will no longer submit annual reports to the Prime Ministry. Annual reports will continue to be sent to the Presidency and Human Rights Examination Commission within the Parliament.

Before this change, the DPL required the members of the DPA to have at least 10 years of working experience in either the public or private sector as well as in NGOs or international organisations. This condition will not be required anymore. Furthermore, Article 21(3)/d of the Law stipulating that "*members who will be appointed to the task shall give their consent and care should be given to have members who have experience in this field*" is also abolished. According to Article 21(5) DPA, the selection of members by the Parliament is initiated with the proposals by political party groups or representatives which is followed by a secret vote in the Parliamentary General Assembly. The procedure concerning the selection of the members by the President, on the other hand, is not envisaged in the DPL. Furthermore, from now on the President shall decide on any investigation about the members of the DPA according to Article 21(11) DPL.

These changes raise questions about the independence of the DPA. The closeness of the DPA to the state organisation casts doubts on the working method of the DPA and the effectiveness of the safeguards for the protection of personal data. For instance, the President of the Republic is the only person to initiate investigations against the members of the DPA. On the other hand, the fact that not all decisions of the DPA are published also undermines its transparency.[121] The independency issue was also raised in progress reports concerning Turkey.[122] It should not be forgotten that the Court of Justice of the European Union has dealt with the issue of "independence" before and has a negative view on the state or governmental control over national data protection authorities.[123]

to a presidential regime were accepted by a majority of 51%. Following the presidential and parliamentary elections held on 24 June 2018, the presidential regime in Turkey was consolidated.

[119]Bakanlıklara Bağlı, İlgili ve İlişkili Kurum ve Kuruluşlar ile İlgili 2008/1 Sayılı Cumhurbaşkanlığı Genelgesi, OJ no. 30479, 15 July 2018.

[120]Under the old system, 5 members of the DPL were selected by the Parliament, 2 members were selected by the President of the Republic and 2 members were selected by the Cabinet of Ministers, which no longer exists.

[121]Küzeci 2018, p. 367.

[122]*See* Sect. 9.3.3.

[123]CJEU, *European Commission (Supported by EDPS) v. Federal Republic of Germany*, Judgement, 9 March 2010, Case C-518/07; CJEU, paras 25–37, *European Commission (Supported by EDPS) v. Republic of Austria (Supported by Federal Republic of Germany)*, Judgement, 16 October 2012, Case C-614/10, paras 37–66; CJEU, *European Commission (Supported by EDPS) v. Hungary*, Judgement, 8 April 2014, Case C-288/12, paras. 47–62.

9.4 Application of the GDPR in Turkey

Turkey is not a member to the EU therefore direct application of the GDPR is not possible. Nevertheless, this does not mean that the GDPR would not have any effect in Turkey. Below, the extraterritorial application of the GDPR in relation to Turkish data processors and possible harmonisation of Turkish Law with the GDPR will be analysed.

9.4.1 Extraterritoriality of the GDPR

Since Article 3 GDPR has a wide territorial scope of application,[124] it may also encompass activities of Turkish controllers. If a Turkish company offers goods or services to data subjects in the Union or monitor their behaviour, it will be subject to the GDPR as per Article 3(2). Such a simple statement may create complications in practice. Therefore, the European Data Protection Board ("EDPB") published the Guidelines 3/2018 on the territorial scope of the GDPR ("Guidelines") to give further explanation and examples as to how this Article should be interpreted. Accordingly, the Guidelines excluded the indirect presence[125] of an establishment in the EU from the application of Article 3(1) GDPR. As to the application of Article 3(2) GDPR, the Guidelines stress that data processing without any method of "*targeting*" would fall outside the scope of the GDPR.[126]

Nonetheless, one should distinguish applicability from enforceability. To that extent, the question remains how to enforce this provision in case Article 3(2) GDPR applies. The GDPR seems to bring a solution to this problem with the requirement to appoint a representative for controllers or processors outside the EU per Article 27. The GDPR also imposes a fine of EUR 10,000,000 or up to 2% of the worldwide annual revenue for those who do not comply with this requirement per Article 83. In spite of this provision, it is very difficult to ensure enforceability in case the processor or the controller do not have assets within the EU.[127] There is a tendency in some Member States to hold the representative liable in order to overcome this problem;[128] however, the efficacy of this approach is also doubted if the representative itself is not

---

[124]The wide territorial scope of the GDPR and its possible application have usually not been objected to in the Turkish literature. The general tendency is to simply point out the extraterritorial application of the GDPR to Turkish or non-EU data processors and controllers. Dülger 2019, p. 195; Çekin 2018, pp. 29–34; Develioğlu 2017, pp. 15–20. In a recent article, the extraterritoriality of the GDPR is rejected from a public international law perspective. Dal 2019, p. 32.

[125]EDPB 2018, pp. 4–12.

[126]EDPB 2018, p. 14.

[127]Däubler 2018, p. 411. For a different reasoning, *see* Brkan 2016, pp. 339–341.

[128]*See* Azzi 2018, para 55; The Author also points out the last sentence of the Recital 80 GDPR confirming this tendency: "*The designated representative should be subject to enforcement proceedings in the event of non-compliance by the controller or processor*".

liable.[129] Given this, the extraterritoriality rule in the GDPR might not be as legally effective as it was designed to be. The pressure for Turkish or other non-EU processors should rather be political or economic.[130] Moreover, Article 28(1) imposes a duty on data controllers to use processors that will meet the level of protection that the GDPR offers. Article 28(1) and Article 28(3) would likely create an indirect effect on processors from non-EU countries.[131] Therefore, they need to abide by the GDPR standards in order to be present in the economic market.

Even if the GDPR is applied per Article 3(2), Turkish data processors can also be subject to Member State Law due to the special reference made in the GDPR in some cases. For instance, the right to demand indemnity in Article 82 GDPR and penal sanctions in Article 84 are subject to Member State Law. There are also other Articles that leave some discretion to Member States.[132] By virtue of these references to Member State Law, Turkish processors may also face additional requirements as per the Member State Law that is applicable.

From a private international law perspective, in a contractual relation involving data processing, if the law applicable to the contract is that of one of the EU Member States, the GDPR is directly applicable. Nonetheless, is the GDPR applicable to a contract whose applicable law is that of a non-EU country? If, for example, parties choose Turkish Law in their contract or Turkish Law is the applicable law in accordance with conflict of law rules, the question would remain whether the GDPR would still be applicable. In a different wording, the issue here is whether rules in the GDPR have an overriding mandatory effect.

Although their comprehensive notion would be hard to give, overriding mandatory rules are rules that are rooted in the public interests of a country, such as the ones regarding economic, political or health policies; thus, are applicable regardless of the choice of law rules or otherwise applicable law.[133] Some rules in the GDPR can be considered as overriding mandatory rules[134] and be applicable regardless of the provisions in the applicable non-EU law given their aim to create a cross-border data protection system. Even in this case, the applicability of the GDPR is not certain under Turkish Law. Pursuant to Article 31 of the Turkish Code on Private International Law and International Civil Procedure ("PIL Code"), "*effect may be given to the overriding*

---

[129] Däubler 2018, p. 411.

[130] Develioğlu 2017, p. 117; For examples of sanctions and other mechanisms for action, *see* Azzi 2018, paras 59–77.

[131] EDPB, p. 10.

[132] *See* Articles 6(2), 8(1), 9(4), 23, 80(2), 85, 88 GDPR, *also see* Wagner and Bennecke 2016, pp. 354–357.

[133] Nomer 2017, pp. 184–187; Demirkol 2014, pp. 16–17; van Bochove 2014, pp. 148–150; Erkan 2011, pp. 83–84; Özdemir Kocasakal 2010, pp. 70–74; Özdemir Kocasakal 2001, pp. 11–12; *see* Article 9(1) of Rome I Regulation (Regulation (EC) No 593/2008 of the European Parliament and of the Council of 17 June 2008 on the law applicable to contractual obligations (Rome I) (2008) OJ L 177.

[134] Lüttringhaus 2018, pp. 73–74. The author states that Article 82 GDPR is an overriding mandatory rule. Däubler 2018, p. 406; Brkan 2016, p. 339. According to the authors, Article 3 GDPR is an overriding mandatory rule.

mandatory rules of a third country which are closely connected to the law applicable to the contract". The article gives a discretionary power to the judge and the judge will take the purpose, nature, content and consequence of these rules into consideration "*whether to give effect to these rules or apply them"*. The ambiguous wording of the said article has led to different interpretations. Some contested that the terms "*may give effect*" and "*apply*" have the same meaning and overriding mandatory rules are directly applied.[135] Others are of the opinion that these two terms have different meanings. According to the latter interpretation of the provision, the term "*may give effect*" connotes the recourse to the overriding mandatory rules as a fact, but not as a legal rule per se. Moreover, "*apply*" refers to the direct application of the overriding mandatory rules as a legal rule to the case at hand.[136] As a result, some authors defend that overriding mandatory rules can only be given effect in a case as fact.[137] In contrast, others emphasize the direct application of them.[138]

Another problem arises if a data breach occurs out of a contractual relationship. In case of a violation of personality rights through data processing or a limitation to the right to have information on personal data, Article 35 of the PIL Code refers law applicable in case of violation of personality rights as applicable. Consequently, the law applicable is the law of residence of the claimant, or the defendant, or the law where the violation has occurred. The claimant can only choose the law of their residence or the law of the country where the violation has occurred, if the defendant is aware of the fact that the consequences of the violation will occur in these jurisdictions. If the chosen law is that of an EU country, it can be concluded that the GDPR is directly applicable. However, if the applicable law is Turkish law, the application of the GDPR as overriding mandatory rules is debatable, since Article 31 of the Turkish PIL is only applicable for contractual obligations.[139]

In any case, Turkey needs to better align its data protection law to the GDPR. Given the GDPR's expanded field of application in accordance with Article 3, especially, when international corporations are at hand, they need to correspond their data protection activities both to Turkish legislation and to the GDPR.[140] Therefore, better alignment with the GDPR would facilitate data protection compliance efforts for these corporations. Furthermore, the harmonisation with the GDPR is one of the future objectives during the candidacy negotiations of Turkey with the EU.

[135] Çelikel and Erdem 2017, p. 441.

[136] Özdemir Kocasakal 2010, p. 75; Demirkol 2014, p. 23; Özdemir Kocasakal 2001, p. 74.

[137] Özdemir Kocasakal 2010, p. 76; Demirkol 2014, p. 23; Kösoğlu 2008, p. 161.

[138] Şanlı et al. 2019, p. 316; Çelikel and Erdem 2017, p. 441. For mitigating views admitting both the application of and giving effect to overriding mandatory rules, *see* Tekinalp and Uyanık 2016, p. 300; Bayata Canyaş 2012, p. 271.

[139] It is suggested that Article 31 of the Turkish PIL shall be applied to non-contractual obligations as well. Vural Çelenk 2018, p. 236; *contra* Şanlı et al. 2019, p. 315.

[140] Develioğlu 2017, p. 20.

9.4.2 Turkey's Harmonisation with the EU and the GDPR

The indirect application of the GDPR aside, it is also possible for Turkey to adopt a new law based on the GDPR in order to ensure harmonisation with EU law as a candidate country for membership. Turkey applied to be a candidate member of the EU in 1987, the candidacy was approved in 1999, and accession negotiations date back to 2005. The closing of some chapters had been on hold unless Turkey recognizes Cyprus as a party to Ankara Agreement.[141] Nevertheless, the accession negotiations are currently frozen.[142]

Turkey's candidacy has also brought the regulation of data protection law as an item for negotiations. Turkey's need to align the data protection regulation with the EU standards concerning Justice and Internal Affairs, was first raised briefly in the 1998 progress report.[143] The need to prepare a separate legislative act for data protection was then shown in the Accession Partnership Document dated 2003, where it was stated that the harmonisation in this area is one of the short-term aims.[144] In the National Program dated 2003, the timeline to prepare the necessary legislative acts was planned to be completed in 2004.[145] Until the adoption of the DPL, the lack of a special regulation on personal data protection was stated almost in every progress report. However, the works could only be completed in 2016, a time when the EU had already made progress regarding data protection and was preparing to accept more advanced rules. The fact that the GDPR was not taken into consideration during the preparations of the DPL is a missed opportunity for Turkey.[146]

The requirements for data protection regulations harmonised with the EU system is twofold: First, personal data protection rules should comply with the EU standards and second, similar practice in terms of data processing by police and judicial authorities is required in order to ensure cooperation in justice and police affairs. Indeed, the 2016 progress report stated that Turkey's adoption of Law on the Protection of Personal Data did not achieve the level of the *EU acquis* because of the vast exceptions applied to data processing and the concerns regarding the independency of the DPA.[147] The 2018 progress report also demonstrated Turkey's need to progress on data protection law to align legislation with European standards and to start negotiations with Europol activities.[148] The latest progress report in 2019 stresses that Turkey needs to harmonise the data protection law with the GDPR and the Directive

---

[141] Agreement Establishing an Association between the European Economic Community and Turkey (Ankara Agreement), 1 September 1963.

[142] Council of the EU 2019 Council conclusions on enlargement and stabilisation and association process. https://www.consilium.europa.eu/en/press/press-releases/2019/06/18/council-conclusions-on-enlargement-and-stabilisation-and-association-process/. Accessed 17 October 2019.

[143] European Commission 1998, p. 35.

[144] The Council of the European Union 2003, p. 45.

[145] Council of Ministers 2003, p. 151.

[146] Dülger 2019, pp. 193 and 195; Çekin 2018, p. 3; *contra* Taştan 2017, pp. 26–27.

[147] European Commission 2016, p. 71.

[148] European Commission 2018, p. 41.

EU 2016/680.[149] The report also mentions concerns towards the powers of the DPA and protection of personal data in law enforcement.[150]

The EU discusses to open negotiations on an agreement regarding the exchange of data for fighting serious crime and terrorism. In a recent resolution regarding the negotiations with Turkey on the exchange of personal data between Europol and Turkey, the European Parliament stressed that data transfer to Turkey bears risks and requested that the future agreement contain specific rules regarding the retention of personal data.[151]

Although its future is now uncertain, the negotiations of this agreement is expected to have a positive effect on developing rules on personal data protection in Turkey. Being a candidate country to the EU, the adoption of harmonised rules with the GDPR will surely be one of the policies in Turkey's future harmonisation agenda.

9.5 Conclusion

The need for adequate protection of personal data is one of the most crucial concerns of the digital society. By adopting the GDPR, the EU has taken an important step forward to create a single market where the subjects are provided with adequate protection concerning their personal data. Following the steps of the EU, Turkey has also made progress in terms of personal data protection and privacy rights by adopting the DPL; however, further harmonisation requires a more cautious approach towards data processing. Especially, as the chapter suggests, the frequent use of personal data in practice should be lessened and the DPA should be more independent. Nevertheless, this chapter also puts forward that the current laws and regulations as well as the case-law provides a comparable level of protection and future harmonisation would not be challenging. The future will show Turkey's further steps to close the gap between the DPL and the GDPR.

Acknowledgements I would like to thank my colleagues Nesli Şen Özçelik, Seda Palanduz, and Sercan Çavuşoğlu for their comments and suggestions to earlier drafts of the chapter. Needless to say, the responsibility for all mistakes remains mine alone.

---

[149] Directive (EU) 2016/680 of the European Parliament and of the Council of 27 April 2016 on the protection of natural persons with regard to the processing of personal data by competent authorities for the purposes of the prevention, investigation, detection or prosecution of criminal offences or the execution of criminal penalties, and on the free movement of such data, and repealing Council Framework Decision 2008/977/JHA, (2016) OJ L 119.

[150] European Commission 2019, p. 31.

[151] European Parliament 2018, especially Articles 7–14.

References

Akgül A (2015) Kişisel Verilerin Korunması Bağlamında Biyometrik Yöntemlerin Kullanımı ve Danıştay Yaklaşımı [The Use of Biometric Methods in the Context of the Protection of Personal Data and the Council of State's Approach]. Türkiye Barolar Birliği Dergisi 118:199–222

Azzi A (2018) The challenges faced by the extraterritorial scope of the General Data Protection Regulation. JIPITEC 126:126–137

Bayata Canyaş A (2012) AB ve Türk Hukuku Uyarınca Sözleşmeye Uygulanacak Hukuka İlişkin Genel Kural [General Rule Regarding the Law Applicable to the Contract in accordance with EU and Turkish Law]. Adalet, Ankara

Brkan M (2016) Data protection and conflict-of-laws: A challenging relationship. EDPL 3(2):324–341

Çekin M S (2018) Avrupa Birliği Hukukuyla Mukayeseli Olarak 6698 Sayılı Kişisel Verilerin Korunması Kanunu [Law No. 6698 on the Protection of Personal Data in Comparison with the European Union Law]. On İki Levha, İstanbul

Çelikel A, Erdem B (2017) Milletlerarası Özel Hukuk[Private International Law]. Beta, İstanbul

Council of the European Union (2003) Council Decision of 19 May 2003 on the principles, priorities, intermediate objectives and conditions contained in the Accession Partnership with Turkey, 2003/398/EC, https://www.ab.gov.tr/files/AB_Iliskileri/Tur_En_Realitons/Apd/Turkey_APD_2003.pdf Accessed 16 October 2019

Council of the EU (2019) Council conclusions on enlargement and stabilisation and association process. https://www.consilium.europa.eu/en/press/press-releases/2019/06/18/council-conclusions-on-enlargement-and-stabilisation-and-association-process/. Accessed 17 October 2019

Dal U (2019) Avrupa Birliği Genel Veri Koruma Tüzüğü'nün ülke dışı uygulama yetkisi ve bu yetkinin uluslararası hukukta meşruiyeti [The extraterritoriality of the GDPR outside the country and its legitimacy in international law]. Kişisel Verileri Koruma Dergisi 1(1): 21–33

Däubler W (2018) Das Kollisionsrecht des neuen Datenschutzes [The conflict of laws of the new data protection]. RIW 7:405–412

Demirkol B (2014) Sözleşmeye Uygulanacak Hukuk [The Law Applicable to the Contract]. Vedat, İstanbul

Develioğlu M (2017) 6698 sayılı Kişisel Verilerin Korunması Kanunu ile Karşılaştırmalı Olarak Avrupa Birliği Genel Veri Koruma Tüzüğü Uyarınca Kişisel Verilerin Korunması Hukuku [Data Protection Law in Accordance with the GDPR and with a Comparison with the Law No. 6698 on the Protection of Personal Data]. On İki Levha, İstanbul

Dülger M V (2019) Kişisel Verilerin Korunması Hukuku [The Law on the Protection of Personal Data]. Hukuk Akademisi, İstanbul

Erkan M (2011) MÖHUK Madde 31 Bağlamında Türk Hukukunda Doğrudan Uygulanan Kurallara Bakış [Overview of the Overriding Mandatory Rules in Turkish Law in the Context of Article 31 of the Turkish Code on Private International Law]. Gazi Üniversitesi Hukuk Fakültesi Dergisi, 15(2):81–121

European Commission (1998) "Regular Report From the Commission on Turkey's Progress Towards Accession", https://www.avrupa.info.tr/sites/default/files/2016-11/1998.pdf Accessed 16 October 2019

European Commission (2016) Commission Staff Working Document, "Turkey 2016 Report". https://ec.europa.eu/neighbourhood-enlargement/sites/near/files/pdf/key_documents/2016/20161109_report_turkey.pdf Accessed 16 October 2019

European Commission (2018) Commission Staff Working Document, "Turkey 2018 Report". https://ec.europa.eu/neighbourhood-enlargement/sites/near/files/20180417-turkey-report.pdf Accessed 16 October 2019

European Commission (2019) Commission Staff Working Document, "Turkey 2019 Report" https://ec.europa.eu/neighbourhood-enlargement/sites/near/files/20190529-turkey-report.pdf Accessed 16 October 2019

European Data Protection Board (2018) Guidelines 3/2018 on the territorial scope of the GDPR (Article 3) – Version for public consultation 16.11.2018. https://edpb.europa.eu/our-work-tools/public-consultations/2018/guidelines-32018-territorial-scope-gdpr-article-3_en. Accessed 27 September 2019

European Parliament (2018) "Resolution of 4 July 2018 on the Commission recommendation for a Council decision authorising the opening of negotiations for an agreement between the European Union and Republic of Turkey on the exchange of personal data between European Union Agency for Law Enforcement Cooperation (Europol) and the Turkish competent authorities for fighting serious crimes and terrorism". COM(2017)0799 – 2018/2061(INI) http://www.europarl.europa.eu/sides/getDoc.do?type=TA&language=EN&reference=P8-TA-2018-0296 Accessed 16 October 2019

Kocasakal Özdemir H (2001) Doğrudan Uygulanan Kurallar ve Sözleşmeler Üzerindeki Etkileri [Overriding Mandatory Rules and its Effects on Contracts]. Galatasaray Üniversitesi, İstanbul

Kocasakal Özdemir H (2010) Sözleşmelere Uygulanacak Hukukun MÖHUK m.24 Çerçevesinde Tespiti ve Üçüncü Devletin Doğrudan Uygulanan Kuralları [Determination of the Law Applicable to Contracts within the framework of Article 24 of the Turkish Code on Private International Law, and the Overriding Mandatory Rules of a Third State]. MHB 30(1–2):27-88

Kösoğlu M (2008) Milletlerarası Özel Hukuk ve Usul Hukuku Hakkında Kanunun 31. Maddesi: Sözleşme ile Sıkı İlişkili Üçüncü Bir Devletin Doğrudan Uygulanan Kurallarına Etki Tanınması [Article 31 of the Code on Private International Law and International Civil Procedure: Giving Effect to the Overriding Mandatory Rules of a Third Country which is in Close Connection with the Contract]. MHB 28(1–2):147–172

Küzeci E (2018) Kişisel Verilerin Korunması [Protection of Personal Data]. Turhan, Ankara

Lüttringhaus J D (2018) Das internationale Datenprivatrecht: Baustein des Wirtschaftskollisionsrechts des 21. Jahrhunderts [International Privacy Law: Building Block of 21st Century's Conflict of Laws]. Jahrhunderts, ZvglRWiss 117:50–82

Nomer E (2017) Devletler Hususi Hukuku [Private International Law]. Beta, Istanbul

Şanlı C, Esen E, Ataman Figanmeşe (2019) Milletlerarası Özel Hukuk [Private International Law]. Beta, Istanbul

Sayıştay (2014) Sosyal Güvenlik Kurumu 2013 Yılı Sayıştay Denetim Raporu [Social Security Institution 2013 Court of Accounts Audit Report]. https://www.sayistay.gov.tr/tr/Upload/62643830/files/raporlar/kid/2013/Sosyal_Güvenlik_Kurumları/SOSYAL%20GÜVENLİK%20KURUMU.pdf. Accessed 16 October 2019

Taştan F G (2017) Türk Sözleşme Hukukunda Kişisel Verilerin Korunması [Protection of Personal Data in Turkish Contract Law]. On İki Levha, Istanbul

TC Cumhurbaşkanlığı Devlet Denetleme Kurulu (2013) Denetleme Raporu: Kişisel Verilerin Korunmasına İlişkin Ulusal ve Uluslararası Durum Değerlendirmesi ile Bilgi Güvenliği ve Kişisel Verilerin Korunması Kapsamında Gerçekleştirilen Denetim Çalışmaları, Table of Contents and Conclusion available at http://www.ttb.org.tr/images/stories/file/2015/ddk_rapor.pdf. Accessed 16 October 2019

Tekinalp G, Uyanık A (2016) Milletlerarası Özel Hukuk Bağlama Kuralları [Conflict of Laws in Private International Law]. Vedat, Istanbul

van Bochove L M (2014) Overriding mandatory rules as a vehicle for weaker party protection in European private international law. ELR 7:147–156

Vural Çelenk B (2018) Üçüncü Ülkenin Doğrudan Uygulanan Kurallarının Haksız Fiiller Alanında Uygulanmasının MÖHUK Madde 31 ile Değerlendirilmesi [Evaluation of the Application of the Overriding Mandatory Rules of a Third Country in Tort Law, in accordance with Article 31 on the Turkish Code on Private International Law and International Civil Procedure]. In: Tarman Derya Z (ed) Genç Milletlerarası Özel Hukukçular Konferansı [Young Private International Law Scholars Conference]. On İki Levha, Istanbul, pp 205–243

Wagner J, Benecke A (2016) National legislation within the framework of the GDPR. EDPL 2:353–361

Yücedağ N (2017) Medeni Hukuk Açısından Kişisel Verilerin Korunması Kanunu'nun Uygulama Alanı ve Genel Uygunluk Sebepleri [Field of Application of the Law on the Protection of Personal Data within the Framework of Civil Law and Conditions for Lawfulness] İÜHFM 75(2):765–789

Yücedağ N (2019) Kişisel verilerin korunması kanunu kapsamında genel ilkeler [General Principles within the Scope of the Law on the Protection of Personal Data]. Kişisel Verileri Koruma Dergisi 1(1):47–63

Başak Erdoğan Research and Teaching Assistant at MEF University, MEF University, Ayazağa Cad., No: 4, 34396, Maslak/Sarıyer/İstanbul/Turkey.

Chapter 10
The United States and the EU's General Data Protection Regulation

Muge Fazlioglu

Contents

Abstract This chapter focuses on U.S. information privacy and data protection laws, their similarities and differences with the EU's General Data Protection Regulation (GDPR), and how the GDPR is likely to affect privacy and data protection in the United States in the years ahead. In contrast to the EU's omnibus approach to data protection, U.S. privacy laws are "sectoral" in nature, meaning that businesses in different economic sectors are subject to different privacy rules and regulations. Several key federal and state-level privacy protections, including the Fourth Amendment and state privacy torts, as well as regulatory authorities, such as the Federal Trade Commission and state attorneys general, shape the boundaries of the right to privacy in the United States. Regarding the interaction between the GDPR and U.S. law, the conflict between the right to be forgotten and the protection of speech and of the press provided by the First Amendment has been a primary concern.

M. Fazlioglu (✉)
International Association of Privacy Professionals, 75 Rochester Ave., Portsmouth, NH 03801, USA
e-mail: muge@iapp.org

E. Kiesow Cortez (ed.), *Data Protection Around the World*,
Information Technology and Law Series 33,
https://doi.org/10.1007/978-94-6265-407-5_10

Attention within U.S. privacy circles has also shifted in recent years toward handling data breaches, defining "privacy harms," and the understanding the interaction of state-level consumer privacy laws—such as the California Consumer Privacy Act of 2018—and legislative efforts at the federal level.

Keywords Data breach · Federal Trade Commission · General Data Protection Regulation · Privacy harm · Right to be forgotten · Right to erasure · U.S. privacy law

10.1 Privacy and Data Protection Regulation in the United States

Information privacy law in the United States[1] is concerned with the collection and use of data by governments and private entities. In contrast to European law, which takes an omnibus approach to privacy and data protection, U.S. privacy law employs a sectoral approach.[2] In other words, most U.S. privacy laws regulate data processing based on the context in which data are used (e.g., healthcare, banking, education).[3] Overall, privacy regulation in the U.S. can be described as highly contextual, sectoral, rooted in provisions in the common law and federal and state laws and statutes,[4] and largely based on private law or affirmative agreements later enforced by federal or state law.[5] Federal statutory enforcement is carried out primarily by the Federal Trade Commission (FTC), while state attorneys general also play active roles in consumer privacy protection. The Fair Information Practice Principles, which provide a standard set of principles that have served as the basis for many privacy and data protection laws, including those in the U.S., EU, and elsewhere around the world, were first laid down in 1973 by an advisory committee of the U.S. Department of Health, Education, and Welfare[6] and later enshrined in the U.S. Privacy Act of 1974.[7]

Over the past couple of years, several new state privacy laws have been passed, including those in California, Nevada, and Maine. The most expansive of these, the California Consumer Privacy Act of 2018 (CCPA), provides California consumers with rights to access, deletion, and opt-out of sale of their personal data, amongst others, while imposing additional obligations on businesses that collect and sell personal information. With the CCPA set to enter into force on January 1, 2020, some

[1] Warren and Brandeis 1890 wrote the seminal article on the right to privacy in the United States. Notably, their arguments drew upon sources of European law, such as the French Penal Code.

[2] Schwartz 2009, p. 905.

[3] Schwartz and Solove 2014, p. 879.

[4] DeVries 2003, p. 285.

[5] Cate 2011.

[6] Sec'y Advisory Comm. On Automated Personal Data Sys., U.S. Dept. of Health, Educ. & Welfare, Records, Computers, and the Rights of Citizens (1973) https://aspe.hhs.gov/report/records-computers-and-rights-citizens.

[7] Privacy Act of 1974, 5 U.S.C. § 552a, as amended.

members of Congress have been working to pass a federal privacy law. Some of these federal legislative proposals would codify this patchwork of state privacy protections into law at the federal level, while others would pre-empt state law by establishing an upper limit or ceiling for privacy and data protection in the United States.[8] As of the time of this writing, however, members of Congress have not reached consensus over which provisions and privacy protections a new federal privacy law should contain.[9]

10.1.1 The Fourth Amendment

The boundaries of the right to privacy in the United States are defined in part by the Fourth Amendment to the U.S. Constitution, which protects individuals against "unreasonable searches and seizures" by the government.[10] If a local, state, or the federal government is involved in data collection and use, an individual's Fourth Amendment rights may be triggered. A privacy claim derived from the Fourth Amendment invokes what is known as the *reasonableness standard* and the *expectation of privacy test*, which originated in the case of *Katz v. United States*. In its decision for the case, the Supreme Court ruled that the government's warrantless eavesdropping on a person making a call from a phone booth exceeded the defendant's subjective expectation of privacy that could be deemed reasonable by prevailing social norms.[11] Thus, privacy claims in the U.S. are usually judged by the standards of an "objective third party," a person with "reasonable sensibilities."[12] In a recent landmark U.S. Supreme Court case, warrantless access by police to historical records in cellphones about the physical location of individuals was deemed to be a violation of the Fourth Amendment.[13]

The U.S. Supreme Court has also upheld the privacy rights of individuals around issues such as birth control, same-sex relationships, and abortion, as a *penumbra* of rights derived or implied by the Constitution.[14] These have also been referred to as "unenumerated" rights to privacy,[15] which, alternatively, are often referred to in European law as fundamental rights.[16]

---

[8]Chander, Kaminski, and McGeveran 2019, p. 37.

[9]Fazlioglu 2019, p. 5.

[10]U.S. Constitution, Amendment IV.

[11]In his concurring opinion, Justice Harlan explained that a reasonable expectation of privacy is indicated by both subjective and objective expectations of privacy. 389 U.S. 347, 361 (1967). But compare this with Kerr 2015, who describes the "subjective expectation of privacy" test as a "phantom doctrine.".

[12]Haynes v Alfred Knopf, 8 F. 3d. 1222 (1993).

[13]Carpenter v United States, 138 S. Ct. 2206 (2018).

[14]Griswold v Connecticut, 381 U.S. 479 (1965); Lawrence v Texas, 539 U.S. 558 (2003); Roe v Wade, 410 U.S. 113 (1973).

[15]Helscher 1994.

[16]While privacy in Europe connotes respect for personal dignity, the meaning of privacy in the U.S. is more inclined towards liberty from intervention by the state. Whitman 2004, pp. 1160–1163.

10.1.2 Sectoral Laws

Perhaps the most notable feature of U.S. privacy and data protection law is the scope of regulation. U.S. privacy regulations are primarily *sectoral* in orientation.[17] For example, different regulations apply to the data processing activities of government agencies and private companies.[18] Moreover, businesses that are located within different sectors of the economy or that process different kinds of data are subject to different rules.[19] Thus, sectoral laws specify the requisite level of protections for discrete data processing activities, from consumer financial transactions, to law enforcement and medical recordkeeping.[20] In essence, sectoral laws treat threats to privacy and data protection as sector-specific or particular to certain kinds of data processing industries or technologies.[21]

The categories of information subjected to heightened processing obligations in the U.S. "are often information which would be considered as being of 'intimate' nature," such as personal health information.[22] Sector-specific federal statutes in the U.S. that regulate the processing of personal data include the Health Information Privacy Portability and Accountability Act (HIPPA),[23] Family Educational Rights and Privacy Act (FERPA),[24] Children's Online Privacy Protection Act (COPPA),[25]

---

[17] Examples examined elsewhere in this study include the Fair Credit Reporting Act (FCRA), Gramm-Leach-Bliley Act (GLBA), and the Electronic Communications Privacy Act (ECPA).

[18] Schwartz 2013, p. 1974. One problem with this distinction, however, is that the line that separates government activity from private activity has become increasingly blurred. For instance, it was reported that 98% of PRISM intelligence, one of the NSA's mass surveillance programs disclosed by Edward Snowden, came from private companies such as Yahoo, Google, and Microsoft. Gellman B and Poitras L (2013) U.S., British Intelligence Mining Data from Nine U.S Internet Companies in Broad Secret Program https://www.washingtonpost.com/investigations/us-intelligence-mining-data-from-nine-us-internet-companies-in-broad-secret-program/2013/06/06/3a0c0da8-cebf-11e2-8845-d970ccb04497_story.html. Accessed 4 June 2018.

[19] Schwartz 2013, p. 1974. For example, the delivery of pre-recorded audio-visuals is regulated by the Video Privacy Protection Act. If the video is delivered by a cable system, however, then the Cable Communications Policy Act applies. Moreover, both laws can simultaneously apply in certain instances.

[20] Swire and Ahmad 2012, p. 32.

[21] Reidenberg 2000, p. 1318; Simitis 2010, p. 139. The U.S. sectoral approach to privacy regulation stands in stark contrast that of the EU, which pursues *omnibus* regulations that impose obligations on all sectors of the economy and both private and public actors. The EU's comprehensive data protection framework is sustained by a "rights-dominated approach" that seeks to broadly and reliably secure the use and collection of data. Moreover, in the EU, the number of directives on various issues, such as health-related documentation, social security, health issues, etc., is increasing.

[22] Gratton 2014, p. 165; Skinner-Thompson 2015, p. 159.

[23] U.S. Dep't of Health & Hum. Serv. (2017) Your rights under HIPPA https://www.hhs.gov/hipaa/for-individuals/guidance-materials-for-consumers/index.html. Accessed 28 May 2018.

[24] U.S. Dep't of Educ. (2018) Family Educational Rights and Privacy Act https://www2.ed.gov/policy/gen/guid/fpco/ferpa/index.html? Accessed 28 May 2018.

[25] Fed. Trade Comm'n (2015) Complying with COPPA: Frequently asked questions https://www.ftc.gov/tips-advice/business-center/guidance/complying-coppa-frequently-asked-questions#General%20Questions. Accessed 28 May 2018.

Gramm-Leach-Bliley Act (GLBA),[26] Fair Credit Reporting Act (FCRA),[27] Cable Communications Policy Act,[28] Electronic Communications Privacy Act,[29] Computer Fraud and Abuse Act,[30] Video Privacy Protection Act,[31] and Genetic Information Nondiscrimination Act.[32] Thus, U.S. data protection and privacy laws apply to particular industries, technologies, and uses of data rather than to the processing of "personal data," broadly defined. In other words, data processing in the U.S. is regulated based on the context in which data are used.[33]

10.1.3 *Privacy Torts*

Privacy torts, which offer fundamental protections for privacy in the U.S., have been adopted by most states through common law or statutes or established by interpretation of their state constitutions.[34] Privacy torts include intrusion upon seclusion,[35] public disclosure of private facts,[36] appropriation,[37] and false light.[38] These torts protect four different interests of individuals that all revolve around "the right to be let alone," as Samuel Warren and Louis Brandeis famously described the right to privacy in an 1890 law review article.[39] The applicability of privacy torts, however, has been somewhat curtailed by the reasonableness standard laid out in U.S. common law as well as by the First Amendment. Indeed, the Supreme Court has struck down

---

[26] Fed. Trade Comm'n (2002) How to comply with the privacy of consumer financial information rule of the Gramm-Leach-Bliley Act https://www.ftc.gov/tips-advice/business-center/guidance/how-comply-privacy-consumer-financial-information-rule-gramm. Accessed 3 June 2018.

[27] Fed. Trade Comm'n (2016) Fair Credit Reporting Act, 15 U.S.C. § 1681 https://www.ftc.gov/system/files/fcra_2016.pdf. Accessed 3 June 2018.

[28] Fed. Commc'n Comm'n (2015) Cable television https://www.fcc.gov/media/engineering/cable-television. Accessed 3 June 2018.

[29] U.S. Dep't of Just. (2013) Electronic Communications Privacy Act of 1986 (ECPA), 18 U.S.C. § 2510-22 https://it.ojp.gov/PrivacyLiberty/authorities/statutes/1285. Accessed 3 June 2018.

[30] Jarrett H and Bailie M (2015) Prosecuting Computer Crimes https://www.justice.gov/sites/default/files/criminal-ccips/legacy/2015/01/14/ccmanual.pdf. Accessed 3 June 2018.

[31] Comm. on the Judiciary, Subcomm. on Privacy, Tech. and the Law (2012) The Video Privacy Protection Act: Protecting Viewer Privacy in the 21st Century https://www.judiciary.senate.gov/imo/media/doc/CHRG-112shrg87342.pdf. Accessed 3 June 2018.

[32] U.S. Equal Employment Opportunity Comm'n (2008) The Genetic Information Nondiscrimination Act of 2008 https://www.eeoc.gov/laws/statutes/gina.cfm. Accessed 3 June 2018.

[33] Schwartz and Solove 2014, p. 879.

[34] Prosser 1960; Privacilla.org (2002) How U.S. state law quietly leads the way in privacy protection http://www.privacilla.org/releases/Torts_Report.html. Accessed 12 January 2017.

[35] Restatement (Second) of Torts § 652B (1977).

[36] Restatement (Second) of Torts § 652D (1977).

[37] Restatement (Second) of Torts § 652C (1977).

[38] Restatement (Second) of Torts § 652E (1977).

[39] Warren and Brandeis 1890.

state privacy laws that do not require the invasion of privacy to be *outrageous* or *unreasonable*.[40] For example, the public disclosure of private facts tort requires publication of a private fact that is *highly offensive and of no legitimate public concern*. Likewise, in intrusion upon seclusion, the breach of seclusion or another private matter must be *highly offensive to a reasonable person*.

10.1.4 The Federal Trade Commission

The processing of personal information in the U.S. is also regulated by the Federal Trade Commission (FTC), which plays a significant role in protecting the privacy of U.S. consumers.[41] It does so primarily through its power to maintain independent oversight of and undertake enforcement actions against unfair and deceptive business practices laid down in Section 5 of the Federal Trade Commission Act.[42] The FTC can provide injunctive relief and impose civil penalties against companies whose practices violate consumers' privacy rights, and the agency today "dominate[s] the enforcement of privacy policies."[43] Although the FTC has succeeded in changing the practices of major companies,[44] it has also been faulted for neglecting to take action on widely-criticized activities that have raised privacy concerns, such as Facebook's online tracking activities.[45]

The FTC is the primary enforcement authority for federal privacy laws such GLBA,[46] FCRA,[47] and COPPA.[48] In recent years, it has also been playing a more active role in consumer privacy protection through its consent decrees, which it issues in settlements with companies accused of privacy violations. For example, in July 2019, the FTC imposed a $5 billion penalty against Facebook, the highest fine ever received by a company in a privacy enforcement action anywhere in the world. The penalty was imposed for Facebook's violation of a 2012 consent decree issued by the FTC, which had required it to give consumers "clear and prominent notice" and obtain

---

[40] Cate 2001, p. 59.

[41] Hoofnagle 2016.

[42] 15 U.S.C § 45.

[43] Solove and Hartzog 2014.

[44] In 2011, the FTC imposed a settlement order on Google requiring it to implement a privacy program because of its misrepresentations around the use of consumer information through its network, Google Buzz. Fed. Trade Comm'n (2011) FTC charges deceptive privacy practices in Google's rollout of its Buzz social network https://www.ftc.gov/news-events/press-releases/2011/03/ftc-charges-deceptive-privacy-practices-googles-rollout-its-buzz. Accessed 10 January 2016.

[45] Rotenberg M (2012) The reform of the EU data protection framework—building trust in a digital and global world https://epic.org/privacy/Rotenberg_EP_Testimony_10_10_12.pdf. Accessed 4 June 2018.

[46] 15 U.S.C. §§ 6801-6809 (2012).

[47] 15 U.S.C. § 1681 (2012).

[48] 15 U.S.C. §§ 6501-6506 (2012).

their "express consent" before sharing their information.[49] After a yearlong investigation, the FTC found that Facebook had deceived its users and undermined their privacy preferences. The settlement order imposes significant privacy requirements on Facebook.[50]

A couple of months later, in early September 2019, the FTC also settled its complaint against Google and its subsidiary YouTube for the illegal collection of personal information from children without parental consent.[51] As FTC Chairman Joe Simons explained, YouTube simultaneously presented itself to corporate clients as being a popular children's platform, while refusing to acknowledge that pages on its platform were targeted at kids so as to avoid having to comply with COPPA. The settlement entailed a $170 million fine, which also set a record as the largest privacy fine imposed against Google as well as the largest penalty ever issued under COPPA.[52]

10.2 The Interaction of the GDPR and U.S. Law

Several notable commonalities and differences exist between the privacy and data protection frameworks of the European Union and the United States. In terms of overlap, privacy laws within both jurisdictions are rooted in the Fair Information Practices (FIPs), which were first laid down in 1973 by an advisory committee

[49] Fed. Trade Comm'n (2012) FTC approves final settlement with Facebook https://www.ftc.gov/news-events/press-releases/2012/08/ftc-approves-final-settlement-facebook. Accessed 6 September 2019.

[50] These include a requirement that Facebook establish an independent privacy committee within its board of directors independent of CEO Mark Zuckerberg. Facebook must also appoint compliance officers who will be responsible for submitting quarterly and annual certifications to the FTC regarding the company's compliance with the order. In addition, the FTC order enhanced external oversight of Facebook by an independent third-party assessor, which will also report to the new privacy board, and required Facebook to conduct "privacy reviews" of every new or modified product or service before implementation. Another important requirement of the order is for Facebook to "exercise greater oversight of third-party apps," which can include the termination of app developers that are not in compliance with Facebook's platform policies or are unable to justify their needs for certain user data. Fed. Trade Comm'n (2019) FTC imposes $5 billion penalty and sweeping new privacy restrictions on Facebook https://www.ftc.gov/news-events/press-releases/2019/07/ftc-imposes-5-billion-penalty-sweeping-new-privacy-restrictions. Accessed 6 September 2019.

[51] Fed. Trade Comm'n (2019) Google and YouTube will pay record $170 million for alleged violations of children's privacy law https://www.ftc.gov/news-events/press-releases/2019/09/google-youtube-will-pay-record-170-million-alleged-violations?utm_source=govdelivery. Accessed 6 September 2019.

[52] Carson A (2019) FTC touts historic YouTube settlement as 'game changer' for COPPA enforcement https://iapp.org/news/a/ftc-touts-historic-youtube-settlement-as-game-changer-for-coppa-enforcement/. Accessed 6 September 2019.

of the U.S. Department of Health, Education, and Welfare.[53] The Organization for Economic Cooperation and Development provided similar guidelines in 1980, which it updated in 2013.[54] FIPs have influenced both EU and U.S. legislation, including the Data Protection Directive and GDPR in the EU, and the Privacy Act, the Fair Credit Reporting Act, and the Children's Online Privacy Protection Act in the U.S., as well as international privacy agreements.

The principles of EU and U.S. privacy law diverge, however, far more often than they overlap. For example, under EU law "a legal basis and a legitimate purpose are always needed before personal data may be processed."[55] By contrast, in the U.S. commercial data may generally be processed "unless there is some legal rule preventing it."[56] Thus, while EU law does not allow data processing without justification, data processing in the U.S. is allowed by default unless it causes legal harm or is otherwise restricted by the law.[57]

10.2.1 The Right to Be Forgotten

A key issue of incompatibility between EU and U.S. privacy and data protection law has been the right to be forgotten. The boundaries of the right to be forgotten, its applicability to search engines, and its effect on other values, such as freedom of expression and access to information, were topics of significant discussions throughout the drafting of the GDPR.[58] Indeed, the potential clash between the right to be forgotten and the values of freedom of expression and freedom of the press protected by the First Amendment has been one of the most important issues in discussions regarding the application of EU law to U.S. publishers and technology platforms.[59] Given that one of the aims of the GDPR was to strengthen the right to be forgotten, the enforcement of erasure requests against U.S. companies is likely to remain a contentious issue at the interface of EU and U.S. privacy laws.

---

[53]U.S. Dept. Health Education and Welfare, Secretary's Advisory Committee on Automated Personal Data Systems (1973) Records, Computers, and the Rights of Citizens https://aspe.hhs.gov/report/records-computers-and-rights-citizens. Accessed 13 January 2017.

[54]Organization for Economic Co-operation and Development (1980) OECD Guidelines on the Protection of Privacy and Transborder Flows of Personal Data http://www.oecd.org/document/18/0,2340,en_2649_34255_1815186_1_1_1_1,00.html. Accessed 3 June 2018. Its eight principles include: Collection Limitation Principle, Data Quality Principle, Purpose Specification Principle, Use Limitation Principle, Security Safeguards Principle, Openness Principle, Individual Participation Principle, and Accountability Principle.

[55]Massachusetts Institute of Technology (2015) Privacy bridges: EU and U.S. privacy experts in search of Trans-Atlantic privacy solutions https://privacybridges.mit.edu/sites/default/files/documents/PrivacyBridges-FINAL.pdf. Accessed 4 June 2018.

[56]Massachusetts Institute of Technology (2015) Privacy bridges: EU and U.S. privacy experts in search of Trans-Atlantic privacy solutions https://privacybridges.mit.edu/sites/default/files/documents/PrivacyBridges-FINAL.pdf. Accessed 4 June 2018.

[57]Schwartz and Solove 2014, p. 881; Schwartz 2009, p. 913.

[58]Rosen 2012, p. 88; Fazlioglu 2013, p. 149.

[59]Wimmer 2018, pp. 565–566.

The right to be forgotten was established in the 1995 Data Protection Directive and allowed users to request "the rectification, erasure or blocking of data"[60] where that data is incomplete, inaccurate, or inconsistent with the directive, and in instances where data processing is not in compliance with the law.[61] This right has been interpreted by the Court of Justice of the European Union (CJEU) to involve the right to request the removal of data that is "inadequate, irrelevant or no longer relevant, or excessive."[62] Article 17 of the GDPR invigorates this interpretation by providing a broader right to the data subject not only to request erasure of personal data, but to halt its further use and dissemination. The GDPR will allow individuals to withdraw their consent for data controllers to process their data.[63] This right creates further responsibilities for data controllers to make certain information publicly available, such as "tak[ing] reasonable steps, including technical measures" to inform other controllers about the individual's request for erasure.[64]

10.2.2 RTBF and the First Amendment

The First Amendment of the U.S. Constitution[65] is the main source of conflict in U.S. law for the GDPR's right to erasure. Historically, the First Amendment has played an important role in defining the boundaries of U.S. privacy law. Because it is a limitation on the exercise of government power—preventing the government from restricting the flow of information—the First Amendment often acts as a hindrance to laws aimed at protecting privacy insofar as those are construed as government

---

[60]Council Directive 95/46/EC, Article 1, 1995 O.J. (L281) (EU).

[61]Council Directive 95/46/EC, Article 12, 1995 O.J. (L281) (EU).

[62]Judgement para 94.

[63]Regulation (EU) 2016/679, of the European Parliament and of the Council of 27 April 2016 on the protection of natural persons with regard to the processing of personal data and on the free movement of such data, and repealing Directive 95/46/EC (General Data Protection Regulation), 2016 O.J. (L.119), Article 17 (1). Nevertheless, the effectiveness of the right to be forgotten as a privacy tool has also been subject to debate. The Advisory Council to Google on the Right to be Forgotten suggests that the ruling does not have the effect of *forgetting* so much as *delisting*, a "process of removing links in search results based on queries for an individual's name." Although search queries containing the data subject's name will no longer return that result or link to the source of publication, search queries using other terms might still bring up that article. When delisted, information is still available at the source, but access to it is reduced. *Report of the Advisory Council to Google on the Right to be Forgotten,* Google, at 4 (Feb. 6, 2015). Indeed, many have emphasized the limited nature of the *forgetting* in this right, which specifically addresses the link between using an individual's name as a search query and the search results referring to certain webpages. Thus, sources linked to the person remain accessible when different search terms are used. Media Policy Project (2014) European Court Rules Against Google, in favor of Right to be Forgotten http://blogs.lse.ac.uk/mediapolicyproject/2014/05/13/european-court-rules-against-google-in-favour-of-right-to-be-forgotten/. Accessed 4 June 2018.

[64]General Data Protection Regulation, Article 17(2).

[65]U.S. Constitution, Amendment I.

actions inhibiting the press or speech.[66] If a court deems that a law or action taken by the government restricts the communication of information, it can be rendered as unconstitutional.[67]

Thus, privacy claims in the U.S. are often trumped by the First Amendment, which has a well-established place in common law. Laws that restrict certain uses of data have also been met by First Amendment challenges. For instance, in the case of *Sorrell v. IMS Health*, the Supreme Court reviewed a Vermont state statute that prohibited the sale, licensing, or exchange of prescriber-identifying information for marketing or promotional purposes as well as its use by pharmaceutical manufacturers.[68] After determining that these data processing activities were essentially a form of "[s]peech in the aid of pharmaceutical marketing,"[69] the Court interpreted the statute as governmental regulation of protected speech, subjected it to heightened judicial scrutiny, and held it to be an unconstitutional violation of the First Amendment.[70]

Even speech that is outrageous or the cause of emotional or reputation harm can receive constitutional protection under the First Amendment. Indeed, the concerns of offended listeners and viewers have been summarily dismissed by U.S. courts.[71] For example, in *Cohen v. California*, a public display of anti-military profanity was found to be protected by the First Amendment. The Court held that if people are made to feel discomfort about certain things, they can "avert their eyes," or endure the speech as an essential condition of freedom.[72] Speech that inflicted emotional pain on others also received special protection under the First Amendment in *Snyder v. Phelps*.[73] Moreover, the First Amendment's protection of truthful expression can also trump claims of reputational harm. As the Court argued in *Bartnicki v. Vopper*, "absent exceptional circumstances reputational harms cannot justify proscription of truthful speech."[74] These exceptional circumstances are extremely narrow. Thus, the risk that negative consequences will flow from the publication or dissemination of information that is truthful has not overcome the First Amendment. Courts have held

---

[66] Richards 2005, p. 1155. Moreover, while the First Amendment limits the government's power to restrict speech, it does not impose an obligation on it to *facilitate* expression. In other words, while the First Amendment inhibits the curtailment of expression, it does not enjoin the law to facilitate speech or access to information. Additionally, narrow exceptions to the First Amendment's limitation on government restriction of the press or speech, such as public safety or national security, exist. Privacy, however, is not among them.

[67] Sorrell v. IMS Health, 131 S. Ct. 2653 (2011).

[68] Sorrell v IMS Health, 131 S. Ct. 2653 (2011).

[69] Sorrell v IMS Health, 131 S. Ct. 2657-2659 (2011), in which it was found that "the creation and dissemination of information are speech within the meaning of the First Amendment."

[70] Bhagwat 2012, p. 879; Bambauer 2014, p. 57; Piety 2012, pp. 4–5; Julin, Isani, and Acosta 2012, p. 882; Massey 2015, p. 854; Richards 2015, p. 1506; Young 2012, p. 917.

[71] Cate 2001, p. 59.

[72] *Cohen v California*, 403 U.S. 15, 21 (1971).

[73] 552 U.S. 443 (2011).

[74] The First Amendment even protected broadcasting an *illegally* intercepted communication of truthful speech on a matter of public interest. 532 U.S. 514, at 534 (2001).

that the "fear that people would make bad decisions if given truthful information" does not justify content-based restrictions on speech.[75]

This potential clash between the right to be forgotten and freedom of expression has also been dealt with recently by the CJEU in its ruling that the French data protection authority CNIL could not compel Google to honour the right to erasure requests across its search engine domains worldwide.[76] As Future of Privacy Forum CEO Jules Polonetsky noted, although the court ruled that European law does not compel search engines to delist globally when the right to be forgotten is asserted, it left room for data protection authorities to pursue such a global delisting "if the privacy balance called for it in a specific circumstance."[77] Given these dynamics, the interaction between the right to erasure and the values protected by the First Amendment remains an area where EU and U.S. approaches to privacy and data protection remain unreconciled.

10.3 Prominent Issues in U.S. Privacy and Data Protection Law

10.3.1 Privacy Harms

State-level privacy torts and the unfairness category of the FTC's Section 5 authority require proof of harm to pass judicial muster. Indeed, privacy harms have been at issue in many U.S.-based privacy discussions, and "information injury" was even the topic of a workshop held in late 2017 by the Federal Trade Commission.[78] The FTC has also brought enforcement actions against companies alleging privacy harm given the lack of "reasonable and appropriate" safeguards to protect consumer data in recent years. While most companies faced with an FTC enforcement action agree to a settlement with the agency, some have pushed back. In one such case, a judge initially dismissed the FTC's complaint against LabMD, a clinical testing laboratory, which the FTC alleged had failed to provide acceptable safeguards against unauthorized access to

[75] Thompson v. Western States Medical Center, 535 U.S. 357, 374 (2002); Sorrell v. IMS Health, 131 S. Ct. 2653, 2659 (2011).

[76] Woods AK (2019) Three things to remember from Europe's 'right to be forgotten' decision https://www.lawfareblog.com/three-things-remember-europes-right-be-forgotten-decisions. Accessed 10 October 2019.

[77] Polenetsky J (2019) The right to be forgotten: Future of Privacy Forum statement on decisions by European Court of Justice https://fpf.org/2019/09/24/the-right-to-be-forgotten-future-of-privacy-forum-statement-on-decisions-by-european-court-of-justice/. Accessed 10 October 2019.

[78] Ohlhausen M (2017) Remarks at the FTC Informational Injury Workshop https://www.ftc.gov/system/files/documents/public_statements/1289343/mko_speech_-_info_injury_workshop_1.pdf. Accessed 3 June 2018.

consumers' personal information.[79] The judge wrote that, at best, the complaint proved the "possibility," not the "probability or likelihood" of harm. In July 2016, the FTC overturned the judge's ruling,[80] but on appeal in the Eleventh Circuit,[81] the U.S. Court of Appeals vacated the FTC's order on the grounds that it was "unenforceable." The case is notable for having successfully challenged the FTC's authority to take action to prevent, mitigate, or redress privacy harms.[82]

10.3.2 Data Breaches

Related to privacy harm, data security has been another prominent topic in U.S. discussions about privacy law and regulation, especially as large corporations continue to be successfully targeted by hackers. In just the past five years alone, Yahoo,[83] Target,[84] eBay,[85] Anthem,[86] Sony Pictures,[87] and JP Morgan Chase[88] have been affected by large-scale data breaches. The most recent widely-reported breach hit Equifax, a credit reporting agency that houses financial information, including social security numbers, for hundreds of millions of U.S. consumers, a breach which the FTC revealed in September 2017 that it is investigating.[89] In July 2019, Equifax

---

[79] Fed. Trade Comm'n (2015) Administrative law judge dismisses FTC data security complaint against medical testing laboratory LabMD, Inc. https://www.ftc.gov/news-events/press-releases/2015/11/administrative-law-judge-dismisses-ftc-data-security-complaint. Accessed 4 June 2018.

[80] Fed. Trade Comm'n (2016) Commission Finds LabMD Liable for Unfair Data Security Practices https://www.ftc.gov/news-events/press-releases/2016/07/commission-finds-labmd-liable-unfair-data-security-practices. Accessed 3 June 2018.

[81] BNA Privacy and Security Blog (2017) Still waiting on 'LabMD' ruling on FTC data security power https://www.bna.com/waiting-labmd-ruling-b73014473153/. Accessed 3 June 2018.

[82] Newman C (2017) LabMD appeal has privacy world waiting https://www.lexology.com/library/detail.aspx?g=129a4ea7-cc38-4976-94af-3f09e8e280d0. Accessed 3 June 2018.

[83] Perlroth N (2017) All 3 billion Yahoo accounts were affected by 2013 attack https://www.nytimes.com/2017/10/03/technology/yahoo-hack-3-billion-users.html. Accessed 3 June 2018.

[84] Kassner M (2015) Anatomy of the Target data breach: Missed opportunities and lessons learned https://www.zdnet.com/article/anatomy-of-the-target-data-breach-missed-opportunities-and-lessons-learned/. Accessed 3 June 2018.

[85] Kelly G (2014) eBay suffers massive security breach, all users must change their passwords https://www.forbes.com/sites/gordonkelly/2014/05/21/ebay-suffers-massive-security-breach-all-users-must-their-change-passwords/#19621fcb7492. Accessed 3 June 2018.

[86] Kolbasuk McGee M (2017) A new in-depth analysis of Anthem breach https://www.bankinfosecurity.com/new-in-depth-analysis-anthem-breach-a-9627. Accessed 3 June 2018.

[87] Silverman R and Fritz B (2014) Data breach sets off upheaval at Sony Pictures https://www.wsj.com/articles/data-breach-sets-off-upheaval-at-sony-pictures-1417657799. Accessed 3 June 2018.

[88] Crowe P (2015) JPMorgan fell victim to the largest theft of customer data from a financial institution in US history http://www.businessinsider.com/jpmorgan-hacked-bank-breach-2015-11. Accessed 3 June 2018.

[89] Fung B and Shaban H (2017) The FTC is investigating the Equifax breach. Here's why that's a big deal https://www.washingtonpost.com/news/the-switch/wp/2017/09/14/the-ftc-confirms-its-investigating-the-equifax-breach-adding-to-a-chorus-of-official-criticism/?utm_term=.77e136c6fe95. Accessed 3 June 2018.

agreed to pay at least $575 million and up to $700 million for its "failure to take reasonable steps to secure its network" leading to the 2017 breach.[90] The funds were earmarked to provide credit monitoring services to affected consumers and to reimburse others who bought them in the wake of the breach.[91] Beginning in January 2020, the company is also required to provide six free credit reports per year for seven years to all U.S. consumers.

Data breach notification requirements are one area where the GDPR's requirements were based on U.S. laws. Notification requirements for data breaches are an important new addition to the EU data protection framework brought about in the Regulation. As with other obligations for data controllers and processors, the GDPR calibrates data breach notification requirements to levels of risk. If a data breach is "likely to result in a high risk to the rights and freedoms of natural persons," the data controller is obliged to notify the data subject.[92] Notification is not required, however, if the data breach does not have any potential to create a "risk to the rights and freedoms of natural persons."[93]

Similarly, some U.S. state laws have explicit provisions that involve considering the "likelihood of harms" for breach notifications. For example, in Alaska,[94] Arizona,[95] Arkansas,[96] Colorado,[97] Connecticut,[98] and Florida,[99] disclosing a data breach to individuals is not required if it is not likely to result in harm to them. Indicative of the sectoral nature of U.S. privacy laws, data breach notification requirements can be found across at least eight separate federal acts.[100]

[90] Fed. Trade Comm'n (2019). Equifax to pay $575 million as part of settlement with FTC, CFPB, and states related to 2017 data breach https://www.ftc.gov/news-events/press-releases/2019/07/equifax-pay-575-million-part-settlement-ftc-cfpb-states-related. Accessed 6 September 2019.

[91] Dellinger AJ (2018) Americans spent $1.4 billion on credit freezes after Equifax breach https://www.ibtimes.com/americans-spent-14-billion-credit-freezes-after-equifax-breach-2665247. Accessed 6 September 2019.

[92] GDPR, Article 34(1).

[93] GDPR, Article 33, Article 34.

[94] Alaska Stat. § 45.48.010(c) (2009).

[95] Ariz. Rev. Stat. § 44-750(L)(1) (2007).

[96] Ark. Code Ann. § 4-110-105(d) (2010).

[97] Colo. Rev. Stat. § 6-1-716(2)(a) (2006).

[98] Conn. Gen. Stat. § 36a-701b(b)(1) (2012).

[99] Fla. Stat. § 501.171(4)(c) (2014).

[100] These include the Privacy Act, the Federal Information Security Management Act, the Veterans Affairs Information Security Act, the Health Insurance Portability and Accountability Act, the Health Information Technology for Economic and Clinical Health Act, the Gramm-Leach-Bliley Act, the Federal Trade Commission Act, and the Fair Credit Reporting Act.

10.4 The Effect of the GDPR on Privacy and Data Protection in the United States: Resolving Issues or Making Things Worse?

The GDPR, which came into force on 25 May 2018, does not only directly apply to the twenty-eight Member States of the EU, but requires non-European businesses and individuals to alter their practices. The territorial scope of the GDPR is no longer limited by the location of the data controller, but is directly applicable to the processing of personal data of data subjects in the EU "regardless of whether the processing takes place in the Union or not."[101] In its interpretation of the scope, the European Commission suggested "for the first time," there is "no legal doubt" about the application of the Regulation to non-EU companies that process Europeans' data.[102] Moreover, the term *processing activities* includes offering products and services, even those free of charge, to Europeans and monitoring their behavior.[103]

American companies that process Europeans' data in this manner must abide by the provisions of the GDPR or face severe consequences. When an infringement occurs, data protection authorities (DPAs) can impose administrative fines, the levels of which vary depending on the infringed obligation.[104] A company that violates the rules on data transfers outside the EU, for example, may be subject to the higher of (a) four percent of a company's annual turnover, or (b) 20,000,000 EUR.[105] A variety of conditions determine the magnitude of the fine(s), such as "the nature, gravity and duration of the infringement" in relation to "the nature, scope or purpose of the processing as well as the number of data subjects affected and the level of damage suffered by them," the negligence of the data controller, the existence of a previous infringement, and other considerations.[106]

10.4.1 Spillover Effects of GDPR Compliance

The GDPR seems poised to enhance privacy and data protection for U.S. consumers as well as Europeans. By imposing higher standards on companies that simultaneously offer goods and services on both sides of the Atlantic, data subjects in the

---

[101] GDPR, Article 3.

[102] European Commission, Factsheet on the Right to be Forgotten Ruling (C-131/12) (2014) https://www.inforights.im/media/1186/cl_eu_commission_factsheet_right_to_be-forgotten.pdf. Accessed 4 June 2018.

[103] GDPR, Article 3(2)(a), (b); GDPR, Recital 23. Behavioral monitoring encompasses the tracking of individuals' online activities in ways that are designed to assist in the prediction of their behaviors, attitudes, and personal preferences.

[104] GDPR Article 53(2), (4), (5), (6).

[105] GDPR Article 83(5).

[106] GDPR Article 83 (2) (a)-(k).

U.S. are positioned to benefit downstream from EU laws and the efforts of EU regulators to change the practices of these companies that process personal data. For example, in the wake of the Facebook-Cambridge Analytica scandal, Mark Zuckerberg announced Facebook would implement GDPR controls not just for users in the EU, but in all markets where the social networking website operates.[107] Microsoft also announced that it would offer the privacy protections mandated by the GDPR to all of its customers around the world.[108] Considering such legal developments, American consumers may be among the beneficiaries of the additional privacy protections that the GDPR was designed to provide to Europeans.

In terms of legislative impact, the GDPR has inspired laws proposed at both the federal and state levels in the United States. In addition to helping to inspire the CCPA, the GDPR was the model for the Washington Privacy Act, a consumer privacy bill that was proposed, but ultimately failed, in Washington state, home to digital giants Amazon and Microsoft. The proposed law borrowed heavily from the GDPR, including its expansive jurisdictional scope, distinction between data controllers and processors, and mandated risk assessments.[109] Moreover, as described in the previous section, U.S. state laws on data breaches as well as the FTC's standards around data security contain requirements resembling the GDPR. Therefore, the efforts of U.S. companies to comply with U.S. data breach notification laws may overlap substantially with their efforts to demonstrate compliance with the GDPR's provisions on data breach notifications and mandated risk assessments.

10.5 Conclusion

This chapter has outlined several of the most important laws and issues in privacy and data protection in the United States, and how those may be affected by the GDPR. Several important differences and similarities between privacy and data protection in the EU and the U.S. exist. Perhaps the most notable difference is in their approach to regulation, vis-à-vis either sectoral or omnibus regulations, each of which comes with distinct advantages and disadvantages.

[107] Rahman M (2018) Amidst data scandal, Facebook will voluntarily enforce EU's new privacy rules "everywhere" https://www.xda-developers.com/facebook-voluntarly-enforce-eu-privacy-law/. Accessed 3 June 2018.

[108] Brill J (2018) Microsoft's commitment to GDPR, privacy and putting customers in control of their own data. Microsoft.com https://blogs.microsoft.com/on-the-issues/2018/05/21/microsofts-commitment-to-gdpr-privacy-and-putting-customers-in-control-of-their-own-data/. Accessed 10 October 2019.

[109] Noordyke M (2019) The state Senate version of the Washington Privacy Act: A summary https://iapp.org/news/a/the-state-senate-version-of-the-washington-privacy-act-a-summary/. Accessed 10 October 2019.

On the one hand, the sectoral approach of the U.S. often leaves new business sectors "free of regulation," such that they can use personal information for commercial purposes.[110] Indeed, data controllers often see the sectoral approach as "an opportunity to limit the restrictions of the intended use."[111] Moreover, opponents of the sectoral approach have argued that it "cannot serve as the basis for a generalized protection of informational privacy"[112] and that it lacks the accountability and enforcement mechanisms to oversee the issues and gaps in privacy legislation.[113] From a more critical perspective, U.S. privacy law has been characterized as "disjointed" and "piecemeal."[114] On the other hand, the patchwork nature of U.S. privacy laws and its accompanying "lack of comprehensive philosophical foundation" has been argued to actually benefit privacy, as it provides flexibility to courts to deal with various fact patterns.[115] Several new privacy laws at the state level, especially the CCPA, as well as the possibility of new federal privacy law, are introducing even greater complexity into the U.S. privacy landscape.

Given the extraterritorial reach of the GDPR, many leading U.S. companies are now faced with the task of complying with both U.S. and EU privacy and data protection laws and must meet the different standards set by American and European data protection authorities. The monitoring activities of several American technology companies, such as Apple, Facebook, and Google, that regularly offer goods and services to Europeans via the Internet, have already come under the scrutiny of European data protection officers. France's data protection authority, for instance, led a probe on behalf of the EU group to review Google's revisions to its policies,[116] and in January 2019 imposed a fine of $50 million euros for violations of the GDPR, including "lack of transparency, inadequate information and lack of valid consent regarding the ads personalization."[117] In addition, government privacy watchdogs from France, Spain, and Italy have joined the Dutch-led effort, accompanied by authorities in Germany and Belgium, to investigate the way Facebook

[110]Schwartz 2013, p. 1979.

[111]Simitis 2010, p. 2000.

[112]DeVries 2003, p. 285.

[113]Swire and Ahmad 2012, p. 30.

[114]DeVries 2003, p. 285.

[115]Schwartz and Peifer 2010, p. 1963; Flaherty 1989, pp. 404–405. As privacy and information policy scholar David Flaherty has explained, sectoral legislation "permits general data protection principles to be shaped in precise, statutory form to suit a particular type of problem and in order to grant specific enforceable rights to individuals."

[116]Matussek K (2015) Google loses most of challenge to German data-privacy order http://www.bloomberg.com/news/articles/2015-04-08/google-loses-challenge-to-german-regulator-s-data-privacy-order. Accessed 4 June 2018.

[117]Commission Nationale de l'Informatique et des Libertés (2019) The CNIL's restricted committee imposes a financial penalty of 50 million euros against GOOGLE LLC https://www.cnil.fr/en/cnils-restricted-committee-imposes-financial-penalty-50-million-euros-against-google-llc. Accessed 6 September 2019.

combines and uses data from its services, such as Instagram and WhatsApp, for targeted advertising.[118]

While seeking to comply with the GDPR, U.S. companies may find areas where existing compliance efforts with U.S. laws can be leveraged to maximize their compliance activities for the GDPR while minimizing the risk of their data processing operations. Laws regarding data breach notifications are an area where this may be particularly true. At the same time, some differences that exist between U.S. and EU seem irreconcilable. The interaction between the right to erasure and the First Amendment is likely to remain a legal challenge, especially if European regulators continue to seek to expand the breadth of erasure requests and to bring more publishers or indexers into the fray. While definitions of privacy harm have been elusive to scholars, lawmakers, and regulators on both sides of the Atlantic, this may be an area where the most progress can be made through increased cooperation and dialogue.

Acknowledgements I would like to thank to Professor Fred H. Cate for his valuable comments and feedback on an earlier draft of this chapter, and to my supervisors at the IAPP, Rita Heimes and Omer Tene, for their useful suggestions. I am also grateful to Kyle Heatherly for his love and support and to Mavi Heatherly for everything that he is.

References

Bambauer J (2014) Is data speech? Stan L Rev 66:57–120

Bhagwat A (2012) Sorrell v. IMS Health: Details, detailing, and the death of privacy, Vt L Rev 36:855–880

Cate F (2001) Privacy in perspective. The AEI Press, Washington DC

Cate F (2011) The growing importance (and irrelevance) of international data protection law. http://www.lcil.cam.ac.uk/news/article.php?.section26&article=1581 Accessed 4 March 2017 (link no longer active)

Chander A, Kaminski M, McGeveran W (2019) Catalyzing privacy law. Georgetown Law faculty publications and other works. https://scholarship.law.georgetown.edu/facpub/2190/ Accessed 6 September 2019

DeVries W (2003) Protecting privacy in the digital age. Berkeley Tech LJ 18:283–311

Fazlioglu M (2013) Forget me not: The clash of the right to be forgotten and freedom of expression on the Internet. Int Data Privacy L 3:149–157

Fazlioglu M (2019) Consensus and controversy in the debate over US federal data privacy legislation. International Association of Privacy Professionals, Portsmouth. https://iapp.org/store/books/a191P000002YpUzQAK/

Flaherty D (1989) Protecting privacy in surveillance societies: The Federal Republic of Germany, Sweden, France, Canada, and the United States. The University of North Carolina Press, Chapel Hill

Google (2015) Report of the advisory council to Google on the right to be forgotten. https://static.googleusercontent.com/media/archive.google.com/en//advisorycouncil/advisement/advisory-report.pdf Accessed 4 June 2018

118 Schechner S (2015) Facebook privacy controls face scrutiny in Europe https://www.wsj.com/articles/facebook-confronts-european-probes-1427975994. Accessed 4 June 2018.

Gratton É (2014) If personal information is privacy's gatekeeper, then risk of harm is the key: A proposed method for determining what counts as personal information. Alb L J Sc & Tech 24:1–90
Helscher D (1994) *Griswold v. Connecticut* and the unenumerated right of privacy. N Ill U L Rev 15:33–61
Hoofnagle C (2016) Federal Trade Commission privacy law and policy. Cambridge University Press, New York
Julin T, Isani J, Acosta P (2012) The dog that did bark: First Amendment protection of data mining. Vt L Rev 36:881–901
Kerr O (2015) *Katz* has only one step: The irrelevance of subjective expectations. U Chi L Rev 82:113–134
Massey C (2015) Uncensored discourse is not just for politics. Vt L Rev 36:845–854
Piety T (2012) "A necessary cost of freedom"? The incoherence of *Sorrell v. IMS*. Ala L Rev 62:1–54
Prosser W (1960) Privacy. Calif L Rev 48:383–423
Reidenberg J (2000) Resolving conflicting international data privacy rules in cyberspace. Stan L Rev 52:1315–1371
Richards N (2005) Reconciling data privacy and the First Amendment. UCLA L Rev 52:1149–1222
Richards N (2015) Why data privacy law is (mostly) constitutional. Wm & Mary L Rev 56:1501–1533
Rosen J (2012) The right to be forgotten. Stan L Rev 64:88–92
Schwartz P (2009) Preemption and privacy. Yale L J 118:902–947
Schwartz P (2013) The EU-US privacy collision: A turn to institutions and procedures. Harv L Rev 126:1966–2009
Schwartz P, Peifer K-N (2010) Prosser's privacy and the German right of personality. Calif L Rev 98:1925–1988
Schwartz P, Solove D (2014) Reconciling personal information in the United States and European Union. Calif L Rev 102:877–916
Simitis S (2010) Privacy – an endless debate? Cal L Rev 98:1989–2006
Skinner-Thompson S (2015) Outing privacy. Nw U L Rev 110:159–222
Solove D, Hartzog W (2014) The FTC and the new common law of privacy. Colum L Rev 114:583–676
Swire P, Ahmad K (2012) Foundations of information privacy and data protection: A survey of global concepts, laws and practices. International Association of Privacy Professionals, Portsmouth
Warren S, Brandeis L (1890) The right to privacy. Harv L Rev 4:193–220
Whitman JQ (2004) The two Western cultures of privacy: Dignity versus liberty. Yale L J 113:1151–1221
Wimmer K (2018) Free expression and EU privacy regulation: Can the GDPR reach U.S. publishers? Syracuse L Rev 68:545–576
Young E (2012) *Sorrell v. IMS Health* and the end of the constitutional double standard. Ver L Rev 36:903–930

Muge Fazlioglu Senior Westin Research Fellow, International Association of Privacy Professionals, 75 Rochester Ave., Portsmouth, NH 03801 USA.

Chapter 11
European Laws' Effectiveness in Protecting Personal Data

Ambrogino G. Awesta

Contents

Abstract The fuel for the digital economy and business is data. Data is being harvested online on an unprecedented scale. Digital enterprises involved in this practice are thus quite active in collecting all sorts of data through pervasive techniques that track and collect huge amounts of information. This practice has drastic consequences for the privacy and security of such data. In order to ensure the security and privacy of those data, European legislators have recently enacted and adopted different legal instruments. However, a mere adoption of laws does not per se guarantee their effectiveness in achieving the intended goal. This presumption underpins the hypothesis of this research which comes down to the following: the mere adoption of legal tools does not automatically guarantee the enhancement of the privacy and security of personal data against online tracking and targeting. By putting this hypothesis to the test, this research attempts to address the question over the extent to which newly created obligations in recently adopted legal tools can effectively enhance and secure the privacy of users' data against the tracking and targeting practices of digital enterprises. To this end, this study will firstly elaborate on the meaning and scope of the concept of privacy. Secondly, the applicability of privacy in relation to technologies that are employed for tracking and targeting in cyberspace is scrutinized. In the third place, we will take a closer look at the impact of obligations that are imposed on digital enterprises by the new legal instruments. Finally, a conclusion is drawn over the actual effectiveness of these instruments in protecting and securing the privacy of users against the technologies deployed by digital enterprises.

A. G. Awesta (✉)
Windesheim University of Applied Sciences, Hospitaaldreef 5, 1315 RC Almere, The Netherlands
e-mail: ag.awesta@windesheimflevoland.nl

E. Kiesow Cortez (ed.), *Data Protection Around the World*,
Information Technology and Law Series 33,
https://doi.org/10.1007/978-94-6265-407-5_11

Keywords Privacy · Cybersecurity · Consent · Tracking · Targeting · Digital enterprise

11.1 Introduction

On 17 March 2018, two leading newspapers, *The New York Times*[1] and *The Guardian*,[2] published articles through which the abuse of users' data by Cambridge Analytica was brought to the public's attention. It came to light that, based on the revelations of whistleblower Christopher Wylie, this company had harvested data from as many as 87 million profiles of Facebook users with the aim to influence and predict elections through political targeting by means of psychographics. Noteworthy is that Facebook had known since 2015 that data harvesting was taking place and yet it had not done much about it, if anything at all. In July, the British data protection authority, the Information Commissioner's Office (ICO), decided to fine Facebook for a rather symbolic amount of £500,000.[3] On 20 March 2018, the Federal Trade Commission (FTC) opened an investigation into this situation, and Mark Zuckerberg was urged to testify before the U.S. Congress, and later in front of the European Parliament.

On 25 March 2018, he broke his silence and apologized for the breach of trust that had occurred with the aforesaid abuse of users' profiles. Yet, this particular data breach did not finally result in a total deactivation of this feature on Facebook. As of June, 2018, all that Facebook could offer on its platform is the following notice: "keep in mind that when you install an app, you give permission to access your public profile, which includes your name, profile pictures, username, user ID (account number), networks and any info you choose to make publicly available. You also give the app other info to personalize your experience, including your friends list, gender, age range and locale".[4] Facebook also emphasizes that "when you connect a business integration to your account using Facebook Login, you also give it permission to access your name, profile picture and any other information you agree to share when you log in. [...] A business integration may also ask for additional info later when you're using a feature that requires it".[5]

---

[1] Rosenberg et al. 2018. How Trump consultants exploited the Facebook data of millions. https://www.nytimes.com/2018/03/17/us/politics/cambridge-analytica-trump-campaign.html. Accessed 5 July 2018.

[2] Cadwalladr et al. 2018. Revealed: 50 million Facebook profiles harvested for Cambridge Analytica in major data breach. https://www.theguardian.com/news/2018/mar/17/cambridge-analytica-facebook-influence-us-election. Accessed 5 July 2018.

[3] Smout 2018. Facebook faces small but symbolic UK fine over data protection breaches. https://uk.reuters.com/article/us-facebook-privacy-britain/facebook-faces-small-but-symbolic-uk-fine-over-data-protection-breaches-idUKKBN1K033N. Accessed 5 July 2018.

[4] https://www.facebook.com/help/187333441316612. Accessed 6 July 2018.

[5] https://www.facebook.com/help/615546898822465?helpref=related&ref=related. Accessed 6 July 2018.

Further, it is not clear what these 'business integrations' are and why Facebook still allows them to access users' data and, if Facebook allows this, how it supervises their conduct in order to prevent similar abuses as those committed by Cambridge Analytica. Noteworthy is that Facebook itself also continues to collect innumerable data, which can be divided into the following categories: information and content the users provide, device information, and information from partners. This social platform also collects personal data, i.e. Internet browsing habits, even if one is not using this platform, a practice which is denoted by the notion of 'offsite tracking'.[6] This company has provided other enterprises, such as Apple and Samsung, access to data about users as well as their friends.[7] However, one has to bear in mind that the aim of the study at hand is not to demonize Facebook, but rather to use it as a mere case-study, since this company has been at the center of the privacy discourse. What is more, it has to be borne in mind that this platform is not alone in conducting those aforementioned activities and, thus, we should not forget that other digital enterprises, such as Google, are also very active in collecting (personal) data[8] through pervasive techniques that track and collect information, with far-reaching consequences for the privacy and security of such data. To guarantee the privacy and security of data, various laws have been adopted. However, a mere adoption of laws does not per se guarantee their effectiveness. More concrete, the hypothesis of this research is that the mere adoption of legal tools does not automatically entail the enhancement of the privacy and security of personal data against online tracking and targeting.

The newly adopted legal tools that are central to the assessment of our hypothesis are the following. First, we have the General Data Protection Regulation (GDPR),[9] which has occupied everyone's attention since its enactment and coming into force. Without detracting from the importance of this legal instrument, we need, however, to keep in mind that the attention paid to this law went at the expense of another legal tool, namely the EU Network and Information Security Directive (NIS Directive),[10] which came into effect at around the same period. Another noteworthy event concerns the ambiguity around the simultaneous entry into force of another legal instrument along with the GDPR, which ultimately did not come into effect. This latter instrument is the regulation concerning the respect for private life and the protection of

[6]Van Alsenoy et al. Draft 25 August 2015 From social media service to advertising network: A critical analysis of Facebook's Revised Policies and Terms, version 1.3. https://www.law.kuleuven.be/citip/en/news/item/facebooks-revised-policies-and-terms-v1-3.pdf. Accessed 6 July 2018.

[7]Serrels 2018. Facebook gave Apple, Samsung access to data about users—and their friends. https://www.cnet.com/news/facebook-apple-samsung-cambridge-analytica-user-data-and-their-friends-data/. Accessed 7 July 2018.

[8]Englehardt and Narayanan 2016. Online tracking: A 1-million-site measurement and analysis. https://webtransparency.cs.princeton.edu/webcensus/. Accessed 7 July 2018.

[9]Regulation (EU) 2016/679 of the European Parliament and of the Council of 27 April 2016 on the protection of natural persons with regard to the processing of personal data and on the free movement of such data, and repealing Directive 95/46/EC.

[10]Directive (EU) 2016/1148 of the European Parliament and of the Council of 6 July 2016 concerning measures for a high common level of security of network and information systems across the Union.

personal data in electronic communications (E-Privacy Regulation),[11] which tends to repeal Directive 2002/58/EC while aiming to align itself with the GDPR. Although these three instruments are independent legal tools, they are at the same time closely connected with one another. This interrelationship is not only anchored in the mere cross-references made in each of these tools, but it has also to be sought in their shared aim of protecting the data-subject in cyberspace by imposing, among others, stricter conditions on the digital enterprises. Yet, a closer look at these instruments would convey a contradictory image with regard to the roles of the aforementioned digital enterprises, which our hypothesis also indicates. Therefore, by putting this hypothesis to the test, the following overriding central question arises: *to what extent do the newly created obligations in the aforementioned legal tools effectively enhance and secure the privacy of users' data against the tracking and targeting practices of digital enterprises*?

In an attempt to arrive at an answer to our central question, the following steps will be taken. Firstly, we have to comprehend the meaning and scope of the concept of privacy. Secondly, we have to scrutinize the applicability of privacy in relation to technologies employed for tracking and targeting in cyberspace. Thirdly, we will take a closer look at the impact of obligations that are imposed on digital enterprises by the newly available legal instruments. Finally, based on the foregoing findings, a conclusion will be drawn regarding the effectiveness of the new legal tools in protecting and securing the privacy of users against technologies deployed by digital enterprises. These steps, which in fact make up the sub-questions to our central question, will constitute the structure of this contribution.

11.2 The Concept of Privacy

The notion of privacy is a very broad one that does not lend itself easily to a single and universal definition. It is rather a container concept that covers different realms of life. Accordingly, the notion of privacy has been defined in different ways but with the same essence on both sides of the Atlantic. Traditionally, the right to privacy has been understood as a right against arbitrary intrusion, i.e. unreasonable searches and seizures by the government, which is currently, given the expansion of the scope of this concept, merely one of its many angles. As a right, this concept covers a variety of realms such as family life, motherhood, procreation, and currently online privacy which is the focus of this study. As to the meaning of this right, which can underpin all those different realms, reference can be made to the reasoning of the Associate Justice Louis Brandeis in his dissent in the landmark case *Olmstead v. United States*,[12] where he states that "the makers of our Constitution undertook to secure conditions

[11] Proposal for a Regulation of the European Parliament and of the Council concerning the respect for private life and the protection of personal data in electronic communications and repealing, Directive 2002/58EC.

[12] *Olmstead v. United States*, 277 U.S. 438 (1928), Nos. 493, 532, and 533.

favorable to the pursuit of happiness. They recognized the significance of man's spiritual nature, of his feelings, and of his intellect. They knew that only a part of the pain, pleasure and satisfactions of life are to be found in material things. They sought to protect Americans in their beliefs, their thoughts, their emotions and their sensations. They conferred, as against the Government, the right to be let alone - the most comprehensive of rights, and the right most valued by civilized men. To protect that right, every unjustifiable intrusion by the Government upon the privacy of the individual, whatever the means employed, must be deemed a violation of the Fourth Amendment".[13] Samuel D. Warren and Louis D. Brandeis have also explained in an article that the "principle which protects personal writings and all other personal productions against publication in any form is the principle of 'inviolate personality'".[14] The classical meaning of the right to privacy, namely, the right to be let alone, can be interpreted to mean that one should be the sole author of his decisions, i.e. to be autonomous in his choices, without the intrusion of others.

Against this background, Louis Henkin wrote already in 1974: "I do not have even an every-day definition of 'privacy' or of the 'right of privacy'. Some may define 'privacy' as the sum of all 'private rights'. Many, however, obviously contemplate a discrete private right of privacy, though they may differ widely as to its character and content. So we find innumerable references to the 'right to be let alone': some contemplate a right to be alone, to be free from unwanted intrusion, to be secreted and secretive: a right to be unknown ('incognito'), free from unwanted information about oneself in the hands of others, unwanted scrutiny, unwanted 'publicity'; a right to 'intimacy' and a freedom to do intimate things. Some offer another kind of definition, a right to be free from physical, mental, or spiritual violation, a right to the 'integrity' of one's 'personality'".[15] And yet, by referring to different judgements rendered by the Supreme Court, Henkin reckons "that the Court cites search and seizure cases as precedent for its new zone of autonomy [which] suggests that it does not distinguish between privacy and autonomy and may be treating them both as aspects of 'the right to be let alone'".[16] According to his analysis, "primarily and principally the new Right to Privacy is a zone of prima facie autonomy [...]".[17]

What is more, in defining the notion of privacy there are roughly two strands of interpretation deployed. "First, privacy as seclusion or intimacy which is often, as a point of departure, spatially defined; other definitional approaches in this strand might be by the types of action or information that might be considered as private by 'substance'. Second, privacy as freedom of action, self-determination and autonomy. Privacy, however, is only split in this sense at first sight: the two strands can be united again in perceiving privacy as protecting the free development of one's personality, that is, self-realisation and autonomy in a wider sense".[18] In this regard, a distinction

[13] Ibid.

[14] Warren and Brandeis 1890, p. 205.

[15] Henkin 1974, p. 1419.

[16] Henkin 1974, p. 1425.

[17] Ibid.

[18] Ziegler 2007, p. 1.

has also been made between the ‘libertarian’ and ‘dignitarian’ views to privacy, both of which are said to be overarched by the principle of ‘autonomy’,[19] which in its etymological sense means ‘self-rule’ or, better perhaps, ‘self-determination’. Hence, “self-governance is the conceptual root of autonomy”.[20] It is on this principle that ‘consent’ is predicated.[21] As it has been rightly argued, “the capacity for self-determination is a necessary feature of agency, which is crucial to the justification provided by consent”.[22] Without going further into a philosophical discussion of these notions, we can already discern that, in a way, autonomy forms the essence of privacy and that this fact is reflected in the notion of consent. This has traditionally found expression in medical law in general and reproductive rights in particular. However, privacy has not only been applied to reproductive and medical cases but, as mentioned above, also to many other realms of life.

When applied to cyberspace, some scholars differentiate between ‘*information privacy*’ and ‘*decisional privacy*’. As regards the meaning of these two notions, it is stated that “the focus of decisional privacy is on freedom from interference when one makes certain fundamental decisions [...]. In contrast, information privacy is concerned with the use, transfer, and processing of the personal data generated in daily life”.[23] Yet, this conceptual distinction is treacherous, because, as the proponents of this distinction are also aware, “decisional and information privacy are not unrelated; the use, transfer, or processing of personal data by public and private sector organizations will affect the choices that we make”,[24] with perilous implications as recently revealed by the case of Cambridge Analytica. Hence, the essence of the right to privacy is decisional and should remain that way, since any alteration of this, no matter how conceptual, is prone to create a fragmentation of self-determination, that is, a lowering of the degree of protection afforded to this concept as a right. Within the context of data protection laws, we can also observe that the emphasis is on privacy as autonomy. This is apparent from the fact that in this field of law, the concept of ‘consent’ is not only applied as a prerequisite for lawful processing,[25] but its application is even subject to further conditions, as we will see in the next section.

[19] Ibid., Whitman 2004, p. 1151.

[20] Miller and Wertheimer 2010, p. 61.

[21] Maclean 2009, p. 9.

[22] Maclean 2009, p. 10.

[23] Schwartz 2003, p. 2058.

[24] Ibid.

[25] Article 6 of the Regulation (EU) 2016/679 of the European Parliament and of the Council of 27 April 2016 on the protection of natural persons with regard to the processing of personal data and on the free movement of such data, and repealing Directive 95/46/EC.

11.3 The Notion of Consent

The concept of 'consent', as the essence of privacy, is the notion through which autonomy is expressed. To be valid, the notion of consent is subject to the conditions that we will discuss in this section. Each of these conditions in turn reveals the fact that consent is in essence the expression of autonomy and self-determination. To comprehend this notion, we will look mainly at its meaning and scope within the three legal instruments chosen for this study.

First of all, we must note that the notion of consent is absent from the NIS Directive. The reason is that this statute does not have as its main objective the protection of personal data. The objective of this directive is rather the achievement of a high common level of security of network and information systems[26] within the European Union. However, the protection of such infrastructure is not separate from, among others, the protection of personal data. This is because a breach of security oftentimes results in data breach. In other words, as this directive states, "personal data are in many cases compromised as a result of incidents".[27] What is more, as far as the moment the processing of personal data is concerned, this directive refers to the European data protection laws.[28] This means that this directive does not deviate from these laws but aims rather to comply with them.[29]

As regards the notion of consent, the GDPR states that "consent of the data subject means any freely given, informed and unambiguous indication of the data subject's wishes by which he or she, by a statement or by a clear affirmative action, signifies agreement to the processing of personal data relating to him or her".[30] In this reasoning, different criteria are mentioned, the fulfillment of which is necessary for the consent's validity. Therefore, further explanation is necessary which will be provided hereafter.

Regarding free and informed consent, reference can be made to the field of biology and medicine such as clinical trials[31] in which the notion of consent has a longer and more profound foundation. In this context, "a widely acknowledged approach to informed consent is analysis of the concept in terms of its basic elements, the most generic of which are information and consent. The information component refers to the disclosure of information and to the comprehension of what is disclosed. The consent component refers to a voluntary decision and an authorization to proceed.

---

[26]For a definition of this notion, see Article 4 of Directive (EU) 2016/1148 of the European Parliament and of the Council of 6 July 2016 concerning measures for a high common level of security of network and information systems across the Union.

[27]Ibid., Recital 63.

[28]Ibid., Recital 79 and Article 2.

[29]Ibid., Recital 75.

[30]Article 4 (11) of the Regulation (EU) 2016/679 of the European Parliament and of the Council of 27 April 2016 on the protection of natural persons with regard to the processing of personal data and on the free movement of such data, and repealing Directive 95/46/EC.

[31]Recital 161 of the preamble of the Directive (EU) 2016/1148 of the European Parliament and of the Council of 6 July 2016 concerning measures for a high common level of security of network and information systems across the Union.

Legal, regulatory, philosophical, medical, and psychological literatures often propose the following five elements as the analytical components of these two generic units of informed consent: (1) competence, (2) disclosure, (3) understanding, (4) voluntariness, and (5) consent. Some writers present these elements as the building blocks of a definition of informed consent: One gives an informed consent to an intervention if [...] one is competent to act, receives a thorough disclosure, comprehends the disclosure, chooses voluntarily, and consents to the intervention".[32] However, these building blocks are not the same as what we can find in the framework of the GDPR, even though in my point of view they have, by way of analogy, to be taken into account.

In the context of the GDPR, according to Article 29 Working Party, these are the minimum requirements for the consent to be informed: 'the controller's identity, the purpose of each of the processing operations for which the personal data are intended,[33] the type of data that will be collected and used, the existence of the right to withdraw consent, information about the use of the data for automated decision-making, and the possible risks of data transfer'.[34] In addition, "when seeking consent, controllers should ensure that they use clear and plain language in all cases. This means a message should be easily understandable for the average person and not only for lawyers. Controllers cannot use long privacy policies that are difficult to understand or statements full of legal jargon. Consent must be clear and distinguishable from other matters and provided in an intelligible and easily accessible form. This requirement essentially means that information relevant for making informed decisions on whether or not to consent may not be hidden in general terms and conditions".[35] What is more, "if consent is to be given by electronic means, the request must be clear and concise. Layered and granular information can be an appropriate way to deal with the two-fold obligation of being precise and complete on the one hand and understandable on the other hand".[36]

As regards the consent that has to be given in freedom, one can clearly discern the notion of autonomy, because in this element real choice and control of the data subject are implied.[37] Accordingly, "consent should not be regarded as freely given if the data subject has no genuine or free choice or is unable to refuse or withdraw consent without detriment".[38] Hence, the autonomy of the data subject is visible not only in the *giving* of consent but also in the *withdrawal* thereof in a broad sense

---

[32] Miller and Wertheimer 2010, p. 56.

[33] Recital 42 of the preamble of the Regulation (EU) 2016/679 of the European Parliament and of the Council of 27 April 2016 on the protection of natural persons with regard to the processing of personal data and on the free movement of such data, and repealing Directive 95/46/EC.

[34] Article 29 Working Party, *Guidelines on Consent under Regulation 2016/679*, adopted on 28 November 2017; as last Revised and Adopted on 10 April 2018, p. 13.

[35] Ibid., p. 14.

[36] Ibid.

[37] Ibid., p. 5.

[38] Recital 42 of the preamble of the Regulation (EU) 2016/679 of the European Parliament and of the Council of 27 April 2016 on the protection of natural persons with regard to the processing of personal data and on the free movement of such data, and repealing Directive 95/46/EC.

of the term. In other words, "a data subject should have the right to have personal data concerning him or her rectified and a 'right to be forgotten' where the retention of such data infringes this Regulation or Union or Member State law to which the controller is subject. In particular, a data subject should have the right to have his or her personal data erased and no longer processed where the personal data are no longer necessary in relation to the purposes for which they are collected or otherwise processed, where a data subject has withdrawn his or her consent or objects to the processing of personal data concerning him or her, or where the processing of his or her personal data does not otherwise comply with this Regulation".[39] What the scope is of a freely given consent, is sometimes de facto hard to determine. For instance, a person can give his consent regarding the processing of his personal data by a telecommunication network operator, after obtaining information about the purpose of this data collection. But what if the operator or the provider of any other digital service wants to submit these data for further processing (to another party)? This was the case in the *Deutsche Telekom AG/Bundesrepublik Deutschland* judgement.[40] First, the European Court of Justice said that "the passing of subscribers' personal data to a third-party undertaking which intends to provide publicly available directory enquiry services and directories constitutes processing of personal data for the purposes of Article 8(2) of the Charter, which may be undertaken only 'on the basis of the consent of the person concerned or some other legitimate basis laid down by law'".[41] However, "[…] the wording of Article 12(2) of the Directive on privacy and electronic communications does not support the inference that the subscriber has a selective right to decide in favour of certain providers of publicly available directory enquiry services and directories. It should be noted in that regard that it is the publication itself of the personal data in a public directory with a specific purpose which may turn out to be detrimental for a subscriber. Where, however, the subscriber has consented to his data being published in a directory with a specific purpose, he will generally not have standing to object to the publication of the same data in another, similar directory".[42] Despite the fact that the passing of subscribers' personal data to third parties is 'subject to the condition that the data may not be used for other purposes than those for which they were collected', a freely given consent can thus mean a loss of control over one's personal data, because one cannot know in whose hands the data might end, which, subsequently, makes, among others, the withdrawal of consent more complicated, if not impossible.

Furthermore, the 'unambiguity' of the consent indicates that "consent requires a statement from the data subject or a clear affirmative act which means that it must always be given through an active motion or declaration. It must be obvious that the data subject has consented to the particular processing".[43] This can be done

[39]Ibid., Recital 65.

[40]Case C-543/09 *Deutsche Telekom AG v Bundesrepublik Deutschland* [2011] ECR I-03441.

[41]Ibid., para 53.

[42]Ibid, para 62.

[43]Article 29 Working Party, *Guidelines on Consent under Regulation 2016/679*, adopted on 28 November 2017; as last Revised and Adopted on 10 April 2018, p. 15.

by means of a 'clear affirmative action' or a 'statement'. Both notions indicate the autonomy of the data subject, as the first notion comes down to the fact that the data subject 'must have taken a deliberate action to consent'.[44] However, this element of consent can cause some confusion in cyberspace, especially when the data subject is tracked or targeted while attempting to use a service. On this issue, we can think of online profiling based on the collected data. The term 'profiling' means "any form of automated processing of personal data consisting of the use of personal data to evaluate certain personal aspects relating to a natural person, in particular to analyse or predict aspects concerning that natural person's performance at work, economic situation, health, personal preferences, interests, reliability, behaviour, location or movements".[45] However, in this case, "the data subject should be informed of the existence of profiling and the consequences of such profiling. Where the personal data are collected from the data subject, the data subject should also be informed whether he or she is obliged to provide the personal data and of the consequences, where he or she does not provide such data".[46] Yet, the provision of information does not per se entail a deliberate action on the part of the data subject.

What is more, the autonomy of the data subject is not unlimited, but ought to give way to higher interests, i.e. the interest of the individual has to serve the general interest. This is a communitarian approach which justifies the confinement of the autonomy of the individual for the sake of the community. We can discern this from the following reasoning in the GDPR: "Where the data subject has given consent or the processing is based on Union or Member State law which constitutes a necessary and proportionate measure in a democratic society to safeguard, in particular, important objectives of general public interest, the controller should be allowed to further process the personal data irrespective of the compatibility of the purposes. In any case, the application of the principles set out in this Regulation and in particular the information of the data subject on those other purposes and on his or her rights including the right to object, should be ensured. Indicating possible criminal acts or threats to public security by the controller and transmitting the relevant personal data in individual cases or in several cases relating to the same criminal act or threats to public security to a competent authority should be regarded as being in the legitimate interest pursued by the controller. However, such transmission in the legitimate interest of the controller or further processing of personal data should be prohibited if the processing is not compatible with a legal, professional or other binding obligation of secrecy".[47] Another example of the aforesaid communitarian approach concerns the circumstance wherein "the processing of special categories of personal

[44] Ibid., p. 16.

[45] Article 4 (4) of the Regulation (EU) 2016/679 of the European Parliament and of the Council of 27 April 2016 on the protection of natural persons with regard to the processing of personal data and on the free movement of such data, and repealing Directive 95/46/EC.

[46] Ibid., Recital 60.

[47] Ibid., Recital 50.

data may be necessary for reasons of public interest in the areas of public health without consent of the data subject".[48]

Thus far, we have been able to see the scope and limitation of the notion of consent in the GDPR. Another relevant instrument in this regard is the *E-Privacy Regulation (draft)*. What is important to emphasize from the very outset is the fact that the adoption of a regulation is due to the fact that, among others, "the implementation of the ePrivacy Directive has not been effective to empower end-users. Therefore the implementation of the principle by centralising consent in software and prompting users with information about the privacy settings thereof, is necessary to achieve the aim".[49] More concrete, "the consent rule to protect the confidentiality of terminal equipment failed to reach its objectives as end-users face requests to accept tracking cookies without understanding their meaning and, in some cases, are even exposed to cookies being set without their consent. The consent rule is over-inclusive, as it also covers non-privacy intrusive practices, and under-inclusive, as it does not clearly cover some tracking techniques (e.g. device fingerprinting) which may not entail access/storage in the device".[50]

Thus, the E-Privacy Regulation attempts to enhance the end-user's control by making clear that consent can be expressed through technical settings and a broadening of the exceptions to the rules of consent. In this regard, the following assessment is made in order to find the right balance: "By centralising the consent in software such as internet browsers and prompting users to choose their privacy settings and expanding the exceptions to the cookie consent rule, a significant proportion of businesses would be able to do away with cookie banners and notices, thus leading to potentially significant cost savings and simplification. However, it may become more difficult for online targeted advertisers to obtain consent if a large proportion of users opt for 'reject third party cookies' settings. At the same time, centralising consent does not deprive website operators from the possibility to obtain consent by means of individual requests to end-users and thus maintain their current business model. Additional costs would ensue for some providers of browsers or similar software as these would need to ensure privacy-friendly settings".[51] The notion of consent is thus a central concept in this regulation, but the meaning and conditions for it are the same as in the GDPR,[52] since this regulation is a *lex specialis* of the GDPR. Therefore, for a more thorough comprehension of this notion, we have to refer back to the elaboration above. How, then, the concept of consent is proportionate to the tracking and targeting possibilities will be discussed in the next section.

---

[48]Ibid., Recital 54.

[49]Explanatory Memorandum to the Proposal for a Regulation of the European Parliament and of the Council concerning the respect for private life and the protection of personal data in electronic communications and repealing Directive 2002/58EC.

[50]Ibid.

[51]Ibid.

[52]Recital 18 of the preamble and Article 9 (1) of the Proposal for a Regulation of the European Parliament and of the Council concerning the respect for private life and the protection of personal data in electronic communications and repealing Directive 2002/58EC.

11.4 Tracking and Targeting

As regards the concept of consent, as explained above, the GDPR states that 'consent ought to be given by a clear affirmative act establishing a freely given, specific, informed and unambiguous indication of the data subject's agreement to the processing of personal data'. The way in which this consent is expressed "could include ticking a box when visiting an internet website, choosing technical settings for information society services or another statement or conduct which clearly indicates in this context the data subject's acceptance of the proposed processing of his or her personal data. Silence, pre-ticked boxes or inactivity should not therefore constitute consent. [...] If the data subject's consent is to be given following a request by electronic means, the request must be clear, concise and not unnecessarily disruptive to the use of the service for which it is provided".[53] This reasoning contains two crucial aspects that need to be discussed. The mere ticking of a box or choice of technical settings cannot do justice to the autonomy of the user, especially when the options to click and/or choose are a priori determined by the service provider. In light of this, usage of and access to the service concerned also often depend on the acceptance of such predetermined conditions. In other words, the techniques described above are prone to disruption. Hence, one cannot say that the expression of consent in the manner described above is, in particular, free and unambiguous.

Noteworthy is that 'unambiguity' assumes deliberation. But in cyberspace where the data subject receives multiple consent requests, which have to be handled through click and swipes, the actual warning effect of consent mechanisms is diminished. This is because consent requests are no longer read: "This is a particular risk to data subjects, as, typically, consent is asked for actions that are in principle unlawful without their consent".[54] One of the options for tackling this problem, as stated in the literature, is the incorporation of consent into the browser settings. However, this means that, as mentioned above, the service provider can determine in advance the options that please him and to which the data subject has to agree if he wants to use the service properly, even if the provided options are disadvantageous for him.

What is more, we read above that the validity of 'consent' entails that 'a statement from the data subject or a clear affirmative act must be present, which means that it must always be given through an active motion or declaration'.[55] This indicates that the data subject has autonomy, because in this context the data subject 'must have taken a deliberate action to consent'.[56] This element of consent, and therewith the autonomy of the data subject, is threatened in cyberspace when we take into account that the data subject is usually tracked or targeted while attempting to use a service.

---

[53] Recital 32 of the preamble of the Regulation (EU) 2016/679 of the European Parliament and of the Council of 27 April 2016 on the protection of natural persons with regard to the processing of personal data and on the free movement of such data, and repealing Directive 95/46/EC.

[54] Article 29 Working Party, Guidelines on Consent under Regulation 2016/679, adopted on 28 November 2017; as last Revised and Adopted on 10 April 2018, p. 17.

[55] Ibid., p. 15.

[56] Ibid., p. 16.

The question is then: how independent and autonomous his decision actually is. For instance, for storing third party tracking cookies, web browsers need to obtain the consent of the user, which, according to the E-Privacy Regulation, requires "freely given, specific informed, and unambiguous agreement to the storage and access of such cookies in and from the terminal equipment".[57] This regulation takes for granted that a consent is affirmative if the user "actively selects 'accept third party cookies' to confirm their agreement",[58] which, again, can be, among others, coercive if the usage of the service is made dependent hereupon. The only option for the user is the possibility to change the default settings for privacy and cookies or to withdraw his consent,[59] even though it also cannot be guaranteed that the penetration of such tools will be prevented or eliminated.

Furthermore, this menace is neither diminished with the adoption of the GDPR nor will it be abated by way of the E-Privacy Regulation, since this latter even states that it "broadens the possibilities for providers of electronic communications services to process electronic communications metadata, based on end-users' consent".[60] This legal instrument also provides "the possibility [for] providers of electronic communications services to process electronic communications data in transit, with the informed consent of all the end-users concerned".[61] The question that arises is then: how informed can the consent be if the average data subject is not aware and schooled in the latest technological developments – such as web bugs, spyware, hidden identifiers, tracking cookies, device fingerprinting and other unwanted tracking tools—that can intercept and process his data (in transit), even though the regulation says that methods for obtaining consent have to be 'user-friendly' which is itself a vague and open-ended notion and thus prone to abuse. This is especially so when such data "may reveal details of an individual's emotional, political, social complexities, including the content of communications, pictures, the location of individuals by accessing the device's GPS capabilities, contact lists, and other information already stored in the device"[62]—and when we take into account 'that, e.g., information may be provided in combination with mere standardised icons'.[63]

Another shortcoming of the GDPR, and with this the E-Privacy Regulation as well, is the absence of a time limit for consent. As Article 29 Working Party attempts to clarify, "how long consent lasts will depend on the context, the scope of the original consent and the expectations of the data subject. If the processing operations change or evolve considerably then the original consent is no longer valid. If this is

[57] Recital 24 of the preamble of the Proposal for a Regulation of the European Parliament and of the Council concerning the respect for private life and the protection of personal data in electronic communications and repealing Directive 2002/58EC.

[58] Ibid.

[59] Ibid., Articles 9 and 10.

[60] Ibid., Recital 17.

[61] Ibid., Recital 19.

[62] Ibid., Recital 20.

[63] Recital 60 of the preamble of the Regulation (EU) 2016/679 of the European Parliament and of the Council of 27 April 2016 on the protection of natural persons with regard to the processing of personal data and on the free movement of such data, and repealing Directive 95/46/EC.

the case, then new consent needs to be obtained".[64] Although the data subject has the possibility to withdraw his consent at any moment, the average user cannot be assumed to know exactly how to do this. The only positive development, albeit not good enough to effectively protect the privacy of users, is the fact that the E-Privacy Regulation requires that the user be reminded every six months of the possibility for him to withdraw his consent.[65]

Another menace posed to privacy with therein the autonomy of the data subject is scientific research, for in this field one deviates from the concreteness of consent. As the GDPR states, "it is often not possible to fully identify the purpose of personal data processing for scientific research purposes at the time of data collection. Therefore, data subjects should be allowed to give their consent to certain areas of scientific research when in keeping with recognised ethical standards for scientific research. Data subjects should have the opportunity to give their consent only to certain areas of research or parts of research projects to the extent allowed by the intended purpose".[66] The case of Cambridge Analytica and the involvement of academia therein is a plain example of this menace.

Based on the foregoing, it can be inferred that the increase in requirements does not per se result in better protection and security of the users' privacy. As we have seen, the requirements concerned only raise the threshold to mere minimum norms that are not sufficient for protecting the autonomy of the data subject. Furthermore, this shortcoming has been exacerbated, among others, with the inclusion of vague and open-ended terms. However, the protection of users' privacy in cyberspace depends not only on the terminology of the law but also on the roles and competences of the enterprises that process personal data. In the next section, the impact of the relationship between these competences and roles and the right to privacy will be scrutinized.

11.5 Obligations of Digital Enterprises

As regards the privacy and security of personal data, the laws under review impose certain obligations on the processors of such data. To what extent these obligations define and confine the power of digital enterprises in order to provide security and ensure privacy will be the central focus of this section.

Firstly, we read in the GDPR that "where processing is based on the data subject's consent, the controller should be able to demonstrate that the data subject has given

[64] Article 29 Working Party, Guidelines on Consent under Regulation 2016/679, adopted on 28 November 2017; as last Revised and Adopted on 10 April 2018, p. 21.

[65] Article 9 (3) of the Proposal for a Regulation of the European Parliament and of the Council concerning the respect for private life and the protection of personal data in electronic communications and repealing Directive 2002/58EC.

[66] Recital 33 of the preamble of the Regulation (EU) 2016/679 of the European Parliament and of the Council of 27 April 2016 on the protection of natural persons with regard to the processing of personal data and on the free movement of such data, and repealing Directive 95/46/EC.

consent to the processing operation. In particular, in the context of a written declaration on another matter, safeguards should ensure that the data subject is aware of the fact that and the extent to which consent is given. In accordance with Council Directive 93/13/EEC a declaration of consent preformulated by the controller should be provided in an intelligible and easily accessible form, using clear and plain language and it should not contain unfair terms. For consent to be informed, the data subject should be aware at least of the identity of the controller and the purposes of the processing for which the personal data are intended. Consent should not be regarded as freely given if the data subject has no genuine or free choice or is unable to refuse or withdraw consent without detriment".[67] In this line of reasoning, we can discern that the threshold for a consent to be informed is significantly lowered. This in addition to the fact that an average user has little to no understanding of the purposes of processing, even if they are not written in jargon, since they are oftentimes too technical and broad in scope. Another shortcoming is that one can lose control over one's data after having given consent, since one cannot know to whom (which third party) the data has, subsequently, been given.

However, the GDPR states that "in order to ensure that consent is freely given, consent should not provide a valid legal ground for the processing of personal data in a specific case where there is a clear imbalance between the data subject and the controller, in particular where the controller is a public authority and it is therefore unlikely that consent was freely given in all the circumstances of that specific situation. Consent is presumed not to be freely given if it does not allow separate consent to be given to different personal data processing operations despite it being appropriate in the individual case, or if the performance of a contract, including the provision of a service, is dependent on the consent despite such consent not being necessary for such performance".[68] Although doubts and critique can be raised about certain aspects of this reasoning, the most conspicuous part for our discussion is that the imbalance between the data subject and the controller is always present, and this latter is not always the public authority but rather the private sector against whom the data subject needs to be protected by public authority.

As regards the notion of consent itself, we have to note that "when consent is obtained via electronic means through only one mouse-click, swipe, or keystroke, data subjects must, in practice, be able to withdraw that consent equally as easily. Where consent is obtained through use of a service-specific user interface (for example, via a website, an app, a log-on account, the interface of an IoT device or by e-mail), there is no doubt a data subject must be able to withdraw consent via the same electronic interface, as switching to another interface for the sole reason of withdrawing consent would require undue effort. Furthermore, the data subject should be able to withdraw his/her consent without detriment. This means, inter alia, that a controller must make withdrawal of consent possible free of charge or without

[67]Ibid., Recital 42 and Article 7.

[68]Ibid., Recital 43.

lowering service levels".[69] Earlier in our study, we analyzed the menace of simplification of consent through click and swipes. The same reasoning concerning the peril and undermining of autonomy holds for the simplification of withdrawal of consent, as we can see here.

What is especially striking is the terminology deployed for categorizing digital enterprises. In the GDPR, the terms '*processor*'[70] and '*controller*',[71] among others, are used. It is the controller who determines the purposes and means of processing personal data, and therefore, the one who bears the final responsibility and liability for the processed data.[72] In the E-Privacy Regulation, the term '*providers of electronic communications networks and services*' is deployed. In the NIS Directive, a distinction is made between '*operators of essential services*' and '*digital service providers*', the cooperation among whom is encouraged[73] for the sake of security, especially if network and information systems are the responsibility of both of them.[74] However, these distinctions can be confusing regarding the allocation of responsibilities, resulting in their diminution, because the role of these parties is not as clear-cut as it is often assumed. To the contrary, these parties oftentimes fulfill a double role. For instance, the providers of electronic communications networks and services can also be the operators of essential services when they provide broadband internet access and voice communications services, both of which are considered essential services.[75] This confusion regarding the capacities of digital enterprises can also impact their duty to obtain consent and fulfill the underlying conditions.

Another vagueness is created when the GDPR requires only the security of processing,[76] whereas the NIS Directive aims at the security of network and information systems. And yet, this latter instrument requires both the operators of essential services and digital service providers to ensure the security of the network and information systems.[77] Again, the question of whether the digital enterprise concerned

[69] Article 29 Working Party, Guidelines on Consent under Regulation 2016/679, adopted on 28 November 2017; as last Revised and Adopted on 10 April 2018, p. 21.

[70] Article 4 (8) of the Regulation (EU) 2016/679 of the European Parliament and of the Council of 27 April 2016 on the protection of natural persons with regard to the processing of personal data and on the free movement of such data, and repealing Directive 95/46/EC.

[71] Ibid., Article 4 (7).

[72] Ibid., Article 24.

[73] Recital 35 of the Directive (EU) 2016/1148 of the European Parliament and of the Council of 6 July 2016 concerning measures for a high common level of security of network and information systems across the Union.

[74] Ibid., Recital 44.

[75] Recital 18 of the Proposal for a Regulation of the European Parliament and of the Council concerning the respect for private life and the protection of personal data in electronic communications and repealing Directive 2002/58EC.

[76] Article 32 of the Regulation (EU) 2016/679 of the European Parliament and of the Council of 27 April 2016 on the protection of natural persons with regard to the processing of personal data and on the free movement of such data, and repealing Directive 95/46/EC.

[77] Recital 52 of the preamble of the Directive (EU) 2016/1148 of the European Parliament and of the Council of 6 July 2016 concerning measures for a high common level of security of network and information systems across the Union.

has taken the appropriate measures to mitigate the risks and has fulfilled its obligations in this regard, which depends on its capacity and roles, is blurred because of the vagueness of the roles they can play. This is especially the case when the directive says that 'the security requirements for digital service providers should be lighter',[78] and that the 'digital service providers should be subject to light-touch and reactive *ex post* supervisory activities justified by the nature of their services and operations'[79] whereby the competent authorities, besides, 'have no general obligation to supervise digital service providers'.[80] This relief gives those digital service providers a lot of freedom and, therewith, contributes to the imbalance between users and providers, thereby putting privacy further at risk.

The NIS Directive further creates an escape route for the digital service provider, because it states that for the question of whether such a provider intends to offer services within the EU, "the mere accessibility in the Union of the digital service provider's or an intermediary's website or of an email address and of other contact details, or the use of a language generally used in the third country where the digital service provider is established, is insufficient to ascertain such an intention".[81] This and other issues that we discussed above provide digital enterprises a lot of leeway instead of increasing their obligations to provide better protection and security for the privacy of users. This is despite the fact that the directive aims to respect fundamental rights and principles, such as the right to respect private life and communications, and the protection of personal data.[82]

Based on our analysis in this section, the conclusion can be drawn that, given the inconsistency in the terminology of the laws under review, the roles and competences of digital enterprises are oftentimes blurred, enabling them to play a double role in order to escape liability and responsibility. This is a direct threat to the right to privacy. Also, the imbalance between the data subject and processor is a dilemma which is not properly mitigated in these laws, and because of which privacy might be further imperiled. Hence, the implications that vagueness and simplification of legal concepts can have on privacy should not be kept out of sight.

11.6 Concluding Remarks

With the advancement of information technology, we have witnessed not only the advantages hereof but also scandals regarding data and security breaches. In response, the European lawmakers have tried to enact different statutes to deal with this kind of menaces. The effectiveness of these laws has been the central theme of our research insofar as it concerns the privacy of data subjects. To this end, the question that

[78] Ibid., Recital 49.

[79] Ibid., Recital 60.

[80] Ibid.

[81] Ibid., Recital 65.

[82] Ibid., Recital 75.

underpinned this research is the following: *to what extent do the obligations in the new legal instruments effectively enhance the privacy of users' data against the tracking and targeting practices of digital enterprises*? In order to answer this question, we have, firstly, seen that the essence of the right to privacy, based on the notion of autonomy, is decisional and should remain that way since any conceptualization will, in the end, result in the alteration of the right to privacy. The decisional character of privacy is evident from the concept of 'consent', whose elements we have discussed in this research for the purpose of determining its scope and effectiveness in cyberspace.

Secondly, the applicability of 'privacy' through the concept of consent in relation to tracking and targeting technologies has been scrutinized. In this regard, we have seen that raising the requirements does not per se result in a better protection and security of the data subjects' privacy. Also, the law in books with minimum standard does not do justice to this right. However, the protection and security of privacy do not solely depend on the terminology in the law, but also on the roles and competences of enterprises that process personal data.

This has resulted in a third step, whereby we were able to take a closer look at the impact of the roles and obligations of digital enterprises on the right to privacy. In this survey, we have come to the conclusion that the threshold for an informed consent is significantly lowered. This is in addition to the fact that an average user has little to no understanding of the purposes of processing, even if they are not written in jargon, as they are oftentimes too technical and fairly broad in scope. This is only one example of the fact that the imbalance between the data subject and controller will always be present. Furthermore, the menace of simplification of consent through click and swipes directly threatens the autonomy of the user. Another problem concerning the laws under review, despite their interwovenness, has been their inconsistency with respect to terminology, as in the categorization of digital enterprises that can have de facto far-reaching consequences regarding the allocation of responsibilities and roles.

In short, the question regarding the effectiveness of the new laws in protecting and securing the privacy of users in cyberspace can be answered as follows. These new laws have come up short in rendering (full) justice to the autonomy of data subjects. And while the results achieved are not to be discarded, one must be aware that they only herald a new phase and beginning in this Information Age, and that more reflections, such as the present study, are needed to improve these laws until they are able to achieve the highest attainable autonomy for data subjects.

References

Englehardt S, Narayanan A (2016) Online tracking: A 1-million-site measurement and analysis. https://webtransparency.cs.princeton.edu/webcensus/. Accessed 7 July 2018

Henkin L (1974) Privacy and autonomy. CMLRev. https://doi.org/10.2307/1121541

Maclean A (2009) Autonomy, informed consent and medical law: A relational challenge. Cambridge University Press, Cambridge

Miller F G, Wertheimer A (eds) (2010) The ethics of consent: Theory and practice. Oxford University Press, Oxford
Schwartz P M (2003) Property, privacy and personal data, Harv L Rev 117:2056–2128
Van Alsenoy B et al. (2015) From social media service to advertising network: A critical analysis of Facebook's revised policies and terms (draft 25 August 2015; version 1.3). https://www.law.kuleuven.be/citip/en/news/item/facebooks-revised-policies-and-terms-v1-3.pdf Accessed 6 July 2018
Warren S D, Brandeis L D (1890) The right to privacy. Harv L Rev 4:193–220
Whitman J Q (2004) The two Western cultures of privacy: Dignity versus liberty. Yale L J 113:6
Ziegler K S (ed) (2007) Human rights and private law: Privacy as autonomy. Hart Publishing, Oxford

Ambrogino G. Awesta Coordinator and Lecturer of the Minor Programme *Cyber Law & Security* at Windesheim University of Applied Sciences, Hospitaaldreef 5, 1315 RC Almere, The Netherlands.

Chapter 12
Data Protection Around the World: Future Challenges

Elif Kiesow Cortez

Contents

Abstract As new technology becomes more integrated in daily tasks, new challenges to the right to the protection of personal data arise. GDPR aims to be technology neutral to make sure that the protection of the personal data does not depend on the techniques used in processing and is adoptable to the use of new technologies. This chapter will focus on European Data Protection Board guidelines and reports to highlight future GDPR compliance challenges to data protection and privacy in three prominent domains: (1) automated decision making, profiling and artificial intelligence, (2) face recognition technology and video processing, and (3) the newly emerged discussions on public health on the use of contact tracing apps with regards to the coronavirus pandemic and COVID-19. This chapter concludes by highlighting the importance of finding a balance between the right to protection of personal data without hindering the use and the development of innovative technologies in the EU.

Keywords Right to privacy · GDPR · Artificial intelligence · COVID-19 · Face recognition · Contact tracing · Corona apps

---

E. Kiesow Cortez (✉)
The Hague University of Applied Sciences, Johanna Westerdijkplein 75, 2521 EN The Hague, The Netherlands
e-mail: e.kiesowcortez@hhs.nl

E. Kiesow Cortez (ed.), *Data Protection Around the World*, Information Technology and Law Series 33,
https://doi.org/10.1007/978-94-6265-407-5_12

12.1 An Overview of Future Challenges

Before the GDPR, within the EU, right to protection of personal data was legislated under the Data Protection Directive 95/46/EC of 1995. This legislation was a "directive" and not a "regulation" and therefore it required every EU member to transpose it into national legislation. This fragmented application of data protection rules therefore created problems both for the citizens and for the businesses willing to operate in or target their products and services to the EU market. For citizens, a fragmented approach might have led to unequal rights to the protection of personal data across member states. For companies, it meant that compliance was very costly due to the wide variation and need to track many different requirements.[1] With the objective of creating a non-fragmented, uniform implementation of EU level data protection laws, the GDPR was adopted in 2016 after four years of strong negotiations.[2]

The GDPR has been at the center of discussions regarding its extraterritorial applicability since it was in the draft stage.[3] Research shows that at that point it was seen as controversial because it required any company, including international companies, that processes residents' data to comply with the GDPR.[4] The extraterritorial applicability might present as an effort to prevent data controllers from circumventing EU regulation by relocating to or contracting third parties from non-EU countries.[5]

A communication by the European Commission reported that the GDPR was to create legislation in line with the EU Digital Single Market Strategy[6] that would protect European citizens' fundamental right to privacy. A European Commission survey from 2015 showed that 67% of the survey respondent EU citizens described themselves as concerned about having no control over the information they provide online as they did not know how this information could be used.[7] A year after GDPR taking effect, in 2019, slightly less, 62%, indicated they were concerned about having partial or no control over the information they provide online.[8] The same survey showed that some were trying to take control over their privacy settings, as 56% of social network users reported they had tried to change their default privacy settings on a social media platform.[9] However, recent research shows that seemingly non-personal data variables such as location data or metadata based on the use of phone services can be used to extract personal data and that such attempts to control privacy provide little protection.[10] Given such vulnerabilities, it is clear that new and emerging technologies pose a threat to individual privacy.

---

[1] Albrecht 2016.

[2] Voigt and von dem Bussche 2017.

[3] Schwartz 2013.

[4] Victor 2013.

[5] Kuner 2010.

[6] European Commission 2015a.

[7] European Commission 2015b.

[8] European Commission 2019.

[9] Ibid.

[10] Schneier 2015; Acquisti et al. 2016.

Recital 15 of the GDPR states that the regulation should be "technology neutral"[11] to make sure that the protection of the personal data does not depend on the techniques used in processing. Therefore the European Commission and the European Data Protection Board (EDPB) regularly issue guidelines on how the GDPR applies to new and emerging technologies. In this chapter, we will focus on EU-level guidelines and reports on future challenges to data protection and privacy in three prominent domains: (1) automated decision making, profiling and artificial intelligence, (2) face recognition technology and video processing, and (3) the newly emerged discussions on public health with regards to the coronavirus pandemic and contact tracing apps.

12.2 Automated Decision-Making and Artificial Intelligence

Working Party 29 was established by Directive 95/46/EC[12] and was replaced by the EDPB to ensure the consistent application of the GDPR.[13] Working Party 29 adopted the latest version of the guidelines on automated decision making and profiling regarding GDPR in February 2018.[14] The EDPB endorsed these guidelines (hereinafter, the WP29 guidelines) during its first plenary meeting in 2018.[15] The guidelines explain that automated decision making brings about many advantages as it increases the accuracy of predictions as well as many risks regarding profiling given that individuals might end up being forced into existing profiles about themselves, which can lead to social segregation.[16]

Article 4.4 of the GDPR defines profiling as "any form of automated processing of personal data consisting of the use of personal data to evaluate certain personal aspects relating to a natural person, in particular to analyze or predict aspects concerning that natural person's performance at work, economic situation, health, personal preferences, interests, reliability, behavior, location or movements." The WP29 Guidelines break this down to the following key aspects: profiling consists of personal data processed through an automated manner with the aim of evaluating personal aspects of the data subject.[17] Individual's right not to be subject to a decision based solely on

[11] For an in-depth discussion on technology neutral law, see Hildebrandt and Tielemans 2013.

[12] EU Directive 95/46: Directive 95/46/EC of the European Parliament and of the Council of 24 October 1995 on the protection of individuals with regard to the processing of personal data and on the free movement of such data, OJ 1995 L 281/31.

[13] EU General Data Protection Regulation (GDPR): Regulation (EU) 2016/679 of the European Parliament and of the Council of 27 April 2016 on the protection of natural persons with regard to the processing of personal data and on the free movement of such data, and repealing Directive 95/46/EC (General Data Protection Regulation), OJ 2016 L 119/1.

[14] Article 29 Data Protection Working Party 2018.

[15] EDPB 2018.

[16] Article 29 Data Protection Working Party 2018.

[17] Ibid.

automated processing, including profiling, which produces legal effects concerning him or her or similarly significantly affects him or her is codified in Article 22 of the GDPR.

Data subjects are often unaware of the amount and the type of information collected about them as well as about how this information can be connected via artificial intelligence technologies to infer their characteristics.[18] The key risk of this type of profiling is that users have no knowledge of or control over their categorization or how interconnected systems treat them based on this categorization.[19]

The WP 29 Guidelines make a distinction between activities that are solely based on automated decision making and those that are based on profiling. By way of illustration, the guidelines explain that speed cameras on highways, which impose fines based on license plates, perform automated decision making but not profiling. But if these cameras were to monitor drivers' behaviors and habits over time and the amount of fine was decided based on repeat of an offense or in light of other collected data about the individual, that would include profiling.[20]

Artificial intelligence also presents a distinct challenge as an advanced form of automated decision making which facilitates profiling based on seemingly insignificant data. Article 9 and Recital 51 of the GDPR indicate that sexual orientation and ethnic origin are sensitive personal data.[21] Kosinski et al. found that combining a list of things a Facebook user has liked with very limited information could be used to predict sexual orientation of the user with 88% accuracy and his or her ethnic origin with 95% accuracy.[22] This study took place in 2013, and as artificial intelligence and data analytics continue to develop, accuracy as well as the range of extractable sensitive information may increase.

As the WP29 Guidelines refer to the fact that profiling can lead to social segregation, it is important to notice that data subjects' profiles are interconnected and this might lead to targeting the data subject with the same personalized advertising and even information on different platforms. Research shows individuals may gain excessive confidence in their points of view because of such targeting of information[23] and that this can lead to extremism and polarization in societies. Future research on data protection and privacy should focus on possible solutions to this problem.[24]

[18] For a discussion on informational identity, see Floridi 2011.

[19] Ibid.

[20] Article 29 Data Protection Working Party 2018.

[21] For suggestions on how legislation should be combined with technology design, see Hildebrandt 2008.

[22] Kosinski et al. 2013.

[23] For a thorough discussion on these risks, see Sunstein 2001.

[24] See Helberger et al. 2018 for a detailed analysis of diversity-sensitive design.

12.3 Face Recognition and Video Processing

The EDPB adopted guidelines on processing of personal data through video devices on 29 January 2020. Thus, guidelines issued by the EDPB can be examined for insights on GDPR compliant practices in processing of personal data through video devices.

Scholarly discussions in personal data protection gave special attention to processing of facial recognition data collected through video devices.[25] Under the GDPR, personal data refers to any information relating to an identified or identifiable natural person. The guidelines highlight that the frequent use of systematic automated monitoring of areas by audio-visual means increases the possibility of identifying the data subjects that use the monitored areas.[26]

In the guidelines, the EDPB first defines the scope of applicability of the GDPR by demonstrating possible scenarios. For example, it states that a person using a personal device or an action camera attached to sports equipment to record activities when on holiday might be protected under the household exemption of the GDPR Article 2(2) (c) even if third parties have been recorded in the background. However, there is specific emphasis that the exemption applies to cases where the recording is shown to friends and family. The guidelines refer to a 2003 decision of the European Court of Justice and states that uploading the video on the internet and making the data available "to an indefinite number of people" does not benefit from household exemption.[27]

Purpose specification is one of the principles of personal data processing under the GDPR Article 5(b). Regarding processing of personal data through surveillance cameras, the EDPB asserts that the purpose of the monitoring should be specified and documented for each surveillance camera. The guidelines also explain that "video surveillance for safety" on its own would not be seen as a sufficiently specific purpose. On the other hand, they state that, according to Article 6(1) (c), where national law requires video surveillance doing so cannot be a violation of the guidelines.

The guidelines describe when a shop owner could install a video surveillance system assuming no national law demands this action and therefore the shop owner would like to use the "legitimate interest" ground under the GDPR Article 6(1) (f) as the legal basis for posting the camera. To establish a legitimate interest in installing the system to avoid vandalism, the shop owner must prove that statistics show that vandalism is an actual threat in the relevant neighborhood; a general threat in the nation of vandalism does not suffice.[28] The guidelines do say that banks and jewelers do not necessarily have to supply neighborhood-specific risk justification to post a camera.

[25] Ringrose 2019.

[26] EDPB 2020, p. 7.

[27] European Court of Justice, Judgment in Case C-101/01, Bodil Lindqvist case, 6 November 2003, para 47.

[28] EDPB 2020, pp. 9–10.

The guidelines state data controllers must balance the interests and fundamental rights of the data subjects and their legitimate interests. The EDPB list some of the balancing factors as the size of the area that is under video surveillance, the type of information that is gathered, and the number of data subjects. According to Recital 47 of the GDPR, when data subjects do not reasonably expect their data are being processed, it is likely that the interests and fundamental rights of the data subject would override the interests of the data controller.

The guidelines emphasize that data subjects can reasonably expect that they are monitored by video surveillance at a bank or ATM but not, for example, in their private garden, in fitness facilities, or in publicly accessible areas dedicated to regeneration or leisure. The EDPB guidelines also state that signs that inform the data subjects of video surveillance are not relevant in objectively assessing reasonable expectations of privacy. Thus, posting a sign saying the area is under video surveillance does not override an individual's reasonable expectation of privacy.

Consent is one of the legal bases for processing an individual's personal data. This might pose problems for entities that want to conduct video surveillance, given the challenges of collecting consent from every data subject who enters the area. Simply entering a marked area would not constitute valid consent on its own unless it is compliant with the criteria of Article 4 and 7.

GDPR Article 9 and the EDPB guidelines provide somewhat contradictory information about the possibility that video surveillance produces health data. According to GDPR Article 9, revealing that a person is using a wheelchair could be seen as health data and therefore fall under special categories of data (sensitive data). However, the EDPB guidelines state that video footage showing health circumstances are not always considered to be sensitive data. While a hospital monitoring a patient's health condition through video camera would constitute processing of sensitive data, video footage showing that someone uses a wheelchair is not per se processing of sensitive data. The guidelines liken intentional monitoring of a patient's health to using video surveillance to detect someone's political opinions, such as union organizing,

The guidelines provide other examples to clarify restrictions. For example, they state that for a hotel to use video surveillance to identify automatically if a VIP guest has entered the property they would have to get explicit consent of every guest in order to scan their faces. However, the EDPB indicates that if a shop is scanning customers only to detect their gender and age, without generating biometric templates of individuals, no affirmative consent is required as this does not constitute sensitive personal data.

EDPB guidelines on processing of personal data through video devices provide several examples on ensuring GDPR compliance with data processing principles and with data subjects' rights regarding the use of video devices. In so doing they indicate that additional measures and restrictions might become applicable in the short run for video surveillance practices. Some new measures suggested in the guidelines include a requirement for informative signs on video surveillance that communicate data subjects' rights and the data's retention period as a condition of video surveillance. The guidelines also include a list of organizational and technical measures to assist

GDPR compliance. As law enforcement[29] and targeted advertising[30] increasing use face recognition technologies, the guidelines would serve to achieve a more uniform approach on processing of personal data through video devices within the EU.

12.4 The COVID-19 Pandemic and Contact Tracing Apps

During the first months of 2020, the coronavirus pandemic became a prominent topic in scholarly discussions about privacy and the right to protection of personal data. One of the main discussion points was contact tracing apps (also known as corona apps) that countries such as South Korea had adopted.[31] In order to provide EU-level guidance to the discussion, the EDPB issued two guidelines regarding COVID-19 and privacy. The first guideline, on 21 April 2020, focuses on the processing of data for the purpose of scientific research in the context of the COVID-19 outbreak[32] and the second guideline concerns the use of location data and contact tracing tools in the context of the COVID-19 outbreak.[33]

This section will only focus on the second guideline regarding the contact tracing tools. The relevant EDPB guidelines refer to the fact that GDPR was designed as technology neutral and that the regulation is flexible enough to apply in the exceptional situation of the current COVID-19 outbreak. The guidelines underline that uses of individuals' data should empower individuals and should be protected from any use that can stigmatize the data subjects. The guidelines highlight that contract tracing apps should be used to gather location data that would enable the experts to better predict the spread of the virus and the apps can also be used to notify the individuals who have been in close contact with an infected individual. The EDPB explains in these guidelines that the effectiveness of the contact tracing tools would depend on several factors such as the percentage of the citizens who would be using the app. They highlight that their position is to keep the use of these apps on a voluntary basis.

Some researchers explain that the use of contact tracing apps can be useful in containing the pandemic because the location data collected by the app would allow governments to track compliance with social distancing measures.[34] Such timely feedback would provide vital information about the efficiency of messages and whether interventions are needed.[35] However, metadata that seems unimportant such

---

[29]Satariano A (2019) Police use of facial recognition is accepted by British court. https://www.nytimes.com/2019/09/04/business/facial-recognition-uk-court.html. Accessed 25 February 2020.

[30]Kuligowski K (2019) Facial recognition advertising: the new way to target ads at consumers. https://www.businessnewsdaily.com/15213-walgreens-facial-recognition.html. Accessed 25 February 2020. Also see Lewinski et al. 2016.

[31]Zastrow M (2020) Coronavirus contact-tracing apps: can they slow the spread of COVID-19? https://www.nature.com/articles/d41586-020-01264-1. Accessed 20 May 2020.

[32]EDPB 2020b.

[33]EDPB 2020c.

[34]Buckee et al. 2020.

[35]Ibid.

as location data can give away information about an individual that would allow identification of them.[36] Many news stories have described how infected individuals in South Korea whose data was shared anonymously were deanonymized and identified by other citizens.[37]

Given that location data can be used to deanonymize individuals, the EDPB guidelines put special emphasis on the anonymization of data, providing three criteria to ensure contact tracing apps comply: (1) it should not be possible to single out the individual, (2) it should not be possible to link two or more data points about any surveilled individual, (3) inference with significant probability. EDPB guidelines express concern that the legitimate need to collect location data to fight the pandemic will cause a ratchet effect where infringement of privacy, once allowed, cannot be disallowed even when the pandemic passes.

The COVID-19 related tracking app rolled out in Germany in June 2020 attempts to accommodate privacy concerns through the adoption of the following design features.[38] First, the real identities of the users are not exchanged, but only anonymized IDs that change several times an hour are exchanged between phones. Second, contact details are not stored centrally, but instead decentrally on the respective smartphones. Exclusively the list of anonymized IDs of the infected individuals is kept on a central server. The identification and matching of users that were close to an infected user for a sufficient amount of time takes place solely on the individual smartphones. Third, the app does not record names, addresses or telephone numbers of users. When a newly infected user chooses to insert that information in the app, the user attests the reliability of this information by scanning a QR code generated by the public health facility that performed the test. A second way to attest the truthfulness of the positive test result is through a phone hotline, through which the infected user obtains a code to be then inserted in the app. This second verification option can be criticized as problematic in terms of the degree of privacy protection, because the anonymization that is upheld with the QR code option cannot longer be guaranteed to the same extent when the infected user dials the hotline.[39]

Currently researchers are working on centralized and decentralized models of gathering data[40] and discussions are taking place regarding which model will protect individuals' privacy while serving the public interest in data gathering to fight the

---

[36] Schneier 2015.

[37] Zastrow M (2020) South Korea is reporting intimate details of COVID-19 cases: has it helped? https://www.nature.com/articles/d41586-020-00740-y. Accessed 20 May 2020.

[38] Federal Government of the Federal Republic of Germany (2020), press release on the "Introduction of the Corona-Warning-App". https://www.bundesregierung.de/breg-de/themen/coronavirus/veroeffentlichung-der-corona-warn-app-1760892. Accessed 17 June 2020.

[39] Spiegel (2020) What IT experts say about the Corona-warning-app. https://www.spiegel.de/netzwelt/apps/corona-warn-app-was-netz-experten-zur-app-sagen-a-2d93fe4d-ce6f-448a-8988-f77d7ec32c6a. Accessed 17 June 2020.

[40] Fraser C, Abeler-Dorner L, Ferretti L, Parker M, Kendall M, Bonsall D (2020) Digital contact tracing: comparing the capabilities of centralized and decentralized data architecture to effectively suppress the COVID-19 epidemic whilst maximizing freedom of movement and maintaining privacy. https://github.com/BDI-pathogens/covid-19_instant_tracing/blob/master/Centralised%20and%20decentralised%20systems%20for%20contact%20tracing.pdf. Accessed 20 May 2020.

pandemic.[41] Further attention by privacy scholars might also be focused on the differences among the national contact tracing apps preferred by EU Member States, their compliance with the GDPR as well as their interoperability after border restrictions are lifted.

12.5 Upcoming Challenges

In addition to the selected technological and current developments that have been analyzed in this chapter, many scholars also paid special attention to how to further develop blockchain technology that is compliant with the GDPR. Blockchain technology gained wider popularity and wider use in the recent years. This also led to an increase in attention to regulatory frameworks that could be applicable for the use of blockchain technology. Some scholarly analysis[42] focused on how or whether the blockchain technology should be regulated, a research question a study for the European Commission DG Communications, Networks, Content & Technology is currently exploring.[43] Regulatory efforts are aiming to find a balance between creating legal certainty for users and investors of this technology without hindering innovation. Finding this delicate balance could lead to different regulatory approaches to blockchain technology emerging across the globe and would be a very fruitful and necessary domain for further research.

12.6 Concluding Remarks

Preserving the right to the protection of personal data in a world marked by increasing digitalization, innovation, and technology-reliant lifestyles constitutes the goal of the GDPR. It seems increasingly clear that this regulatory effort will frequently require additional clarifications and situation-specific refinements as circumstances evolve and change, as exemplified by AI-supported enhanced information gathering technologies or crises such as the current pandemic. Whether current efforts, like the GDPR, are likely to achieve the fine balance of adequate privacy protection without stifling innovation dynamics and without watering down the right to protection of personal data, will continue being an exciting area for legal and interdisciplinary research to tackle in the coming years.

---

[41] Criddle C and Kelion L (2020) Coronavirus contact-tracing: world split between two types of app. https://www.bbc.com/news/technology-52355028. Accessed 20 May 2020.

[42] Finck 2018.

[43] Study on Blockchains: Legal, governance and interoperability aspects (SMART 2018/0038), Study on Blockchains (2020.0931), version 27 March 2020.

References

Acquisti A, Gross R, Stutzman FD (2014) Face recognition and privacy in the age of augmented reality. J Privacy and Confidentiality 6(2):1

Acquisti A, Taylor C, Wagman L (2016) The economics of privacy. J Econ Lit 54(2):442–492

Akerlof G (1970) The market for lemons: Qualitative uncertainty and the market mechanism. Q J Econ 84:488–500

Albrecht JP (2016) How the GDPR will change the world. Eur Data Prot L Rev 2:287

Buckee CO et al (2020) Aggregated mobility data could help fight COVID-19. Science (NY) 368(6487):145 https://science.sciencemag.org/content/368/6487/145.2

European Commission (2015a) Communication, "Commission to the European Parliament, the Council, the European Economic and Social Committee and the Committee of the Regions: A Digital Single Market Strategy for Europe", COM (2015) 192

European Commission (2015b) Special Eurobarometer 431 (June 2015). http://ec.europa.eu/public_opinion/archives/ebs/ebs_431_sum_en.pdf Accessed 16 January 2020

European Commission (2019) Special Eurobarometer 487a (June 2019). http://ec.europa.eu/public_opinion/archives/ebs/ebs_431_sum_en.pdf Accessed 16 January 2020.

European Data Protection Board (2018) Endorsement 1/2018. https://edpb.europa.eu/sites/edpb/files/files/news/endorsement_of_wp29_documents_en_0.pdf Accessed 25 February 2020

European Data Protection Board (2020a) Guidelines 3/2019 on processing of personal data through video devices, Version 2.0 29 January 2020. https://edpb.europa.eu/our-work-tools/our-documents/guidelines/guidelines-32019-processing-personal-data-through-video_en Accessed 25 February 2020

European Data Protection Board (2020b) Guidelines 03/2020 on the processing of data concerning health for the purpose of scientific research in the context of the COVID-19 outbreak, Version 1.1 30 April 2020. https://edpb.europa.eu/sites/edpb/files/files/file1/edpb_guidelines_202003_healthdatascientificresearchcovid19_en.pdf Accessed 20 May 2020

European Data Protection Board (2020c) Guidelines 04/2020 on the use of location data and contact tracing tools in the context of the COVID-19 outbreak, 21 April 2020. https://edpb.europa.eu/sites/edpb/files/files/file1/edpb_guidelines_20200420_contact_tracing_covid_with_annex_en.pdf. Accessed 20 May 2020

Federal Government of the Federal Republic of Germany (2020), press release on the "Introduction of the Corona-Warning-App" https://www.bundesregierung.de/breg-de/themen/coronavirus/veroeffentlichung-der-corona-warn-app-1760892 Accessed 17 June 2020

Finck M (2018) Blockchains: regulating the unknown. German Law J 19(4): 665–692

Floridi L (2011) The informational nature of personal identity. Minds Mach 21(4):549–566

Hildebrandt M (2008) Profiling and the identity of the European citizen. In:Hildebrandt M, Gutwirth S (eds) Profiling the European citizen. Springer, Dordrecht, pp 303–343

Hildebrandt M, Tielemans L (2013) Data protection by design and technology neutral law. Comput Law Secur Rev 29(5):509–521

Kosinski M, Stilwell D, Graepel T (2013) Private traits and attributes are predictable from digital records of human behaviour. P Natl Acad Sci USAmerica 110(15):5802–5805

Kuner C (2010) Data protection law and international jurisdiction on the internet (part 1). Int J Law Inf Technol 18(2):176–193

Lewinski P, Trzaskowski J, Luzak J (2016) Face and emotion recognition on commercial property under EU data protection law. Psychol Marketing 33(9):729–746

Ringrose K (2019) Law enforcement's pairing of facial recognition technology with body-worn cameras escalates privacy concerns. VA Law Rev Online 105:57

Schneier B (2015) Data and Goliath: The hidden battles to collect your data and control your world. WW Norton, New York

Schwartz P (2013) The EU-US privacy collision: a turn to institutions and procedures. Harvard Law Rev 126:1

Sunstein CR (2001) Republic.com. Princeton University Press, New Jersey

Victor JM (2013) The EU general data protection regulation: Toward a property regime for protecting data privacy. Yale Law J 123:513

Voigt P, von dem Bussche A (2017) The EU general data protection regulation (GDPR): A practical guide. Springer International Publishing, Cham

Wachter S (2018) Normative challenges of identification in the Internet of Things: Privacy, profiling, discrimination, and the GDPR Comput Law Secur Rev 34(3):436–449

Welinder Y (2012) A face tells more than a thousand posts: Developing face recognition privacy in social networks Harv J Law Technol 26:165

Dr. Elif Kiesow Cortez is a senior lecturer and researcher in data protection and privacy regulation in the International and European Law Program at The Hague University of Applied Sciences (THUAS), the Netherlands.

Ingram Content Group UK Ltd.
Milton Keynes UK
UKHW020137050723
424579UK00003B/167

9 789462 654068